'Glynn Christian's book has all the ingredients of succ᷈— written with the first-hand passion of the hero's descendant, who ᴵ᷈ ᴬ his ancestor's footsteps and so came closer to the original. This deeply researched and highly readable book must become the classic account [of the story of Fletcher Christian]'

> Robin Hanbury-Tenison OBE
> Explorer, Gold Medallist, Royal Geographical Society

'It is exclusively due to Glynn Christian's investigative efforts that we know Charles Christian (his brother) participated in a mutiny and that Fletcher must have known about it—a major contribution to *Bounty* research.'

> Dr Sven Wahlroos, *Bounty* historian, author of *Mutiny and Romance
> in the South Seas: A Companion to the Bounty Adventure*

'. . . undoubtedly the best written account of *Bounty* for many years . . . And for once this is a book which has something new to offer readers. The second part of the book . . . the author's journey to Pitcairn . . . is a masterly story, honest and frank and beautifully told.'

> Gavin Kennedy: Bligh biographer
> author of *Bligh* and *William Bligh: The Man and his Mutinies*

'No one has ever delved so deeply into Christian's background . . . sources are skilfully woven into the text without diverting the reader's attention from the facts . . . one shares the author's thrill of discovery.'

> *Oceans Magazine*

'Tells a fascinating tale'

> *New York Times Book Review*

FRAGILE PARADISE

THE DISCOVERY OF FLETCHER CHRISTIAN, BOUNTY MUTINEER

GLYNN CHRISTIAN

ISBN: 1-59048-2506

First published in 1982

Cover photograph of Pitcairn Island by Glynn Christian.

DEDICATION

To the people of Pitcairn Island

Contents

Maps and Tables

Maps and family tree by George Jordan

Acknowledgements

Hundreds of people all round the world co-operated to help me discover Fletcher Christian. Some helped financially, some gave practical labour, others were supportive when times and bank accounts were bleak. Each was essential to whatever success this book enjoys.

My biggest debt of gratitude is owed to Ewan Christian of Newbury who unhesitatingly gave me exclusive access to the family papers in his keeping. His generosity was the key to the yesterdays behind the door, and I thank him most sincerely for his altruistic kindness.

The scholarly guidance and advice of Rolf du Rietz in Sweden, and of Bengt and Marie-Thérèse Danielsson in Tahiti were of major importance: it was flattering to have such eminent interest too.

In England I was fortunate indeed to have the proximity of Stephen Walters, and of Derek McDonnell from Bernard Quaritch Ltd. They both found books, sources and other opinions for me.

Robin Hanbury-Tenison, Tim Severin, Nigel Winser and Shane Wesley-Smith of the Royal Geographical Society helped with the expedition; and where would I be without Mary Crowley of Ocean Voyages Inc. of Sausalito? Or, especially, without successive managers of Coutts & Co., Cavendish Square?

Financial assistance came from *Now!* magazine, Fisher & Paykel Ltd., Konica Cameras, Supertravel and Bernard Quaritch Ltd. Metal detectors were given by C-Scope. Friends who provided funds were friends indeed. I am most grateful to Richard Broome, Greg James, Gregg Scott, and my parents.

A special 'Ta' to Pat, Keith, Gerald, Grant, Garth and Susan Christian who subsidised my research in Sydney with bed, board, beer, barbecues and beaches.

Three years' travelling around the world meant many beds were given, often more than once. In the United States Sally Brady, Katie Stapleton, Judy Popkin, Kurt Weyrauch, Jesse Parker, David Williams and Fred Baumeister all welcomed me. On Norfolk Island Bernie and Mary Christian-Bailey did me proud. On Pitcairn Island it seemed I was everyone's guest, but I stayed with Tom and Betty Christian and no one has ever been more welcomed or better looked after anywhere—even if chickens do peer at you while you are in the bath! In England I stayed most with the irreplaceable Marika Hanbury-Tenison or with David and Lindsay Quysner.

Naturally, support in one way or another was most forthcoming from the family or from those with especially close associations. As well as from my immediate family, especially sister and brothers, there was invaluable encouragement from Michael Curwen and his family, from Edward and Susan Curwen of Belle Isle, from Sir Clive Edwards, Bt, of Milntown, from Edward Corteen of Ballasholague, IOM, and from Arthur Christian of Tiburon, California.

Amongst the countless libraries and institutions consulted, none is so special as the Mitchell Library in Sydney. The Admiralty Library, London, was equally co-operative. The Manx Museum, Douglas, has been ceaselessly helpful and thorough under the guidance of Ann Harrison. Brian Jones and his staff at the Record Office in Carlisle were reliable and uncomplaining. P. Ll. Gwyn-Jones, Bluemantle Pursuivant at the College of Arms was both fascinated and fascinating as we connected and corrected the family trees. Paul Stephens helped tremendously with details of eighteenth-century political and naval life.

Not one of these many kindnesses would have been any use without the talents of those who sell and make books. My thanks to Julian Bach, my agent, for his initial encouragement. Thanks to my editors, Upton Birnie Brady and Caroline Tonson Rye for their continuous enthusiasm, generosity and patience. Most of all, thanks to Michael Brook, researcher, sailor, surveyor and friend *extraordinaire;* this book would truly have been impossible without his unselfish and (often unrewarded) labours.

For this second edition of *Fragile Paradise*, new friends and colleagues have given sterling support. Fiona Henderson and Heather Curdie of Transworld prodded, pushed and persuaded me into new areas and their caring editing has eliminated previous errors and done as much as possible to avoid new ones.

In Britain, artist Adrian Teal spent many years researching how Fletcher Christian might have looked and was exceptionally generous in allowing me both to use his research and to publish the fascinating image in the colour photographic section which resulted from his collaboration with noted artist/artistic anatomist John Lockett.

On Norfolk Island Marie Bailey, Gillian Reckitt and Nina Stanton, director of the Kingston Museums, are first amongst many equals, and Shane Quintal gave generous access to his unbeatable collection of photographs. In New Zealand, my sister Faye helped to clarify Polynesian life wonderfully: my brothers Bruce and Ross and their wives Dale and Sheryl have been exceptionally hospitable, as has Max Cryer. Cousins Susan, Grant and Jeanette kept faith during a difficult year for them in Sydney, and in the United States cousin Curtis is a terrific detective and loyal enthusiast. And nothing would have been possible without the quiet support of Chris Beech.

To list the other generous and enthusiastic people who lent me documents, or pictures, sent me information, answered letters, gave me bed or board, tried to raise funds, sailed, typed, read or otherwise encouraged would be unfair. Lists suggest some order of merit, and there is none. It was all needed and it is all appreciated.

Introduction

'*I look forward to the day when there is no longer the urge to cast Bligh or Christian as black or white. They are men who are remembered. Few men who are remembered can have been wholly one or the other*'

Those were the last words I wrote in the first edition of *Fragile Paradise*, and I believe them just as passionately twenty years later. This second edition brings both men even more colourfully to life, with fascinating new insights into what drove them from passionate friendship to ultimate personal betrayal in the world's most famous mutiny.

The mutiny aboard *Bounty* on 28 April 1789 was the revolt of one man against another, Fletcher Christian against William Bligh. It was their relationship which caused the mutiny and, on balance of the evidence of the men who were aboard *Bounty*—the only men we should heed—it was Bligh's treatment of Christian which drove Christian to it.

Every new facet added to our understanding of one man enhances our understanding of the other. Yet, until this book, what really happened on board *Bounty* was limp-footed history, only half told. Almost nothing was known of Fletcher Christian, and any analysis of his relationship with Bligh could only be speculative at best.

Fragile Paradise changed that, and now I can add even more meat to the bones of Fletcher Christian. Careful new readings of *Bounty*'s Logs will also create new sympathies for the unprecedented harshness with which Bligh treated him after *Bounty* sailed from Tahiti. The suspicion that Fletcher might have been insane is also faced squarely for the first time. Armed with expert medical knowledge and the benefit of deeper research and hindsight, psychologists and medical professors have helped to provide explanations for his behaviour which totally change our perspectives of both men.

Fletcher's challenge to survive on uncharted Pitcairn Island in the South Pacific was unprecedented for a European. It has taken more than 20 years of research for me to realise Fletcher Christian's settlement might have failed without the extraordinary resilience and skills of his Tahitian consort Mauatua, and her companions. The Polynesian women whose blood is in my veins were the ones who truly made his dream into reality, who made Pitcairn Island and, later, Norfolk Island, possible. I should not have told the story of Fletcher Christian without including these women. This time they are here, and they enrich the life-story of Fletcher Christian immeasurably.

Fletcher Christian's life after the mutiny, and the many versions of his death, have added fuel to the burning curiosity about him for more than two centuries. To make some sense of this mystery I adventured in the same waters he did, also felt the sudden catch of sails atop unfathomable waves on the slow, lonely swell of the South Pacific, and tried to imagine a future without escape on the rock of Pitcairn Island. Walking on its steep volcanic hills brought me astonishingly closer to him, and to a greater discovery of myself.

Fragile Paradise has been an extraordinary life-long exploration for me, one which continues. For this is the ultimate story to prove truth is stranger than fiction. Fletcher Christian and his fateful adversary William Bligh were real men, both complicated, both flawed. To me these old sailing companions are both heroic visionaries who did magnificent things in spite of enormous adversity. Even if they had not met I am certain we would have heard of them. But they did meet, and made thrilling history in the remote waters of the South Pacific, history which can at last be told with more insight.

To me, the excitement of history is that it brings people back to life, and it is the complexity of these two lives which makes their true story and the outcome of their raw passions so poignant. Here, I hope you will discover and understand why Fletcher Christian mutinied against William Bligh, and blame neither.

Christian Family of Milntown, Isle of Man & Ewanrigg, Cumbria

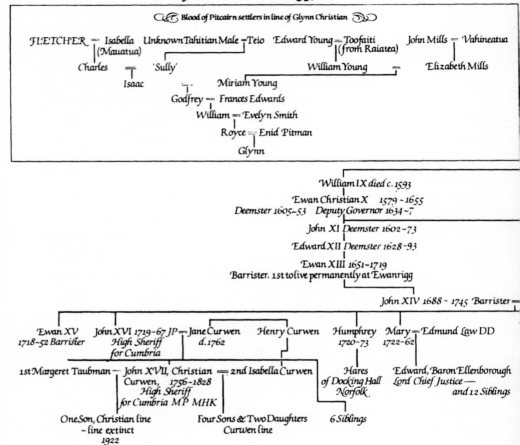

Blood of Pitcairn settlers in line of Glynn Christian

FLETCHER = Isabella (Mauatua)   Unknown Tahitian Male = Teio   Edward Young = Toofaiti (from Raiatea)   John Mills = Vahineatua

Charles   'Sully'   William Young   =   Elizabeth Mills

Isaac

Miriam Young

Godfrey == Frances Edwards

William == Evelyn Smith

Royce == Enid Pitman

Glynn

William IX died c. 1593

Ewan Christian X   1579~1655
Deemster 1605~53   Deputy Governor 1634~7

John XI Deemster 1602~73

Edward XII Deemster 1628~93

Ewan XIII 1651~1719
Barrister. 1st to live permanently at Ewanrigg

John XIV 1688~1745 Barrister =

Ewan XV   John XVI 1719~67 JP = Jane Curwen   Henry Curwen   Humphrey   Mary = Edmund Law DD
1718~52 Barrister   High Sheriff   d.1762   1720~73   1722~62
                     for Cumbria

1st Margeret Taubman — John XVII, Christian == 2nd Isabella Curwen   Hares   Edward, Baron Ellenborough
                       Curwen, 1756~1828   of Docking Hall   Lord Chief Justice —
                       High Sheriff   Norfolk.   and 12 Siblings
                       for Cumbria MP MHK

One Son, Christian line   Four Sons & Two Daughters   6 Siblings
~ line extinct   Curwen line
1922

John MacCrysten I, Deemster 1408 b.ca.1368

William MacCrysten II, Deemster 1417 MHK 1408~48

John McCrysten III Deemster 1448~98

John McChristen IV Deemster Died c.1511

John V Deemster Died c.1533

William VI Deemster Died c.1535

Ewan VII Died c.1539 MHK

William VIII Died c. Deemster 1568

John, 1st Protestant Vicar of Maughold, I.O.M.
Edward Christian, Capt. R.N., Governor 1628~39
Died in Prison 1660/1

William (Illiam Dhone) b.1608 executed 1622/3
Receiver~General, Governor

Edward 1 = Eleanor of Castile
King of England 1239~1307

14 Generations

Bridget Senhouse of Netherhall, d.1744

Charles = Ann Dixon & 6 Siblings
1729~68   1730~1820

John   Ewan   Jacob   Edward   Mary   Charles   FLETCHER = Isabella   Frances   Ann   Humphrey
1752~91   1754~57 1756~7   1758~1823   1760~86 1762~1822 25th.Sept.1764 (Mauatua)   1766   1766   1767~90
Attorney   Barrister   Oct.1793   d.19th Sept.1841 (twin)   (twin)
                                        Chief Justice
                                        of Isle of Ely
                                        Professor of Laws

Thursday October = Sussanah (Teraura)   Charles   =   'Sully'   Mary Ann
Oct.1790~21 April 1831   1791 ~ 4 Jan 1842 d.7 Mar 1826   Oct 1793~2nd Jan 1866

        7 Siblings   Isaac   =   Miriam Young
                    26 Apr 1825 31 Oct 1877 30 Aug 1829 25 Nov 1911

15 Siblings   Godfrey b.28 July 1849 = Frances Edwards (American)

Linda   Nita   William = Evelyn Smith   Anabelle   Sarah   Renée   Charles   Glynn   Francis
                          (New Zealander)

    Royce = Enid Pitman   Colin = Nola Rowlands   Keith = Patricia Barber
    1918   1917

Glynn Bruce Faye Ross   One Son, Two Daughters   Three Sons, One Daughter
1942   1944   1947 1948

I

The Right to Rule

1

Bravery in Retrospect

I was nine when I learned I was descended from Fletcher Christian. My teacher that year at Auckland's Owairaka Primary School was Mr Jackson, a rare man, able to conjure up in the minds of children the reality of times past. To me he revealed that history is simply the lives of other people. By exciting those untrammelled senses of romance and adventure that the young enjoy before the afflictions of puberty, Mr Jackson helped me to realise that I, marooned in the suburbs of Auckland, was linked to men and women who had been affected by the discoveries of Drake, the invasion of William the Conqueror, the rise and fall of the Romans. I became so stimulated that I desperately wanted to know just where the men who made me had been when, say, Queen Victoria was crowned or when Columbus reported back to Ferdinand and Isabella.

With an impatience that made eating impossible I waited for my father to return home from work, so I could ask: 'Are we . . . am *I* descended from anyone famous?'

By remarkable coincidence, MGM's 1930s *Mutiny on the Bounty* with Clark Gable as Fletcher Christian had been re-released that very week. Rather than rehearsing to me the story himself, my father arranged that I should be taken to see the film; and then Mr Jackson let me tell the class about it two mornings in a row.

There was a dramatic improvement in my playground status, which I did everything to encourage, and being the smallest and most easily bullied kid in school became marginally more bearable, except when I believed everything the papers said about Fletcher Christian and claimed I had royal blood. You do not have royal blood and live in Owairaka and talk about it.

The story of the man who stole one of the king's ships from William Bligh and then went to live with semi-naked women on a remote South Pacific island was too much properly to absorb, too dramatic for me really to feel part of it. But pieces did help explain some of the confusion that discoloured my childhood, as until then I had been troubled about why my grandfather looked so different and why he was so tall— I hardly grew as high as his belt before he died. When he talked with his sisters it was a language that even my father, his eldest son, could not understand. His extraordinarily idiosyncratic English I attributed at first to plain ignorance. He made singular words plural and vice versa, saying he had lost his 'glass' when I knew he meant his spectacles. He was decidedly different, and children hate being associated with difference. So, for all the status it offered, talking about Fletcher Christian had to be tempered until I was able to understand the difference and appreciate the specialness of my grandfather and his equally overpowering sisters, my great-aunts. It took me another five years to learn that, almost universally, other people found them fascinating.

Like most men whose grandparents are dead I deeply regret I did not know my grandfather better. I should have learned how to speak his special language, a mixture of eighteenth-century English and eighteenth-century Tahitian, the language with which Fletcher Christian talked to his wife and children. I should now love to hear more of the lilting English, idiosyncratic certainly, but peppered with wonderful words and accented softly, like men of England's West Country. But I was frightened of his size and learned what I could from Aunt Renée, the smallest of his sisters. She told me what she would—not what she could—and explained without knowing it some of the extraordinary aspects of myself that had made me a shy and frightened child.

From my earliest days I was aware of the ease with which ecstasy could overtake me as soon as I was alone under the sun or in the thick, evergreen New Zealand bush. I could lie for hours on hot grass or under trees or beside flowers, entertained to the point of bewildered fulfilment just by being there, by the heat and the smells. Sometimes I took off my clothes to walk freely and secretly in the bush or along a beach, and had done so since I was seven. It was physical and sexual and I knew it; but it was imperative.

The absorption of the fact that Fletcher Christian's wife, my great-great-great-great-grandmother, was Tahitian, and that the family had lived on Pacific islands for generations, helped to explain that my instinctive fascination with the sun, the tropics and the fruits and flowers made by them was perfectly natural. It was my heritage and from that time I developed an enormous but very private sense of pride in what made me different.

It reinforced what Mr Jackson had taught, that links with the past are more than names on paper and faded photographs. I had started a search which I now see was as much for myself as for Fletcher Christian.

Fletcher Christian had two sons and a daughter, Mary, who was first written of as the 'Fair Maid of the South Seas' but who died a crabby old spinster. His sons were Thursday October and Charles, and were the only sons of the *Bounty* pirates who, like their fathers, married full-blooded Tahitian women. Thursday married a much older widow of one of the mutineers, and Charles married Sully, who had arrived on Pitcairn Island as an infant with *Bounty* in 1790. So all of Fletcher's grandchildren were three-quarter Tahitian, explaining why, of all the *Bounty* families, the Christians are most likely to show or feel their Tahitian ancestry.

Charles's son Isaac was born on Pitcairn in 1825, but by 1856 the island was considered unsuitable to support its population of 187. Queen Victoria, who had always taken an interest in the Pitcairners, and who had sent them gifts, including an organ, agreed that the *Bounty* descendants, forgiven the sins of their forefathers, should be given Norfolk Island, which sits temperately between Australia and New Zealand.

Norfolk Island had been the British Devil's Island, the ultimate punishment for men transported from Great Britain for stealing bread or killing others. For decades it was a cesspool of sodomy, massacre and exploitation; but now, deserted apart from a few caretaker ex-convicts, it was to be settled by the world's most fascinating and God-fearing community. Most of them hated it on sight. The sparse, green, rolling hills, spiked by lofty Norfolk pines, peppered with the sedate Georgian masonry of the prison and surrounding village, were no match for the lush ruggedness of Pitcairn. There were not even any coconuts for milk and the stuff that came out of cows, as well as being difficult to obtain, was considered unhealthy. Several families returned to the tropic remoteness of Pitcairn as soon as they could, a retreat that was based neatly upon blood lines. Those Christians descended from Thursday October returned, the family of Charles stayed.

Isaac, my great-great-grandfather, married Miriam Young. Their son too was named Isaac, but to avoid confusion was known by his second name, Godfrey, a tradition that has been continued in the family up to this day. Isaac-called-Godfrey grew to manhood at a time when Norfolk Island was an important and busy whaling centre. Eventually he owned his own ship and married an outsider, Frances Edwards, the daughter of an American whaler. Her mother was a Flowerday, and so she was a granddaughter of the Hansens, the first white children born and brought up in New Zealand: thus the marriage linked the blood of two of the South Pacific's earliest European families.

Godfrey and Frances had the typical large family of the time, one of whom was William, my grandfather, a favourite son and a favourite brother, known through his youth as Sunny for his good nature and smile. Aunt Renée told me stories that I first disbelieved, but I heard them from other sources, too. Grandfather William first tried to stowaway on his father's whaler when he was eight. He was tall and muscular enough to pass for twelve or thirteen, by which time you were certainly expected to earn your living in those tough times. He managed to get aboard undetected but made the great mistake of trying too hard, and lit up a pipeful of tobacco, his first. Nausea exposed what his light boy's voice had not, and he was returned home.

The stories of his bravery and individuality as a young man would fill a book. He did go to sea and by the time he was twelve was a hand harpoonist. Later he sailed with the Bishop of Melanesia to South America and was aboard the cable ship *Iris* during the First World War when Count von Lucknow was arrested. When he went to New Zealand in 1916 he married Evelyn Smith, descended from an Irish soldier who was a very early settler in New Zealand. My father, William and Evelyn's eldest son, was born in 1918.

Once I had the descent in my mind I was able to work out that Fletcher Christian was my great-great-great-great-grandfather, but that was all I knew. After I left school I worked in radio and television, and, although I should have known better, thought of Fletcher only in terms of Gable. When, in the early sixties, Marlon Brando announced he was making a new version of the film, I was reassured to hear how much research he said he had done on Fletcher Christian. It was all a terrible disappointment. The dandified gentleman portrayed by Brando was possibly more accurate than Gable's character (he had first refused to play the part, feeling that pigtails and knee breeches would damage his masculine screen image), but the fiery immolation with which Brando ended the character's life caused me infinite pain and trouble. Too many people believed it to be the way Fletcher Christian had really died and maintained that my claim to descent was bogus.

There seemed to be no book that would tell me the truth, or a consistent version of any part of the story. Was Bligh the tyrant that my great-aunts said? Who would tell me if Fletcher Christian was from the Isle of Man or Cumberland? Who knew what had become of him? It became increasingly important that I should know all these things.

By September 1965, already successful as one of New Zealand's first full-time radio and TV scriptwriters, I was frustrated, feeling I could go no further in that country. Spontaneously I decided to leave. Six weeks later I was aboard RHMS *Ellinis*, bound for Southampton. Apart from £10 my parents had given me, the money I carried was borrowed. I knew only one person in England and hardly knew why I was going. I had made one of those unpremeditated decisions that irrevocably changes a life, the kind of decision that has to be right whatever happens.

A few loyal friends considered it a brave and ambitious move. In retrospect I can see it was, especially for a young man who still blushed easily and who could not go to a pub by himself until over thirty years old. At the time, I was aware only of being fired by absolute fear of failure or ridicule. With each battle I fought to survive in England I was even more determined not to return to New Zealand until I had achieved something that made my leaving worthwhile. My thoughts turned to Fletcher Christian often as I realized his decision to take *Bounty* had put him into the same situation. More and more I wondered if it might be in any way possible to discover why he had made that one decision that so irretrievably changed his life.

On the surface I could not compare myself with Fletcher Christian. He apparently came from a privileged background and was physically strong and athletic. Yet when I visited Tahiti on my way to Europe, I knew at once that my intoxication with nature came from my Tahitian ancestry, and that first day on Tahiti remained one of the most precious experiences of my life. Having established one connection with the past, I hoped that knowing more about Fletcher Christian might explain some of my other, wilder ways and the paradox of self-doubt and ambition. If this were possible it had to follow that there were other men and women in my background whose traits and personalities would allow me to see myself simply as a link in a continuing chain, rather than as a rootless adventurer. That is precisely what has happened. My discovery of Fletcher Christian has proved far more rewarding than I dared imagine, for in unearthing his background and motivations I discovered my own. And through that I know the rest of my life will be immeasurably richer.

2

The New Generation

There never was a mutiny *of Bounty*. Rather there was a revolt of one man against another, Christian against Bligh, with some of *Bounty*'s men joining in later. Logically that clash can only be understood if the passions and perversities of both men are chronicled. Until now this has not been done.

To those who understand such things, Fletcher Christian is known as one of the finest English navigators of his time, a shining pupil of Bligh, who in turn reflected the brilliance exhibited by Captain James Cook. When Bligh and Christian sailed off to the South Seas in 1787, they carried one of the first chronometers perfected by Larcum Kendall. The very one is on view in Britain's National Maritime Museum and still functions accurately. With this invention, which made it possible to discern longitude accurately for the first time, Fletcher Christian safely sailed the pirated and under-manned *Bounty* on an epic 8,000 mile mid-Pacific voyage in search of a haven. He journeyed as far west as Fiji and discovered Raro-tonga. Early in 1790, he located and settled on Pitcairn Island, which was known but incorrectly charted.

Pitcairn Island was possibly the first closed community in which white men could choose women only of another colour. It was a volatile mixture of men and women who knew little of each other's culture, even less of their language. The descendants of these ill-matched pioneers became the most God-fearing and admired community on earth, an inspiration both to Queen Victoria and her missionaries.

Christian was a law-breaker, a mutineer, a pirate, a blackbirder, and possibly a fool. He was also an important explorer, the founding father of a unique people and, like so many of his powerful family and so many others in the eighteenth century, a courageous social pioneer. What Rousseau dreamed, Christian did.

The books and pamphlets of the proselytizing Victorian Church—and Hollywood—have made Fletcher Christian a star. He is a hero of protest and escapism whom you might as easily find yourself discussing on the white sands of the Gulf of Siam as in Westminster, the U.S. Capitol, Teotihuacan, or the Australian Outback. I have.

But who was Fletcher Christian?

Fletcher Christian was born to Charles and Ann Christian in the farmstead of Moorland Close on 25 September 1764, and carried over the hill to be baptized in Brigham Church the very same day, something which happened only when a baby was not expected to survive. Either he was born sickly, or there was an epidemic of some kind in the purlieus of Cockermouth.

Not far from Cumbria's Lake District, Moorland Close sits snug on the long gentle brow of a great green hill that slopes, ultimately, to the slow River Derwent, the Cocker, and the town of Cocker-mouth. When dialect was common it was called Mairlandclere and was 'a quadrangular pile of buildings in the style of a medieval manor house, half castle and half farmstead', originally fortified against Lowland reivers who came to plunder, wreck and, time permitting, rape. The peace brought to the Borders by the accession of James I of England had existed for well over a century when Charles Christian and Ann Dixon began their married life at the Close on 2 May 1751, and they had every expectation of comfort

and peaceful prosperity. The marriage was quite in keeping with
their station in Georgian society and both were in possession of
their inheritances—Ann's was Moorland Close. Her father, who
was a dyer but described as a gentleman, was her co-heir and lived
with them.

The strictures of primogeniture meant that younger sons, even
of the richest families, had to marry an heiress; even so, many were
forced also to embrace the equally rewarding bosom of the church,
the comradeship of the armed forces or, *in extremis*, what we now
call the professions. Charles, Fletcher's father, was the fifth son of
John Christian, the fourteenth documented head of the ubiquitous
Christians of Milntown on the Isle of Man and Ewanrigg in Cumberland. They were an extraordinarily prosperous and powerful clan
with fingers firmly in every temporal, pastoral or spiritual pie—at
home and abroad—that might feed their ambitions. Charles had two
sources of income: one from inherited shares in his family's mining
and shipping interests; the other from his practice as an attorney in
Cockermouth. In the Christian family, the pursuit of a legal career
was no sign of impecuniosity but the proud following of a tradition
that had its roots deep in the past.

With financial security and scion status, Charles was seriously
eligible. But good sense and the convention of the time prevented
him using his pecuniary stability as a spur to indiscriminate matri-
mony or, worse, love; one generally married for the comfort of a
fortune and looked elsewhere for the exercise of the libido. In Ann
Dixon, Charles was fortunate to find a woman who offered both.

Ann's mother, Mary, was a Fletcher and, though not as rich as
the Christians, they had been in Cumbria far longer. Her grandfather was descended from William Fletcher, the builder of Cockermouth Hall (now a parking lot), who had succoured Queen Mary
of Scotland when she fled her mutinous realm. He gave her clothes
and cloth of red velvet out of pity for her state; and she gave him
thanks.

Unusually, Ann seems not to have had a fortune in cash, but was heiress to the farm her mother owned. It offered a potential husband a roof and an income, and gave her distinct market value. Jane Austen's female characters are not untypical for being introduced by their fortunes rather than their faces; without the former, the latter was valueless.

Once, the house and outbuildings had been clustered inside a tall, strong, red-brick wall iced with crenellations. A thin, rutted road ran under the long east side. In this wall was the main entrance, guarded by a high, square watch-tower with a pointed roof. To enter you had to dismount and walk through a succession of low narrow doors under the tower, a lesser version of the defences of a medieval castle.

Then in 1709 the Fletchers built a new house outside the battlements, a simple solid building of elegant proportions in honey-coloured, dressed stone (now hideously stuccoed). The partly-eviscerated quadrangle was planted as an orchard and garden, emulating the walled wonders of espalier and asparagus seen on the estates of the noble and rich; a startling conceit for a modest moorland farm. Still, the battlements did provide protection from biting northerly winds that damaged young plants quite as badly as invaders' boots had once done. They also made the most seductive setting imaginable for the adventurous fantasies of children and for the social delusions of their parents; from certain angles the house looked positively stately. In the 1860s, there were still those who remembered seeing some of the medieval buildings within the wall, but they are all gone now.

To Charles Christian, who had been brought up in Ewanrigg, a mansion with forty-two bedrooms, any disadvantages of size or facility at Moorland Close were outweighed by its being an easy ride from his birthplace; his brother Humphrey was forced to move to Norwich to marry a suitable fortune.

Charles and Ann were twenty-two and twenty respectively when they married, and they had ten children, six of whom survived to adulthood, a good record for the time. The names they chose show interest and awareness in their families' past, and an assured belief either in tradition or the generosity of relatives to young namesakes.

John, Ewan, Jacob, Edward, Mary, Charles, Fletcher, Frances, Ann and Humphrey were all named, in that order, for brothers, uncles, aunts, sisters, and grandparents, mainly names which the Christian family had used since the fourteenth century. Ewan and Jacob died within weeks of each other early in 1757, of some unrecorded infantile affliction: Frances and Ann were twins who survived but a short time. There might have been even more children, but three months after Humphrey was born, Charles senior died and was buried in Brigham on 13 March 1768, beside his wife's grandfather.

Charles's tomb, arguably the showiest in the graveyard, indicates the importance attached to being a Christian, dead or alive. The inscription reminds the reader he was not only of Moorland Close but was also the son of John Christian of Ewanrigg. It is an elegant table grave with turned legs and, at its head, a massive, moulded rendering of the family coat of arms with its unicorn-head crest. Strictly, the arms should not have been there, for the family was not granted them officially until 1788, but they had been displayed for generations and accepted as genuine, a common enough happening with Manx families where the Heralds, perhaps heeding stories of rude law and discomfort, had never made a Visitation.

When the august *Gentleman's Magazine* of March 1768, reported Charles Christian's death they described him as Coroner for Cumbria. This is untrue. Coroners there were, unusually, in the direct appointment of Lord Egremont, incumbent of Cockermouth Castle, but no Christian appears in the list of his appointees.

The death of Charles must have been expected. On Valentine's Day 1768, he made his Will, declaring himself weak of body and leaving everything to Ann. With nice feeling for that saint's day, and perhaps with that charity that approaching death so often encourages, he pays Ann pretty compliments. To her he committed 'the custody and tuition of the children with whom it hath pleased God to bless us during their respective minorities, not doubting but as she has approved herself to me the best of wives she will also prove the best of mothers'.

On the third of May 1768, Ann, a widow at thirty-six, and her father, Jacob Dixon, both giving Moorland Close as their address, swore that 'the Paper Writing to you now shown' was the last Will and testament of Charles and paid the large sum of £800 to the Keeper General of the Exchequer and Prorogative Court of Robert, Lord Archbishop of York. This was a bond to ensure they carried out the provisions of the Will, paying creditors and funeral expenses. Ann was also expected to show 'a true and perfect inventory of Goods, Rights, Credits, Cattles and Chattles'; this so that there could be no pleading of false poverty to avoid payment of just debts.

Most authors write that Ann now retired to Douglas on the Isle of Man, but this is nonsense; those who repeat this particular tale then go on to tell of Fletcher's school days in Cockermouth! Was he put into a foster house at four years old?

The fatherless children, aged from fourteen to three months, were reasonably provided for and the Close was a going concern. They had a resident maternal grandfather and there seem to have been plenty of Dixons ready to turn a hand on the farm. Ann took the children's tuition seriously, for her children had been left more than possessions. They were the new faces of an extraordinary heritage, part of the newest generation of a family that had prospered for 400 years.

Most families point proudly to men of power or wealth or influence in one generation or another; some might even trace one or all of these attributes for several successive lives or in related family branches. But there are few, royalty and nobility not excepted, that can claim the combination of all three in ever-growing strength and in an unbroken line of direct male-only descent from the mid-fourteenth century, before which most records are suspect anyway. The Christians could. It is so unusual for a progression of fathers and sons to have so much strength for so long a time that it had marked relevance to anyone born into that family. It would have been impossible for Fletcher, Charles's and Ann Christian's seventh child and sixth son, not to be influenced by this heritage.

3

Men of Man

It seems perfectly possible that the Christians have been on the Isle of Man for almost a thousand years. The name has variously been prefixed with Mc or Mac, a Celtic device, but the family is unquestionably of Scandinavian origin. There are conflicting theories, but the most likely is descent from Gillocrist Mackerthac, a Norwegian noble, sent to Man in 1238 as a sort of trouble-shooter. His descendants would have inherited the power and the land with which he was invested, and that would neatly explain the Christians' emergence in the earliest records as major landowners and politicians in the north of the island, the only pocket of notice-ably Scandinavian clanship, names and customs.

Another historian linked us to one Gillocrist, foster brother of King Godred II of Man. In 1154 land was exchanged between that king and the Priory of St Bees on the Cumberland coast, which might explain how Fletcher Christian's forefathers owned, from an unknown date, Manx property known as Staffland and the Barony of Maughold, names identifying them as having once been ecclesi-astical holdings.

When Godred Crovan, a fugitive from Iceland, conquered Man in 1077 he landed in the north of the island and fought a famous battle at Skyehill, now Scafell. It is he who introduced the Tynwald parliament and divided the island into the six districts that remain today. Perhaps it was then the Christians came to own their ancestral home Milntown, which lies tucked in a glen on the side of Scafell. They even owned that historic hill too, for untold centuries. The truth is still fugitive, but without the dedicated struggle of the Christian family over the centuries, the Isle of Man and the Tynwald, its open-air parliament, would not be the unique things they are. Today, all laws passed by the legislators, a freely elected House of Keys, must still be proclaimed from the Hill of Tynwald at St Johns, as has been the custom for over a millennium.

The round, stepped Tynwald Hill, eighty feet in diameter and twelve feet high, is reputed to be constructed of earth from all parts of the Scandinavian kingdom to which Man once belonged, but it could equally be of Druidic origin, for their legal and civil offices and officers are as clearly reflected on the island as those of the Vikings. From the steps of this hill, a stirring thing whatever its origins, the island's chief judge, the First Deemster, reads the new laws in Manx and English on Midsummer Day, that no man can plead ignorance of them and no official can secretly impose his own rule.

The earliest Christian I could positively trace as an ancestor of Fletcher Christian was such a First Deemster. There is such a plethora of Williams, Johns, and Ewans among the Deemsters of the Christian pedigree that they are numbered according to succession rather than by generation. This Deemster, John Christian I, who with his son Deemster William II, signed a declaration against the Scrope family claim to the island in 1408, held the post if not by accepted hereditary right, then by tradition too strong to break. There can be no doubt that beyond him other Christians, whose names are lost, performed the Tynwald duties we see today.

The Isle of Man requires two Deemsters, one for the north, one for the south, with the first, from the north, being by far the more powerful. As Chief Judges they are responsible for the judicial side

of life. The office has always been of the greatest dignity and importance, and its inherent Manxness is nowhere better illustrated than
in the last part of the Deemster's Oath, '. . . I . . . do swear that I
will, without respect of favour or friendship, love or gain, consan-
guinity or affinity, envy or malice, execute the laws . . . betwixt
party and party, as indifferently as the herring backbone doth lie in
the midst of the fish.'

As well as their own Deemster Courts which were truly the
backbone of daily life and its strife, the Deemsters sat on every
other court. Perhaps their most difficult role was that of being the
main buffer between the people and the Lord or King of Man,
usually via his representative the Governor. Even on Tynwald Hill
they are positioned between the Lord of Man and his people while
the other officers of government are spread on either side.

Neither the laws nor their interpretation began to be written
until 1594. The Deemsters practised Breast Law, their announcement, 'We give for the Law' being based solely on unwritten precedent to which they alone had full access. It would have been a
dangerous thing to give such unfettered power to an untrained man,
perhaps one who did not clearly understand that even the juries
(Enquests) went to great lengths to avoid imposing the death
penalty, though ears were lopped off with abandon. So the Manx
allowed the post to become hereditary, at least in the case of the
Christians.

When James, seventh Earl of Derby and uncrowned king of Man
went to the island in 1627, he found the Christians firmly holding
their inherited lands and influence, impervious to the politics of the
rest of the world. Later, concerned for the future of his family,
who had lost their English estates when Civil War broke out in
1642. James wrote at length to his son Charles.

There be many Christians in this country—that is Christins,
the true name; But they have made themselves chief here,

wherefore if a better Name could be found they would likely
pretend unto it ... But it is not so much that so many be
called Christians, as that by Policie they are crept into the
principall Places of Power; and they be seated round about
the Countrey and in the Heart of it; they are matched with
the best Families; have the best Livings [that is farms] and must
not be neglected.

There were three 'pretenders' that the earl and his son could not
neglect. At that time the First Deemster was Ewan Christian X. He
was twenty-six when he was appointed in 1612, and was to remain
in office for fifty years.

Ewan was probably the most diplomatic of all the Christian
Deemsters, for he held power during the troubled time of the
Commonwealth. Although cousins, nephews, and sons were punished, imprisoned and put to death, he escaped all such retribution.
Yet he was by no means cool of temper. The records are full of
tales of litigations, charges and counter-charges, with the Deemster
often admitting guilt and paying a bloodwite for having struck
someone with whom he disagreed.

Ewan Christian X's private life seems to have been fully as passionate as his public one. Lord Derby, in the document mentioned,
says:

Someone in a pleasant humour says he thought the Deemster
did not get so many Bastards for Lust's Sake, as in Policie, to
make the Name of the Christians flourish ... It is very true
that there be many Bastards here in this Isle: and he is to be
wonder'd at who wonders at it. Be sure it would be very well
if that Law were here as in other Places that all knowne Bastards were called after their Mother's names ... they are
subject to make Factions ... Men of the same Name will side
with one another against any Body.

If the Christians didn't own your land, or marry into your family, then they had children by your daughters, children who took the surname Christian and who then stuck by the family in times of strife.

Lord Derby quickly got the Christians on his side by appointing another 'pretender' governor. This was Edward Christian, first cousin of Ewan X. At twenty-two, in 1612, he sailed with a flotilla of the East India Company, charged with capturing the trade of Western India from the Portuguese. After remarkable adventures during which he had been kidnapped and threatened with death, he returned three years later as commander of one of the vessels and an extremely successful man. Back in London he was arraigned for having made a private fortune and for having 'carried himself too proudlie'.

Yet, it suited both Derbys and Christians to have Edward as Governor; they could run the island virtually as they wished. But Edward's love of profit and status became troublesome and the earl removed him from the governorship. Then, hearing rumours that Parliament supporters might attack Man, he gave Edward charge of the milita.

Edward took over Peel Castle and set up a training camp. At the same time there were riots throughout the island about the tithing system. The new Governor, John Greenhalgh, wanted to impose martial law, but Edward refused his troops. Judging his own situation more dangerous than that of the Crown, Lord Derby sailed back with English troops to quell the island's 12,000 people. Edward Christian was charged with sedition and brought to trial. With the help of his cousin, Deemster Ewan, he got off reasonably lightly. Instead of being executed, he was fined 1,000 marks 'and his bodie to perpetual imprisonment or untill hee shall be relapsed by the said Lord'.

Ewan, aware of the delicacy of his position, now made over Milntown to his son John, and the small estate of Ronaldsway (the present Manx airport) to William, his youngest son, commonly known as Illiam Dhone (Brown-haired William). William—the third 'pretender'—had been a member of the House of Keys and steward of the Abbey, and by 1648 he was Receiver-General, responsible for the Derbys' finances. In 1649, after the execution of King Charles, Parliament asked Derby to surrender the island, and when he refused simply gave it to Lord Fairfax, who did nothing to claim it.

In August 1651, Derby moved to the mainland to continue fighting, leaving the government in the hands of his wife, and the remaining militia in the command of William Christian. Then, in September, Derby was captured in Chester. Knowing the island could not hold out against Cromwell, Lady Derby wrote offering to surrender it in return for the release of her husband. The Manxmen were not pleased. They had never been part of the British Isles and never wanted to be; they would consider surrendering, but on their own terms. On 19 October 1651, 1,800 Manxmen met at Ronaldsway; they agreed to oppose Lady Derby, and within ten days had taken over all the forts on the island except her Castle Rushen. Meanwhile, Lord Derby had been executed in Bolton, on the 15th.

The Commonwealth fleet, under the command of Colonel Duckenfeld, shortly arrived at Ramsey, close to Milntown. A deputation of four men, led by John Christian acting as Deemster on behalf of Ewan X, his father, offered surrender without bloodshed in return for 'laws and liberties as formerly they had'. There was no immediate answer; instead William Christian of Ronaldsway was enlisted by Duckenfeld to present a request for surrender to Lady Derby. Was he a traitor to his liege, or was he a patriot, behaving in the manner best suited to secure what he could on behalf of the people of Man? Did Duckenfeld enlist him because Illiam Dhone controlled the forts and the people and had made some kind of deal at the expense of the Derbys? This is but part of the controversy which surrounds Illiam Dhone. Lady Derby was arrested and the Isle of Man became part of the Commonwealth.

England wanted to dispense with the office of Governor, but found that several courts would be unconstitutional, so William was appointed to the position, retaining that of Receiver-General. Ewan X had recently died, but the two Deemsters were William's brother John XI and his nephew Edward XII, John's eldest son. Once more the Christians of Milntown had a firm grip on the island.

When Charles II was restored to the throne, Charles, eighth Earl of Derby, tried to tempt him to return confiscated Derby properties. The king was persuaded that to do this would be a breach of the Act of Indemnity. In a revenge by proxy, Derby accused William Christian of plotting against his father and signed a mandate 'to all his officers, both civil and military, to bring William Christian to account for all his illegal actions and rebellions on or before the year of our Lord 1651'. That is, Illiam Dhone was to be tried for his actions during the time of the Commonwealth, something which no one other than the regicides had undergone.

William denied the right of the court to try him, but Derby argued that the Act of Indemnity pardoned only crimes against the English Crown and that it was possible separately to be guilty of treason against the King and Lord of Man.

In spite of the efforts of William's brother, Deemster John XI, and his eldest son, Deemster Edward XII, Illiam Dhone was shot on 2 January 1663 at Hango Hall within sight of his home. King Charles was incensed at this formalized murder and Derby was ordered to pay damages and to restore Ronaldsway to William's sons. Everyone else involved was punitively fined and Deemsters John and Edward were reinstated. But the Derbys' malevolence continued and in 1770 Illiam Dhone's descendants left Man to flourish in Ireland and Virginia. For several generations more, the Christians spent their time equally on Man and in Cumberland and Ewan XIII was the first permanently to settle at Ewanrigg on the mainland.

When Ewan's son, John XIV, was twenty-nine, he married Bridget Senhouse, who was directly descended from Edward I, and Queen Eleanor of Castile.

There was great prosperity at Ewanrigg during the life of John and Bridget. They built the kennels and huntsmen's quarters of beautifully dressed and pointed limestone when hunting became formalized and *de rigueur* for the gentlemen of the area. Men were heard to comment that the Christians' kennels were better than most people's houses; the ruins of the building make this unquestionable.

John's and Bridget's grandchildren were remarkable for their talents and attainments. This generation, which included Fletcher, was almost without exception the high point of the Christian family.

Their eldest daughter, Mary, married in 1740 the Reverend Edmund Law, DD, taking a fortune of £3,000, which made her more than an ordinary bride. Within the family she is remembered for always referring to her thirteen children as her baker's dozen and also for the resolutions she made on the April evening before she was wed, aged eighteen.

RESOLUTIONS OF MARY CHRISTIAN UPON THE DAY OF HER MARRIAGE

I resolve:

1. Never to contradict my dear Husband without it be quite necessary and then with the greatest good nature I am mistress of.
2. To serve God more sincerely than I have done in the state I am now about to leave and to lead a life suitable to the Blessed calling of my Husband.
3. Never to fret or fall into a Passion about small matters but to have always a cheerful heart, knowing my blessings much exceed any troubles that can possibly befall me, and in all

dangers to commit myself and family to an All-Wise Providence, and then to be easy about the event.

4. I likewise resolve to lay aside all fondness for dress but to be always neat and clean.

5. I resolve to be very active and never for the sake of saving myself a walk to neglect anything, though it be never so great a trifle.

6. I resolve to be very frugal and never to put my Husband to any needless expense.

7. I resolve to be very kind to my servants, as well to their souls as to their bodies, and always to give exact orders and never to be in a passion if they not be executed.

8. I resolve to treat my friends kindly, but never extravagantly, and to be full as glad to see his relations as my own.

Thus would I live
Thus would I die
And when this world I leave
To Heaven I'd fly.

Mary Christian 28 April 1740.

Almost half a century later on the same date her nephew Fletcher would enact something totally inimical to her piety and morality.

Mary's children, Fletcher's first cousins, were an illustrious brood. The eldest surviving son, John, became Chaplain to the Duke of Portland, Lord Lieutenant of Ireland, and then successively Bishop of Clonfert (aged only thirty-seven), of Killala and of Elphin. Edward became Chief Justice of England, the last to have automatic cabinet rank and elevation to the peerage. He was the first Baron Ellenborough, and made fun of his younger cousin, Edward Christian of Moorland Close, all his life.

Ewan, Joseph and Thomas Law all started their careers in India; Ewan made a fortune, Joseph died there, and Thomas left the East

India Company for America where he was befriended by George Washington and married his granddaughter.

George Law became yet another bishop, eventually occupying the see of Bath and Wells. The youngest of the Laws was Joanna, who kept up the Indian connection begun in the sixteenth century by marrying Sir Thomas Rumbold, Governor of Madras for three years from 1771.

Humphrey—the youngest brother of Mary and of Charles, Fletcher's father—went to Docking, Norfolk, to marry Elizabeth Brett. Through complicated genealogical arrangements their eldest son, just eight years older than Fletcher, inherited Docking Hall provided he changed his name to Hare. Hares still live in the fine old Hall, with portraits of Christians as their ancestors, and consider changing their name back to Christian.

John and Bridget's eldest son was Ewan XV. He worked with his mother's family, the Senhouses of Netherhall, to extend the family mining interests and began with them the expansion of the tiny seaside hamlet of Elnefoot into Maryport, soon to become one of the country's most important ports for trade with the New World. Ewan died unmarried and was succeeded by his brother, John XVI, who had married into the rich Curwen family, one of the ten oldest names in the country, but a family who had never distinguished themselves until they became connected with the Christians; they had two sons and six daughters, the eldest of whom was only sixteen when Mrs Christian died in 1762. Four years later John himself died in Petty France in Gloucestershire and eleven-year-old John XVII inherited. This rich young man was to become John Christian Curwen and was a ward of his uncle Henry Curwen.

John Christian XVII was well cast as head of this generation although only eight years older than his first cousin, Fletcher. He was perhaps the most influential of all Christians and certainly made the greatest contribution to national life. At nineteen he married Margaret Taubman in Kirk Malew on the Isle of Man. Margaret was seven years older than he and was also his sister-in-law, for her brother had married John's eldest sister, Dorothy. They lived on Man for a while at the Bowling Green, Margaret's parents' house, where their only child, John XVIII, was born in 1776. She died after two and a half years of marriage in 1778. John remained on Man a while as he was elected to the Manx House of Keys in 1777.

John left the island in 1779, saying it had been created solely to plague anyone who had dealings with it and his son was mainly brought up by his Taubman grandparents. During the next two years he spent wildly to rebuild Ewanrigg. Soon after Margaret died, his old guardian Henry Curwen also died, leaving his only daughter Isabella, then aged thirteen, to the care of John's sisters, Bridget and Jane. Isabella was splendidly rich, heiress to Workington Hall and huge mining interests. She attracted titled and rich suitors as she grew up and undoubtedly was noticed by Fletcher Christian on her visits to Ewanrigg. Her trustees humoured her with such gifts as the island in the middle of Windermere, eventually named Belle Isle after her. A rich merchant had shown much nerve by commissioning a round house to be built on it, but he was so mocked for his 'pepper-pot' folly that it was advertised for auction and bought in the spring of 1781 for Isabella at 1,640 guineas, less than half the amount expended upon it.

Isabella always had an affection for her 'prodigious' cousin John and in spite of every distraction, including smart schools in London, her wards could not cope with her. John and she fell in love, he returning at intervals from Europe to see her. She was a Ward of Chancery and, for reasons never made clear, the Lord Chancellor forbade them to marry. This was a red rag to such spirited and financially independent young people. They sped secretly to Edinburgh and were married at the Gaelic Chapel on 9 October 1782, and, whatever the law thought, there was a high old time at Ewanrigg on the 10th, when John's sisters danced with the servants. They married again on 4 November, at the Parish Church of

St Mary Magdalene, Bermondsey. Isabella was seventeen and John was twenty-six. He gave her a diamond costing £1,000 and they went to Paris and the South of France with Bridget and Jane still in attendance.

John now abandoned Ewanrigg, which he had extended and given an entrance hallway of marble into which he could, and did, drive a coach and four. He went to live at Workington Hall and added crenellations, as well as making Belle Isle into a blissful summer retreat. Apart from leading a brilliant social life in London and the provinces with his wife, John energetically developed the mining interests of the Christians and Curwens. He pioneered the distribution of free milk to the poor, began the first Agricultural Society, and was MP for Carlisle for many years. When the British Parliament first legislated to introduce Social Security in 1912, John was given fulsome credit for having been first to devise and to operate the equivalent of National Insurance. 'The first person to subscribe,' said John Christian Curwen, 'must be the worker who was going to benefit, the second must be the employer and the third, the state'. This was exactly the scheme that was adopted and with his Friendly Societies John Christian Curwen had run such schemes on his estates. It is little wonder that his cousin Fletcher grew up with revolutionary ideas, it was simply the Christian way.

Like so many of his predecessors, John fought for those less fortunate than himself and took his pleasures among them, too. At one political meeting in Workington he reminded his audience that he was like a father to them all. There was much laughter when a woman called out that he was indeed father to at least half the town! John and his sisters knew and cared for the family at Moorland Close and Fletcher saw and was told the import of the large number of family portraits that hung in the great red-brick house of Ewanrigg. He could not help seeing his cousin's benevolence, industry and charity and he must have known too the wilful Isabella, rich and beautiful, less than a year older than himself, and the obvious object of a young man's affections, especially those of someone with ambition.

So, for uncountable generations, the Viking-rooted Christians had been First Deemsters of the Isle of Man. They owned the best land, made the best marriages, wielded almost unlimited power, ruled by ancient right, might and an army of bastards. Political expediency in the difficult (for them) aftermath of the Commonwealth and Restoration saw the family move their seat to Ewanrigg, high on a cliff in Cumbria. While keeping all their land and most of their influence on Man, they were safe from the bloody thrusts of the island's politics, and could concentrate on filling coffers rather than coffins. Now, late in the eighteenth century, they were almost at their zenith. The sons being prepared to inherit were destined to become memorable men in the corridors of Westminster, the Inns of Court, the Cabinet, the peerage, the palaces of the Church, the governments and commerce of India and both Indies, the highest ranks of the Navy and the Universities and, most unforgettably, the newly discovered islands of the South Pacific.

4

Brothers in Bankruptcy

Being a younger son of a well-to-do family is a pretty good way to grow up; you learn by watching your elders' mistakes and the mistakes máde upon them, so you may drift through puberty into adulthood blameless, but knowing. As your parents become more financially secure you enjoy the education and pleasures of their superior indulgence. There is no reason to think this was not the pattern for Fletcher Christian. He had both a mother ambitious for her sons and the example of his many cousins to follow, the collected addresses of whom were an almanac of everything rich and grand in Cumbria.

It was suggested in C. S. Wilkinson's *The Wake of the Bounty* that Fletcher's future was always to take over Moorland Close, and that this is why he was so named. Precedent shows his sister Ann was the most likely legatee; if not her, then the older John. The plan was for Fletcher to go to university, probably Peterhouse or St John's at Cambridge, just as the Christians always seemed to do.

His childhood world was one of adventure and action. All about were streams to fish, hills to climb, woods, nooks, crannies, glens and valleys to explore on the piebald horse that, until recently, you could see painted on a door of the farmstead. The horizon in every direction is one of mountains, powerful and pastel, as only Cumbrian peaks can be; and there were wonderful battlements of red brick in the backyard. Fletcher was undoubtedly stimulated by the outdoors and activity, for all who knew him agree he was strongly built and athletic, proud of his muscular and acrobatic abilities. Stories have been published of his playing truant from school to do boyish things, but I have never been able to trace these anecdotes to their sources, likely as they seem.

Fletcher's primary school was the small Parish School of Brigham, in a room in Eller Cottage on the High Street; the dwelling stands today in a cosy garden, but the name of his Dame is forgotten.

Then Fletcher was accepted as a pupil at Cockermouth Free Grammar School, a dour stone building which stood at the entrance of All Saints Churchyard. It had been founded in 1676 and was free to all from Cockermouth, although term fees and other costs were normally paid, which generally meant that the poor did not go after all. Cockermouth was not too badly off, for it was a busy little place. The Main Street was then a cobbled road and the houses mostly low thatched whitewashed cottages. The chief occupations were agriculture, hat making, tanning and weaving; these last three all used plenty of water and the houses of the tradespeople were clustered close to the river banks, off Main Street and Kirkgate. Many of the cottages were primitive enough still to have an outside staircase to the upper floor bedrooms. None of the churches seen now was then built and most of the big buildings were public houses or coaching stations. The grand blue stone and tile houses of the successful merchants and landowners were spread farther away from the busy and doubtless smelly centre, except for Cockermouth Castle itself.

The route Fletcher rode from Moorland Close to the Grammar School is difficult to follow today, as it has been slashed by fences and highways, but it meets Cockermouth's Main Street exactly opposite the beautiful house of John Wordsworth, father of the poet

William and his limpet-like sister Dorothy. Much has been made of Fletcher Christian and William Wordsworth being contemporaries at the Free Grammar School, but Fletcher was six years older than William and schoolboys rarely fraternize over such a wide age gap; even brothers do not.

The Grammar School, typical of the time, combined instruction in the principles of religion with courses in Greek, Latin, English and a wide range of mathematical subjects, including trigonometry and navigation. The terms were 5 shillings for entrance and 6 shillings a quarter. You were expected to pay more for entrance if you were from prosperous stock, but children of the poor could pay just this minimum sum, known as a cockpenny.

Fletcher then followed his brother Edward to St Bees School, close to Whitehaven. Founded in 1583 by a charter of Queen Elizabeth I, it was a venerable and respected institution by the late eighteenth century, closely linked to The Queen's College, Oxford (which now owns Moorland Close). In Fletcher's time, probably 1777–79 or so, it was still one building, which now forms the school's dining hall. The ground floor was the schoolroom, the top floor contained the headmaster's quarters and offices for the governors. Boarders were accepted at thirteen guineas a year, fifteen guineas if the long holiday was included. Few boys can actually have boarded at the school itself, there being virtually no extra space, and the majority would have lodged privately in the tiny village.

School was from seven in the morning until eleven, and from one until five. Unless they had leave to play, the scholars then had to walk home 'two by two together so far as their way lyeth . . .' On Saturdays they had to spend two hours writing, whilst being examined on the Catechism in 'English, Latin or Greek, according to their capabilities'. But these were young gentlemen from the finest Westmorland and Cumbrian families. It was not all discipline and examination. On 13 October 1778 the *Cumberland Pacquet* recorded, 'Last week the young gentlemen students at St Bees gave a very elegant ball to the ladies of Egremont and other neighbouring places. Upwards of thirty couples danced country dances, and the whole was conducted with the greatest propriety'.

When Fletcher Christian's brother Edward was publicly defending him after the mutiny, he pointed out in Fletcher's defence, that he had 'stayed at school longer than men generally do who enter the Navy, and being allowed by all to possess extraordinary abilities, is an excellent scholar'. This is not quite the truth. Fletcher seems certainly to have been as clever as his brother avers, but he stayed at school because he had no intention of going into the Navy until such a choice was forced upon him by the mismanagement of his elder brothers, Edward included.

While Fletcher was at St Bees preparing to move on to higher education, his security, social and financial, was whisked from beneath him. His mother was bankrupt, Moorland Close was to be sold and it was largely the fault of those from whom he should have been learning how to manage.

Each of the three brothers alive at the time plays an important part in the new knowledge we have of this dramatic reshaping of Fletcher's expectations. The eldest, John, is least known and the most selfish. He was admitted to Lincoln's Inn on 29 June 1771, when not quite nineteen, and became a Fellow Commoner at Peterhouse on 2 February 1773. He was up for at least three years, for in the diary of Jane Christian, his first cousin, she writes on 19 June 1776, 'Coz. J. Christian called going to Cambridge next week.' He did not graduate but practised as an attorney in Cockermouth and in London, where he seems to have had offices in several Inns of Court as well as in Pall Mall. In Cockermouth he had very grand premises, the palisaded double-fronted building once (and now) known as the Swan Inn, right on the Market Place, complete with seven rooms for lodgers, a variety of parlours with marble chimney pieces, stablings, a dovecote, a dairy, and the right to four seats in a church pew. From surviving letters it can be inferred that John took some control of the family affairs once he went into business, probably because he expected to inherit; if not, the Close was, at least, security for borrowed money.

Edward Christian, five and a half years younger than John, is the best known of the trio, eventually becoming both the chief public defender of Fletcher and *bête noire* of Bligh, as well as Chief Justice of the Isle of Ely, Professor of the Laws of England at Cambridge, a founder of Downing College, Professor of Law at East India College, Commissioner for Bankrupts and an authority whose published opinions, notably in *Blackstone*, brought him considerable income. He is better remembered in the Inns and Halls as a reliable bore and an eccentric of electrifying inventiveness.

The *Dictionary of National Biography* says: 'He disappointed the high expectations of future distinction which had been formed from his university career and gradually sank so low as to become the subject of practical jokes.' He had been admitted a Pensioner at Peterhouse, where his uncle Edmund Law had recently been Master until his elevation to the riches of the Bishopric of Carlisle. On 4 November 1777, Edward was admitted Foundress Scholar, was BA in 1779, 3rd Wrangler and 2nd Chancellor's medallist and MA in 1782. He was a Member's Prizeman in 1780 and a Fellow of St John's from 1781 to 1789. When he died in 1823 he was said to be 'in the full vigour of his incapacity'.

It was Edward who had the closest contacts with the Wordsworths. He was Headmaster of Hawkshead Grammar School from July 1781 until July 1782, while William was a pupil. Perhaps because of this he was one of the counsel for William and Dorothy Wordsworth in their case against James Lowther, later first Earl of Lonsdale in 1791. Lowther had employed their father as agent and owed the Wordsworths £5,000 when he died. Lowther would not pay this to the Wordsworth estate so there was a huge, scandalous case at the Carlisle Assizes. Lowther retained forty counsel but the Wordsworths could afford only four, led by Edward Christian. Dorothy wrote of him:

'We have got a very clever young man on our side, but he is young and he will not have much authority . . . (but) . . . he has zeal for our interests.' As well as zeal he must have had more authority than Dorothy thought, for the case was won. The wicked earl still refused to pay and it was not until his more honourable heir succeeded that the Wordsworths got their money.

The brother closest in age to Fletcher was Charles, born in 1762, and so only two years older. Of him nothing was known until my discovery of a document detailing 600 years of family history and of a copy made earlier this century of Charles's now lost holograph autobiography. This document makes him a vital new witness to the story of Fletcher Christian.

In 1779, Fletcher's mother and older brothers had to admit finally there was something terminally wrong with their finances. Privately, Ann had been struggling for years and what seems to have happened was this: her elder sons had borrowed heavily against the estate in the interest of their careers and university educations with absolute disregard for reality. It was irresponsible, especially to their younger brothers and sister. Whatever happened, John and Edward would still have their smart Cambridge education and their Inns of Law, but if something went wrong, Charles, Fletcher and Humphrey would have no hope of such education and their sister Mary would have no hope of marriage, for she would have no fortune, a far worse disability.

Ann and her family had suffered vagaries of fortune even when Charles Senior was alive; he was either a bad attorney or a bad farmer or both. In 1752 he borrowed money from his eldest brother, John XVI, and also leased two plots of land from him for £24 a year. By 1755 Charles and Ann Christian had to discharge a debt to Thomas Brunsfield by giving him most of the extra pieces of land they had bought, but by the time Charles died thirteen years later, they had again been acquiring land, from the Fletchers of Cockermouth.

The records of the family, such as they are, exist because first Charles and then his widow and children regarded the head of the family as a pit full of money as deep as the coal mines he developed so well. Even when John Christian XVII was still a minor, he was lending Ann's eldest son John sums of £400 at reduced rates of interest, with the approval of his guardian Henry Curwen. No reasons for the loans are ever given in the records but they must have been personal ones, perhaps for education, as by 1772 Ann again owed Brunsfield a serious amount of money. This time she was bailed out by Roger Fleming, a mariner of Cockermouth, who paid £600 and got the deeds of their plot called Simonscales in return. I can only surmise that Brunsfield was some kind of regular and too-trusting supplier to the farmstead.

In December 1773, nine-year-old Fletcher Christian became a brother-in-law for the first time when John married a woman identified only as Ann. The younger Ann's name appears on a document signed on 17 December together with that of her aunt, Mary Hardy of Wisbech, Cambridgeshire. Mary had given John £400 on the condition that Ann junior be given an income of £30 per year. The capital was secured against the Close, but by 1775, John and his mother mortgaged the place for £1,500 to James Christian. James was a Manx Christian, born at the family's ancestral home, Milntown. He had made a fortune in business in London, where he was well known as Master of Grigsby's Coffee House. The respite for Moorland Close was short and troubled. Although James's fiscal spirit was healthy and willing, his physical state was not and in July 1778, he was dead, aged seventy-three.

There were distressing deaths for Fletcher to witness close to home, too. In August 1777, John and Ann's first child, a son called Charles, died, and a few days after Christmas 1778, their daughter Maria was also buried in Brigham churchyard. After this they seemed to have given up for there are no further records of births or deaths. By 1779, Ann's father, Jacob Dixon, was also dead but this had not made her absolute mistress of Moorland Close. The dead man had left his interest to his youngest sister, Frances, now married to Patricius Senhouse of the Fitz; and she expected an income of £20 a year. Presumably to ensure such incomes for them both, the two women, aunt and niece, rented the troubled property to John XVII, whose first wife had also died early in 1779, supposedly from measles she caught from nursing her young son. But the women were clutching at straws.

On 9 March 1779, Ann Christian was 'carried to Carlisle for her son's debts' (John's presumably) and shortly afterwards the executors of James Christian wrote saying that they wanted their money to pay his bequests to charity. John put his grand house in Cockermouth up for sale. A large advertisement appeared on the front page of the *Cumberland Pacquet* on Tuesday 19 October, describing its facilities and attractions and it continued each Tuesday until 9 November.

John XVII had to step in and he offered the executors on Man a moiety of Moorland Close, retaining the other half as his own security for monies he had already paid out. The executors agreed in principle as the putative value of the moiety of £750 suited their purpose, exactly half the mortgage having somehow been repaid. Months of niggling followed, for the Manxmen wanted the value of the Moorland Close moiety proved by public auction.

The Letter Book of Charles Udale, painstaking and loyal agent to John XVII, and John's letters from Brussels (he was making the grand tour), show their patience with Ann and the extraordinary lengths they took to help her avoid such an auction, which would expose her plight to the public gaze and, apparently, antagonize an already spiky Frances Senhouse.

Some time early in 1780, the family resigned themselves to admitting defeat. By now Ann was in debt for the staggering amount of £6,490. 0s. 11d, which can be multiplied by at least forty to obtain the modern equivalent. Ann owed money everywhere, so did her elder sons. As well as Moorland Close, everything else had to go, and James's executors still insisted on the auction.

The moiety of the Close that John XVII had publicly to encash was advertised in the *Cumberland Pacquet* on 14 March 1780. It was to be sold at Cockermouth's Globe Hotel on Monday, 10 April. No one wanted a moiety of a bankrupt farmstead, and John Christian XVII cut further negotiations short by remitting the Manx executors a few shillings less than £750. He then took over all the family's possessions, including their sheep and wood, which brought him assets valued at just over £4,500, two-thirds the value of the debts he was paying.

For John XVII, there was still no end to it. Edward Christian was writing to him, first hoping that some arrangement could be made so that one day 'some of us may be in such circumstances as to think it a desirable object to redeem the place of our nativity, which has been so long in my mother's family—but if ever we should have such fortune, I hope at the same time we should have honesty enough to pay off as far as we were able the debts of the farm and restore your loss.' Edward announces in the same letter that he had just been elected a Fellow of St John's, worth some eighty guineas a year, and from that he hoped generously to allow his 'poor mother twenty guineas a year'; the catch was that the annuity was actually to come from John and be repaid by Edward!

Ann had £20 a year from some other source (almost certainly John Christian) and Edward goes on to say that with the total of £40 his mother would be able to live comfortably anywhere, sharp and urgent advice for she was still threatened with arrest for some of the debts. Edward suggested the family might remove to the Isle of Man 'or any other place, if they could be prevailed upon'.

John agreed to finance the extra twenty guineas for his aunt, as seen by his account books. Only two years after John had bailed Ann and her family out of debt, she and her eldest son again owed him money, another £888. 6s. 4d.

With no home left in Cumbria, Ann Christian, now aged thirty-nine, went to live in Douglas with her annuity, her daughter and her two youngest sons, Fletcher and Humphrey. Charles had joined the West Riding of Yorkshire Militia in Liverpool and by 2 May 1780, he was marching to Leeds and planning to be a surgeon.

If Fletcher Christian had not known much of his Manx background before, or did not know there was a long ballad written about Illiam Dhone, one of his most famous ancestors, he would now have learned quickly. In the same year a broadsheet of 'The Ballad of Illiam Dhone' was privately printed and widely circulated for political reasons. It was known and widely sung anyway, but now you would have had to be very sheltered indeed not to know the story, particularly if you were a Christian, or related to them. And most of the Manx were one or the other, or said they were.

Among those on the Isle of Man during 1780 who would also have been reminded of the Christians' long history was Richard Betham, the Collector of Customs, as well as the naval officer who was shortly to marry his daughter, Betsy. His name was William Bligh and he had earlier been based in Douglas for several years. Now, after returning from his voyage to the South Pacific with Cook, he was again in Douglas.

The island was so small that everyone knew of the Christians, including Bligh. This is when he either first met Fletcher Christian or at least heard of him. Among the places where he had stayed in Douglas was the Nunnery, where his hostess was Dorothy Christian Taubman, Fletcher's first cousin. It was her husband who was finally to bring these two men together.

But for the moment Fletcher Christian had still not decided to join the Navy. The move to Man had dramatically illustrated to him the difference between his previous expectations and the new reality. Once he had had a position and future in society. Now he had neither, unless he re-created them himself.

5

'Riot ... obscenity ... drunkenness ... debauchery'

I n 1780, Douglas, chief port and township on the Isle of Man, mustered few more than 2,500 people, but life was gay with public assemblies for dances, with card parties, dinner parties and tea parties.

The island was in somewhat of a muddle. In 1765 the passing of the Revestment Act meant the British Crown owned the regalities and customs duties of Man, which it had purchased from the Duke of Atholl, the successor to the Derbys. The King of England was now the King of Man, but the island's prosperity was smashed because until then the island had fattened itself on the profits of smuggling. This was unpopular with the British who sorely missed the lost revenue. When ports and towns were suddenly swarming with British Customs Officers, the Manx saw it as personal betrayal by Atholl.

By the time the Christians of Moorland Close arrived, things were simmering down and Douglas was a port from which the Royal Navy could strike out at smugglers from Ireland on their way to England.

The new family had as a co-citizen Thomas Scott, immediate younger brother of Sir Walter, by whom the author was supplied with the material for *Peveril of the Peak*; Thomas had planned his own literary work on the subject, but wearied of the task of transcription. The Heywoods, who had sold the Nunnery to the Taubmans, had returned from Whitehaven in 1779, to live on The Parade, the newest and most fashionable part of town. Peter Heywood, the family head, had once been Second Deemster, but now returned as Seneschal for the Duke of Atholl, who retained personal interests on the island. With Peter Heywood Senior were most of his ten living children, including six-year-old Peter, later to sail with Fletcher on *Bounty*.

Herring fishing and the curing of the rock-hard red herrings (kippers were still to be invented) were the basis of any industry to which the lower classes, no longer smugglers, could apply themselves, and during winter their boats were drawn up on the pebbly sweep of beach, for the herring is one of the few fish that is at its peak in midsummer. There was a small Old Pier, a small shipyard and a small brewery, and St George's Church was just being completed. Most of the houses were on the flat land and the hills upon which boarding houses and bed-and-breakfast hotels today cluster were then farms and gardens.

There was a regular packet service between Whitehaven and Douglas which helped bind the ties between Cumbria and the island and the many families who had members on both sides of the water, the Christians included. Excitement for the richer young was confined to one another's company and the occasional great storm in which they might watch men and their boats being lost in the harbour. At the Pier, the Royal Navy's ships were constantly calling, on their way to and from chasing recidivist smugglers. Privateers brought in their prizes, recruiting parties and press gangs were about, and riots by the 'uncivilized' were not unknown. The year 1780 also saw the formation of the first regiment of the Royal Manx Fencibles and, in 1781, John Wesley preached in Douglas Marketplace, both events to remember in their own way.

A regular and important user of the packet from Whitehaven was Jane Christian, sister both to John XVII and Mrs Taubman of the Nunnery, Fletcher's first cousins. Jane's diaries show she was constantly at the opera in London, at Windsor, buying and commenting upon fashions, dining with the Duke of Norfolk in St James's Square, seeing the Prince of Wales and the Duke of Clarence at soirées and masquerades and St James's Palace. She regularly joined the knights, bishops, ladies and lords of her acquaintance and her family for teas and dinners of twenty-five people or more. When the season was over she travelled by 'easy stages' from country house to inn to family dwellings all over England, several times eating each of three meals in a different house and sleeping in a fourth. Considering coach fares were equivalently far higher even than today's exorbitant railway prices, the cost must have been staggering. But like all her sisters she had a fortune of some £3,000 and an income from shares in the ships and mines the family continued to buy. For a long time the sisters shared a house in Whitehaven.

Wherever Fletcher Christian was at this time he could not have avoided knowing what was happening to John, Jane and others of the Ewanrigg family, either at first hand or through the gossip that warms and enlivens all small towns and which could scarcely have ignored the island-wide entertainments arranged when Jane sailed in from Whitehaven.

⋯⋰⋱⋯

From Edward Christian's assertion that his brother stayed at school longer than normal for someone planning to go to sea we could infer that Fletcher remained at St Bees, boarding in the village. In *The Life of Vice-Admiral William Bligh* by George Mackaness, Fletcher Christian is said to have actually been aboard HMS *Cambridge*, in 1782–83, during which Bligh was the vessel's sixth lieutenant. But assiduous searching and diligent cross-checking does not reveal Fletcher's name on the muster sheet of *Cambridge* and so the years 1780 to April 1783 remain a mystery. It is quite likely that he remained at school until the end of 1782 and sailed only between Whitehaven and Man.

Remembering that he later called his Tahitian wife Isabella, and that the names of Fletcher and Isabella Curwen have been linked in a number of romantic theories, it is no surprise, six months after Isabella secretly married John Christian XVII, to find Fletcher signing on as a midshipman aboard HMS *Eurydice*, Captain George Courtney. The date was 25 April 1783, and the ship was moored at Spithead.

The Navy considered merit far more important than the Army, where you could buy yourself in, up, down or out. Wellington said at least three-quarters of army commissions were so filled. Officers of ships were highly trained specialists with enormous responsibility, both for the king's men and his money. There was no equivalent charge on land and you could actually be dismissed from the Navy for incompetence; you could also go all the way up to being a full admiral, whoever you were, something inconceivable in the Army.

Many a common man had risen to the rank of naval officer on merit and examination and the service was one of the few means of acceptable upward social mobility. 'It is no disgrace', said the anonymous writer of *An Inquiry into the Present State of the British Navy* . . . (1815), 'to the post captains of the English Navy who have many lords amongst them, that these are also the worthy offspring of tailors, shoemakers, farmers, ale-house keepers, sailors, pilots, haberdashers, milliners, in fact every calling under the sun.' This would have been unthinkable in the Army and it was precisely the opportunities for the satisfaction of real ambition and for social mobility offered by the Navy that appealed to Fletcher Christian. It was the finest—and only—way he could follow the path of service and position that his background demanded.

Eurydice was a 6th rater, with twenty-four 9-pound guns and although built at Portsmouth only two years before, was of an almost archaic design. She alone of the many types of ship in the Navy could still be manoeuvred by rowing. She was 114 feet long and 32 feet wide, but had oars 113 feet long, each manned by a group from among her 140 men, 25 of whom were marines to keep order and discipline.

When Fletcher joined, the ship was loading stores and being generally overhauled, for she had just returned from the West Indies, where in the previous October she had captured the French brig *Samea*. She was not going to sail again until October 1783, and during the six months Fletcher was first aboard he would have seen much of the worst aspects of naval life. For although officers and young gentlemen like himself had some shore leave, the seamen, guarded by armed marines, did not; hence the custom of allowing women on board. Among the most enlightening pages of Ian Ball's *Pitcairn, Children of Bounty*, are those that illustrate this vicious aspect of naval life. Ball quotes a document privately printed in 1821 and submitted to the Lords Commissioners of the Admiralty. It was entitled *Statement Respecting the Prevalence of Certain Immoral Practices in His Majesty's Navy*.

It has become an established practice in the British Navy to admit, even invite, on board our ships of war, immediately on their arrival in port, as many prostitutes as the men, and in many cases, the officers may choose to entertain to the number, in the larger ships, of several hundred at a time; all of whom remain on board, domesticated with the ship's company, men and boys, until they again put to sea.

The tendency of this practice is to render a ship of war, while in port, a continual scene of riot and disorder, of obscenity and blasphemy, or drunkenness, lewdness, and debauchery. During this time the married seamen are frequently joined by their wives and families, (sometimes comprising daughters from ten to fifteen years of age) who are forced to submit to the alternative of mixing with these abandoned women, whose language and behaviour are usually of the most polluting description; or of foregoing altogether the society of their husbands and parents. These all inhabit the same deck, where whatever their age or sex or character, they are huddled promiscuously together, eating, drinking and sleeping without any adequate means of separation or privacy for the most part without even the slightest screen between their berths; and where in the sight and hearing of all around them, they live in the unrestrained indulgence of every licentious propensity which may be supposed to actuate inmates of this description.

A Naval Officer of large experience asserts that from the time he entered the Navy, about twenty-eight years ago (1787?), he had served in no ship in which, while in port, the custom of permitting women of the very worst description to come and remain on board was not tolerated, and even encouraged, by the Commanding Officer. The Lieutenants and grown Midshipmen were obliged to sit at table and associate with them and to be witnesses to the debauchery and indecency which took place, not only there but among the men also. It was even common for the women to employ all their arts to debauch these youths who generally were caught in their snares, and became their prey.

The authors 'boldly and confidently' attacked the normal defence of the toleration of prostitutes aboard His Majesty's ships, a cry that if women were not permitted the men would turn to one another, the penalty for which was death. The authors said, 'if there really exists a danger of this kind in the Navy, it arises more from the very practice which we have been reprobating ... What can be more *unnatural*, more contrary to all the feelings of our common nature than the open, undisguised, unblushing promiscuous concubinage which now takes place. Is not the person . . . tutored in this school of impurity and licentiousness . . . less likely than others to shrink from any other abomination which may be suggested to his mind?'

Their point is good, for men and women *are* easily brutalized. The report seems to have had little effect, and if it had been implemented the mutinies of 1797 might have flared again.

Young Midshipman Christian would at least have been familiar with the seamen, if not with their life aboard ship. Many, if not most, of the men on *Eurydice* wore pigtails, and those who could not grow one would pin on a false tail of teased oakum, the fibre used for caulking, which was made by unravelling rope. Some of the prettier or more forward men affected curls or lovelocks over their ears, like women of high fashion, and many wore gold earrings. These were part of a sailor's superstition, supposed to improve eyesight as well as to ensure a burial if a body was mercifully washed up on a Christian shore. Some captains forbade them on the grounds that they were un-English.

Each man had two hammocks, one in use and one clean; they had to be scrubbed of the inevitable infestation once a week. (Those not members of a watch had to be out of their hammocks by 7.30 am; if not, the hammock was cut down.)

The horror of the food is worse than most imaginations permit. Ship's biscuit, euphemistically called bread, was the most liberal ration. They were cooked in the royal bakeries attached to the dockyards at the rate of seventy a minute. Each biscuit was about 5 inches in diameter, thick, brown, well cooked and stamped in the centre, which was therefore even harder than the rest. They should have been made of wheat flour and some pea flour, but bone dust was thought often to have been added. It is likely. The eighteenth-century bakers, in an effort to please the lust for ever whiter bread, commonly added alum, which gave a harsh bitter flavour. They also mixed in chalk, lime, poisonous white lead, animal bones, and, it was charged, bones from the charnel houses. Those who had some sympathy for their customers included jalap, a purgative Mexican root, to counteract the costive effect of the alum.

The pea flour content of the biscuits never blended evenly but clumped together in threads or lumps of incredible hardness which could not be bitten through until age had softened the biscuits. When old, they developed a musty sour taste and became the perfect breeding ground for weevils and maggots, which in hot weather multiplied to an unspeakable degree. You could ask the cook to rebake the biscuits but it was more common to eat them in the dark, when the eye and the stomach were less consciously assaulted. It is said an enduring memory of naval service was the dull thumping rhythm of mealtimes which filled this darkness, as men methodically thumped their biscuits onto the table before each mouthful, hoping to dislodge what wildlife they could. If you bribed the cook, and it paid to, he might sometimes pound the biscuits with sugar and pork fat to make a sort of cake.

The salted beef and pork were worse; there was not even the brief pleasure of enjoying it relatively fresh at the outset of a voyage. The naval custom was that old meat had to be eaten first and the ship's company could expect to finish barrels of salted meat returned from other ships or which had been turned up in some forgotten corner of a warehouse. After several years in salt, even the best meat is unwholesome, shrunken and stone hard. There were wholly believable rumours that the mahogany-coloured stuff was horsemeat; Negroes who walked near victualling yards were said to disappear. The beef was worse than the pork but sailors could carve curios out of either. Both are said to have taken a good polish.

Each four pound piece of 'meat' was likely to be mainly bone, gristle and fat, and the provisioners packed the casks short anyway, so that a sailor's pound was said to be only twelve ounces. To ensure he had something approaching a good serving, from time to time a man might trade and hoard his ration over several days.

The water quickly became slimy, foul with algae.

Breakfast was supposed to be burgoo, or porridge, but even a naval surgeon had said it was cruel to expect men to eat it. Most was given to the pigs and other animals on board, for the combination of bad oatmeal, filthy ship's water and the inattention of the cook made it wicked stuff. You could elect not to take this or any other ration and draw money or save credit for purchases in port; many did when it came to breakfast's oatmeal. As an alternative some would boil burnt ship's biscuit in water to make a thick, dark paste which was sweetened with sugar, when available, and called Scotch coffee.

Raisins and currants and flour were carried among the provisions and the messes would be given these in lieu of meat one day a week to make those boiled duffs and puddings which are still favoured by the English. Other substitutes might be rice instead of biscuit or the equally foul cheese, oil instead of cheese, sugar instead of rancid butter. Each mess of six to eight men shared one table which was hooked to the beams when not in use and fixed between the guns when it was.

It is easy to see how the alcohol which was so liberally distributed was important to fill the stomach, to give some suggestion of nutrition, and to dull the senses and any sensitivity that might be left. Seamen were allowed a gallon of beer a day, while it lasted, then a pint of wine; curiously most seamen preferred white wine to the more robust reds and service in the Mediterranean was unpopular because they got only red. They were also issued grog twice a day; this was one part of rum to three of water, a pint of the mixture per man and, at lunch, lemon juice was added as an anti-scorbutic. It was common to save this allowance for regular and painful binges, especially at Christmas time.

Drunkenness, or some degree of stupefaction, was common and

it was not thought unusual if one-third of a ship's company was less than capable of an evening.

For the new men and boys aboard *Eurydice*, the six months they spent in port at Spithead would have avoided an early introduction to the worst of the food and drink. In port, captains were more or less obliged to supply fresh meat, vegetables and soft bread. Both in port and at sea the officers and young gentlemen fared only slightly better than the crew.

Eurydice sailed for India on 11 October 1783, to help mop up a battle with France. Fletcher Christian had just turned nineteen and probably had enough sense and good advice to have laid in a store of treats for himself. In a few months he was likely to be looking forward to eating biscuits and salt meat in much the way more experienced sailors did; for just as the free sex life in port brutalized their libidos, the food on board brutalized and dulled their palates.

Horrible or not, life at sea was what Fletcher Christian had chosen, perhaps despite the following figures: Between September 1774 and September 1780, 175,990 men had been raised for the Navy. Of these, 42,000 had 'run', leaving the number of men who served at 134,000, in round figures. Of these, 1,243 were killed in action and an appalling 18,541 were lost through sickness and disease, more than one in every seven. It is an average of sixty men a week for six years. In 1803, Lord Nelson said the life of an average naval man was finished at forty-five.

Able seamen of the time were paid 6 shillings a week, the ordinary seaman four shillings and nine pence, but deductions for clothing, extra food and support of a family at home easily halved this. Although the men often got a month or two's pay before they sailed on a long trip, the balance was usually held in arrears, often for two years or longer; even if the ship was paid off, they might not get all they were owed. The rates of pay and the inefficient system of payment had not changed since the days of the Commonwealth over one hundred years before.

6

'A superior pleasant Manner'

urydice sailed for India via Madeira and Table Bay, where Cape Town is sited, at the southern extreme of Africa. On 16 November they crossed the equator and David Laird, the master, noted, 'In order to celebrate the joyful event of crossing the Equator, the ship's company performed the ceremony of paying tribute to Neptune according to the usual custom of dunking into the sea those who had not crossed the line before'. This was always dangerous and it was to be forbidden when Fletcher next crossed the equator southwards with William Bligh.

In Madras in June, Captain Courtney noted the arrival of a big East Indiaman called *Middlesex*. Fletcher's brother, Charles, was to serve as surgeon in this ship—what happened to him gravely affected Fletcher's future.

Madras was a large town surrounded by a wall and a ditch. The English had slowly constructed Fort St George on the sea-shore into a jumble of an irregular shape, but the houses inside were only inhabited during siege. The countryside around the town was fragrant with the gardens of the white residents, which could be reached by a handsome brick bridge over the river south of the fort. The native quarter was called Black Town and presented a spectacle of dirt and filth. None of the streets was anything but black earth, which mixed with the wasted fluids of men, animals, river and heaven to form stinking mud that engendered infection and allowed free passage only to the whimsical and awkward local carriages, drawn by two oxen. Perhaps it was the viscosity of the mud that required the palanquins of the rich to be carried by six slaves; in Bombay, it took only four, but they were bigger men, apparently.

Madras cloth of cotton was hawked to visitors; so were very fine handkerchiefs of large checked pattern, excellent colouring and a peculiar fineness. The Indian ships in the harbour were known as *Parias*. They had masts of teak and rope of coconut hair and were extremely cumbersome, weighing up to 600 tons even though only used for coastal sailing. An English captain of the time said, 'If their hull be defective, the manner of rigging them is not less so'.

In Anjango, Fletcher was on the Malabar coast where he would see the vines of black pepper and a strange variety of green dove. In the countryside along the river that ran by the small fort, men amused themselves by hunting snipe, woodcock, hare and wild hogs. Here the ship traded and the men sweltered, for although the climate of the Malabar coast is generally warm and moist, in April and May it is insufferable. The ship had also been in Masalaputnam and Tellicherry and then with Sir Edward Hughes' squadron had sailed to Bombay in November 1784. There, salt water was distilled into fresh water and the squadron sailed back to Woolwich spending four weeks in Table Bay, where the only fresh water available was contaminated with whale oil and whale sperm, three weeks at St Helena and a night at Ascension. By June 1785, they were home. Fletcher had been aboard for more than two years and had spent eye-opening months seeing the lives and customs of the East. He had also performed his duties as a midshipman well. When *Eurydice* was in Madras, on 24 May 1784, Fletcher was made acting lieutenant after only one year's service, and an AB was promoted to take his place. It is to two of Fletcher's brothers whom we must turn for amplification of this early example of patronage by a superior officer.

When Charles Christian was in India in *Middlesex* in 1786, he met Thomas William, who had been surgeon aboard *Eurydice*, and on his return from India Charles met another unnamed officer who had sailed with Fletcher. Both these men corroborated to him Fletcher's own assertions. Charles reports that Fletcher was said to be strict, but 'ruled in a superior pleasant Manner'.

Fletcher's other brother, Edward, also reports of *Eurydice* in 'The Appendix' he wrote to Stephen Barney's *Minutes* of the trial of the *Bounty* mutineers. He says that when Fletcher returned to Woolwich he was met by a relative, whom he told he had been extremely happy under Captain Courtney's command, saying he had been entrusted with a watch all the way home. Edward, like Charles, gives us a quotation supposedly from Fletcher's own mouth: 'It was very easy to make one's self beloved and respected aboard a ship; one had only to be always ready to obey one's superior officers, and to be kind to the common men, unless there was occasion for severity, and if you are when there is a just occasion they will not like you the worse for it.'

Fletcher's 'pleasant rule' and the respect of the men aboard *Eurydice* was not much use to him, for peace had been concluded and in just a few days he had been paid off. Fletcher made up his mind to be appointed mate of a West Indiaman, feeling he had the necessary qualifications. He had to turn to friends and use family influence, a simple matter. It was the Season in London and most of the most useful people would have been there. Through his own endeavours or an introduction, Fletcher was treating with a merchant in the City when Captain Taubman arrived from the Isle of Man. His wife, Dorothy, Fletcher's first cousin, had died eighteen months previously in January 1784, but Taubman obviously felt an obligation and said he would write to William Bligh, a man whom he knew well, who owed him a favour or two, and who I think already knew of Fletcher. Taubman suggested to Christian that it would be very desirable for him to serve under so experienced a navigator as Bligh.

Bligh returned a polite answer, saying he was sorry he could not take Fletcher Christian, as he had his full complement of officers. Edward Christian said that, of his own accord, and presumably in writing, Fletcher Christian observed to Bligh, 'wages were no object, he only wished to learn his profession and if Captain Bligh would permit him to mess with the gentlemen, he would readily enter the ship as a fore-mast man until there was a vacancy amongst the officers,' adding, 'we midshipmen are gentlemen, we never pull at a rope; I should even be glad to go one voyage in that situation, for there may be occasions when officers are called upon to do the duties of a common man.' Prophetic words.

Bligh had no objection and under the terms suggested, Christian sailed one voyage with him. It is easy to get the impression that this first voyage was embarked upon within a short time of Christian's arrival home from India, but a period of some fifteen months intervened. To explain this, it is now time to introduce more fully William Bligh.

The Bligh family comes from Cornwall, and in June 1967 I went there to make a television documentary about William Bligh, the family's most famed son, commander of the mutinous *Bounty*, Governor of the restive colony of New South Wales. After a baffling search for the exact place of Bligh's origin it seems that his father, Francis, was born in St Tudy, and that William was born in Plymouth; at least he was baptized there. In the family Bible, his entry into the world is given as 9 September 1754, and the church of St Andrew in Plymouth records his baptism on 4 October.

William's father, Francis, had a distinct and developed taste for the wives of dead men, marrying a series of widows, the first of whom, Jane Pearce, was William's mother; she died before he was sixteen, and he was the single child of this marriage.

The power of the movies is such that it is constantly necessary to reiterate that the picture of Bligh as some upstart red-neck who rose to position from before the mast, although possible, is wrong. This assassination of character had its beginnings at the end of the eighteenth century, and the Christian family cannot be said to be entirely free of involvement. Some of the charges still brought against Bligh are difficult to disprove, for if his father attracted widows, William Bligh attracted dispute. As well as the mutiny aboard *Bounty*, he was court-martialled and convicted of using abusive language to a junior officer, was involved in the fleet-wide Nore mutiny, and was also ignominiously removed from his governorship of New South Wales, after another mutiny. He was, and is, controversial. But his naval background was impeccable, remarkable only because the man had every possible degree of education to suit him for the career, but not one advantage of patronage or service that was not dearly earned through personal endeavour or slavish devotion to duty.

William Bligh first appears in the Admiralty records on 1 July 1762, aged seven years and nine months, as servant to the captain of HMS *Montrose*. Being registered at such an early age was a ploy to ensure rapid promotion later in life. A man had to serve at least six years at sea before he could qualify as a lieutenant. If his family had friends on the quarterdeck, he would be entered early on a ship's books and would be serving his time while actually labouring over copy books and eating cosy teas with mother in the nursery. The other end of naval promotion was equally absurd. Once a man had been promoted to post captain, exertion or appearance at sea became academic. Progression up the charts through all the degrees of admiral was automatic as those at the top toppled under the regular increase of

braid and port-engendered disease. It was *far* more unusual for Fletcher
Christian to have waited until he was eighteen to go to sea, than for
Bligh to begin his service at sea aged seven.

As to there being servants aboard, an Admiral of the Fleet on a
large ship was entitled to an entourage of fifty! A captain was
allowed four servants per each 100 men of his ship's complement.
Other officers, from lieutenants to cooks, surgeons, carpenters and
boatswains were allowed one or two servants according to the size
of the vessel in which they served. Often these servants were exactly
that, hairdressers, tailors, footmen and artists. But many were
serious young men under that officer's direct patronage, boys who
planned a naval career and who were starting the best way of all,
under the special and noticeable protection of a single officer. It
was a two-way affair. The patronage you gave helped your career
and social life quite as much as the patronage you received. William
Bligh was always acutely aware of this, but it was years before he
could use it to his advantage.

Young Bligh's putative service aboard *Montrose* lasted six months,
but every little bit helped. It was 1770 before he was aboard HMS
Hunter, a 10-gun sloop on which he was rated as able seaman, but
almost certainly served as a midshipman, an everyday bending of
the rules that is, again, unremarkable. Fletcher Christian was offering to do it under Bligh's command years later.

Bligh was fifteen when he joined *Hunter*, and his mother was
dead. Mackaness suggests that the legendary problems of stepmoth-
ers and the feeling of desertion by his father, so easily aroused in
the breast of the lone adolescent, may have been the reasons for
Bligh now going to sea.

His nominal rating as AB lasted only six months and on 5 February 1771 he was appointed midshipman; in September of the same
year he was transferred to the 36-gun HMS *Crescent*, serving aboard
her for three years until 23 August 1774, and it is likely that this
is the time during which his naval education was largely absorbed.

On 2 September 1774, William Bligh signed on in HMS *Ranger*, again as an AB, there being no place for a 'middy'. *Ranger* was based at Douglas, Isle of Man, her duty to hunt and apprehend smugglers in the Irish Sea, under the eye of Richard Betham. HM Collector of Customs. It was an assignment offering neither spectacular career opportunities nor adventure. The ship spent most time being repaired, so Bligh sensibly capitalized on inactive service by improving his experience ashore, equally important for naval advancement.

As he approached his coming-of-age, William Bligh presented a striking, even beautiful appearance. For a man, he had skin of a surprisingly lambent, marble-whiteness that was commented upon most of his life. To that was added the startling combination of piercing blue eyes and raven hair. His face was quite broad, but in proportion to the length of his head, and he had a nose as noble and fine as his skin demanded. The firm set of his chin was shadowed by a dark beard and contrasted strangely with lips that had never grown out of their childish cupid's bow. All in all, it was an appearance that demanded attention; but it was to be no advantage.

By the end of September 1775, a few weeks after turning twenty-one, Bligh was re-entered on the books of *Ranger* as a midshipman, a post he held until March the following year.

His eighteen months of duty on and about the Isle of Man had been very useful. The Isle of Man was only a small fish in the seas of Bligh's ambition, but he eagerly baited and secured his hook. His father was probably able to give an introduction to Richard Betham, being a Customs man himself, and Betham's daughter Elizabeth seems to have been a willing and enjoyable social partner. But now Bligh had to go to the further side of the world with the hero who was to be his idol and touchstone, James Cook. The experience was finally to hone Bligh into a great but flawed sailor, unable to recognize his own insensitivity to other men's problems.

7

The Merchant Service

Whatever the naval diligence required of a midshipman aboard an antiquated vessel engaged in anti-smuggling measures in the king's latest insular acquisition, Bligh must have performed it well and with some publicity, for on 14 July 1776, he sailed to the South Pacific as master of *Resolution*, flagship of James Cook's third voyage.

The position of master aboard a ship was senior and responsible. He was in charge of actually sailing the ship, and also oversaw the correct stowage of the hold. He had to be a man of great seamanship, with above average ability in navigation; both attributes were certainly true of William Bligh. The wonder is how and why he was chosen from his Manx obscurity. It seems likely that Cook saw journals or charts prepared by Bligh when at the Admiralty fitting out his ships and chose him from this evidence of ability. At the time, William had just sat and passed his lieutenancy exams. His certificate is dated 1 July 1776, and states: 'He produces Journals kept by himself kept in the *Crescent* and *Ranger*, and Certificates from Captains Henshaw, Morgan, Thompson and Lieut. Samber of his Diligence, Sobriety and obedience to command. He can splice, Knott, Reef a Sail, work a Ship in Sailing, Shift his Tides, keep a reckoning of a Ship's way by plain sailing and Mercator, observe by Sun or Star, find the variation of the Compass, and is qualified to do the duty of an Able Seaman and midshipman.'

From Bligh's many charts, journals and letters that survive, we know that he was gifted both in powers of observation and the ability to set what he saw on paper in words or pictures. The journals he kept as a midshipman, part of the training in observation required of all young gentlemen, were bound to have been exemplary.

Bligh's voyage with Cook, during which the Hawaiian Islands were discovered and Cook was murdered, was both the final ingredient and the crystallization of the complex character that was William Bligh. Cook's influence can be seen in so much of what was to come that Bligh's time with him must have been filled with hero worship and adulation, as well as a sense of severe personal loss on his death. Bligh always said that Cook's death might have been averted if men on the beach of Kealakekua had done their duty, or had been of the calibre expected of naval officers.

It was Cook who introduced new ideas of shipboard hygiene and food to the Navy and between voyages in 1776, he was elected to the august Royal Society and awarded their Copley Gold Medal for his paper on the subject. Bligh was one of the few who adopted the ideas, perhaps because he had seen them employed to his own advantage when sailing under Cook. There was another, ugly side of Cook that Bligh also seems to have copied—temper. Cook was renowned for his vile temper and extraordinary cruelty; he flogged men more often and for less than Bligh ever did, yet inspired a devotion that bordered on veneration. Bligh was equally famed for his outbursts of invective, but his personal abuse was wounding in a way that Cook's foul language never was.

Bligh made no bones about the cover-ups he thought were employed to smudge the facts of Cook's murder as he saw them, and he was bitter because charts he made were attributed to other hands. Airing such opinions in public, when the rest of the officers agreed to tell a different story, was probably why, mortifyingly, he was the only man excluded from the general promotion when the expedition returned home in 1780. Passing the lieutenant's examinations did not automatically give a man this rank; there were many who served for years as midshipmen before being commissioned into full service and given the leg up towards being post captain. Some men who had passed their examinations never became lieutenants at all.

Already his own worst enemy, Bligh returned from his first South Pacific voyage clearly demonstrating the basis of his many future downfalls. Confident always of a faultless personal morality, he thundered at the weakness of others and the weapon he invariably mounted was that of an acerbic and wounding tongue.

So, experienced, travelled, confident—but snubbed—he returned to life on land, first in the West Country of his birth, then back to the Orkneys, where a family called Stewart had recently welcomed him when *Resolution* had called. Eventually he returned to the Isle of Man, where he would quickly find himself at home again with the Taubmans, Christians and Bethams . . . and with a wife.

Elizabeth Betham Bligh has had nothing but good said about her. Indeed it is hard to fault any naval wife of the time who remained loyal, domestic and fruitful. She was her father's second daughter, educated and vivacious, befitting the family's background of cultural connections with Scotland. By January, all was arranged and, both in their twenty-seventh year, they were married on 4 February 1781, at Kirk Onchan, just outside Douglas.

Ten days after his marriage Bligh had to leave his wife, called back to active service of a different kind. He was appointed master of *Belle Poule*, a captured French ship which had been returned to service against her former proprietors. The battle in which he participated at Dogger Bank early in August was enough for him finally to be promoted to lieutenant. As such he was transferred briefly to *Berwick*, then as fifth lieutenant aboard *Princess Amelia*. In March 1782, he went to HMS *Cambridge* as sixth lieutenant and stayed aboard her until January of the following year. This ship took part in the relief of Gibraltar and Bligh was paid off and placed on half pay in January 1783.

Once more Bligh returned to the Isle of Man where, on just two shillings a day, he could barely afford to feed the family. Expecting some overdue new appointment that might prevent them settling permanently, they moved into lodgings. By May, already expecting their first child, the Blighs managed to move into a house of their own, while Bligh was writing everywhere for an appointment. Not unnaturally he decided to see what his wife's family connections might bring.

Elizabeth's mother was a Campbell and included among her relatives an Uncle Duncan. Duncan Campbell was an influential and a rich man, a merchant trader and a plantation owner in the West Indies as well as the proprietor of convict hulks. He was also involved in the slave trade. But few as yet had conscience about such connections and William and Elizabeth Bligh were grateful for the interest of a man who seemed to offer more open doors to advancement than anyone else they knew. Bligh was extremely grateful for the interest shown in him by Campbell, who was to become a regular correspondent, adviser and mentor.

Campbell advised Bligh that to hedge his bets he should obtain official permission from the Lords of the Admiralty for leave to quit the kingdom. That way he might be able to join the merchant service, for Duncan Campbell, ever the opportunist, saw in this nephew-in-law someone to whom he could entrust his ships and his business in the West Indies. At £500 a year William Bligh was happy to comply; he moved his family to Lambeth, close enough to the Admiralty so he could show his face as often as he wished, and then in succession commanded *Lynx*, *Cambria* and *Britannia* for Campbell. Apart from his duties aboard, he was responsible for actually finding cargoes to be carried home, in competition with others. His letters to Campbell are a constant apology for bad business and lack of contacts, complaints about the weather and a retailing of misfortunes, as well as the usual affirmations of friendship and duty and a listing of compliments that had to be given; even in the context of eighteenth-century correspondence which is verbose and emotional, the letters of Bligh always seem to slop over the boundaries of taste, convention and the manner of the period and into a stagnant pool of self-pity and unctuousness.

Fletcher Christian sailed under Bligh only in Campbell's ship *Britannia*. In April 1786, Bligh was still commanding *Lynx* and in Caribbean waters, so Fletcher was certainly not with him then. There are no letters I know of that come from *Cambria* that might fix the dates of that command; but there is a letter dated 30 November 1786, in which Bligh writes to Campbell about his great difficulties getting down the Channel at the start of another voyage. I think this is likely to be a letter from *Britannia*, at the beginning of the first voyage Bligh and Christian made together.

The sailing time to and from the West Indies was four to six weeks each way and allowing about the same time for trading once there, an average round trip can be reckoned to take three to four months. There would have been a turnaround time in England, too. We know that Bligh and Christian sailed on two voyages in *Britannia* and at the end of the second returned to England in August 1787; thus it seems that Fletcher had waited over a year before he achieved his desire to sail to the West Indies with William Bligh.

Later in 1793, after Bligh had returned from his second breadfruit voyage to the South Pacific, he made a note that Fletcher Christian had been with him in the merchant service for three years. This is impossible. The maximum could have been only two years and on all other evidence, including Bligh's, the period was actually nine or ten months. Bligh's memory often played tricks to his own advantage.

However long it took, Fletcher Christian was eventually aboard *Britannia* with Bligh, a man just ten years older than himself and with whom he could talk at length about so many things, the Isle of Man in general, his family in particular. He sailed on the first voyage as an ordinary seaman, but ate with the midshipmen and officers. This was the spirit Bligh appreciated and it was no bad thing to have a Christian in his debt.

Life in the merchant service was much easier than in the Navy, as a comparison of Bligh's income clearly indicates. Discipline was important for everyone's safety, but flogging and food favouritism were all less severe than in the king's service. Edward Christian tells us that when Fletcher Christian returned from his first voyage with Bligh, he said he had shared the labour of the common men, but had also been helped by Bligh, who had shown him the use of charts and instruments, furthering Christian's knowledge of navigation. Fletcher added that although Bligh was very passionate, yet he prided himself on knowing how to humour him. So far, so good.

When we get to the scant knowledge we have of the second voyage, stories begin to diverge. Edward says Christian was taken out as second mate, that when he returned he did not have enough time to see any relatives but that in letters he had made no complaint about the captain. He quotes anonymously Lebogue, who had sailed with the men both to the West Indies and to the South Pacific, who was asked if Bligh's treatment of Christian had always been the same. The man answered, 'No, it would not long have been borne in the merchant service.'

Lawrence Lebogue was an illiterate sailmaker from Annapolis, USA, and at forty, one of the oldest men who also signed on in *Bounty*. When Edward Christian and William Bligh were sniping at each other in pamphlets in 1794, Lebogue told Bligh he had never made the statement that Fletcher could not have borne Captain Bligh's conduct much longer, because, 'I knew Captain Bligh was always a friend to Christian when he sailed with him to the West

Indies as well as afterwards . . . Captain Bligh was the best friend Christian ever had.'

But Lebogue had never been accused of saying that Christian could not bear Bligh's treatment aboard *Bounty*, he simply said he was treated differently aboard *Britannia* and *Bounty*.

This confirms two points: the first, that men in the merchant service, because they were not serving under armed guards, expected better treatment and had it in their power to demand it, or to take some kind of redress, without being hanged for mutiny. It also shows that Bligh behaved differently when employed by the king; perhaps Fletcher Christian did, too. At least, if you can believe another story, it is certain that the behaviour attributed to Christian by Edward Lamb, also aboard *Britannia*, would never have been borne on a *naval* vessel.

Edward Lamb, had been 'in the ship Brittanic [sic] when I was chief mate and eyewitness to everything that passed.' Lamb first refutes Edward Christian's assertion that Fletcher was second mate, saying he was put upon the articles as gunner but that Bligh had wished him to be thought of as an officer. This confusion may, of course, have been caused by Fletcher Christian, wishing his relatives to think his progress was rather more grandiose than it was; it is as likely that it was simply Edward Christian getting mixed up between Fletcher's actual position and the duties he was expected to do. Mr Lamb continues, 'When we got to sea, and I saw your partiality for the young man, I gave him every advice and information in my power, though he went about every point of duty with a degree of indifference that to me was truly unpleasant; but you were blind to his faults, and had him to dine and sup every other day in the cabin, and treated him like a brother in giving him every information.'

Edward Lamb goes on to give a tantalizing extra picture of Fletcher Christian and his relationship with women as, 'then one of the most foolish young men I ever knew in regard to the sex'; his shipmate, Lebogue, was one of those who remembered Fletcher always having a girl with him in Tahiti.

Virtually all the evidence we have about Fletcher Christian, for and against, is written with hindsight. If Lamb had been well treated by Bligh he might have felt obliged to repay a debt of gratitude by fudging his memories of Fletcher Christian; or perhaps they were perfectly clear and he was simply jealous of the young man who received all the captain's special attention? Either is likely but I think a combination of the two is more so, for nowhere else are we given the remotest suggestion of Christian slacking his duty. There may be something in the man's surname; Mackaness suggests there was contact between the Bethams and Charles and Mary Lamb. It would be strange indeed if Bligh had not looked to his relatives and friends for support; Edward Christian did, when he was defending his brother.

Only one thing is certain about the *Britannia* voyages—Bligh and Christian were firm friends and well pleased with one another.

8

Bountiful Breadfruit

O f all the breathtaking things you were expected to believe about the South Seas when the first explorers returned in the mid-eighteenth century, two stood out. The first was the sexual licence of the Polynesians, and the second, a more suitable subject for drawing-room conversation, breadfruit: the bread which grew upon trees. It must have seemed unfair that the British, unquestionably the most civilized of Christian nations, had to labour (and pay) for their daily bread whereas indolent pagans of the South Pacific were given it *gratis*, just as the Lord's Prayer suggested it should be.

The Standing Committee of West India Planters and Merchants was particularly interested in the virtues of this plant. While making their fortunes out of sugar plantations in the Caribbean, these men were also put to the unfortunate expense of feeding the slaves from Africa who did the work (the natives of the area having been exterminated for their hindrance of progress and other men's fortunes). Bananas served the purpose most of the time, but storms easily destroyed these delicate plants, which are herbs, not trees, as they have no true trunk; they are supported by tightly rolled leaves. This meant the additional trouble and expense of buying or storing grain and other foodstuffs, particularly from the eastern coast of America.

Tiresome and expensive. They had enough problems trying to diversify their economy from being so dependent on sugar.

In 1760, the Society of Arts offered a premium to encourage cinnamon production and for the rest of the eighteenth century such emoluments were extended to other tropical products like cochineal, silk, indigo, cotton, cloves, camphor and coffee. Indeed the whole world was being combed for botanical specimens that would benefit civilization, and specimen gardens were established in the West Indies to complement Kew, Chelsea and Edinburgh.

It did not take the Standing Committee long to realize the possibilities of the breadfruit tree. A couple of trees fed a tractable native for a whole year, cost nothing, and as well as being of a tropical disposition were also strong and hardy. The idea must have been intoxicating, so much so that in 1775 the Committee soberly announced they were prepared to pay all reasonable costs of a captain willing to transport breadfruit plants from Tahiti to the West Indies; they even suggested how it could be done. There were no takers and anyway, the colonizers of America ungratefully took it into their heads to be independent. The breadfruit offer was swamped by martial news, and provisions from the States became increasingly expensive.

American Independence meant that the transportation of breadfruit became more important and as soon as the Atlantic had resumed a semblance of normality on both its shores, the Standing Committee got to work in London, starting what would now be called a PR campaign to convince king and country that their needs were of national importance and that the solution should be funded out of public monies. They, being nothing but poor farmers and traders (and having had time to think about their first offer of standing some of the costs), could look only to their government for salvation.

Being men of the world, the Committee knew the way to the king's purse was through his advisers and they set about flattering Sir Joseph Banks, who was President of the Royal Society and the king's chief but unofficial scientific adviser on everything to do with the South Pacific.

As plain Mr Banks, he had been on Cook's first voyage to the South Pacific and at Tahiti, in 1769, had gone so far as to eat breadfruit. Nothing then happened concerning the South Seas without the inclusion of Mr Banks, who was created a Baronet on 24 March 1781. By early 1787, Banks had the news that breadfruit plants to the value of £2,000 had arrived in the French West Indies, adding fire to the English West Indian complaints that their government was interested only in taxing them.

At first, a ship that had transported felons to Botany Bay was to collect plants from Tahiti and David Nelson, a botanist, was put in charge of plans. By March, Banks had changed his mind and thought an independent vessel, fitted under his supervision, would better suit the purpose.

The king was enchanted, and quickly gave his blessings and orders, which he signed on 15 May 1787. The Admiralty Lords were not pleased, they had war on their minds, but as the king was more than a little involved, they supplied ample funds, but little time or thought, thereby dooming the expedition from the outset.

Lord Sydney, one of the Principal Secretaries of State, wrote to the Lords Commissioners of the Admiralty on 5 May 1787, detailing the exact nature of the voyage. Four days later on 9 May, the Navy Board was ordered to purchase a ship not exceeding 250 tons. As nothing was found suitable among the 600 ships of the king's Navy, advertisements let it be known that the Board would inspect vessels offered for sale the following Wednesday; they also suggested to the Lords that someone acquainted with the expedition might attend with their own officers.

By 16 May, the Navy Board had six ships to consider and quickly chose a snub-nosed coastal trader built in Hull, only two and a half years old, called *Bethia*, and lying at Wapping Old Stairs on the Thames in London. The asking price was £2,600. Sir Joseph Banks arranged to meet Mr Mitchell, assistant to the Surveyor of the Navy, aboard the ship to give his approval. Meanwhile the Officers of Deptford Yard gave their assessment of the condition and value of *Bethia*; in their opinion she was valued at £1,820. 12s. 8d. plus £64. 15s. for anchors that had been offered with her, a total of £1,895. 7s. 8d. The sum eventually paid seems to have been £1,950.

Within days she was at Deptford Naval Yard and by 6 June had been rechristened *Bounty*, more a reflection of the expectations of personal gain she would bring to the West Indian planters than an indication of any national benefit from her voyage. Still, she was a ship without precedent, marking a creative new twist to administrative thinking. *Bounty* was bent neither on scientific exploration nor on colonial conquest, she was simply to bear the fruits of such endeavours from one part of the world to another. Before all this she had to be adapted, both for the voyage itself and for her special task as a floating greenhouse. There was much to do and the Lords Commissioners were munificent, refusing nothing asked of them.

First there was the matter of sheathing. The sailor's worst enemy, by far, was the shipworm—*Teredo navalis*—a voracious beast that effortlessly negated man's efforts to sail vast distances unless notice was taken of it. *Teredo* worms could eat up a hull in a very short time. The simplest solution was to sheathe the hull in more wood, which could be replaced as it was eaten, and *Bethia/Bounty* had been so treated, having an outer hull of planks some 1¼ inches thick, secured by iron nails. This did for coastal work but was not suited to a voyage to the South Pacific, so *Bounty* was resheathed with English copper and all her fastenings were made of copper or bronze, an enormous but sensible expense.

Then there were the masts and sails. Ships ordered to the South Seas always carried less sail than when on other duties, so *Bounty*'s masts were shortened, giving her rather less top weight and a lower centre of power.

There were very strict rules about the number of officers, men and guns that a ship might carry, according to its exact definition. The Admiralty had written on 6 June, to advise these things, as well as to announce the ship's new name and status as an armed vessel. She was to have four short-carriage 4-pound guns, ten half-pounder swivel guns. Her complement was to be twenty officers and twenty-five able seamen, forty-five men in all.

If ever you see the latest reproduction of *Bounty*, built in New Zealand, you will be hard put not to stand aghast. It is exact. And it is small and ugly and impractical. You need little imagination to infer the appalling conditions of life at sea at the time, nothing unique to *Bounty*, but certainly contributory to what was to happen.

Bounty was to journey around the world under sail, yet at only 91 feet long she was hardly bigger than many a diesel-powered pleasure craft that today carefully hugs the coast. Her maximum width of 24 feet 4 inches makes her sound squat, an impression not altered by knowledge of her almost flat nose and upright stern. In reality the effect is not like that, as she is very tall for her length, carrying much more above the waterline than you might expect possible. Most surprising of all to the modern sailor, there is no superstructure of day cabins or galleys. Everything but steering and sail handling went on below the flush main deck—cooking, eating, sleeping and the storage of supplies, both live and dead. This microcosm of self-sufficient life was carried on in virtual darkness and impossible cramp. There were no portholes; fresh air and light came only through the three-foot hatches to the ladderways when conditions were suitable. Otherwise there was neither, except when men changed watch, every four hours.

Officers and gentlemen abaft the mast had headroom of 7 feet and for a few of them the doubtful advantage of tiny airless cabins, ventilated only by slits in the doors. The ABs before the mast had only 6 feet 3 inches and shared one open space which directly abutted the galley and the pens in which goats, pigs and sheep were often kept. In this room they ate and slept.

Banks had recommended that the great cabin, which was to be used as a greenhouse for the breadfruits, should be extended from its original depth of 11 feet (it stretched the width of the stern of the ship) to as far forward as the rear of the aft hatchway, trebling it to 30 feet.

Bligh himself was excluded from the great cabin by the arrangements for the breadfruit and so thirty-nine of the forty-five men had to live for months on end with an average space of 30 square feet. The other six were down companionways in even smaller cells on platform decks where headroom was only 5 feet.

To give the planners their due they had increased the accommodation by building these two platform decks in the hold. They had to compromise, for the hold was to carry enough provisions for many months. But these new decks, called cockpits, did relieve the congestion on the lower deck considerably. The new fore cockpit accommodated the boatswain and the carpenter as well as the sailroom and the storeroom of the boatswain, gunner and carpenters. The aft platform had cabins for the botanist, the surgeon, the captain's clerk and the gunner, as well as a steward room, captain's storeroom and a sloproom for spare clothing. The added usefulness of the aft cockpit was that by boring holes through the floor of the greenhouse directly above, water which drained from the pots could be collected in barrels below. So far more space had been added than that taken by the new greenouse, a point never made before. But it was not enough.

To those more interested in botany than humanity, the arrangements for the breadfruit plants were wonderful. Having first had its deck made expensively waterproof by lining it with lead, the new room was then furnished with fine raised platforms, the planks of which had been adapted to hold earthenware pots. Four gangways provided access. Around the walls was suspended a line of similar potholders; they were even five and six deep against the stern windows so that instead of the original plan for 500 pots, they ended with accommodation for '629 pots in all' each carefully drawn and counted on the plans dated 20 November 1787. There were gratings on the decks and scoops in the sides to provide fresh air. A stove was installed to keep the plants warm on the voyage around the Cape.

From the plans we can also see that the pantry, Bligh's responsibility as purser, was directly beside his cabin on the starboard side of the ship. He also tells us that he had a place near the middle of the ship to eat in. This was against the bulkhead that divided the ship from the pantry on the starboard side, precisely at the aft of the main hatch, about fifteen feet forward of the mainmast. It is not clear whether this was actually a room and probably it was not, looking at the space available. More likely it was simply divided on either side by canvas screens from the berths of the mates and the midshipmen. Here also the arms chest was kept. It was exactly midway between the captain's cabin and that of the master with only the ladderway between them.

As to the messy business of the men's more personal functions, most urinating would have been over the side and into the sea. There was privacy and a sedentary position for defecating; for the men there were heads on either side of the bowsprit and Bligh had his own privy, which hung over the stern precisely where Fletcher Christian stands in the famous image of the mutiny by Robert Dodd.

The approved scheme of complement for HM Armed Vessel *Bounty* was as follows:

1	Lieutenant to command	1	Quartermaster's Mate
1	Master	1	Boatswain's Mate
1	Boatswain	1	Gunner's Mate
1	Gunner	1	Carpenter's Mate
1	Carpenter	1	Carpenter's crew
1	Surgeon	1	Sailmaker
2	Master's Mates	1	Corporal
2	Midshipmen	1	Clerk and Steward
2	Quartermasters	25	Able Seamen

This made a total of forty-five men. But the eventual complement was not thus balanced. A servant of the system of patronage, by which he himself had gained command of *Bounty*, Bligh would find himself forced to adapt, further weakening the usefulness of a crew whose structure was, by any account, unsuitable for such a voyage, although probably adequate for a ship of its size. The main criticism of the complement is that there was no space for marines to ensure discipline, thus there was no back-up of brute force in case of trouble or of any physical incapacity of the commander and his officers that might lead to trouble.

It should be noted that even though they had been appointed by the date the list was supplied, there is no mention of Nelson, the botanist, or Brown, his assistant.

❦

Fletcher Christian and William Bligh, on their second voyage together aboard *Britannia* were quite ignorant of the excitements planned when they arrived back at the Downs on 5 August where they were met by Campbell. But next day Bligh was writing fulsomely to Banks, with whom he had had no previous recorded contact.

> August 6, 1787
>
> Sir, I arrived yesterday from Jamaica and should have instantly paid my respects to you had not Mr. Campbell told me you were not to return from the country until Thursday. I have heard the flattering news of your great goodness to me, intending to honour me with the command of the vessel you propose should go to the South Seas, for which, after offering you my most grateful thanks I can only assure you I shall endeavour, and I hope succeed, in deserving such a trust. I await your commands, and am with the sincerest respect, Sir, your obliged and very Humble Servant.
>
> Wm Bligh

Thanks to Duncan Campbell, Bligh had a patron of status and substance at last. Not having one in the past had hampered his promotion terribly, and he clung tenaciously to Banks for the rest of his life.

Campbell had been one of the most ardent supporters of an official breadfruit expedition, although with his fortune based on slave trading and exploitation he could have paid for it single-handedly. The Committee having been so successful as to have the king sign orders for the purchase of a ship, it was easy for Campbell then to press the case of Bligh, both an employee and a nephew-in-law. He went to Banks, of course.

It is likely Banks would have sniffed out Bligh anyway, for few men had the relatively low rank of lieutenant as well as the necessary experience of the South Seas. Bligh's time as master of Cook's *Resolution* showed him to be an excellent navigator and scientific man, capable of making charts, calculating, sounding and negotiating; to Banks, Campbell was able also to recommend him as a businessman, a quality expected of the commander of *Bounty*.

Bligh was appointed on 16 August and took command at Deptford on 20 August. Bligh found his new ship far from complete and from any point of view he was better off where he had been, but ambition can be an imprudent master.

In the merchant service with Campbell, Bligh earned £500 a year plus what he made in private dealing (if he weren't so engaged he would have been most perverse). Working for the king he would be paid only 4 shillings a day, plus what he could make out of also being purser, a basic income of £73 per annum, on which to support a wife and three children. The difference was enormous and goes a long way towards explaining why Bligh was so pernickety about his money and interests. The voyage made promotion virtually certain and this was important to his pride, a point he clearly demonstrated before he sailed. There was another matter for pride, too. In his capacity as commander of a naval vessel he was for the first

time in a position to help others towards naval preferment, a heady
and treacherous thing. It was all too easy to be blinded by social
position and to hire a man for his friends rather than for himself.

When *Bounty* finally came out of dry dock at Deptford on 3
September the carpenters and joiners remained on board, well
behind schedule, and endlessly delaying the start of the voyage, a
not unfamiliar situation with these trades.

The frustrations connected with equipping *Bounty* for her voyage
were shared by everyone. Sir Joseph Banks was hounded by Sir
George Yonge, Secretary for War and a botanical enthusiast, who
said he thought Bligh was almost totally unaware of his responsibilities in the South Seas. Banks replied, 'I am not a little alarmed
at the rect. of yours: if Capt. Bligh is not sufficiently instructed and
the purpose of the voyage consequently in danger of being lost,
blame must lay somewhere and no one is so likely to support the
burthen of it as your Hmble servant.'

The full and largely unknown correspondence between Yonge
and Banks (now in the Museum of Natural History, London) reveals
many surprises and suggests that Bligh was playing the two men off
against one another. It is impossible that Bligh, a stickler for pro-
cedure, would accept the command of a ship without first ensuring
it was worthy of his talents and ambition.

Yet he seems to have told Yonge that Nelson, the gardener, was
responsible both for provisioning the ship and for instructing Bligh
as to his duties!

Naturally, Bligh wanted to make his mark on his ship and he
found fault whenever he could, which was seldom. On 15 September, he wrote to Banks regretting progress was slower than
expected, 'owing to a great struggle to get the masts and yard
shortened—a circumstance I am happy I persisted in'. He was subsequently proven wrong, as in the South Pacific he had to raise
royals, small sails that fly high above the normal square rigging.
The ballast of iron bars was also reduced, from 45 tons to 19 tons,

for he was certain that too much deadweight in the bottom caused the misfortunes of many a ship in foul weather.

He was also very unhappy about the complement of three small boats and, with an uncanny foresight, he requested they be exchanged for others. The biggest, the launch, was 23 feet instead of 20 feet, and thus able to carry another four men; there was also a 20-foot cutter and a 16-foot jolly-boat. Once they had been stowed on *Bounty*'s deck, there would hardly be room for the entire complement to be on deck at once, what with steerage, hatches, chicken coops and ladderways all taking up space as well. There was no escape from the gloom and cramp of the quarters to broad and sunny decks aboard *Bounty*.

On 9 October, Bligh told Banks that the ship had been sent down to Long Reach and there the guns and gunner's stores were loaded; he also thanked him for the present of a sextant of noticeably good workmanship.

Bligh took a special interest in provisioning his ship, for he had advanced and definite ideas about health and diet. The Navy Board ordered *Bounty* to be victualled with one year's supply of all provisions except beer. Only one month's allowance of the beverage was to be put aboard; wine and spirits were taken in lieu of the rest, for they would last longer and better, and beer could be made on board. Bligh decided he should provision for eighteen months. On 18 September the Admiralty instructed the Navy Board that in response to requests (presumably from its commander) the ship could have additional supplies and the Commissioner of Victualling was directed to supply 'Sour Krout, malt [dried], wheat and Barley [instead of oatmeal], sugar [instead of oil], juice of wort [condensed brewing malt], and salt for salting fresh meat and fish'. Bligh was given freedom to arrange the quantities of each and a week later there was further approval of five hundredweight of portable soup, something normally supplied in quantities sufficient only for the sick.

By 10 October, all the trading goods had been purchased, too, and Bligh had been allowed the sum of 100 ducats for his use in places he would visit after leaving the South Seas. As the request to the Admiralty for funds for these items came from Lord Sydney, one of the Principal Secretaries of State, and Bligh's signature stands at the bottom of the list, it can be safely assumed that Bligh's experience had been used to compile it and the Admiralty was simply to pay up; but Banks' knowledge of the Pacific was doubtless called upon too.

This is what was taken for trading:

Toeys or Chissels in sizes;	No 1—32 dozen
	2—54 dozen
	3—44 dozen
	4—46 dozen
	5—58 dozen
	234 grose as per pattern
Knives in wood handles and sheaths	4 grose
Spike nails of 6 inches	3 cwt
3 inches	2 cwt
10 inches	3 cwt
Hand saws	4 dozen
Small Bar Iron	6 cwt
Hatchets in sizes	14 dozen
Gimlets	10 dozen
Coarse flat files	10 dozen
Rasps	9 dozen
Looking glasses at 3d or 6d each	14 dozen
Common white glass beads	30 lbs
Common blue glass beads	30 lbs
Common red glass beads	20 lbs
Drops for earrings—stained glass	22 dozen
Coarse shirts	6 dozen

The 'chissels' were of a special design, plans for which were included in the document, just the attention to detail we should expect from Banks and William Bligh.

By 10 October Bligh had bought everything with expedition and economy. In exchange for the invaluable breadfruit they were taking £125. 6s. 4d. of trading goods.

BOUNTY'S COMPLETE COMPLEMENT

Joined ship	Age	Names	
1787			
20 Aug.	—	Lieut. William Bligh	commander
	—	John Huggan	surgeon
	—	John Fryer	master
	20	Thomas Hayward	AB to 1 Dec. 1787 then midshipman
	—	David Nelson	botanist
	—	William Brown	assistant botanist
27 Aug.	—	William Cole	boatswain
	—	William Purcell	carpenter
	—	William Peckover	gunner
	40	Lawrence Lebogue	sailmaker
	24	Henry Hillbrant	AB
	26	John Samuel	clerk
	21	George Stewart	midshipman to 30 Nov. 1787, then AB: acting master's mate to 2 March 1788
	15	Peter Heywood	AB to 23 Oct. 1790 then midshipman
29 Aug.	36	William Elphinstone	master's mate
	30	Peter Linkletter	quarter master
31 Aug.	30	Isaac Martin	AB
	36	Joseph Coleman	armourer
7 Sept.	28	Charles Churchill	master-at-arms
	20	Alexander Smith (John Adams)	AB
	21	Fletcher Christian	master's mate to 2 March 1788 then acting lieut.
	25	Thomas Burkitt	AB
	21	John Millward	AB
	25	Thomas McIntosh	carpenter's mate to 31 Dec. 1787 then carpenter's crew
	29	John Mills	gunner's mate
	27	James Morrison	boatswain's mate
	26	John Williams	AB
	22	John Sumner	AB
	15	John Hallet	midshipman
	17	Robert Tinkler	AB
7 Oct.	28	James Valentine	AB
8 Oct.	27	George Simpson	AB to 14 Oct. then quartermaster's mate
	21	Robert Lamb	AB
	19	Thomas Ellison	AB
13 Oct.	34	John Norton	quartermaster
16 Oct.	36	John Smith	AB
23 Oct.	27	William Muspratt	AB
	37	Matthew Thompson	AB
	21	Edward Young	AB, but sailed as midshipman
16 Nov.	—	Michael Byrne	AB
21 Nov.	—	Charles Norman	carpenter's crew to 1 Jan. 1788 then carpenter's mate
28 Nov.	—	William McKoy	AB
	—	Matthew Quintal	AB
6 Dec.	—	Thomas Denman Ledward	AB to 11 Dec. 1788 then acting surgeon

9

A Laudable Recovery

It is strange that Bligh, a man dogged in the pursuit of his duty to the king, allowed himself to sail with neither the muscle he needed to man the ship nor the muscle he needed for discipline. Gavin Kennedy, in his biography of Bligh, makes the point extremely well, showing that by attending to the fancies of others, as well as to a few of his own, he appeared to dilute the strength of his crew. Instead of the twenty-five able seamen to sail *Bounty*, that is to stand watch and to manhandle the sails, the ship had only thirteen, one of whom was Michael Byrne, an almost sightless Irish fiddler Bligh hired to inspire the men to dance nightly for their health. The berths that should have gone to other ABs had been whittled by such arrangements as the employment of five midshipmen instead of the two allowed. As well, there had to be an armourer to oversee the guns, an official requirement; there was a commander's cook (a bit of swank, surely), a steward, and at the last moment an assistant surgeon—all signed on as Able Seamen. The latter appointment was a most sensible precaution, for the surgeon was a sot who had been foisted on Bligh with a degree of insensitivity to the voyage that borders on criminality. He seemed perfectly useless up to his death on Tahiti. But to be fair to the

man, who was liked by the Tahitians, we only have Bligh's word
of his disabilities.

The two gardeners were also men whose berths had to come out
of those allotted to ABs, although the instructions of William
Brown, one of the gardeners, make it clear he was to stand watch.
As to the sailing duties of the rest of the 'extras' we have no exact
knowledge. But the midshipmen were certainly not expected to haul
ropes and climb masts and I doubt if a commander's cook or an
assistant surgeon would; a blind violin player could not. It looks as
though the ABs were in for an even tougher time than usual, but
this was not actually the case. Scurvy and other diseases caused far
more thinning of the seamen's ranks than favouritism ever did. It
was not unusual for a ship to return from a long journey with less
than half its original complement.

Bligh's belief in his methods of feeding and hygiene at sea may
have allowed him to play deliberately with his crewing, in arrogant
trust that there would always be enough men to sail the ship. Or
perhaps twenty-five ABs really were too many and it was, like so
many aspects of Georgian life, simply a form that had to be gone
through and was *always* adopted. It is unlike Bligh to do himself
down, and I think the latter is most likely; the real problem was
not of manpower but of not having either more commissioned officers or some marines aboard.

Gavin Kennedy offers some interesting observations about the
later actions of the replacements of the men who deserted *Bounty*
before she sailed; there was plenty of opportunity for them to
change their minds and futures thanks to the slowness of the arti-
sans. Nineteen of those assigned to *Bounty*, pressed or transferred,
did not sail with her. Three were transferred to other ships and
sixteen 'ran', including all the pressed men. Of the replacements,
all volunteers, six became mutineers of whom Young, McKoy and
Quintal, were hardliners who sailed off to temporary oblivion in
the pirated ship. Although nothing official was announced to her

crew until she was well into the Atlantic, rumours and assiduous questioning made the destination of this extraordinary vessel common knowledge.

Volunteers for such a journey must have been inquisitive, adventurous and footloose by nature and thus were far more likely to want to stay in the Pacific than men who had been wrenched from their homes by a press gang. It should be added, to balance Kennedy's remarks, that these last minute replacements were particular malcontents, that of the nine men who went to Pitcairn one was Brown, appointed to the ship before Bligh, and another was the American, Isaac Martin, who signed up on 31 August, a week before Fletcher Christian. *Bounty* is thought to have been the first ship of the Navy ever to have sailed with no pressed men aboard; perhaps her crew of volunteers was yet another reason why her capture by mutineers was so simple it seemed inevitable?

Bounty was also competing for men with a general muster, for there were new problems in the Netherlands and the Baltic. To career minded naval officers the approaching battles were a boon, for war meant faster promotion. The drawback was obvious. War also meant the possibility of death, and sensible ambition includes some time for the enjoyment of one's achievements. I am persuaded that many a volunteer who sailed aboard *Bounty*, careerist or not, had the voyage in mind as an adventurous and possibly profitable way to avoid permanent interruption to his plans.

Bligh would have liked another change aboard *Bounty*, one more important than ballast and boats. He wanted promotion, both as a right and because he then would have one—or two—lieutenants under him, which in his later opinion would also have ensured there would be no disciplinary problem. Bligh actually wanted promotion to full captain, that is post captain, which would automatically have given him lieutenants, without whom he was the only commissioned officer on board. He would have accepted the lesser promotion to master and commander and wrote directly to Banks 'considering that I was going out of the immediate chance of promotion and the great advantage of being in the beginning of a war . . . I have been constantly in service for eighteen years and I hope that may have some weight with his lordship . . .'

Bligh continued to write about promotion from *Bounty* with a decided whine to his quill as long as he could send letters. But, although moral right was certainly on his side, there were rules and regulations about what rank could command what type of ship. It was impossible to bend them and Banks was either incapable of forcing the issue, or felt he had done quite enough for his new protégé, who begged obsequiously. Added to his burden of difficulties with the Admiralty and the delaying of his ship's departure, the snub to Bligh's sense of justice must have made him feel well justified to sit and sulk. Having no other commissioned officer aboard forced a solitariness of command upon him.

His father-in-law, Richard Betham, sympathized with Bligh and agreed he should be promoted but pointed out what was common knowledge. In peacetime virtually no promotions were made other than at sea. Betham told Bligh he should expect to be given sealed orders that were not to be opened until he had crossed a certain latitude. It was good advice, but promises were not enough for Bligh. He could not get lieutenants or new insignia out of salt air.

He must have been very glad to see, perhaps had even encouraged, the slow growth of a coterie of young men aboard who were in some way associated with his past or his family, and who could thus be expected to show respect over and above that normally commanded by a mere lieutenant. If others did not know their duty to him, Bligh was certainly showing that *he* understood the duties of patronage.

George Stewart was the first of these young men to come aboard. He arrived as a midshipman on 27 August, but was rerated down to AB on November 30, when young men more deserving of the title had been employed; of course he continued to serve as a young gentleman, not as an AB, and the demotion was a matter of paper administration. Stewart was from the Orkneys and someone had moved fast to get him on *Bounty* only two weeks after Bligh's appointment. When *Resolution* had called at Stromness in the Orkneys in 1780 on her way home from the South Pacific, Bligh had been well looked after by the Stewart family and promised interest to George, aged thirteen at the time. The boy had not gone to sea but at twenty-one quickly took advantage of knowing Bligh; presumably Bligh wrote to him for nothing had been published in the newspapers that would have told Stewart of the voyage.

On the same day that Stewart arrived, Bligh also welcomed fifteen-year-old Peter Heywood, whose case had been pleaded by Bligh's father-in-law, who had long known of the plans, through Duncan Campbell. Peter's father in Douglas, Isle of Man, had suddenly fallen from the security and profit of being Seneschal to the Duke of Atholl. Betham wrote saying he thought young Peter 'ingenious . . . a favourite of mine and indeed everybody . . . I hope he will be of some service to you, as far as he is able in writing or looking after any necessary matters under your charge.' Richard Betham also emotively underlined the duty he felt towards the Heywoods and how great would be their disappointment if he had not applied to Bligh successfully; emotional blackmail was disguised only by the thinnest turn of phrase. Bligh acquiesced, so yet another family connection—and his father-in-law—were obliged to him.

Then it was Betsy Bligh's turn. She recommended fifteen-year-old John Hallet, the brother of a friend from London, whose father had written. Mackaness tells us the fourth midshipman, twenty-year-old Thomas Hayward from Hackney, then a salubrious agricultural village, also came through her influence.

Thus, four of the five men who were to sail as midshipmen came directly through Bligh connections. A fifth Bligh connection was Robert Tinkler, who was recommended by John Fryer the master. As the lad was actually Fryer's brother-in-law, Bligh could hardly refuse. The four young gentlemen were embarked, Peter Heywood having stayed with Elizabeth in Lambeth, by 7 September. If Bligh had later cause to regret having any of them on board he had only himself to blame, which might explain some of the vitriol he directed towards them.

On the same day the quartet of midshipmen was completed one of Bligh's best friends, his first protégé, also came aboard. Fletcher Christian was to sail as master's mate.

Two other faces were familiar to him too, Lebogue the sailmaker and young Tom Ellison, who was to serve as an AB. Both had been on *Britannia*. Ellison, small and thin, was of special interest to Duncan Campbell.

Six weeks later yet another young man was signed on as an AB but would sail as a midshipman. Edward Young was 21. Born on St Kitts in the West Indies, he was perhaps a mulatto and described as having 'a bad look'. Bligh says, in the journal he later wrote during his epic open-boat voyage, that he was recommended by Sir George Young, 'a Captain in the Navy'. It has long been claimed Edward was the nephew of Sir George Young Bart, later an Admiral. But a note made by the Admiral's son says: 'It was unpardonable to say Young was my father's nephew—or mine! There was an Edward Young, son of George, the son of the Rev. James Young and a first cousin once removed of the Admiral, who may have been this man'. Bligh gives no further amplification, except to note Edward Young 'proved a worthless watch'.

Fletcher Christian's age is given on the muster sheet as twenty-one, but this is not true. He was twenty-two and would be twenty-three just weeks later, on 25 September. In absolute contrast to Bligh's pallor, Fletcher Christian was brown skinned and dark haired. He was 5 feet 10 inches and his body was muscular, marred only by a slight outward bending of his knees, which the breeches of his midshipman's uniform would emphasize into the appearance of being positively bowlegged.

Christian and Bligh had more in common than their past and their connection with Man. They also had similar expectations of the future and a belief in an inherent right to rule other men. Fletcher Christian's was based on the birthright of centuries; Bligh's was based on the authority he donned with his uniform.

Bounty had a remarkably young crew, with most under thirty; Bligh at thirty-three was one of the oldest, perhaps by design. But for Fletcher Christian to have his position quite so young is startling. The master, Fryer, was thirty-four and newly married; the other mate, William Elphinstone, was thirty-eight. Christian must have been indebted to Bligh for an excellent recommendation, and he must also have been an excellent man at his job. When he returned he was virtually certain of becoming a lieutenant, years before Bligh had reached the same rank.

Already Fletcher Christian had been to Africa, India and the West Indies. He had never been in trouble, indeed he had been singled out for special favour by Captain Courtney on *Eurydice*, and by Bligh on *Britannia*. For a young man whose world had been ripped from under his feet only eight years before, he had made a laudable recovery. If he continued the same way he would easily replace all he had lost.

10

Animals, 'fierce and resentful'

The twin aggravations of a dilatory Admiralty and obstructive weather delayed Bligh far more than the fiddling craftsmen. He sailed *Bounty* as far as Spithead on 4 November, having written to Banks on the way to say it would have given him much pleasure to have shown him the ship, as 'I flatter myself she is the completest that has sailed on any expedition'.

The weather was then perfect for Bligh to sail down the Channel, and continued to be so for three weeks. Yet he still did not have his sailing orders, and without those he could only fret and write fine phrases, inspired by a not unreasonable exasperation.

But for Fletcher this delay proved a boon, for it gave him the opportunity of an unexpected meeting with his brother Charles, who was returning to Spithead from Madras in the East Indiaman *Middlesex*. So anxious was Fletcher to take advantage of this chance crossing of paths that he hired a small boat and boarded *Middlesex* as she was still sailing. He had much to tell. Their only surviving sister had died that year, and so had Uncle Edmund Law, Bishop of Carlisle.

Charles must have been equally surprised and pleased to see Fletcher. He had been away for almost twenty months. The two brothers, and one of *Middlesex*'s officers who had once been in the Navy, went ashore and spent the evening and night there.

Their meeting is discussed in Charles's unpublished autobiography. Although writing nearly twenty-five years later, Charles appears to remember the impression Fletcher made in vivid detail; it was, after all, the last time he saw his brother.

> ... he was then full of professional Ambition and of Hope. He bared his Arm, and I was amazed at its Brawniness. 'This,' says he, 'has been acquired by hard labour.' He said, 'I delight to set the Men an Example, I not only can do every part of a common Sailor's Duty, but am upon a par with a principal part of the Officers.
>
> I [Charles] met with a Surgeon [Thomas William] in East India who had gone out with him in the *Eurydice* Frigate, commanded by the Honble Captain Courtney, and also with an Officer on my Return to London who had sailed in the same ship with Fletcher. They corroborated to me his Assertions— Captain Courtney had appointed him to act as Lieutenant [by giving him charge of a watch]. They said he was strict, yet as it were, played while he wrought with the Men—he made a Toil a pleasure and ruled over them in a superior, pleasant Manner to any young Officer they had seen.

If this were all Charles tells us it would still be an important addition to the sparse first hand material we have about Fletcher Christian. In fact, there is much more to tell, for like all men writing about themselves, Charles had left something vital out of the document, not in any way to obscure facts, which were well known at the time, but because the details were both painful and largely irrelevant when he wrote his autobiography. He did refer to the problem in enough detail to show he was not hiding it completely.

I am persuaded that few men [i.e. himself] had a stronger propensity to Beneficance or possessed a greater share of Benevolence, or a more anxious Disposition to be pleasing and
serviceable to all Classes of the Community until a chagrined
Turn of Thought arose, *the offspring of the Middlesex East Indiaman
Voyage*. In that Ship, as well as in every other Ship or in every
House . . . it might be a peace-preserving Mean to have the
following Mottoes always placed conspicuously . . .

'Beware of whom you speak, to whom, of what and where.'
'Give every Man thine Ear, but few thy Voice.'
'Take each Man's censure, but reserve Judgement.'

. . . The Precepts and Doctrine of our Religious inculcate the
Forgiveness of Injuries, but when Men are cooped up for a long
time in the Interior of a Ship, there oft prevails such a jarring
Discordancy of Tempers and Conduct that it is enough on many
Occasions by repeated Acts of Irritation and Offence to change
the Disposition of a Lamb into that of an Animal fierce and
resentful—What can not the Power of Provocation bring to pass
on Land, where there is a free Range of Separation?

These references and one other, which is more relevant later, led
me to look further into the voyage of *Middlesex*. The Captain's Log
can be seen in the Archives of the India Office in Whitehall. There,
in the entry for 5 September 1787, is the origin of the canker that
distressed Charles for the rest of his life. Incredible as it may seem,
there was a mutiny aboard *Middlesex*, and Charles Christian was cited
as one of the officers involved.

Charles Christian was in his fiftieth year when he wrote about
his life, in his mother's house in Douglas, Isle of Man, in 1811. He
wrote his account in letter form, as a defence against rumours that
he had forged banknotes on the island. He relates fluently and pic-
turesquely in non-consecutive episodes a life packed with adventure
and emotion.

A superficial look at his autobiography might easily lead a browser to dismiss Charles Christian's tales of misfortune and persecution as the delusions of a paranoiac; indeed, this is exactly the impression of the two women who found and read the document early in this century. Such an interpretation, if confirmed, would clearly cast suspicion on the veracity of the evidence and careful consideration had to be given to the possibility that it was the work of a man deranged; but after much thought and research I cannot see that this is likely. For Charles both prefaces and punctuates his autobiography with an open willingness to believe he might be in some way mistaken or responsible for his bad fortune, and that is certainly not the manner of paranoiac.

Clearly Charles was an eccentric and possibly he had a personality which made him a natural butt of malicious humour. But throughout his troubled life he never lost his extraordinary strong optimism or Christian faith.

After joining the West Yorkshire Militia in 1780, where he remained for three and a half years, he spent two years at the Medical School in Edinburgh. Although only in his twenties, Charles was an avowed celibate. Like many over-informed medical men he was convinced he would never live out the following year and used this reason to excuse his constant desertion of the women to whom he was attracted, some of whom were very rich and very interested. Perhaps as a result of a romantic attachment, in February 1786, Charles signed on as surgeon on board *Middlesex*, commanded by Captain John Rogers. She was bound first for India, then Macao on the China coast. By the time she had left Madras for England on her return, she must already have been an unhappy ship.

5 September 1787 was a day of many a lamb turned into 'an Animal, fierce and resentful', and a time of great fear. At 6 pm Captain Rogers reports that he confined W. Greace in irons for presenting a loaded pistol to his captain's breast, and for threatening he would put the first man to death who touched him. The

first officer, Mr G. Aitken, was dismissed for aiding and assisting the mutiny's commission. Three hours later Mr D. Fell, the second officer, was also dismissed for 'drunkenness, Insolent Language and striking at his captain on the Quarter Deck'. 'At this time I dismissed the Surgeon, also in the conspiracy.'

Aitken and Fell were actually locked away, for on 7 September, Captain Rogers reported they broke out of their cabins but were reconfined 'to prevent further evils'. It can only be presumed that Charles was locked up too.

If this had been the Navy, Greace, Aitken, Fell and Christian would have been court-martialled and if found guilty of mutiny, could have been hanged from a yardarm. But this was private shipping. Their action was neither against the king, nor was it a civil offence, having occurred at sea, which is why Charles was able to leave the ship when it arrived in Spithead; on 14 November, he was paid £52.12s.2d. back pay. Nonetheless, there were actions at the disposal of the Captain within the framework of the East India Company, and its Court of Directors, but from the minutes of the EIC's Court of Directors for 19 October, we learn the astonishing fact that Captain Rogers had not made an official report of the mutiny. The Directors resolved that his actions were reprehensible in that he had not entered in the Company's Log (quite separate from that of the Captain) 'the several transactions relating the behaviour of his officers in September' and he had not advised immediately on arrival his dismissal of the chief and second officer. The action of the officers was considered 'extremely censurable' and they were each suspended from further service with the East India Company: Aitken for three years, Fell and Charles Christian for two years, and Greace for ever. However, the Company obviously felt Rogers was more than a little to blame. The Court met again five days later on 20 October, to punish him. He was fined the very large amount of £500 (which was to be used by Poplar Hospital) and suspended from trading and profiting for one year.

Fletcher's last conversations with his brother, then, must have been about mutiny. More than that, they were probably about the duty of officers towards their men and the actions that could be taken against captains who were cruel or thoughtless. No wonder Fletcher remained ashore all night—the conversation in Spithead must have been riveting.

On 10 November 1787, Bligh wrote it would be hard if instead of some good reason for being detained he were to discover it was simple oversight by the Lords of the Admiralty: he later said they all deserved to be punished for precisely that sinful attitude towards his expedition. He was subjected to a further fortnight of tedium and complaint before his sailing orders finally appeared. Immediately the wind, which for weeks had been favourable, changed. On the 28th, the crew were given two months' pay in advance and *Bounty* tried to sneak off during a brief change of wind. But she was forced into St Helens, on the Isle of Wight, across from Spithead.

Bligh was well aware of the hardships that lurked at the tip of South America. Every day of delay made them more frightening. At this rate he would be attempting to round the Horn when every force of the southern elements would be against him. He was confident of the ship but already practising that ill-advised habit of belittling the character of his complement. On one hand he noted his 'men and officers all good and . . . happy under my directions'; on the other, he was doubting their ability to stand the snow, sleet and gales of the Horn.

By 3 December, *Bounty* was ignominiously back in Spithead. There was only one ray of cheer. Bligh expected that once this voyage was over, all his 'concerns over money would have been solved' and his 'poor little family' would be financially secure. The bait of future solvency was certainly a stimulus to success and might explain the extra edge Bligh gave to his carping about exertion and excellence, but it makes some of his later actions, which demonstrably threatened success, even more difficult to understand. Three days later, still wheedling for promotion, he attempted again to clear the Channel. This time *Bounty* was blown almost to the French coast and scuttled back to St Helens for shelter, many of her crew suffering severe colds. Bligh was not prepared to risk further 'damaging the ship or hurting the health of my men and officers' and waited until events augured better for his departure. The added time in port gave him a welcome chance to consider further his orders to reach Tahiti by the shortest route, that is via the Horn: he knew failure to carry out orders would reflect badly on his character rather than on the Admiralty, and he was in no mood to be fodder for them, writing to Campbell, '. . . they took me from a state of affluence from your employ with an income of five hundred a year to that of Lieuts pay of 4/- a day to perform a voyage which few were acquanted with sufficiently to insure it any degree of success'.

With success as important for his family as for his reputation, Bligh determined that the Horn out of season was too big an obstacle to risk without the backing of alternative orders. He wrote to Banks asking if he could coax discretional orders from the Admiralty. This time there was no hesitation; it was a reasonable request and their Lordships' permission was almost mandatory, all things considered. Bligh had his new orders within two days, allowing him to sail via the Cape of Good Hope if he arrived too late to breach the Horn.

Only on 23 December did the winds move to the east. Bligh once more said goodbye to Betsy, who had come to Spithead; they had managed some secret and unexpected time together.

On the very first afternoon after departure a seaman fell from a yard while unfurling the main top gallant sail, but saved himself by a herculean lunge at a stay. Christmas Eve was a day of gales. But

Christmas was altogether calmer and the festival, which everyone aboard had expected to celebrate in sub-tropical waters, was marked by the issue of extra rum to accompany beef and plum pudding.

Then for three days and nights, cruel steel grey Atlantic rollers smashed over the struggling ship. On the 27th, her stern windows collapsed under the weight of gale-driven salt water. The icy flood that raced through the ship broke an azimuth compass and Bligh only managed to save the precious time-keeper and his navigational instruments with great difficulty. The men were further tormented; chilled, wet and frightened, they had not even the comfort of hot food, for the stove could not be lit. Instead, rations of grog were added to their beer and they had to fill up with biscuits. There was nothing else.

When the storm abated, anxious stock was taken of the damage. Extra spars had been washed away and the ship's three vital boats had been damaged. Their repair had to take priority—in case there was another such storm, or worse. Seven full hogsheads of beer lashed together on the deck had disappeared and two casks of rum had split, their contents dribbling into the bilge. Most seriously, the water which had crumpled the stern had contaminated *Bounty*'s vital supply of biscuit, stored directly below the Great Cabin; it would all have to be checked and laboriously repacked.

Bligh concentrated on drying the men's gear, their bedding and the ship's interior. When the stove was finally lit, two men from each watch were detailed to wash and dry clothes. The hatches were opened to air the ship and the lower decks were rinsed with vinegar to dissuade the growth of mould and mildew. By 31 December, men were still sorting and repacking the spoiled bread and hoisting planks from the hold to repair the boats.

When they opened some barrels of meat, four 4 lb. pieces were missing from the pork and three 8 lb. pieces from the beef, but this was expected by men in the king's navy.

On New Year's Day 1788, the sorting of the bread was finished but a whole cask of cheese was found to be rotten already. Still, the weather was fine enough to complete repairs to the rigging and to clean. Men were put to drawing yarn and making mats and all sails were set. They were on their way at last. The superstitious on board may have been forgiven for wondering if the storm had been an ill portent, as if someone was trying to prevent the voyage, or at least warn them of worse to come.

Twelve days after leaving England, *Bounty*, almost shipshape once more, sighted Tenerife, dominated by the snowcapped peak of Mt Tiede, a volcano that still smoked ominously. This was *Bounty*'s final civilized opportunity to repair, replenish and replace before heading for South America. It was also a much needed respite after the unpleasant and frustrating start, which apart from the sheer discomfort, had prevented officers and men settling into the routine of mutual trust and companionship upon which all their lives depended.

Bounty anchored in the roads of Santa Cruz, the island's capital, on the morning of 6 January. Bligh immediately sent Fletcher Christian to pay the captain's respects to the island's Governor, a Spanish grandee named Marqués de Branchforte. This is early and positive demonstration of the faith Bligh placed in Christian and of his favouring the dark young man. It was not unusual for Bligh not to have made first contact with such a nobleman himself. But the first mate, Elphinstone, might have been thought better suited than Christian for such a diplomatic mission; but we do not know of the social or physical recommendations of the latter. Still, Fletcher Christian was not going to protest when given such a flattering duty. Without it he might not have gone ashore on this beautiful sub-tropical gem of the 'Fortunate Isles'.

As representative both of Bligh and King George, Fletcher Christian had been directed to tell the Marqués that he would be saluted by *Bounty*'s guns, provided an equal number were fired in return. The reply he carried back was recorded as being extraordinary. His

Excellency said he returned an equal number of guns only to persons equal in rank to himself. Bligh omitted the ceremony with no further comment; he had met his match in sensitivity of public image.

None of this hindered Bligh's tasks there, but the lack of supplies at an unfavourable time of the year did. Indian corn, potatoes, pumpkins, and onions were scant and twice the summer's price. Beef was scarce and inferior, ship's biscuit cost 25 shillings a hundred pounds and chickens were an outrageous 3s. each. Even the sub-tropical fruits, normally so prolific, were in pitiful supply— a few dried figs and bad oranges. Water was bought at five shillings a ton, delivered.

Ferrying goods out to *Bounty* was risky, so Bligh treated with local boatmen, arranging to have everything handled by them. Wine was the only thing which gave Bligh some cheer. It was good and it was plentiful. Thinking it would be better for his men in the tropics than spirits he bought 863½ gallons. He also took aboard two hogsheads of the very finest quality Canary wine, at £15 a pipe, for Joseph Banks, judging it 'not much inferior than the finest London Madeira'. It would be considerably improved by the slow changes in temperature as it crossed the equator and returned.

Exercising his passion for recording detail, Bligh scratched pages of what men allowed ashore in Santa Cruz might see. Nelson was sent off looking for plants and natural curiosities amid the banana trees and the flowers that brighten the place even in winter. The log and Bligh's published narrative of the journey reveal observations on anchorage and the sea bottom, local precautions against smallpox by inoculation and quarantine, the ill-paved, but light and airy streets, and the admirable charitable institutions. But the patronizing cluck of a protestant work ethic is revealed in Bligh's comments about the latter's help for some of the island's poor men, who were encouraged by the governor and a clergyman into some employment:

By this humane institution a number of people are rendered useful and industrious, in a country where the poor, from the indulgence of the climate, are too apt to prefer a life of inactivity, though attended by wretchedness, to obtaining the comforts of life by industry and labour.

Bligh too would have problems with indolence on Tahiti, when even he was seduced by the indulgent climate into relative inactivity.

After five days at Tenerife, *Bounty* sailed toward the coast of Brazil with Bligh recording the ship's company all in good health and spirits; the exception was himself. As well as commander of the ship, Bligh was the purser, in charge of the ship's accounts and thus of the food stores. It was not unusual for the posts to be combined on a small ship but such autocratic control of supplies was open to enormous abuse, a fact both known and expected by the others aboard.

Everyone who has been at sea will know that food is one of the most explosive subjects aboard ship. Meals are one of the few pleasures hard working men expect. They regard food as their reward. Seamen are more sensitive about food, and its quantity, than men and women ashore can possibly imagine, and stories about it are always exaggerated.

Bligh's situation was unenviable. He had to balance not only his books but also the conflict between what the seamen thought were their rights and what he thought practical to give them, allowing for delays and damaged stores. It would be obvious to Bligh from the start that he would be suspected of cooking the books rather than enough food; and indeed he was.

I think most criticism hurled at Bligh about his meagre portions, stealing or substitutions is ill-founded. Certainly he expected to make some profit from the pursery and we know how important he felt this to be. Even if he were slightly dishonest he considered his men's health at least as much as his own pocket. That *Bounty* had such a record of good health is proof enough that his men never suffered from any profiteering Bligh might have enjoyed. Yet there were some problems, and he mentions them in a curiously frank letter to Duncan Campbell, who could naturally be expected to be sympathetic and knowledgeable about such matters. It should also be noted that Bligh continues his unworthy cry that he has no assistance worth mentioning, the transparent ploy of a man begging for sympathy and blaming others as a precaution against later failure, but hardly the way to engender loyalty or comradeship on the ship:

> . . . Having much to think of and little or no assistance, my mind is pretty well employed, and as my pursing depends on much circumspection and being ignorant in it with a worthless clerk, I have some embarrassment, but as I trust to nothing or anyone and keep my accounts clear, if I fail in the rules of office I do not doubt of getting the better of it . . . Tom Ellison improves and will make a very good seaman . . .

11

A Boy at the Horn

Once they were away from the Canary Isles, Bligh set about his final arrangements. He had to tell the men aboard officially where they were bound. Telling them he had no way of knowing the length of the voyage—not even to the nearest six months—he announced he was cutting the bread allowance by one-third. There was nothing sinister in this. In his journal Bligh explains that he had noticed men usually only ate two-thirds of what was given them and by saving the rest he could ensure there was something for later. Clear though the logic is, and even though the men were assured that any such shortage would be made up to them in cash at the journey's end, there were bound to be grumbles. They were also told all their water was to be filtered through a drop stone purchased in Tenerife. Finally Bligh said he had been assured that promotion would come to all on their return to England.

In a decision that benefited everyone on board Bligh also organized the ship to stand three watches, instead of the usual two. By the latter system no man who was part of a watch was ever able to sleep more than four hours; thus at times of danger when all hands were called, he might be on duty for twelve or more hours without rest and with none to look forward to. With three watches the men were on four hours and off eight, so even if there was an emergency they had a good chance of rest as well. Men who were well rested were healthier and more likely to react with alacrity to the orders of their superiors, who were equally well rested.

The arrangement also meant there was time for sheer relaxation, although Bligh insisted this take the form of dancing rather than indolence. He must have planned to switch to three watches even before he sailed from England, having gone to much trouble to find Byrne, the almost blind fiddler who was expected to play for several hours each evening from 4 pm, a time of day when even most men on watch could join in. Dancing as a form of exercise was continued on board English naval ships until this century, as early photographs testify.

Each watch needs an officer to command it, and Bligh gave charge of the new third watch to Fletcher Christian, a great compliment, even though such responsibility had been given him before, when he was much younger and on a considerably bigger ship, *Eurydice*.

On Thursday 7 February, *Bounty* crossed the equator and Bligh allowed all the usual customs and pranks performed upon those who had never done so before, except the ducking, which he considered brutal. The officers had to pay forfeits of rum to the men, which Bligh agreed to reimburse, and there was a special spirit of comradeship during the evening's dancing.

The south-east trade wind was now fresh and steady and the weather dry. More of the ship's bread was put into casks to protect it from vermin, an experiment of Bligh's which proved most successful. For almost a month Bligh wrote mainly of marine matters and how he felt ships should be maintained in tropic waters. By the end of February, they were only 100 leagues from Brazil and the great jungle-clad continent of South America. A westerly wind carried to *Bounty* some of the jungle's jewel-like butterflies, and insects which looked like the English horsefly. Only a week later the weather had turned cool enough for the men to lay aside their tropical clothing; on one day there had been a drop of eight degrees Fahrenheit. Now everyone began wearing the heavier clothes Bligh had ordered be bought in England.

Just a month after being put in charge of the watch, Fletcher Christian was further honoured. On Sunday 2 March, after inspecting the cleanliness of everyone aboard (he cut their grog rations if they were dirty), Bligh conducted Divine Service, at which the Articles of War were always read, and announced he had given Fletcher Christian a written order to act as a lieutenant.

There have been countless comments that this was unfair to Fryer, an insult, in fact. This is not true. It would have been flying in the face of all naval precedent to promote a master at sea. The position was extremely important and responsible; the master was chosen with perhaps more care than any other man on board, and had to have an outstanding degree of seamanship. If such a man was promoted to other duties, who then would take over?

Fryer would not have expected the promotion, and never once said he did. The only man who might have been miffed was Elphinstone, who was first mate and already thirty-eight. But not having been promoted to lieutenant by that age, he should sensibly have resigned himself to a career of permanent midshipmanship. Fletcher Christian was thought the best man for the job, and that was that. He had carried out his extra duties aboard *Eurydice*, *Britannia* and *Bounty* satisfactorily and his promotion was an expected reward. George Stewart, reportedly a highly gifted mariner, was promoted to Christian's old post and henceforth was acting master's mate.

Bligh obviously thought he needed support of a special kind, and at this stage trusted Christian more than anyone else. Having Christian as acting lieutenant should have made Fryer's job much easier, as he would have had his contact with Bligh lessened. It would be unwise of me to overlook the possibility that Fryer *might* have been upset by Christian's promotion. The evidence can certainly be interpreted that he was, and Bligh seems to say Fryer behaved spitefully thereafter. Yet, as there is absolutely no precedent that I can find for the promotion of a master while at sea we must dismiss this as the reason for any disenchantment—real or imagined—shown by Fryer subsequently.

Some other reason must be forwarded for the tension between Fryer and Bligh. If Bligh was publicly voicing the doubts about his officers that he was writing privately in his cabin, and if he included the master among those he belittled, it is no wonder the excitement of the voyage and respect for its captain were quickly cancelled for such men as Fryer who, unlike Fletcher Christian, had not learned to humour the passionate William Bligh.

Bligh's precautions were almost faultless but his disappointments (almost certainly imaginary or avoidable) were to multiply. He had hoped to complete the voyage without punishing a single man; but he might better have tried to walk to Tahiti. His care of the men's health and comfort, his attention to the hygiene and conditions aboard were considered by Bligh ample, if not abundant, reason to expect exemplary behaviour. But hardened seamen are not so easily bought. A week after Christian was made acting lieutenant, Bligh had reluctantly to order Matthew Quintal flogged for insolence and contempt of Fryer. According to the Articles of War, which Quintal had heard read every Sunday, Bligh had no choice. He was sentenced to two dozen lashes, inflicted by the scholarly and articulate boatswain's mate, James Morrison.

The voyage south aboard *Bounty* did not consist entirely of suspicions of theft and flogging, although MGM would have us think so. That whatever unpleasantries had happened were commonplace and unnecessary to report, is perhaps best seen in a previously unknown account of *Bounty*'s voyage from Tenerife to the Cape of Good Hope, which I discovered in the *Cumberland Pacquet* of 26 November 1788 (in the adjoining column, Fletcher's cousin John Christian XVII is thanked for his gift of £2 by the convicts of Carlisle jail). Although the author is anonymous, he is almost certainly the midshipman Peter Heywood. He was distantly related to Fletcher Christian and the two families must have known one another socially on the Isle of Man. Age difference notwithstanding, the men struck up a firm friendship, with a degree of hero worship by Heywood that he acknowledged even later in life.

The full printed dispatch, over a column in length, is introduced by a paragraph which summarizes *Bounty*'s intentions.

Extract of a letter from a midshipman (aged sixteen) on board his Majesty's ship 'Bounty', commanded by Capt. Bligh, now on her voyage to Otaheite under the immediate patronage of His Majesty . . . for the purpose of conveying . . . that valuable production of the vegetable kingdom, the BREAD FRUIT TREE . . .

BOUNTY, Simon's Bay in False Bay (Cape of Good Hope) June 17, 1788.

I shall give you a short account of our passage since leaving Teneriffe [sic], and of the exceeding bad weather we experienced off Cape Horn. I do assure you, the account which Lord Anson gave of it is very true, and not in the least exaggerated, as has been generally supposed; and the report which Captain Bligh will give (as most likely his voyage will be published) will (I dare venture to affirm) correspond with mine in every particular; and perhaps deter future navigators from attempting to double that Cape at so improper a season of the year.

We left Teneriffe on Thursday the 10th of January, after staying there four days. I wrote to you from thence by a Spanish packet, which was to have sailed in two days for Cadiz. After we left Santa Cruz, we shaped our course westerly towards the coast of Brazil, and from that road, till we got into the latitudes of the 30s we had the most pleasant weather imaginable and always plenty of fish. I have drawn one of every sort we caught, and also such birds as I could get a good sight of: so that I hope, by the time I come home, I shall have a tolerable collection.

On Saturday morning, the 16th of February we saw a sail, which next morning we came up with, and found her to be a South Sea Whale-Fisherman, bound for the Cape of Good Hope. In a few days afterwards, we got out of the north-east trade, entered the variables and now and then met with a gale that used us rather roughly, and which went very much against the grain, being so uncommon in the delightful climate we left behind.

The number of large whales which we daily saw, in running down the South American Coast is wonderful; and two or three of them at a time frequently came alongside to windward of the ship and blew the water all over us; and were thereby so troublesome, that, to make them set off, we were obliged to fire at them with muskets charged with ball. They frequently bore three shots before they offered to stir. On Saturday morning the 23rd March at 2 o'clock, we made the land Tierra del Fuego bearing south-east and by this bearing found ourselves in sight of land above Cape St Diego, and of course too far to the windward of Staten Land, to attempt going through Straits le Maire, as the wind was south-west, so we immediately halted off east.

At noon the east part of Staten Land made its appearance. This land is exceedingly high; the summits of the mountains are chiefly rocks, most of them entirely covered with snow and have altogether a very wild and desolate appearance. The only natives belonging to it, and which we saw in vast numbers, are seals, porpoises, and whales; and the birds are wild ducks, albatrosses, quebrantaussoes, petrells, and many other sea birds. Cape St John which is the east point, is in the latitude of 54.47 S. And 63.47 W. We had pretty good weather for a day or two after we left the land; but as soon as we were clear of it we began to feel the effects of the Cape Horn climate!—from the 25th of March till the 18th of April, was one continued gale as it seldom ceased for four hours together. During the 29 days we were beating off the Cape, we had to encounter the most violent storms that I suppose were ever experienced; and I can safely say, the wind was not 12 hours easterly during that time, and we never had more canvas spread than close reefed top sails; but most chiefly, when not lying to, reefed courses. The porpoises we caught off the Cape were thought delicious morcels; and a sea pie, made of albatross, (which, you may judge, must be very fishy, when caught above 100 leagues from the land) went down very well. After beating above three weeks, to no purpose, and the ship at last beginning to be leaky, so as to oblige us to pump every hour; and many of the people being ill, by the severity of the weather, and want of rest, (there being seldom a night but all hands were called three or four times) the captain, on the 18th of April, in the forenoon, thinking it dangerous, and very improper to lose so much time, bore down for the Cape of Good Hope, to the great joy of everyone on board. [Bligh says this happened on the 22nd.]

Peter Heywood's description of Bligh's attempt to round the Horn suggests only a small part of the terrifying ordeal the 90 foot ship of wood endured. Bligh wrote on 2 April that, 'the storm exceeded what I had ever met before'—and there were another three weeks to go.

The next day he reported the snow was no longer lying on the decks but came in large flakes. The hail was sharp and severe. The entire ship was battened down. The only access to the lower deck was through the aft hatchway and Bligh's own mess place. By the 12th Bligh had given up his cabin at night which allowed those who had no dry bed due to leaks to sleep in comfort. He did everything he could to keep the ship warm and dry and ensured no man went on watch in wet clothes.

When at last he knew his men could take no more and as the danger of their position increased, with more and more men injured or ill with rheumatics and other complaints, Bligh ordered the ship to bear away toward the Cape of Good Hope and ordered fresh hog meat to be served. They had carried poultry, sheep and hogs in great numbers but almost all had been victims of the weather. His men had been decidedly affected and Bligh exerted himself to improve their 'jaded' health. He made each man have a breakfast of hot wheat with sugar and a pint of sweet wort (a malt extract) a day, plus fine old rum, sauerkraut, mustard and vinegar. At first some of the men were worse after abandoning the Horn, which only reaffirmed that he had turned away just in time.

The ship's problems were not solved by the joy of a following wind and better weather. It was only with the greatest difficulty they could light a fire or get anyone to bear the smoke below. Four men had to take turns getting the dinner boiled, in the utmost pain, notwithstanding every endeavour to prevent the smoke. Three petty officers and two men were seized with violent sickness, vomiting and severe headaches which, added to those already sick, meant *Bounty* had twelve men out of service. The foresail is generally supposed to be the cause of a ship's stove smoking when going before the wind, but hauling it in made no difference and Bligh regretted not bringing a small caboose for cooking on deck.

Now let Peter Heywood complete his narrative and take his ship to the tip of Africa.

From that day, till we made this land, we had the wind constantly from the westward so that we had only been a month and three days making the run between the two Capes, which was I dare say, as great a run in the time, as ever was performed; and I

have the happiness of telling you that the *Bounty* is as fine a sea
boat as ever swam. She does not sail very fast; her greatest rate
is 8 or 9 knots; but once she went ten, quartering, which is
quite sufficient. We made the Table Land on the 23rd of May
and anchored in this bay on Saturday night following.

We shall leave this place in about a fortnight and proceed
for Van Dieman's Land, to wood and water; afterwards to
New Zealand; and then to Otaheite.

I suppose there never were seas, in any part of the known
world, to compare with those we met off Cape Horn, for
height, and length of swell; the oldest seamen on board never
saw anything equal to them, yet Mr Peckover (our gunner)
was all the three voyages with Captain Cook.

On his way to the Cape of Good Hope, Bligh had tried to find
Tristan da Cunha, but could not. His arrival at the Cape was marked
by a salute to the fort, which was satisfyingly returned by an equal
number of guns. The distance of their berthing at False Bay from
Cape Town was not an inconvenience and possibly helped the men
concentrate on making the needed repairs. The entire ship had to
be recaulked; every piece of the stores and provisions checked.
Fresh meat and vegetables with soft bread were served daily and
Bligh was rightly proud to note that though other ships were arriving with sick crews, tales of dead men and outbreaks of scurvy, he,
having braved a longer and more horrifying voyage, had delivered
his ship with every man in excellent health.

It took thirty-eight days before they were refitted and provisioned,
and *Bounty* sailed at four o'clock on the afternoon on Tuesday 1 July.
She saluted with thirteen guns which were again returned. Those who
were superstitious about their departure from England should have
been shivering at this 'unlucky' number. It was the last time Fletcher
Christian was ever to see a European settlement; and if one of his shipmates can be believed, he had not enjoyed it much.

It is revealing nothing to remind even the newcomer to this story that Fletcher Christian was to found the remote community of Pitcairn Island and that there is a mystery about when and where he died. One of the seamen who sailed with him signed on as Alexander Smith but later reverted to his real name of John Adams, which is how I refer to him. It is from him that we have most of the versions of Christian's death and later I will apply myself to the reasons he gave so many conflicting stories. Naturally Adams was asked for, and gave, his opinions about the mutiny which led to the founding of Pitcairn Island. In the last and most reliable of these accounts—although all are suspect—he mentions something about the Cape of Good Hope that always stuck in my mind. Adams told Captain Beechey in 1823 that Christian was under some obligation to Bligh and that their 'original quarrel' happened there and 'was kept up until the mutiny occurred' in a greater or less degree:

> Mr Christian . . . was under some obligations to him [Bligh] of a pecuniary nature, of which Bligh frequently reminded him when any difference arose. Christian, excessively annoyed at the share of blame which repeatedly fell his lot, in common with the rest of the officers, could ill endure the additional taunt of private obligations: and in a moment of excitation told his commander that sooner or later a day of reckoning would arrive.

I knew that Fletcher was obliged to Bligh for his posting to *Bounty* and for his promotion to acting lieutenant. But if the relationship were to have been complicated by financial dependence, nothing would be more certain to sour the friendship, especially if Bligh were continually carping about it. The idea of money as the reason for the mutiny was again current late in the nineteenth century but curiously because it seemed to come from the family of George Nobbs, an 'outsider' who married Christian's granddaughter Sarah, it was largely dismissed: the source of the story is precisely what should have made historians listen more carefully.

Cape Town was certainly a place where Fletcher might have needed money—to spend on entertainment, to buy private stores of food, or simply Hottentot souvenirs for his friends and family. Letters I discovered in Carlisle showed he had brought shells from the West Indies to his cousin Jane, the diarist and socialite who regularly visited Man. Once I knew, as other writers have not, that Fletcher's family had lost their fortune, it became obvious that he might have needed to ask Bligh for money in Cape Town. Bligh would have enjoyed making Fletcher squirm, reminding him of everything he already owed to his captain.

My later discovery of proof that Christian did indeed borrow from Bligh puts a new complexion on their relationship. Bligh's papers in the Mitchell Library, part of a special collection of *Bounty* material within the State Library of New South Wales, Sydney, made sense at last of the story. According to both the mutineer Adams and Fletcher Christian's Pitcairn descendants, Christian and Bligh's 'original quarrel' was based on money.

As the two men sailed away from Africa, any change in their relationship must have been very unsettling. *Bounty* was now isolated in a way that we can barely understand today. She had no means of communication with the outside world. The southern Indian Ocean was vast and offered no hope of a friendly or practical port of call in case of emergency or disaster. Bligh was master of a small piece of Great Britain, remote and afloat in the immensity of the Indian Ocean. Ahead lay only vaguely known coastlines and the even bigger Pacific Ocean. This was the time when Bligh's system of management would face its greatest test. Because he considered himself alone and unaided, labelling his officers incompetent, he assumed unnecessarily full responsibility for the ship and the success of the expedition. It was a matter of overriding personal compulsion. The question was, would his methods prevail? Were they really a carefully thought out plan? Or was his series of seemingly humane gestures really further proof of the cowardliness that underlies every bully?

The ship's passage from the Cape of Good Hope to Adventure Bay in Tasmania took several weeks. Peter Heywood said that Fletcher Christian enjoyed demonstrating his strength and could make a standing jump from inside one barrel directly into another. He would hold a heavy musket at arm's length and ask that it be measured as absolutely straight. At other times he helped Heywood complete the education that had been interrupted, with lessons in mathematics and classical languages. It is no wonder Heywood sympathized with Fletcher Christian.

The ship had enjoyed westerly winds during its passage, but they were boisterous, sometimes bringing hail and snow, sometimes running seas so high that once the helmsman was thrown over the wheel and badly bruised. They stayed for a couple of weeks in Adventure Bay, contacting the Tasmanian aboriginals, seeing eagles, blue herons and parrots. They caught fresh fish. Mr Nelson measured a tree of thirty-three and a half feet in girth and picked up an opossum measuring 12 inches from its ears to its tail, which was the same length again. Fletcher Christian and William Peckover, the gunner, were in charge of the important wooding and watering parties.

A garden of fruit trees was planted, presumably for future ships. Near the watering place they planted onions, cabbage roots and potatoes, presumably for the locals, who—Bligh agreed with Cook—could best be described as being 'a dull black', for they painted themselves with a kind of soot, laid so thickly over their faces it was difficult to say what they looked like. The native Ti-tree was in great abundance, and Bligh wrote that they gathered and dried it for use as tea and because the thin branches made excellent brooms.

What Bligh omitted from his *Narrative of the Mutiny*, although in this instance it was fully recorded in his Log, was the problem he had with William Purcell, the carpenter.

On 26 August, Purcell directly refused to assist with certain general duties, such as hoisting water into the hold. This was probably a sulk, for Purcell had already earlier felt Bligh's disapprobation of his conduct with the wooding party. Astonishingly, Purcell had answered back 'in a most insolent and reprehensible manner'. Bligh should have confined him until he was tried, but that could not be until the ship returned to England. Loath to lose the assistance of an able-bodied man, he sentenced him instead to labourer's duties aboard the ship. Like an errant schoolboy, Purcell was given a 'chance by his future conduct to make up in some degree for his behaviour . . .'

But Purcell did not labour on board, somehow convincing Fryer, who was in charge of these duties, that he was either exempt because he was a warrant officer, or because he had carpentering to do. Refusing to do as he was ordered was mutiny, or near enough, and if *Bounty* had not been so far away from civilization Purcell would have been in the deepest trouble. It was a vital moment for Bligh and he could not ignore the event. He gathered evidence from all those involved—useful for a trial in the future— and then ordered that until Purcell worked as commanded he should have no provisions; severe punishment was promised to any man who dared assist him. Purcell was 'immediately brought . . . to his senses'; but he had not been punished as he should have been.

Bligh rationalized this with his usual reference to duty. It is important to note that, whereas almost every writer continually carps about how overcrowded *Bounty* was, Bligh was of the opposite opinion.

His Log says: 'It was for the good of the voyage that I should not make him or any man a prisoner. The few I have even in the good State of health I keep them are but barely sufficient to carry the duty of the ship, it could answer no good purpose to lose the use of a healthy strong Young Man in my situation. I therefore laid aside my power in the particular for the good of the Service I am on, altho' it continued in force with equal effect.'

Bligh was deluding himself. His power can no longer have had 'equal effect' if he had not used it when challenged so severely. No single man is vital to a ship. The carpenter could just as well have been lost overboard, or have died of scurvy; the expedition would have gone on. Considering their 'State of Health' Bligh already had more men to sail *Bounty* than would normally have been the expected case.

For the good of the voyage Bligh probably should have confined Purcell, demonstrating, instead of writing about, his power. He was not allowed to flog Purcell, so he was saved that decision. My impression is that he hated inflicting any sort of punishment; but not on any humanitarian grounds. Bligh recoiled from it because of his own insecurity and cowardice. Such people need desperately to be appreciated and this is thought more likely if they forgive rather than punish. By not confining Purcell, Bligh had side-stepped a personal crisis but laid a firm foundation for a bigger one.

Morrison, who left two accounts of the voyage, also writes of events in Adventure Bay adding that here also were sown seeds of eternal discord between Lieutenant Bligh and some of his officers. Bligh 'found fault with the inattention of the rest, to their duty, which produced continual disputes everyone endeavouring to thwart the others in their duty and in this way they found their account and rejoiced in private at their good success.' It seems a remarkable situation: no man doing his duty through any sort of responsibility but to win points off one another and to avoid Bligh's criticism. Bligh's was the rule of a bad-tempered schoolmaster, petulant and niggling. I cannot believe that Purcell would have behaved so unless Bligh had helped create the situation himself. It is inconceivable that a warrant officer would deliberately sabotage himself in the early days of a long voyage if there were not both provocation and some hope of getting away with it.

On 9 October, Bligh was to sign the expense books of the boat-swain and carpenter, thus formally approving them as correct and ensuring the responsible warrant officers were paid properly at the end of the voyage. Fryer, the master, also had to sign the books, something which was done every month or so. This time, Fryer refused, unless Bligh first signed a certificate saying his, Fryer's, behaviour had been blameless throughout the voyage, which was not even half completed. It was gross impertinence and Bligh had to be authoritative. Telling Fryer he did not approve of any man doing his duty conditionally, Bligh ordered all hands aft and read the relevant Articles of War. Fryer's bluff was called publicly, and 'this troublesome man saw his error and before the ship's company signed the Books'.

Fryer had capitulated; but like Purcell he had not been punished. Neither did he take up Bligh's offer to allow him to write his reasons for not wishing to sign the books at the page where he subsequently put his name. Morrison is no help in explaining the circumstances, writing that Fryer did not wish to sign 'for reasons best known to himself'.

What might those reasons be? Why should the master of a vessel on an outward voyage put himself in great danger of present imprisonment or later court martial unless he felt he had excellent grounds for feeling righteous? There is the distinct possibility that Bligh was being too generous to himself in some of his pursing 'circumspections' and that Fryer was offering to swap oversight of this for the certificate of good behaviour. But a mutually beneficial arrangement could have been made privately, with no mention of a certificate. Why the certificate?

I can only presume that by long study of Bligh's own behaviour, Fryer did not expect Bligh to be fair to him on their return. It is easy to see how a man could reach this decision; Fryer, working so close to the captain, would be a regular target of Bligh and would certainly know of his habit of belittling and insulting everybody, regardless of their true worth and ability. Perhaps encouraged by Bligh's demonstrated weak attitude towards punishment Fryer became an opportunist, seeing a chance to protect his career from Bligh's unfair criticism.

Bligh might have thought himself a humanitarian by not punishing Fryer, and could easily have rationalized it as being for the good of the expedition—far more believable in the case of a master than that of Purcell the carpenter. In reality, the captain of the ship had only underlined his own weaknesses for all to see, and remember. He was ripe for exploitation, especially by those to whom he had been most unpleasant.

12

Ten Months to Tahiti

Fryer was not the only man who made Bligh angry on the last weeks of crossing the Pacific. Huggan, the surgeon, was suspected of sabotage or at least of insubordination. Three days before the Fryer incident Bligh was incensed to find James Valentine near death, the result of infection after blood-letting from an inflamed arm. It was monstrous that it had happened at all, infamous that he had not been told. Once more it seems all the officers were to blame for not having let him know what was happening, and in this Bligh was probably correct. Yet remember, Morrison wrote that every man was simply trying to do his job with as little trouble as possible; in other words they were trying to avoid Bligh.

Of course, there was little or no knowledge of antiseptic practice in tropical waters and there was always danger in spite of Bligh's excellent precautions. So the poisoning was not necessarily the fault of the surgeon; the infection could have happened independently, and been the fault of Valentine himself. But Huggan or someone else should have alerted Bligh earlier.

Valentine died on 9 October, the same day Fryer refused to sign the books. Were the events related?

A few days later Huggan declared that three men were suffering from scurvy. Bligh had said the appearance of scurvy on a ship was a 'disgrace'—yet here were three cases. Or were there?

Huggan had been severely castigated by Bligh for Valentine's death, and might have been attacking his captain in return. It is possible that the men did have scurvy in its early stages, and for a rather sad reason. Almost none of the 'new foods' that Bligh had purchased contained the vital vitamin C. They certainly gave a broader spectrum of vitamins and minerals than the usual ship's diet and dramatically improved general health aboard. But if a man were lax or silly about what he ate, scurvy was still a distinct possibility—especially if he did not take his lunchtime grog.

To Bligh the idea was impossible. The men had rheumatics—or something. He fed them essence of malt and increased the vigour of his routine for health and hygiene. The situation on board became ever more ludicrous and childish. On Sunday 19 October, Bligh described the muster of all hands thus: 'I think I never saw a more healthy set of Men and so decent looking in my life.' Anyone who has been aboard a sailing ship for some time would find that hard to believe!

That evening he even supervised the dancing—the men were going to be healthy at any price. Extraordinarily, two men refused to dance. When Brown, the assistant gardener, said he could not dance because of pains in his legs, Huggan backed him up by diagnosing scurvy. Bligh could find no symptoms. At least this is what he wrote in his Log.

The continuous tussle over diagnosis, perhaps aided by mischievousness of some men and encouraged by knowledge of Bligh's unwillingness to punish, continued for weeks. The atmosphere was one of suspicion and discontent, but of a silly schoolboy nature rather than anything threatening or malevolent. With every day Bligh's authority and dignity were further undermined.

It is sad to see this happen to any man, even when he is the victim of his own attacks. It can be sadder for some of those around such a man. For more than a year William Bligh had been a mentor and guide to young Fletcher Christian, perhaps even a father figure. Now, the sight of this man being humiliated and tormented must have been excruciating. Fletcher Christian was as likely as any to have been lashed by Bligh's tongue and so had the dreadful double pull of being faithful to a friend and loyal to his suffering brother officers. No man likes to be associated with an object of fun and Fletcher Christian, sensitive to undeserved criticism, must have observed Bligh's behaviour with considerable distaste and unease.

Bligh could have avoided all this nonsense about diagnoses and treatment simply by insisting Huggan stop drinking; Huggan's continued inebriety and incapacity was just as insolent as the actions of Purcell and Fryer. Again, Bligh seems to have been too cowardly to attack front on. On 21 October, he asked Huggan to stop drinking 'in a most friendly manner' but Huggan was insensible to the suggestion. In his private Log Bligh clearly bears out my belief that he shrank from punishing anybody, hoping that problems would disappear simply because of his superior caring. He wrote on 21 October: 'The Surgeon kept his Bed all this day and always drunk without eating an ounce of food. If it is ever necessary this should be publickly known, I may be blamed for not Searching his Cabbin and taking all liquor from him; but my motive is that . . . hoping every day will produce a change in him, I forbear making a public matter of my disapprobation of his conduct, in expectation as he has done many times this voyage, he may turn sober again.'

This really is absurd. How can a captain consider himself responsible if, once he has identified a problem, and knows the solution to it, he simply sits back and hopes the man will independently come to his senses? It is inviting every other man aboard to behave as he will. It is clear that there can have been no discipline aboard *Bounty* other than what the men sensibly wished there to be.

Two weeks after Valentine had been buried at sea, *Bounty* made the final manoeuvres that would bring her to the sanctuary of

Tahiti's lagoons. Bligh swept his ship east of the island's position and then turned to sail westward, exactly as the Polynesians did. On Saturday 25 October, they reached the physically boring island of Mehitia, sixty miles east of Tahiti, and at 6 o'clock the same evening finally saw the tips of Tahiti, illuminated in the last moments of the sun.

Conscious of his duty to the expedition's success, mindful of his reputation for scrupulous attention to detail, and ever solicitous of his men's health, Bligh ordered the ship's complement to be examined by Surgeon Huggan, for 'it was not expected that the intercourse of my people with the natives would be of a very reserved nature'. Huggan pronounced a clean bill of health, suggesting no one aboard *Bounty* was venereally infected. This may have been true; it may not.

It is puzzling to me why, in view of the importance of not upsetting the Tahitians by introducing further venereal disease, Bligh did not resort to the opinion of his more sober assistant-surgeon, Thomas Ledward. It is perhaps another example of the captain's blind belief that inflexibly following the rules was the greatest service he could perform for his masters, the finest example he could show his men.

Quite who had which venereal disease aboard *Bounty* and from whom is fascinating—but pointless—to conjecture. We know most of the names of the men who were infected at one time or another—almost half those on board—but we do not know when they had it. Careful detective work by other authors indicates that some of those appearing on the ship's venereal list had been treated on the outward voyage. Perhaps it was not VD but self-generated, non-specific urethritis, common enough among lonely men, especially those on a poor diet. Few, if any, doctors even suspected there was a variety of sexually transmitted diseases so there is no way we can now know.

Of course, Bligh was right to be so careful. He knew sexually transmitted disease now existed on Tahiti, but he did not want the responsibility of worsening it. Any man found infected would have been prohibited from free alliance with Tahitian women, so bribery may have encouraged the surgeon's clean bill, possibly as deliberate sabotage. Still, even if Huggan's opinion of universally sound genitals was as questionable as his insistence upon the presence of scurvy, Bligh had done his duty and he had written it all down. He also gave strict instructions about general behaviour and bartering, and the crew were told they must not reveal that Cook was dead.

At 4 am on Sunday morning, *Bounty* hove to, waiting to get a final fix at sunrise. Point Venus and Matavai Bay were only four leagues away, and in these last hours of isolation the *Bounty*'s men were vexed by slow, variable winds.

As the sun rose behind Tahiti, the ink-green shadow of the startling, lava-crumpled land they were skirting gradually focussed into three dimensions. They saw the monumental black precipices which rise from valleys of deep, twisted emerald. Stupefying rock pinnacles, isolated steeples and mile-long slopes hurl themselves into the sky in such unweathered confusion that man may never set foot on most of them. Slowly the morning mist lifted to form sun-gilt clouds, and the Englishmen could see thin, high waterfalls which appeared to merge with wisps of smoke from early morning fires.

By the time the ship carefully drifted through the reef it was 9 o'clock and she was overwhelmed by a welcome of gift-laden canoes. The number of men and women aboard *Bounty* grew so that Bligh could not identify his own people. It was a journey's end as intoxicating as the physical surroundings.

The black beach that edged the crowded lagoon of Matavai Bay was, itself, unremarkable, a gentle, shallow curve, just over a mile long, of volcanic sand notable for its fineness and intrusiveness. As Fletcher Christian looked to his right he would see the naked and rufous outpost of cliff called One Tree Hill. To his left, the extremity of the arc was formed by the low flat peninsula called Point

Venus, which would be the expedition's land base and which had been Cook's. Behind the beach the land is flat, or almost so, for some distance and watered by a river that spills limpid and fresh water from the interior into the salt-blue Pacific.

At that time such detail was blanketed from Fletcher Christian's view by thick garden, owing little to the artifice of man, a wonderful perfumed complication of tropical creeper and vine, a muddle of tall coconut, great breadfruit, orange and vee-apple, mango, hibiscus and gardenia, plantain, banana and sweet potato. Each man lived with his family independent of others, contented and commanding in his corner of paradise.

Fletcher Christian could only guess at these pleasures. But even such expectations and the excitement of the press of brown bodies, the garlands of scented flowers, the gifts of fresh fruit and meat and vegetables, would not engage all his attention. For behind the blue water and the green thickets, the land gathers itself into deep folds and sweeps with no further preparation into two gigantic, raw peaks, that stab the clouds and stun the senses. Neither the mountains of Cumberland nor any of his past landfalls would have prepared Fletcher Christian for these first impressions of the island with which he would forever be connected.

It was Sunday, but there was to be no rest. The gifts, the visitors, the insistent questions and constant assurances of goodwill increased as the severe tropical shadows lengthened. Bligh noted sourly that only chiefs of lesser rank came to greet him on the first day and that most seemed more anxious to know the fate of Cook, for they had heard some rumours of his death from the visit of a previous vessel. Bligh wanted to move *Bounty* to a safer and more permanent anchorage but dared not do this while so hindered with visitors. He deferred the operation until the earliest hours of Monday, finally anchoring in seven fathoms of water a quarter mile from the shore of Point Venus. This dawn start may not have been widely appreciated; for although Bligh ensured that all Tahitian men left the ship overnight, any woman who wished was welcome to stay. If a man was attractive or insistent enough to persuade two to stay with him, no one would say nay.

It was only a matter of days before Bligh was satisfied with formal receptions by those he thought the most important chiefs. In fact he was mistaken in the relative ranks of some, but managed quickly to be invited to take as many breadfruit as he wanted, in return for the gifts that were being so freely distributed. By Sunday 2 November, Bligh had paid his respects to the child Tu, regarded by him as supreme chief, and henceforth nothing was thought likely to hinder the collection of breadfruit shoots. Early that day Fletcher Christian was sent with a party of eight men to erect a tent on Point Venus. This was to be the nursery and, with the help of officials from the local districts, Bligh fixed a boundary over which Tahitian men and women were not to cross without permission. The chiefs were happy to oblige, even helping with the policing of the site, for they had persuaded themselves Bligh was actually assisting them by taking breadfruit to his king on their behalf; it was a surprisingly easy way to pay for metal tools, and they did not want Bligh to reconsider.

Christian's shore party included Peter Heywood and William Peckover, the most experienced Polynesian visitor, who had been here on all Cook's voyages. He spoke excellent Tahitian and had a perfect understanding of the Polynesian mind, so was placed in charge of all the trading and purchasing of provisions, a sensible precaution which neatly avoided the inflation caused by competitive buying. Nelson and Brown, the botanists, were naturally members of the permanent shore party but the other four, probably ABs, may have been rotated from among the entire complement.

The day to day activity of repairing a ship after such a long voyage gave many of the *Bounty*'s men ample opportunity to make friends of both sexes; it was said that soon few were without a *taio*, a blood brother whose family immediately became theirs. As well as the freedom to have women aboard each night, Bligh allowed two men shore leave each day. So, most of the time, the majority lived on the ship, hotter and more airless than ever.

With his second-in-command permanently on shore, Bligh, or Parai as he was known locally, was completely responsible for the ship, entertaining and protocol. He quickly discovered a routine that would continue throughout his stay. On board he entertained chiefs and their wives to huge meals, often having to put the food or the wine (for which the Tahitians quickly developed a taste) into the mouths of the rulers; most feasts were accompanied by gift giving. On shore he was royally entertained with ceremonies and presentations. He was carried over rivers, dragged up streams in canoes, danced and sung for. Women dropped all their clothes, leaving them as presents. The boy Tu was carried out for a mutual inspection across a river. He was too sacred to be approached closely, even by Tahitians. Bligh wrote everything down for he was as assiduous a questioner as his hosts. Throughout he wore his full dress uniform with its lace and skirted coat. At many ceremonies he was draped in bark cloth, a great honour that added both to his dignity and the heat engendered by his heavy coat of finest English wool. It was too much, even for an Englishman and a naval lieutenant. Several times he felt faint, a situation aggravated by the crowds who stood close. They had to be waved away.

But for all his application Bligh was really only writing about life in Tahiti. He was not living it. If certain customs did not suit his temperament or inclination he adapted them to his way of thinking; whereas every Tahitian and the rest of the *Bounty* men were expected to bare their shoulders in the presence of royal personages or at certain places belonging to them, Bligh removed only his hat, saying that was the way he would salute *his* king. Bligh was an Englishman abroad and what he wrote was for the record. But some of his men, Fletcher Christian included, were daily living more and more as Tahitians, or Polynesians at least. For a few, it was the way they would live the rest of their lives.

Half of *Bounty*'s men would never see England again. Some would die horribly, their blood seeping into the already-red soil of Polynesian islands. For the moment the gods, pagan and Christian, were in their heavens and benevolence prevailed. After sailing 27,086 miles, at sea for the best part of ten months, *Bounty*'s men were more concerned with earth than heaven. Not one would have argued if told he were already in heaven.

II

Fettered Freedom

13

Free Love and Death

The Tahiti in which Fletcher Christian and his shipmates found themselves was the stuff of legends, even though the English had been going there only for some twenty years. Apart from the nudgings and winkings of a prurient press, few people today have easy access to knowledge of what eighteenth-century Tahiti was really like; fewer still can imagine the full effect it must have had on an English officer brought up on the strict diet of Bible, Latin and Greek thought adequate preparation for exploring and conquering society and the globe.

No Tahitian ever wore the grass skirt of today's dancing troupes. There was no cannibalism and none of the excesses of nudity, poverty, slavery, squalor, riches and disease that Fletcher Christian encountered in India, Africa and the Caribbean. Instead, he found himself confronted by everything Rousseau had said was possible and preferable—a tall, noble race of golden men and women with few, if any, old, maimed and unwanted. Food grew abundantly with little attention and great variety.

Most disconcerting of all for Fletcher Christian, these charmed creatures were draped in yards and yards of snow-white cloth, like fancy-dress togas. It was as though the sirens and heroes and farmers and sailors of his classical education had been resurrected, or had never died.

These golden gods and goddesses were no figment of the imagination; they were flesh and they were willing to share its pleasures, provided the rather strict rules about such things were understood. If they were broken, the miscreant could be bludgeoned to a *post flagrante delicto* death.

Traditionally, the influence of Tahitian life is blamed for the mutiny, yet few writers have bothered to give their readers any details. Thanks to the self-righteous voyeurism of Bligh and the anthropological interest of Cook, Banks and James Morrison, among others, who excused their detailed observation of sex and paganism by reference to a Christian reforming zeal, we know a lot about ancient Tahiti. There are such modern, thick, scholarly volumes as Douglas Oliver's *Ancient Tahitian Society* on the subject, and thinner, more accessible ones, like Bengt Danielsson's *Love in the South Seas*, all of which repay the reader with glimpses of a life that, although cruel to those who were not considered suitable, was the nearest to Eden that earth has recently seen. Bligh even tells us that when *Bounty* arrived there were no mosquitoes, and that would be paradise enow.

Because I do not know what Fletcher Christian and his plant-nursery team did from day to day in their tents and coconut groves, it would be dishonest to paint a detailed picture of their life. So I shall tell you of what they saw and heard and what influenced the people with whom they were in daily contact. These are the morals and mores that Fletcher took with him on *Bounty* and they are part of my heritage from Pitcairn and Norfolk Islands, the two communities that still thrive on the mixture of English and Tahitian blood that he precipitated.

Tahiti in the 1780s had no single king; the idea had never occurred to the inhabitants. It was a series of small competitive clandoms, each managed by a ruling class of a few families, numerous gods and presumably, goddesses. This was the *ari'i* class and the top people of most districts were related in one way or another, so there was essentially a royal family but no overall sovereign. Each district's chief was so sacred that his hair and nail clippings, faeces and urine had to be hidden lest mortals use them to cast spells upon his family. All that a chief's feet touched belonged to him, so when he was about on his business he was carried shoulder high. When you saw him you were expected to bare yourself to the waist; it was expected even of the buttoned and collared English officers.

The Tahitians were eminently practical and did not let such things as living gods interfere with day to day convenience. Thus, *ari'i* chiefs and chieftainesses were not carried about all their lives, for this was a class bred strictly for maximum height and weight accompanied by minimal colour, all marks of the regality and divinity they claimed. Men and women were regularly over six feet tall, towering over the average pale Englishman; even the lesser classes of Polynesian would have done so. Once an heir had been born to an *ari'i* chief, and pronounced worthy of life by virtue of his size and colour, he was proclaimed sovereign, allowing his parents to walk freely and unacquisitively while he, lighter of mass and hue, became the darker man's new burden. The child Tu had a living father and grandfather. He was not the paramount chief Bligh thought him to be. But later, helped by firearms brought by *Bounty*, he achieved this position, when he changed his name to Pomare and consolidated the rule of the sole Tahitian dynasty.

To ensure the continuation of privilege and the purity of their noble lines, marriage with the darker and smaller lower classes was forbidden, although the *ari'i* men might use their women for pleasure. Incestuous relationships, otherwise anathema to the Tahitian, were arranged for hierarchical reasons within the ruling class. Marriages between half brothers and sisters were considered ideal.

There was enormous prestige in being a chief, but power struggles were usually controlled within each clan by delegating most duties and privileges to other families, so that although one man had the position, others wielded much of the power. It worked extremely well until the introduction of European firearms and ideas of a sole monarchy.

One aspect of *ari'i* life, emulated also by others, most clearly showed the self-indulgence and leisurely life on Tahiti: ritual fattening. At intervals, a group or an individual would retire to a special thatched building in a pleasant place and do nothing but gorge on starches and rich pork and keep out of the sun, emerging fat to the point of grossness, pale to the point of divinity.

It was not just the *ari'i* who were careful about the colour and number of their children. Abortion and infanticide were as common as eating, and it is likely that far more children were killed at birth than ever survived. There are documented stories of women who claimed to have lost up to eight children without qualm or regret. Certainly the majority of girl children would be smothered before they gasped their first lungful of fragrant Tahitian air. We may shudder; but birth control was vital to the community's balance and well being, a lesson being applied to western society centuries too late. As in modern times, some of the foetal and infant deaths were to hide indiscretions that blurred the parents' accepted place, and upset an accepted and acceptable pattern.

Mechanical or chemical birth control was unknown and *coitus interruptus* unthinkable, but abortion was readily induced by herbs and a method of deep massaging, more a slow, intrusive pummelling, which must have worked by dislodging the foetus and its placenta from the wall of the womb.

Absolute freedom of self expression and a supervised independence within an indulgent, extended family were the promises given to those children allowed to live. Their birth, like the activity that had led to it, was probably watched by others; certainly parturition was generally regarded as a public entertainment, and the undivided rooms of the low, cool houses made concealment of intercourse impossible. Although children knew their real mother and father, they would each have many more surrogates, all called by the same name. Within the immediate family and relatives, children were virtually public property from birth. The only drawback from the child's point of view was that all six of the men or women called parents might choose to chastise him at once! It was actually very rare for children to be severely reprimanded and Bengt Danielsson says it would have possibly resulted in a pitful of food being specially cooked for the child, as an apology for having his dignity, or bottom, affronted. Morrison says that if a mother hit a girl for screaming while she was being tattooed, the mother would have been put to death; but this is unsubstantiated.

For all the pallor of the parts of their skin that had not been tanned, Fletcher Christian and his fellow officers had little chance of physical entanglement with the daughters of the *ari'i*, who had to protect the purity of their Polynesian bloodlines. Even though so little visited, the Tahitians had already decided on conventions for the comforting of visiting ships based on the convenient breakdown of both the crew and their society into three strata. The captain was allowed, indeed expected, to bed only the wife of a chief. Bligh never seems to have brought himself to conquer these mountains of corpulence. On the other hand, he was such a stickler for protocol and so prissy it is just as likely that he did, but was simply too nauseated to wish to be reminded of such horrors by having to record them for posterity and the public in his Log and journal. What *would* Betsy and the girls have thought? He was lucky here to have the precedent of Cook, who either avoided or concealed the truth of his royal duties, too.

The officers of a ship were given considerable freedom among the unmarried women of the aristocratic *ra'atira*, the important class of landowners and minor chieftains and this is how we know the background of the woman who later went with Fletcher Christian to Pitcairn Island. Ordinary seamen had to make do with the women of the *manahune*, the labouring class, a generally happy mutual arrangement, for there were more of them and they were freer to give affection than the others; in return they wanted only copper nails.

Sensuality was not the sin Christianity taught it to be, not on Tahiti. It was free and easy and constant, but stories of uninhibited public couplings and universal concupiscence are largely exaggerated. Any that can be verified are applicable only to the dark-skinned *manahune* women, who naturally took every chance to gain status by having a white, and thus, in their eyes, an upper-class, lover. This, in spite of having to overcome the horrors of the *Bounty* crew's foreskins, pubic hair, rotten teeth, execrable manners and a mantling of body odour and halitosis, all abhorrent to Tahitians who constantly plucked all their pubic hair, bathed twice daily and had magnificent teeth. Much as I would like to see Fletcher Christian as combining the best features of his re-creators—Flynn, Gable, Brando and Mel Gibson on film, David Essex on stage—he and Bligh and the rest undoubtedly stank. Washing was never a primary interest of the English, and rinsing clothes in salt water is hardly enough to banish months of sweat and grime. Incursions into their health, teeth, gums and hair by the malnutrition and vitamin deficiency of earlier voyages would not have been cured by Bligh's more sensible provisions. A twentieth-century observer of the welcome afforded these men might well feel the hospitality of the Tahitian women exceeded that expected of even the politest hostesses.

Tahitians chose with whom they lived at an early age and because nothing social or sexual was hidden, and there were no enormous time-consuming responsibilities to the family or community and no rules about what the age of maturity was, they could grow up at their own speed, entering adult life and activity when it suited them. Parents would as easily suggest that a fractious child should masturbate as today's might offer a Coke or a TV show. Children emulated copulation and played 'Mothers and Fathers' to a realistic extreme, little girls using soft unripe coconuts as infants, which they would drop from between their thighs with appropriate grunts, and to the cries of approval of their playmates.

What we call teenagers formed gangs and went off to live at one another's houses, or co-habited wildly and communally in one they had constructed themselves. For as many years as it pleased them they devoted each day to sport, music, dancing and love, sowing *and* reaping their wild oats until such time as one of their partners seemed more attractive than the others and marriage was considered. In many ways this self-policing stage was an extended initiation rite: there were few others except for tattooing for both sexes and circumcision for the boys.

Male circumcision on Tahiti was based on extremely ancient religious grounds, largely forgotten, but had been continued both as a tradition and because health considerations had been attached to the operation, as they still are today in many countries. On Tahiti, the penis was supercised rather than circumcised. When the boy was judged old enough, probably by the appearance of pubic hair, he was attended to by a man who specialized in the operation, possibly on the family marae, the equivalent of a private chapel in a big country house. The upper foreskin was stretched over a shell or piece of smooth curved wood, then quickly slit with a shark's-tooth knife and ashes applied to the wound to stop the blood flow. It was not terribly painful but the boy would limp and wince for a day or two to tell everyone of his new status. If he was royal it was more of an ordeal for others than for him. While a prince was being slit on his ancestral family marae, one or more human sacrifices were suspended from the sacred Toa tree by sennit strings through their ears under the direction of the high priest of the holiest marae, the equivalent of England's Westminster Abbey or Canterbury Cathedral.

From this time on, the boy was expected to cover his penis in public. To reach full maturity and not be supercised was considered perfectly disgusting and you were shunned by women and laughed at by men.

Fletcher Christian and his compatriots were among the first Englishmen to submit to the agony of extensive tattooing. The *Bounty* men who returned to England, including young Peter Heywood, introduced the custom to sailors at large, who so universally adopted it as their own that Polynesians now wearing tattoos are pitied for their slavish following of European customs. Tattooing (the word is an anglicisation of the Tahitian *ta'tau*) was a painful and dangerous process, infection from which could be debilitating or fatal. Both boys and girls were tattooed and the latter were not considered suited to take their place among women until they had been so decorated. There were meanings to some of the marks, but generally they were purely decorative and without them any claim to beauty was hollow. The *Bounty* men took to it almost immediately. Sir Joseph Banks gives the earliest description of what was done, and how.

The colour they use is lamp black which they prepare from the smoak [i.e. ash] of a kind of oily nut used by them instead of candles; this is kept in cocoa nut shells and mixt with water occasionally for use. Their instruments for pricking this under the skin are made of Bone or shell, flat, the lower part is cut into sharp teeth from 3 to 20 according to the purposes it is to be used for and the upper fastned to a handle. These teeth are dipped into the black liquor and then drove by quick sharp blows struck upon the handle with a stick for that purpose into the skin so deep that every stroke is followed by a small quantity of Blood, or serum at least, and the part so markd remains sore for many days before it heals.

I saw the operation . . . performed upon a girl of about 12 years old, it provd . . . most painful . . . every stroke . . . hundreds of

which were made in a minute, drew blood. The patient bore this
for about ¼ of an hour with most stoical resolution, by that time
the pain began to operate too strongly to be peaceably endured
she began to complain and burst into loud lamentations . . . she
was held down by two women who sometimes scolded, sometimes beat and at others coaxed her.

This particular tattooing session lasted over an hour and was to
decorate one of the girl's buttocks with the solid black thought so
attractive. When she eventually submitted to the additions that
curved up from the base of the spine across the small of the back
the pain would be worse, but this was the decoration most highly
prized and commented upon.

Bligh mentions briefly 'tattows' of the men who later took his
ship; Fletcher Christian had a Garter star on his breast, and tattooed
buttocks. It is likely he was persuaded to enter so fully into Tahitian
life that he submitted to the painful blackening of his entire buttocks, the sign of an initiated Polynesian male, indicative of the time
he had to himself and the closeness he felt to these people.

14

'The third person was more horrible'

U nfettered passion was tempered by practicality for the young Tahitians who easily absorbed the tenets of survival during childhood. The three necessities of life in Tahiti were food, clothing and shelter and as there was none of the artifice and complication required by Europeans, instruction was consequently very simple, too. Proficiency was expected in the best methods of cultivating breadfruit, bananas, plantain, yams and other roots. The young learned the best baits, the seasons and places to lure each type of fish, what could be eaten from the sea and what could not. They would know how to rear dogs, swine and fowls, and women were instructed in a social polish of sweetness and grace that attracted men to them and which they passed on, to the improvement of the manners of their swains. Young girls were taught early on how to beat the bark of the mulberry tree into the white cloth which they so gracefully wore, and which was used to furnish their houses and beds. Boys were expected to know each plant and tree and the use of its leaves or timber for making habitations, boats, paddles and sails. Tahitian women taught their daughters that the way to avoid pregnancy was to change partners constantly, advice possibly based on nostalgia rather than wisdom.

Fletcher Christian would have recognised the universal dual morality of males, who were allowed to spread their amours far and wide while inhibiting those of their wives. Not that they were so badly off; as well as her husband a Tahitian woman was free to enjoy sex with all his brothers and his *taios* or blood brothers as well as with his honoured guests. It is through a misunderstanding of this carefully policed intra-familial freedom that stories of licence have originated. There has also been a misconception of Polynesian ideas of hospitality and the relative unimportance they attached to sexual favours. Visitors were often appalled at the ease with which a man offered his wife to his guests; one missionary who refused, and then foolishly stayed to sleep, wakened to find his endowments being handled and discussed by women who thought his refusal indicated he did not have the usual impedimenta of manhood; he was so anguished by this rape of his righteousness that he was never mentally the same again.

Homosexuality, although noted on other Pacific islands, was never recorded as being prevalent or in any way common on Tahiti other than by Bligh. Except for the *mahu*. They were males who had been brought up as females, who walked, talked and dressed as women, and performed almost all the duties of the sex. It should be noted that they were limited in number and, unlike modern transvestites, the *mahu* did not choose their way of life themselves but were chosen at an early age. This was sometimes done because there was a shortage of feminine help in a family group and a boy child was then sacrificed to the hearth. Sometimes the boy was chosen because he had a small penis and the status of being a *mahu* was considered some compensation for the disappointment.

Bligh wrote that he had closely examined a *mahu* or two, and said that their genitals were somehow pulled back between their legs and seemed to have shrunk. Other men, he said, obtained pleasure between the *mahu*'s thighs and he also made oblique reference to further aberrant sexual practices—possibly bestiality—-

which he believed were rife. No other evidence either of intra-crural ejaculation or of the penetration of animals has ever been reported but this does not necessarily diminish Bligh's opinion.

There was no shame in being a *mahu*, indeed there was rank and advantage, for many were senior servants to chiefs, who were forbidden women attendants. Most were available for sexual purposes, but only performed fellatio.

Daily life for the Tahitians had little pattern to it, other than bathing at least twice in a cool stream and preparing the one meal of the day. You might fish, you might garden or pick a little fruit, change a flower in your hair or stroke oil into it. You plucked your pubic hair out, cleaned your teeth, then possibly enjoyed a massage with scented oil. Some time during the year women had to pound for days at the bark of the mulberry tree to make tapa cloth. But other than being clean and fragrant, food was probably uppermost in your mind. Although men could and did perform intimacies of the most physical nature with women, and allowed their wives to do the same with other men, women could not touch much of men's food. It was men who prepared daily the great earth ovens, men who placed the food on the heated stones and covered it with banana leaves and more earth until it was cooked. Men and women ate separately, for if a woman were to touch a man's cooked food it was thrown away; if a woman touched his eating implements they had to be reconsecrated or replaced. It was tabu for men to wear cloth over which women had walked.

But perhaps Tahiti's most startling customs were associated with the *arioi*.

They were bands of men and women sworn into a secret society devoted solely to pleasuring themselves and others. All three classes of Tahitian men and women were permitted to join, starting at a position in the ranks equal to their origins. An *arioi*'s status at any time was identified by the type and positioning of cabbalistic tattooing.

Wherever the *arioi* went they had to be welcomed and fed without stint, easily depleting the reserves of a small community or island within days; but to deny them could mean death. In return, the host was royally entertained. Men competed with javelins and at archery, and these were really preparations for war. Real stars did extraordinary acrobatics with their penises. William Bligh was horrified by this particular performance and, like the spoilsport he was, asked that it be terminated. But he gagged down his horror long enough to record what he *had* seen.

> ... they suddenly took off what clothing they had about their hips and appeared quite naked ... the whole business now became the power and capability of distorting the penis and testicles ... The person who was ready to begin had his penis swelled and distorted out into an erection by having a severe twine ligature close up to the *os pubis* applied so tight that the penis was apparently almost cut through.
>
> The second brought his stones to the head of his penis and with a small cloth bandage he wrapped them round and round up towards his belly, stretching them at the same time very violently until they were near a foot in length ... the two stones and the head of the penis being like three small balls at the extremity.
>
> The third person was more horrible than the other two, for with both hands seizing the extremity of the scrotum he pulled it out with such force the penis went in totally out of sight and the scrotum became shockingly distended (as far as the knees) ...
>
> In this manner they danced about the ring for a few minutes, when I desired them to desist and the Heiva ended, it however afforded much laughter amongst the spectators.

Men and women of the *arioi* rehearsed favourite stories, songs and dances, performed to torrents of percussion under the golden

light of great flares. The lasciviousness of some of the dances stimulated orgies, but consummation was normally discreetly veiled in
the bushes. There could be absolute abandon, for the *arioi* were not
permitted children, and any produced were killed at birth. The *arioi*
were the ultimate and infallible pressure valves of a society that
relished personal freedom, but clearly understood that freedom only
works if policed by the strictest of rules.

But in time of war, *arioi*, trained by their martial games, were
prohibited all sexual adventure. All their energies were directed to
battle.

Not only the *arioi* stimulated orgies, nor were they the only ones
who danced. There were also the informal, spontaneous dances of
the young, often of groups who were loving freely together anyway.
A high point of life was the *heiva*, a formalized festival where hundreds of men and women would sing and dance, each in perfect
unison as they went through actions both acrobatic and sexual that
flabbergasted their first visitors and which have the same effect on
modern ones.

⁓⁕⁓

Little of their duties would disturb the enjoyment of Tahitian life
by Fletcher Christian and his shore party. Sexual liaisons would be
trouble free and at night they could abandon themselves to the
Tahitian ethos as long as they kept at least one pair of eyes on the
encampment. Conveniently, pleasure came searching for them and
so comfort and duty might be pursued concurrently. Even when
day broke and work was to recommence there were hordes of
willing workers to do most of it.

15

Titreano

I t is generally assumed that *Bounty* stayed at Tahiti for six months because when she arrived the season for collecting breadfruit plants was over. This is not true. There are many varieties of breadfruit, one of which is in season throughout the year. Additionally, breadfruit do not reproduce by seeds but by shoots or suckers which spring from the roots of established trees, in the same way as bananas. Soon after their arrival Nelson pronounced that the collection of plants could begin.

The collection of some 800 breadfruit shoots was in no way a laborious or daunting task, indeed for Fletcher Christian it was barely a task. Work began on 7 November, when 110 shoots were collected. By the 15th they had 774. So in a fortnight *Bounty*'s men had done what they had come to do. After waiting another month to complete repairs and to make sure the shoots had all taken successfully in their new situation, *Bounty* could have sailed home. Instead she stayed a further twenty weeks. There has been much speculation about this, including criticism of Bligh for what seems nothing more than shameful self-indulgence.

Bounty was the first British ship to be at Tahiti during the rainy season, or summer, which lasts approximately from November to

April. This is also the hurricane season and even today small sailing ships prefer not to be on the Pacific in the worst of these months. As well, Bligh was expected to return via the Endeavour Straits between Australia and New Guinea. If he sailed at the end of December from Tahiti he would be attempting to enter the straits when the wind blew relentlessly from the west, hindering him as badly as when he tried to round the Horn. To protect his ship and cargo he dare not risk sailing across the Pacific during the rainy season; even if he succeeded, he would be prevented from continuing west through Endeavour Straits by head-on prevailing winds. From every point of view the success of the project could be accounted probable only if he delayed at Tahiti until weather conditions improved. Of course, none of this would have happened if he had been able to leave England months earlier and sailed round the Horn. Bligh was detained at Tahiti not through his own wishes but as a result of the sloppy inattention his mission was given in England in 1787.

But if the delay is not surprising, the use Bligh made of it is. It is perplexing that he did not keep his men more attuned to life at sea by embarking on short surveying expeditions to close island groups. Even allowing for the treacherous changeability of the weather it would have seemed that Bligh's thirst for discovery would have sent him exploring. Instead he contented himself with discoveries on shore, daily hob-nobbing with those he thought the island's sovereign families.

Bligh's royal progress was not without tedium and startling reminders that rulers here had highly individual attitudes to life and love. He was especially exercised to hear whispered that the servant who normally put the food into the mouth of Teina, the father of Tu, was also the lover of his wife, the masculine Queen Itia who scorned gifts of beads and mirrors, demanding nails and iron. Although her husband was six feet three inches, he was vacillating, lethargic and a whiner, but not Itia. So determined was she to prevail over the others who came to visit that she first arranged for all the gifts Bligh gave them to be kept on board *Bounty* in a specially constructed chest. Then, in case Bligh stopped giving when the chest was full, she daily transferred a number of the contents, so the chest always had room for something else. Teina and Itia supervised Bligh's munificence to chiefs from other districts and he noted they were not as generous as he would have been.

Early in December, when routine might have been settled, a startling thing happened. The wind changed and Matavai Bay became as rough as the open sea. *Bounty's* hatches were lashed and the crew remained on board as the ship rolled and pitched furiously. Storm-water swelled the river which ran along Point Venus, threatening to flood the greenhouse of breadfruit shoots. By midday on 6 December, the wind had abated just enough for Teina to risk the waves and tearfully clamber aboard *Bounty*, not to see if Bligh were well, but regally to wish everybody on board farewell before their ship was dashed to the shore and they all perished. Nelson also struggled out to report that Christian's team had diverted the stream by means of a swiftly dug channel and that the plants were safe.

No serious damage was found on board or ashore, apart from a sharp deterioration in the precarious health of surgeon Huggan. On the 9th, he was wanted ashore but when an officer went to fetch him he found him helpless in his dark and fetid cockpit-cabin, from which he had not moved for days. Sensing the stupor was something more than drunkenness, the officer ordered Huggan to be moved into better air and light, but this was more than his ravaged constitution could stand and he quickly expired. He was buried on Point Venus in a grave that Tahitians dug facing east–west as they had been taught by Catholic Spanish visitors. Ledward, so long the locum, was appointed surgeon.

With no precedent for staying at Tahiti in these months, Bligh did much questioning and found the storm *Bounty* had just ridden out was by no means a freak. Matavai Bay became positively dangerous between November and April, the entire rainy season. He resolved to move to one of the sheltered bays of Moorea, an idea greeted with public and private horror. The chiefs of Tahiti's competitive districts were still jockeying for status and also knew there was much more treasure from England aboard. They barely wished to share with one another, let alone with another island.

Most anxious of all the chiefs was Teina. He had been half promised some muskets and Moorea was the home of his arch enemies. If they should get the muskets and the friendship of the Englishmen his ambition of overall sovereignty for his family and his son Tu would be dashed. In an act of histrionic genius and injured pride, such as only a manipulative Polynesian can muster, he accused Bligh of ingratitude and of treachery. Wailing and wheedling, he said Bligh was risking the life of his crew, the friends of Teina, if he sailed to the home of the rascally Mooreans. Why not, he asked, simply move around the corner to the district of Pare.

Bligh was not convinced, but walked over One Tree Hill to inspect the suggested harbour and found it was rather a good idea. Quickly the ship was prepared and Fletcher Christian was ordered to transport the breadfruit pots to *Bounty*, which seems an unnecessary labour. The breadfruit might have remained where they were, for the new anchorage was only a few miles away. If the move really was necessary they might simply have been carried; there were hundreds of volunteers to help.

As it was, the short move to Toaroah harbour almost dashed the entire endeavour—ship, men and breadfruit. Just as *Bounty* slowly approached the entrance to her new anchorage a combination of bad observation by Fryer, from the crow's nest, and the tardiness of the launch crew in throwing a line aboard *Bounty* meant she went aground on a coral shoal inside the reef. Luckily she was not holed, a result of her copper sheathing and snail's pace. To make matters worse her crew also bungled the relatively simple matter of getting her off and the simple change of anchorage took a whole day of tedium and effort.

I cannot help thinking this was caused by the whole crew's restiveness. Gavin Kennedy blames Christian, saying he must have been in charge of the slow launch, and the grounding could also have been entirely Fryer's fault. But what was the captain doing? It takes more than one man to jeopardize the safety of a ship and all are under the command of the captain. The teamwork that seems so effortless at sea rapidly dissipates in port and only slowly rekindles. Those who point convenient fingers at Fryer or Christian might equally wonder if Bligh had given orders as concise as they might have been, or consider that he could have been more assiduous in keeping his men up to action-station pitch. In any case, it is extremely dangerous to move through reefs and shoals unless the sun is directly above, giving a clear view of underwater hazards. *Bounty* was sailing in the mid morning, not an optimum time. Perhaps personal fault is why Bligh's reports of the incident mention only Fryer and no other officer and why they resound with rather too much protestation of his innocence. He is not protecting Christian but himself.

When *Bounty* was anchored and buoyed in Toaroah harbour, there were celebrations all around. The acquisitive Teina and Itia were jubilant. Not only was Bligh still in Tahiti, but he and his ship were now in the waters of their own Pare district, giving increased status and even greater opportunities of obtaining muskets—or anything else.

Teina ordered his holy men to perform a sort of thanksgiving ceremony. Bligh in turn ordered Christmas celebrations for all on 28 December, which included a demonstration of the power of the ship's weapons. Teina, the timid giant, was perfectly terrified by their noise, and thus resolved even more firmly to own some.

Fletcher Christian's new breadfruit camp was not much different from that on Point Venus, though the surroundings were somewhat less salubrious. On a small point of land, just a few minutes' walk from the camp, was the main marae of Teina's family and district.

It horrified Europeans because it was covered with the bones of sacrificial victims and was the site of ceremonies that required interminable, chilling chants. And they could not avoid seeing the bodies of the sacrificed simply by averting their eyes.

In fact, it was forbidden to kill on the marae itself. Thus, there was understandable unease throughout the community when there was a ceremony requiring a cadaver or two. Often they were collected over an unnerving number of days or weeks, and the mere knowledge that one tribute had been killed was never the signal for release from constant vigilance. Women who suspected their husband or son might be chosen kept an especially close watch on their men. There was no ritual foreplay to the killing. The first the victims or their family knew about it was when the man was felled with a sudden cruel blow to the head. If a woman were quick enough to touch the body before it could be whisked away to sacred places, it was desecrated, and the female could then take it for private mourning and burial. If the victim had been especially choice, she might find herself conjoined in his state of oblivion. But even dead women were not allowed onto a marae.

The costumes the priests of the marae wore were as extraordinary as the things they did there. Helmets of sennit and feathers were ten feet high. With their cloaks and draperies and festooned staves the men looked like gorgeous beasts as they rode across the lagoons, fluttering and erect, on platforms built onto rich canoes.

For four more months Fletcher Christian and his precocious young friend Peter Heywood were surrounded by the exotic life of Tahiti, day and night, sacred and profane. They had little to do but enjoy themselves. Certainly there were watches to be kept over the obediently flourishing plants, but Nelson and Brown were the experts and the shoots were primarily their concern.

Fletcher Christian was known as Titreano, for this was the closest the Polynesian tongue could come to his family name. As he walked he would hear his new friends call constantly, inviting him to eat, to drink, to talk, to join the acrobatic games of children and men that he enjoyed so much—wrestling, javelin throwing, stilt walking and kite flying. With Heywood's gift for learning Tahitian as an example, he doubtless answered in their own tongue. He would drink coconut milk or the narcotic yava, fish under blue skies or by torchlight from canoes, wear garlands of perfumed flowers as fragrant oils were massaged into every muscle, rub noses in greeting, and sit cross-legged on piles of soft tapa at gargantuan feasts while dancing girls graphically and energetically indicated where, and precisely how, he should next direct his attentions.

It is quite incorrect to say, as many writers have done, that Fletcher Christian had nothing to do with Tahitian women; he simply had no special attachment at this time.

Fletcher Christian and Peter Heywood soon became part of the community. Heywood was proficient enough at the language to commence a dictionary and both men submitted to tattooing. John Adams too was highly tattooed, and among those who found themselves enamoured of one woman rather than several were George Stewart and Charles Churchill.

After the melancholy of their extended voyage, the men from the northern hemisphere appreciated food as much as women. The European has no difficulty in taking to the bland sweet diet of the South Pacific, high in starch and flesh. There was plenty of pork and fresh fish and fruit, and vegetables cooked in the same pit were sometimes plain, sometimes made into a sort of pudding wrapped in banana leaves. Bligh even wrote the recipe of one, a mixture of grated taro and coconut milk; nowadays you are more likely to eat it on Pitcairn Island. And of course everyone wanted to try the breadfruit.

Growing on stately trees with deep green glossy leaves, not dissimilar to the 'swiss cheese' plant or monstera, each melon-like fruit hangs free from the tree on a long thin stalk. When ripe the skin, reminiscent of plucked poultry, turns a pastel green-yellow.

It was usually baked in the pit ovens, peeled and eaten warm, when it is not unlike freshly baked bread or sweet potatoes. In times of plenty a pulp of the flesh would be stored, then it would ferment, improving its keeping qualities but doing little for its flavour. But the breadfruit and its tree provided more than just food.

The light, easily worked wood was widely used for surf boards, drums, and the bows and sterns of canoes, and occasionally inside houses, even to make furniture. When solidified the milky sap, which exudes whenever any part of the plant is damaged or broken, provided chewing gum for children. As a liquid it could be used to produce a shine on tapa cloth, to glue together gourds for drums, or as a caulking material for canoes.

You can eat a breadfruit with more or less preparation at every stage, from green to very ripe. Nowadays the breadfruit is cooked in hundreds of ways and is especially popular cut into strips and deep fried to make breadfruit chips.

Bounty's crew filled out and regained strength and health on the abundance of food. Fletcher Christian, naturally olive-skinned, looked as though he had been born on the island. With his height, his colouring, his easy manner and willingness to enjoy the physicality of Polynesian life rather than observe it, Titreano must have been a welcome and popular guest.

16

An Individual Problem

I f the journals of Peter Heywood had survived we might know what Christian and his cronies did in more detail. But would it change our view of the story all that much? Tahitian life was not the cause of what became the most celebrated mutiny of all time. It simply served to remind men like Fletcher Christian that there was an alternative to a life of insult and humiliation from an unhappy, vain and petulant captain, even if he had once been a friend. Although ambitious and determined to be a success, Fletcher Christian had never wanted or expected to go to sea. And all his shipmates were volunteers, more adventurers than sailors. The long, golden sojourn on Tahiti was enough for them to slough off the narrow, simple acceptance of discomfort and community that was the lot of the eighteenth-century seafarer. In Tahiti they were given time to become individuals once more, a state a responsible sea captain would have obviated by regular exercise, discipline and the employment of good sense. Individuals cannot sail a ship.

While *Bounty* swayed in the pleasant breezes of a sheltered bay in the midsummer months, Fletcher Christian dallied ashore and Bligh niggled, noted and entertained aboard. As long as the bread-fruit grew and the royal visitors kept coming, Bligh evinced little interest in his men, although he did order the construction of more tubs and pots so more specimens could be collected.

When his calm was disarrayed Bligh was inordinately irritated. Yet nothing his crew did was really so astonishing, considering the attractions of Tahiti, the length of their stay and the slackness of discipline. The petty tasks found for the men each day were no substitute for sailing. His officers and men could not be the paragons Bligh expected, and it is remarkable they did not cause him a great deal more trouble. The most serious exasperation was the discovery, at 4 am on 5 January 1789, that some men had deserted. The watch relief found the duty officer, Midshipman Hayward, asleep on duty, which was not unusual even though the penalty was death. But this time the launch, the ship's biggest boat, had gone. Bligh roused the ship for an immediate roll call and found three men missing—Charles Churchill, the master-at-arms, John Millward, a seaman, and William Muspratt, Bligh's cook. Hayward was immediately put into irons and Bligh subsequently blamed the desertions on his entire officer complement, calling them neglectful and worthless. The missing men had managed to escape with eight muskets, probably for use as barter goods to ensure the secrecy of their hideout. How they obtained them has never been adequately explained, for Fryer should have kept and guarded the keys to the arms chest; he may have given them to Coleman the armourer, which was more mutually convenient.

Although hot for action, Bligh was prevented from setting off in pursuit. Informants from shore, anxious to help in case they were rewarded, told him the launch had been abandoned in Matavai Bay. The runaways had taken a local sail-canoe and headed for the atoll of Tetiaroa, some thirty miles north. Teina's braver and more trustworthy brother, Ariipaea, agreed to lead a search party but was prevented from leaving for a whole week by bad weather. The fugitives had not returned when Bligh discovered something even worse; some of the new and unused sails stowed aboard were rotten.

Neglect of a ship's sails was scarcely less serious than desertion. Rotting sails may have been the fault of the master and boatswain but they were ultimately Bligh's responsibility. Their discovery was an affront to Bligh's vanity, a reminder perhaps that he had been paying too much attention to his noble guests and not enough to the well-being of his ship. It is well known that Bligh's deserved reputation as an extraordinary sailor was based on his ability to cope with serious threats to a ship's safety; in calm weather and in port he could be a perfectly ordinary, rather lax, commander.

When the runaways were eventually found and arrested bravely by Bligh himself, they were treated leniently, even though Bligh said he found in their possessions a list of men who planned to mutiny, and stay in Tahiti by damaging the ship in some way. Bligh later wrote to his step-nephew Lieutenant Francis Bond that Christian's name was on the list. Christian laughed when challenged and Bligh believed his rebuttal at the time, although he came back to it when defending himself in later years. I think there is rather more imagination than fact in the story. By no means every man aboard *Bounty* was able to write, and those who could would know that lists of would-be mutineers are not the thing to make. If there ever was a list it was not of mutineers, nor even of runaways, but it comforted Bligh to think of it thus.

At other times tools and equipment were missing from *Bounty* and Bligh ordered a Tahitian to be flogged far more severely than he had punished any of his own miscreants. There was a mystery about how one of the ship's lines were cut—was it the result of friction of coral; was it part of the plot to hole *Bounty* so the stay would be extended; was it a Tahitian trying to revenge his *taio* Hayward, whom he did not think should be in irons?

Bligh did have to flog some of his men in Tahiti but this is unimportant except for the leniency he showed, tempting admirers of Bligh to cite this as proof of his humanity. Here I agree with Kennedy in suggesting it is more likely that harsher punishment would have meant better discipline. The fact that many of the hard-line mutineers had been flogged by Morrison on Bligh's orders is grossly overplayed. Flogging was as much part of naval life as weevils in the biscuits. If there is any conclusion to be made from the later action of those who had been flogged (lightly) it is simply that they were the most hot-headed aboard.

By the end of February the tropical idyll was ending and Bligh was preparing his ship and the breadfruit plants for the return voyage. He made an all out attack on cockroaches and insects and let cats have free run of the ship. Accommodation for the extra tubs of specimens was made out of part of the chicken coop behind the ship's wheel. Furious rain interrupted preparations for almost two weeks until, on 25 March, Bligh sent the cats ashore, told the sailors they could take only as many souvenirs as could be stowed in their private chests, and ordered a thorough search for stowa-ways. Over one thousand flourishing breadfruit plants were ferried to their floating home and pens were filled with twenty-five pigs and seventeen goats. It was not until 4 April that a wind suitable for *Bounty*'s departure arrived. Bligh loaded up gifts for King George. Teina finally got his muskets and some rounds of ammu-nition as well as some pistols and the ship's two dogs, Venus and Bacchus. His tears were for his future safety and fortune rather than at the departure of Parai and Titreano. And with masterly succinct-ness Bligh recorded: 'at five o'clock . . . we bade farewell to Otah-eite, where for twenty-three weeks we were treated with the greatest kindness and fed with the best meat and finest fruit in the world.'

Not having discovered any new islands on his eastward trek across the Pacific, Bligh hoped he would fare better as he headed west. He should have made rather better preparations. For if the breadfruit and other plants were obedient and collectively servile, *Bounty*'s comple-ment was not. The first few days at sea, even after as little as a week on shore, can be agony as men attempt to smother their individuality.

As well as seasickness there can be the additional discomfort of renewed homesickness. Such talk of home and hearth may seem pointless on a wooden sailing ship half way around the world from both, but it was better than contemplating the awful dangers of the voyage ahead. The contrast between the safety of the land and the danger of the sea has probably never been greater than that experienced by *Bounty*, for few crews were so ill-prepared for a journey such as they were beginning.

17

Threats of Eruption

Bligh's greatest responsibility was now to see his officers and men settled down to a reliable, safe routine. To sail home, they would pass through dangerous waters, so, taking advantage of the relative safety of the Pacific, he set them to practise handling sails and lines, preparing themselves for the alacrity required in coping with the frightening squalls amid the sunken dangers of Endeavour Straits. Their exertions were in earnest when they were once caught by a sudden strong wind.

On 13 April, *Bounty* discovered an island they found to be called Aitutaki, but it was two days before the weather was calm enough to allow three of its inhabitants to board. They fell on their knees to kiss the all-too-receptive feet of Bligh, giving him pearl-shell breast plates, which hung from their necks by braided human hair. In return for such obeisances they were given knives, beads, a boar and a sow; they had no previous knowledge of the delights of pork. That evening, perhaps another omen, a whirlwind ripped past the ship, almost turning her back to face the way she had come.

Fresh breezes alternated with calms and opposing currents, so it was not until 23 April that they reached Nomuka (now Anna-mooka), a low island on the eastern limits of the Friendly Islands, known nowadays as the Tongan Islands. It had been discovered by the Dutchman Abel Janszoon Tasman, who, Morrison reports, had reduced the islanders to good behaviour. Their goodness had not lasted, for now they were fractious, rude even. They tried to take casks from men collecting fresh water, they grabbed at the axes of men chopping wood. They had become so insolent and heedless of the effect of firearms that they countered any threat from the *Bounty* men by a menacing raised club or spear.

Bligh was acquainted with the men of Nomuka from his visit with Cook, but he failed to see that the social chitchat he enjoyed with them on board was different from encountering them in ugly mood beneath the green tropical canopy of their island. It was not just the islanders' mood that was ugly.

The men and women of Nomuka were of average size and well made. The women were judged handsome but 'knew how to set a price on their favours'; naturally, the *Bounty* men were interested in more than wood and water. The women were not tattooed but had circles of weals burned into their shoulders by hot sticks of bamboo. The men were tattooed from knee to waist, so it looked as if they wore tight breeches. They all wore just one piece of cloth tied about the waist. Both sexes dressed their hair with lime or burnt shells, which although originally black soon turned to red, purple or white. Morrison tried to be fair about the overall impression given by these people, saying the men's countenances were open 'yet they have something in it that gives an unfavourable idea to strangers: perhaps this might have been heightened in our eyes by their actions which did not correspond with their name'. This last reference is to their misnomer as Friendly Islanders, one which Bligh was eager to believe.

The constant prodding and teasing of the working party by the tattooed and multi-hued islanders was more than exasperating, it was frightening. It is very important to remember that this was the first time any of them had been threatened by armed Polynesians.

Fletcher Christian, who was in command of the watering party, found the attentions of the martial islanders such that he and his men could not carry on with their duty, and informed Bligh accordingly. Bligh is said to have damned him for a cowardly rascal, asking if he were afraid of a 'set of Naked Savages while he had Arms'. Fletcher Christian replied, 'The Arms are no use while your orders prevent them from being used.'

The contradiction by Bligh and the cross words the two men exchanged was not the first clash since they left Tahiti. Fryer said that while they were working the ship in case of later difficulty Mr Bligh and Mr Christian 'had some words when Mr Christian told Mr Bligh—"Sir your abuse is so bad that I cannot do my duty with any pleasure. I have been in hell for weeks with you"'; several other disagreeable words passed which had been frequently the case in the course of the voyage.' It is not clear if by 'the voyage' Fryer means the journey from England or simply the time since they had left Tahiti. There is no reason why close friends on board a small ship should not disagree; feuding is often a sign of friendship, and nothing much should be made of it. But being in 'hell for weeks' is a different matter altogether. If there had not been the Tahitian interlude, Christian might have said 'in hell for months' for the disagreements seem to have begun in Cape Town. On 26 April, the day after being called a cowardly rascal, Christian was again collecting water with a party of men. Bligh ordered Fryer to go and hurry the party along.

The watering hole, previously used by Cook, was a quarter of a mile inland from the beach, which was crowded with islanders. Fryer had to ask directions from the two men who were guarding the party's boat, for there seemed to be several paths through the plantations in front of him. A good looking man and woman, whom Fryer understood to be chiefs, took his arm to lead him to the pool. Fryer gave orders that the crew who had rowed him ashore were to take the boat far enough off shore to be out of harm's way, and he then went inland. He met Matthew Quintal rolling a cask of water to the boat, surrounded by islanders. Fryer accompanied him back to the shore, saw the cask loaded and then returned with Quintal.

They were met by the same man and woman. This time they indicated Fryer should join them to eat. He excused himself but gave the woman a gift of a jew's harp and a few small nails. Almost immediately Quintal cried out, 'Mr Fryer, there is a man going to knock you down with his club.' Turning, he was surprised to find the young chief indeed brandishing a club above his head. The chief escaped into the plantations, somehow dissuaded from his murderous intentions, although Fryer was not armed even with a stick.

Reaching the watering hole Fryer noted Christian was getting the casks filled as quickly as he could, but there were islanders all about who frequently heaved stones. One chief repeatedly pointed a very long spear at Fletcher, who was armed with a musket and bayonet. In this tense situation Fryer ordered Christian to get the casks down to the boats empty or full, and using bribes of nails, employed some of the troublemakers to help. On the beach they found even more aggravation. Fryer's boat had ignored his orders and, instead of standing off with oars, had anchored with a grapnel. While they were playing tricks with the boys and girls someone had stolen the grapnel.

Fryer asked several chiefs what had happened and was told the anchor had been taken by men from another island and that they had already paddled away with it. When Bligh was informed 'he was very warm about the loss of the grapnel' and said he would detain some of the chiefs on board until it was returned. Fryer said it was unfair to trouble the men aboard or to hold them, as they could know nothing of the anchor or its loss. He added they had plenty of grapnels on board and plenty of iron to make another— he did not feel the loss was great, and by reasonable standards it was not. But Bligh was not being reasonable. 'The loss not very

great Sir, by God! Sir if it is not great to you it is great to me.'
Fryer's reply to this outburst was that he was sorry about the loss,
but that being sorry was no use in righting the situation. Bligh
purposefully pursued vengeance.

The two boats were cleared and hauled in and the anchor heaved.
As Fryer was supervising the unfurling of some sails, Bligh unexpectedly ordered the ship's men to arms. Assuming there was insurrection of some kind, for there were still islanders aboard, and
canoes at the side, Fryer dashed from his duty to Bligh, to learn
his commander had taken prisoner the chiefs aboard. Two of the
men were of an extremely high-ranking family and Bligh had
bragged about their visit to his ship. Keeping four, he sent a relieved
fifth back to shore. Once he was in a canoe this man made signs
to crewmen aboard *Bounty* that the anchor had been carried off to
another island. This man was ignored and Bligh, conscious that many
of his men were awkward and uncommitted about bearing arms in
such an unnecessary circumstance, threatened them, calling them a
'Parcel of good for nothing Rascals', saying he would 'trim them
all'. When the chiefs protested against their arrest they were sent
down to peel coconuts for Bligh's dinner, a terrible insult, but Bligh
was in an insulting mood. With four other men and stout sticks he
claimed he could easily disarm the ship's entire complement; he
even aimed a pistol at William McKoy, threatening to shoot him
for not paying attention to this mindless tirade.

By four in the afternoon the canoes following *Bounty* had fallen
astern except for one double-hulled vessel. This was filled with
women and men, including Nomuka's oldest chief, all of whom
were weeping and injuring themselves in a terrible and bloody
manner. One struck himself with a paddle blade several times with
a sound that could be heard at a considerable distance. This was
their way of showing grief, and most people, including children,
had lost much hair and a finger or two in self-immolatory mourning.

At last Bligh admitted defeat, and ordering the canoe alongside, he gave the freed chiefs some presents. Their resentment was plain to see, but there was little they could do to revenge the insult. The general opinion aboard *Bounty* was that if a weakly manned ship were subsequently to call at the island it would pay handsomely for Bligh's treatment of the chiefs.

It was amazing, quite irrational behaviour. It makes nonsense of claims that Bligh was always diplomatic in his dealings with islanders. Bloodshed was only just avoided and Fryer had no doubt that if Bligh had gone ashore his fate would have been that of Cook. He would have been murdered. If this is typical of Bligh's behaviour, if he constantly gave silly orders and then used them to insult and aggravate his crew, there were few men of dignity who could honestly feel respect for their captain. For Fletcher Christian, it must have been horrifying. But he was more than an observer. He was right in the firing line and worse was to come. For Bligh's irrationality *was* typical.

Only conjecture can suggest the root of Bligh's behaviour but it is likely a final breakdown in his friendship with Fletcher Christian was troubling him and he was struggling for renewed personal status. It needs a brave face to cope with losing a companion in a closed company. But a brave face need not necessitate swagger and insolence towards those whose safety and keeping is in your hands.

Bounty now sailed overnight towards Tofua but with difficulty, for the wind dropped almost to a calm. As they approached the island they could see Tofua was erupting, belching vast columns of smoke and flame. Bligh, smarting from his defeat at the hands of the Nomukans, continued his search for status at the expense of others.

There are anomalies of date in the known versions of what happened next but these are easily explained by naval customs. At sea the day began and ended at noon, so the afternoon, evening and night of a certain date preceded its morning. In the accounts of the events on *Bounty* while becalmed within sight of the volcano of Tofua, some men used naval time and some civil.

What is particularly important is that Bligh's published accounts do not mention what happened next but everyone else gave it great importance. Fryer and Morrison agree that some time on 27 April Bligh, walking about the quarter deck, found further opportunity to torment his officers. It was his opinion that a pile of coconuts stacked between the guns had shrunk overnight—he meant some had been stolen. The coconuts are said to have been his personally, although they may have been purchased by him for ship's stores. Either way, Bligh would consider their loss an affront to his rank. Fryer was sent for, it apparently having been his responsibility to stow them. Fryer agreed the store seemed less than before, but thought the men could simply have flattened them by having to walk over them during the night. Such an easy and simple explanation was not to Bligh's liking. He wanted names.

Bligh ordered every coconut on board to be brought on deck and subjected each man who owned some to the most mortifying cross-examination: 'How many coconuts did you buy?' 'How many did you eat?' How could any man admit to theft under such circumstances, even if he were guilty? Fletcher Christian, behaving like the gentleman he thought Bligh to be, was deeply wounded. 'I hope you don't think me to be so mean as to be guilty of stealing yours?' Bligh retorted, 'Yes, you damned Hound, I do—you must have stolen them from me or you could give a better account of them.'

Multiplying his insult to Christian by lumping his second-in-command with the other officers, he turned and damned them all, calling them thieves and scoundrels who joined the men to rob him.

Edward Christian, when collecting evidence about the mutiny and the preceding events in London some years later, had access to this version. But he also spoke to many other men who had been aboard *Bounty*, none of whom were mutineers. The accounts they gave him confirm and extend the story and must be considered primary evidence. Of course every source must be treated with at least a grain of suspicion, for memories often make heroes out of men who were only bystanders. But such defenders of Bligh as Madge Darby and Gavin Kennedy tend to dismiss Edward Christian outright, especially for concealing who told him what, as though he were fudging the evidence. What he was doing was protecting the men who spoke freely to him. Without his guarantee of anonymity they would not have spoken. Edward wanted to show that the motives for mutiny attributed to Fletcher by Bligh were fanciful. Throughout, Edward is loud and clear in his condemnation of the mutiny, and was perfectly aware his brother was a mutineer. But he did feel his brother, unable to utter a word in his own defence, deserved to have other memories of the event published. From the stories of men who were there, Edward deduced a far more dramatic and personal confrontation between his brother and Bligh.

As officer of the morning watch from 4 am to 8 am, Fletcher Christian was in his hammock asleep when Bligh began his coconut affair. Nonetheless, he was summoned. When he arrived Bligh accosted him thus: 'Damn your blood you have stolen my coconuts.' Christian answered: 'I was dry, I thought it of no consequence. I took one only and I am sure no one touched another.' 'You lie, you scoundrel, you have stolen one half!' was Bligh's rejoinder.

Naturally hurt and agitated Christian asked why he was treated thus. Bligh shook his hand in his face and said: 'No reply,' but he continued to call him a thief and other abusive names.

This version amplifies those of Fryer and Morrison. It was injury of the deepest and most unforgivable kind to be accused of petty theft in such arbitrary and public fashion. After all, Christian was allowed free access to Bligh's spirit supply simply by asking John Smith for the keys—if he were allowed alcohol, why not a coconut? They had been bought at the rate of twenty for an iron nail! It speaks badly of Bligh that he did not even hint at the coconut incident in his account of the events; there was no way he could come out of it well and he knew it.

The importance of the coconut incident is also accepted by Fletcher's brother Charles as the final, irrevocable insult. In his autobiography he writes with much emotion: 'What scurrilous abuse! What provoking insult to one of the chief officers on Board for having taken a coconut from a heap to quench his Thirst when on Watch—base, mean-minded wretch!!'

Bligh's behaviour, first over the grapnel at Nomuka and then over the coconuts cannot be considered normal, even if it was an every-day event. Officers and gentlemen required public respect, what-ever they might have done. Without it they were unlikely to be heeded by the seamen. By humiliating publicly his officers Bligh was encouraging the inefficiency he hated. Yet any inefficiency to which he could reduce his officers served to make himself appear the better sailor and more self-righteous man.

One of the threats Bligh made during the coconut incident was that he would see to it that only half his officers and young gentle-men would return home: they would be made to jump overboard before they got through Endeavour Straits, or they would be left behind at Jamaica. It was all very childish and terribly cruel. When he added that his officers were to have their grog rations stopped and their allowances of yams reduced, he was still not finished. He confiscated some of his officers' coconuts to replace those he thought stolen (whoever had taken them he considered it the incon-trovertible fault of his officers). Then he told them that if they stole from him tomorrow he would reduce their yam rations even further. In other versions this threat was made to all the men.

The officers gathered together and murmured. The seamen, fearful their private yam stores would be Bligh's next target, set about hiding as many as they could.

If the momentum of events was not so dramatic this extraordinary moment would be laughable. There was Bligh nursing feelings of persecution in his cabin. His officers whispered in astonished groups. And his men scurried about secreting food like nervous squirrels. England and sanity were even farther away than they had seemed when *Bounty* sailed from Tahiti, weeks before.

Twenty years after first writing this chapter I have discovered much more about how Bligh actually ran *Bounty* after sailing from Tahiti. Bligh's own records make it clear he consciously imposed a divide and conquer regime that was contrary to every acceptable norm of naval discipline but which was a common thread in his management style throughout his career.

Even the most disruptive serviceman would agree that when discipline is even-handed mutiny is unlikely. Discipline was a way of life for eighteenth-century sailors, and they did not fear or resent flogging anywhere near as much as we might today. Bligh had done no one any favours by flogging far less often than he might during *Bounty's* long absence from Britain: it was probably seen as weakness rather than kindness. But when Bligh did flog, he often ordered more than the 12 lashes at a time that a captain at sea was allowed to inflict (as he did to the men who tried to desert *Bounty* in Tahiti). This added an appearance of cruelty and unkindness to weakness. It was all against the very rules Bligh so constantly called upon to support his every action, and from the crew's point of view it was ill-disciplined of their captain.

Bligh's famous 'ungovernable' temper always blew hot and cold so that men were singled out who had not really offended, and it is documented again and again how he would treat officers as common seamen, an insult to the confidence of both. To all that must be added his infamous bad language, not an accepted part of naval life as you might think. Articles of War XXIII and XXXIII expressly warn against 'reproachful or provoking speeches' and behaviour 'unbecoming to an officer'. Sir John Barrow, an administrator in the Admiralty during Bligh's time said: 'It is difficult to believe that an officer in His Majesty's service could condescend to make use of such language to the meanest crew, much less to gentlemen'. It was ill-disciplined of a captain to do it, and not only did it diminish officers in the estimation of the lower ranks, but the quality of the work of common sailors was hurt because, in the words of John Fryer, *Bounty's* Master, 'it could not be done with any pleasure'.

The continuous blurring of the status of officers and ordinary seamen is what James Morrison believes sowed the seeds of 'eternal discord' between Bligh and *Bounty's* crew. According to his journal, this began at Adventure Bay on the way to Tahiti. There Bligh made officers and able seamen alike collect wood and water. When Bligh joined them ('only to criticize', according to Purcell), he left the ship in the hands of seamen and came on shore with a guard of armed able seamen. Both on land and sea, responsibility for duties and status were blurred and this broke the rules these men lived by, undermining both officers and seamen. Only Bligh thought fit to keep and advertise his rank.

After *Bounty* sailed from Tahiti, Bligh's pathological need to boost his sense of superiority by shattering the confidence of his officers and men was being fully exploited. It seems to have begun in earnest after April 12, when he punished John Sumner for neglect of duty, for from that day he worked everyone extra hard for no practical reason. 'Cleaning down below' was ordered daily rather than the usual every two to four days a week. Significantly, these chores were always done during morning watch, of which Fletcher Christian was officer. In addition Bligh's log shows that Christian was supposed also to oversee small arms practice on a *daily* basis, something not mentioned once in the log on the outward voyage. Cleaning and mending hammocks, normally ordered only once a week, was also expected daily. As well as being targeted for personal abuse by Bligh, Christian was also expected to shoulder far more than his fair share of duties.

Of course it is right that Bligh should want his ship clean, tight and tidy, and he had neglected to keep up standards in Tahiti. But the extra work he now ordered was well beyond that, a spiteful punishment for everyone but himself—and it all had to be done in Christian's morning watch. Perhaps this explains some of what Christian meant when he later said to Bligh: 'I have been in Hell these weeks past and am determined to bear it no longer'.

To this seemingly unwarranted daily extra labour, you must add Bligh's insulting behaviour to Christian and others of the ship's company with accusations of theft and his personal sniping at Christian about debt. This was an unhappy ship from top to bottom, indeed 'ripe for anything'. The contradictory orders on Nomuka, where once again Christian and other officers were made both to look publicly foolish and put at risk, continued what Bligh began long before in Adventure Bay.

So, it was not because her officers and crew were undisciplined that life on *Bounty* was profoundly unhappy. It was because Bligh himself was undisciplined and unable to demand respect or to expect the same in return. The real problem was not Bligh's command but his lack of command. Christian's solution would mean the sacrifice of his honour, his family and his future. The day of reckoning he had foreseen was almost here.

18

Mutiny

The atmosphere aboard *Bounty* was never worse. Every officer and man was oppressed or affected. None more so than Fletcher Christian. As his brother Charles had clearly discussed with him, each man has a breaking point and Fletcher Christian had reached his. There had to be some change.

Later the same day, Purcell, the carpenter, learned Bligh had once more abused his second-in-command. Christian ran forward from the quarter deck with great tears welling from his eyes. Purcell stopped him, asking what had happened: 'Can you ask me and hear the treatment I receive?' Christian said.

Purcell suggested he had received the same treatment but Christian disagreed. As a warrant officer Purcell could not be flogged. He had a degree of protection when he defended himself to Bligh. Christian reminded him, '. . . but if I should speak to him as you do he would probably break me, turn me before the mast and perhaps flog me, and if he did it would be the death of us both, for I am sure I should take him in my arms and jump overboard with him.'

Trying further placation Purcell reminded Christian it was only for a short time longer. But Bligh's continual threats about what he would do to his gentlemen in Endeavour Straits bothered Christian—going through them would be hell, and he was no longer prepared to endure such treatment.

It is clear that Fletcher Christian was torn between a determination to do his duty and the manly requirement to defend himself. As master's mate he was only a superior midshipman and so, although acting lieutenant and second-in-command, Fletcher Christian could be flogged, whereas the petty officers, the tradesmen aboard, could not. He dare not defend himself the way Purcell did. It was typical of Bligh to take advantage of Christian's vulnerability, driving him to the very limits of self-restraint. It was bullying of the most conscious and pernicious kind. If Christian ever were to defy Bligh he would lose his chance of promotion on their return; but by not defying him, he would seem weaker to Bligh and thus a target of further abuse. It was blackmail. And, doubtless, Christian was also tortured about his financial obligations to Bligh.

As Christian wept he protested: 'I would rather die ten thousand deaths than bear this treatment. I always do my duty as an officer and a man ought to do, yet I receive this scandalous usage.' Bligh was to say later that Christian did *not* do his duty and that he had put the ship in great danger just a couple of weeks after leaving Tahiti.

'Flesh and blood cannot bear this treatment,' Christian cried. It was the only time men on board had seen him in tears—'He was no milksop,' said one, something even his literary foes would concede.

Through inflexible responsibility to duty and in defence of his dignity, Fletcher Christian was not prepared to descend to battle with Bligh. Instead, he decided to leave the ship. It was rash, and it was desertion. But it was brave, and it allowed him to keep his pride intact while making an unmistakable comment upon Bligh. From my understanding of Georgian gentlemen and their codes of behaviour this would have been considered honourable, at least by officers who were gentlemen. Duelling with one's superior was out of the question at sea, and England was too far away to issue a challenge that might be settled there.

Late in the afternoon, a sultry sullen time of a tropical day, Fletcher Christian gave away his Polynesian curios. He tore up his letters and papers and threw them overboard. He wanted no one to know the intimacies of his misery. If Christian had planned to mutiny well in advance of the event, as Bligh always preferred to believe, there was no need to do such a thing. Even if he wished to leave the ship but still attack Bligh, he would have left the documents intact. They must have been full of descriptions of his treatment and could have been distributed among his allies for use on the ship's return home. But although Christian had taken umbrage there is no evidence that he was bent on revenge as malicious as his own torture had been. His plan was to escape with maximum dignity and as little added ill-feeling as possible.

The men to whom he turned for help were Purcell, the carpenter, William Cole, the boatswain, George Stewart and Hayward. Later events make Hayward seem a surprising choice. Strange situations make stranger unions, and confronted with an emotional and determined Christian, who was master of his watch and a mess-mate, Hayward would have been hard put to refuse. There was too much general sympathy for Christian for Hayward to dare side against him at this stage.

These men and others, who told Bligh and Courts of Justice they knew nothing of Fletcher Christian's initial plans to leave the ship, were lying to save their lives and future careers. Even to discuss mutiny was dangerous. But when Fletcher Christian was involving others in his plans he had no thought of mutiny. He simply wanted to escape his misery. Still, helping an officer desert his duty was almost as serious an offence against the Lords of the Admiralty and no one would freely admit it. In the super-charged atmosphere of insult and injury in the small, almost becalmed ship, Christian went about his business quietly, but secrecy was impossible.

The most noticeable of Christian's preparations was when he was seen going in and out of the fore cockpit with George Stewart, a part of the ship neither would normally visit. He was collecting nails and other barter items from Purcell. These can only have been associated with a plan to escape, for *Bounty* was not due to call at any other island where such goods would be useful. He also collected wood and binding; now his plans were firm enough for him to let his confidants know he was going to slip overboard and sail away on a raft.

Of course this seems impractical, insane. But perhaps Fletcher Christian was simply 'doing something'? Arranging a method of escape could have been a therapeutic exercise. This achieved, he might well have been content. It is a common action in tense situations, and the danger inherent in his supposed plans did not mean Christian was stupid or rash. He may never have been completely convinced about the plan: his preparations went observed but he used the flimsy excuse to stay on board that there were too many men on deck at night for him to leave in secrecy.

Sensing Christian's lack of conviction and knowing the grave danger of such a venture, George Stewart risked everything to help his friend. He humoured Christian, supporting him when he most needed fellowship, keeping an eye on him, so that nothing really dangerous or suicidal would happen. Christian was an excellent navigator and sailor and with his farming experience and long stay on Tahiti, he was capable of self-sufficiency in Polynesia. He knew a passable amount of the language too. There was enough practicality in it for the scheme to work and Stewart could never be certain Fletcher would not make the attempt.

Christian hoped he would be picked up by a local canoe and if the Friendly Islanders were suitably disposed he could either stay with them or become one of the first independent South Pacific beachcombers. At least these islanders were unlikely to be cannibals, and a lone man with few or no valuable possessions would probably be assimilated by the easy hospitality of the Pacific. There was never any suggestion that either Tahiti or a woman was the reason for his desertion or his ultimate goal. No man aboard the ship ever entertained that idea except Bligh, who was always the last person to know what another man thought.

As evening passed into night, Christian lashed two masts from the launch to a plank and hid some left over pork and breadfruit. These rations were accidentally found by Tinkler, one of his messmates, who thought they had been secreted as part of a prank.

Bligh later poured scorn upon Christian's plans. What else could he do? He had no perception of his officer's misery and if Christian had left *Bounty* Bligh would have been permanently insulted. There were plenty of sympathizers on board to publicize the reasons if *Bounty* returned without Fletcher Christian. From Bligh's point of view losing an officer would be quite as serious as losing a ship.

With extraordinary insensitivity Bligh sent his servant John Smith to invite Fletcher Christian to join him for supper. Bligh also expected him to dine with him the following day. All Bligh's officers took turns at his dinner table, attending once every three days, dinner being served at midday. But Christian was regularly invited to supper in the evening as well. It was out of the question that Christian should accept and he sent a message which politely saved Bligh's face, saying he was unwell. Bligh believed him, sensing nothing wrong. This was by no means just a personal snub by Christian. All the officers agreed they would never again join Bligh at his table; Fryer and the late Dr Huggan had come to that decision more than a year before on the outward voyage.

When it came to the point, poor Smith asked others to replace Christian. Hayward broke ranks and agreed, for which he was hissed by his brother officers, still smarting over the confiscation of their coconuts by Bligh; but Hayward needed to flatter the captain and make up for his falling asleep on duty at Tahiti or he would never be promoted.

Night had fallen with its tropical suddenness. There was only a little wind and the accompanying rain and clouds cleared by 10 pm. Bright moonlight then complemented the weird glow of the volcano. Bligh came up from his airless cabin to leave his orders for the night with Fryer, who comments that at the time he was on speaking terms with his captain, 'but I am sorry to say that that was but seldom'. They discussed the breeze and the youthful moon. If all went well they would reach the coast of New Holland with the waxing moon, greatly increasing their safety and speed of passage through the dreaded Endeavour Straits. At midnight Peckover and his watch relieved Fryer's men. Included among those now responsible for the ship were Edward Young and George Stewart. Fryer, Peter Heywood and the others went down to sleep; but a man who should have been sleeping was not. Fletcher Christian, due on duty at 4 am was awake and restless.

Had he really been watching for an opportunity to take his raft but been deterred by the number of men on deck, entertained by the volcanic eruption and cruising sharks? Or was he hesitating simply because he was perfectly aware of the dangers and hoped someone would sympathize and talk him out of it? The latter is far more likely and it can be shown actually to have been the case.

When the men from Peckover's watch went to waken those of Christian's at 4 am, they found Christian had gone to bed less than an hour before. Confused by lack of sleep, exhausted by the emotions of the last twenty-four hours, Christian still got up to command his watch. Duty had to be done. Until this moment George Stewart had been able to watch his friend but now he wanted to sleep. First, he again soothed Fletcher Christian, pointing out the unlikelihood of any chance of survival if he left the ship. In any case, he added, if Christian left, the ship would be in a worse state, the men were 'ripe for anything'.

Did George Stewart mean the men were ready for mutiny? And that his friend should lead them? It is absolutely out of character and the only evidence that supports this is subsequent conjecture. Stewart had no motive to suggest mutiny. He was a strict disciplinarian, a stickler for duty, undoubtedly his reason for humouring Christian into staying at his post. He did have a regular girl friend on Tahiti to whom he was very much attached, but a woman on a South Seas island was no reason for such a talented young man to abandon friends, family and career. Stewart would know full well that even to suggest such a thing was in itself mutinous.

The simpler explanation is that he was cajoling, using any and every appeal to Christian's loyalty to his friends, telling him in return there was enormous sympathy for him on the ship. If Christian stayed, the men would help put things right; there are always methods, and, apart from the sneaky Hayward, the officers had already quickly demonstrated their defiance by refusing to eat with Bligh.

Even that minor insurrection by the officers was dangerous to mention, but Stewart was adamant in wishing Christian to stay, both for his own safety and for that of the ship. Christian was looked to for leadership and sympathy far more than Bligh. And it must be rigorously remembered that no man ever blamed Christian for what he was about to do or felt personally injured by it. Plenty were willing to blame or seek revenge upon Bligh but not one did the same to Christian, whatever their loss or distress.

Apparently satisfied he had once more mollified Christian, Stewart retired. Mutiny was far from his mind. Although many men aboard *Bounty* later persuaded themselves—or were persuaded—that Stewart consciously suggested mutiny, his friend Peter Heywood always firmly declared that Stewart did not mention the subject even obliquely when talking to Christian. Heywood and Stewart subsequently spent many months together when they could have discussed the conversation in detail, and Heywood had plenty of opportunity to tell the truth in later life, after Stewart was dead. He thought the imputation of Stewart's guilt distasteful, an insult to the memory of a fine sailor and an upright young man. It remains so.

If Stewart did not think of mutiny, Christian certainly did. It was the alternative he had been seeking. It was the most invidious revenge he could wreak upon his tormentor. His breaking point had been passed and all thought of duty dissipated. By the time he was on deck the idea, normally so forbidden, suddenly became simple and practical. At some fatal moment he must have thought: 'Why should *I* go? Why shouldn't *Bligh* leave instead?'

Put like this it did not even sound like mutiny. And had not Charles, his own brother, been forced to act against another captain for the same reasons?

Fate and the natural disinclination of Hallet and Hayward to work hastened Christian's resolve. Hayward was already asleep on the empty arms chest on deck. Hallet had not even appeared. With no other officers to gainsay him, the ship was Christian's for the taking and from this moment his course was set.

At first Christian carried out his normal duties, for he needed assistance and time and thought to choose those likely to be receptive to the idea.

As well as the somnolent midshipmen Hawyard and Hallet, the men on Christian's watch were the gunner's mate John Mills, the carpenter's mate Charles Norman, plus Isaac Martin, Thomas Burkitt, Thomas Ellison and Matthew Quintal, all ABs.

In fine weather this morning watch is one of the most enjoyable at sea, combining a satisfying domesticity with the pleasure of daybreak. The South Pacific air is cool and silken, refreshing with its promises of breakfast, comforting as the rising sun quickly warms. Christian ordered the usual activities to commence. The lines were all neatly coiled and a gangplank unslung to gather water for washing the decks. The rhythm was interrupted only by the banalities of any crowded community. At an early hour William Muspratt, Bligh's cook, was chopping wood on the deck and Byrne fumbled his myopic way up to remonstrate against the thumping which resounded unnecessarily through the quarters below. And then a shark was spotted. Hayward and Norman hung over the edge to watch the threat of its languid motion and malevolent upright fin.

Assessing the men of his watch, Christian settled upon Quintal as the first to approach. Only 5 feet, 5 inches, Quintal was strong and muscular, and is said to have been the only AB who had a permanent attachment in Tahiti. He was heavily tattooed on the backside and elsewhere. Already Christian must have realized the result of the mutiny would be permanent residence in the South Seas. Talking to Quintal he turned the conversation to those pleasant Tahitian times, eventually insinuating his plan of taking the ship and demonstrating his seriousness by showing he had slung a lead weight about his neck. If he failed he would throw himself overboard to drown. This stark illustration of possible tragedy—failure would mean certain death for Christian and any who helped him—frightened Quintal and he refused to help. But the black-bearded American, Isaac Martin, who heard Quintal's protest, thought it a capital idea. He willingly assumed responsibility for raising a party. Quintal quickly changed his mind and became an ardent supporter of Christian.

As the light and warmth of the Pacific sun slowly spread westwards, the heat of Christian's passion for revenge increased and kindled support throughout the creaking ship. Hidden amid the protests of sun-warped timbers, the whispers of revolt in the ears of drowsy men were as varied as those who made them. Some thought Bligh was to be put overboard to fend for himself on Tofua. Others believed he was to be confined and taken back to England with Christian in charge of the ship. Plenty were willing to believe the captain was mad. Others thought they were returning to Tahiti. Any inducement was used to recruit men and little of this was known to Christian, who would not have cared. He simply wanted men.

At this early stage there can have been no definite formulation of ideas. Once he could well have considered taking Bligh back to face his superiors in England. But now he wanted to be rid of him, together with Hayward, Hallet and Samuel. The appeal of the South Pacific life certainly added impetus and fire to his resolve and to gain the supporters he needed to execute his simple plan. With just enough men to guard the ladderways he could achieve the exodus of four undesirables with speed and economy.

Christian's reasons for ridding the ship of Bligh are obvious, and Hayward and Hallet were universally unpopular for their arrogance. Christian probably now despised Hayward, a member of his own watch, for eating with Bligh the night before. Samuel was Bligh's clerk and connected in everyone's mind with the issuing and cutting of rations. He was an obvious target for the displeasure of the seamen and Christian doubtless listened to their request in regard to him.

Raising a gang went smoothly and caused no alarm; those who did it knew exactly who would be game. Then they needed arms. Here they were helped by a small but significant breaking of the rules. Fryer, as master, was supposed to keep the keys of the arms chest, but they were actually in the care of Coleman the armourer. This was a sensible arrangement, but it was against the rules and Bligh may not have known about it. Thus, it was all too simple for Christian to shake Coleman awake and ask for the keys, saying he wanted to shoot a shark; Coleman suspected neither the man nor the hour. Christian was in charge of the watch, he was second-in-command, and if Coleman were that suspicious he could have stumbled into the morning light to see the fortuitous shark. Coleman handed over the keys and went back to sleep. Christian went gloating to his arms chest.

There he found the sleeping Hallet, who was smartly hastened to his duty, suspecting nothing other than further chastisement for his lethargy. As if to reassume some semblance of dignity, Hallet started giving orders as soon as he was on deck. It was his turn to oversee the catering for his mess that week and he asked Burkitt to draw the three chickens that were hanging on the mainstay; fresh poultry was one of the few food advantages the officers had and the coops were on the privileged deck space at the aft of the quarterdeck, alongside Bligh's private lavatory.

Once they were crowded around the open arms chest, Christian and his men quickly agreed on a course of action. Someone's call for caution was heeded; the cutlasses, pistols, muskets and bayonets were only to be deterrents. There would be bloody threats; but there was to be no bloodshed. Christian had exchanged his plan to leave the ship with little fuss for a plot to rid the ship of Bligh equally simply. It would take more force, that was all.

It would have been so easy for Christian to strike or murder Bligh that morning or at countless other times that accusations of his having little or no control of his temper cannot be supported. It is little realized how often this kind of thing happened on naval ships at the time, for few of these bloody incidents are now remembered. Although acting illegally, and perhaps in the grip of a temporary mental breakdown, Fletcher Christian demonstrated himself to be a man of self control and a firm supporter of accepted norms of conduct. It was Bligh who was out of control, infecting others—including Christian—with ideas of abnormal action. It was so universally believed that his mind was unbalanced that plans to confine him or take some other unusual action were accepted without question by almost all those to whom they were initially put. The lack of protest or action by others may mean they were equally unsurprised, even if unapproving.

As the insurrectionists started to remount the fore ladderway, they were seen by Hayward, who asked why they were armed. He was peremptorily told that the captain had ordered them to exercise at dawn. Not believing this story, he started aft, apparently to warn the sleeping Bligh that something was amiss. William McKoy, tattooed and scarred from knife fights, had been loading his musket on deck. He banged it heavily three times on the deck to hurry his companions from below, warning them that Hayward suspected their intention.

Christian quickly emerged carrying a musket with a fixed bayonet and a cartouche box in his sweating left hand, a cutlass and pistol in his right. He ordered Burkitt to take the pistol. When the raw-boned heavily-tattooed man wavered, Christian yelled in fury: 'Damn your blood lay hold of it.' From this moment on, Christian kept his dark-skinned face stern, 'darker than thunder', and by constantly threatening death and injury, kept everyone in fear of him, including his own party. Hurriedly the group caught up with Hayward. 'Damn your blood Hayward, Mamoo!!' said Christian, using the Tahitian word to tell him to hold his tongue, and threatening him with a drawn cutlass.

Slowly Christian descended the aft ladderway, without disturbing Fryer, who slept directly opposite Bligh. Followed by Burkitt, Mills and Churchill, he burst through the habitually open door of Bligh's cabin, waking his victim with a flourish of naked steel and shouting, 'Bligh, you are my prisoner!'

19

A Question Answered

In the breathless few seconds it took to take in the scene, Bligh shouted, 'What's the matter? What's the matter?' When he saw the cutlass blade at his throat he yelled: 'Murder!' It was a natural conclusion. Christian was wild-eyed, beaded with sweat, and dishevelled. Churchill, one of the tallest men on the ship, towered; he had to stoop his balding head much of the time, and now held his illicit weapon in hands that bore the unsightly scars of severe scalding. Mills, as tall as Churchill, was, at forty, one of the oldest men. Burkitt's face was the more menacing for its deep smallpox pits.

Bligh's shouts did not disturb the midshipmen who slept so close. Fryer was already awake, and the prisoner of John Sumner and Quintal. The brace of pistols which was his responsibility was taken from him but was of little use to either party, for he held no suitable ammunition.

Churchill shouted up the ladderway for rope to bind Bligh, Hayward's interference had made them forget it. No one moved. Churchill called up, 'You infernal buggers—hand down a seizing or I'll come up and play hell with you!' Mills cut some line and sent it down. Unable even to don 'trowsers' Bligh, his hands bound tightly behind him, was hustled up on deck by Christian, Churchill, Martin and Adams.

Immediately he was up the ladderway Bligh demanded from Christian, 'What is the meaning of all this?'

'Can you ask, Captain Bligh?' Christian answered. 'Can you ask when you know you have treated us officers and all these poor fellows like Turks?'

Fletcher Christian made the cause of the mutiny perfectly clear to Bligh from the first moment he was asked to explain. Treating people like Turks meant working them like slaves, and everyone on board would have understood this at once.

Christian stood with Bligh just forward of the ship's wheel. In one hand he held the end of the rope binding his prisoner, in the other was a bayonet which he had exchanged for the cutlass and now pointed at Bligh's breast. To young Tom Ellison, just a few yards away at the wheel, Christian seemed like a madman. His long black hair hung loose and his shirt collar was wide open, exposing the deep brown of his tanned and tattooed chest. His eyes flamed with vengeance. As he stood with Bligh his prisoner, every barbaric action and poisoned word aimed at him would have churned through his mind. Comparing his hell aboard *Bounty* with the calmness and order of life on Tahiti would reinforce his conviction that he was justified in the arrest of his wicked commanding officer.

The rope that so securely bound Bligh's wrists had also caught the tail of his night shirt. Burkitt did not like to see his captain stand exposed, the strange ivory-whiteness of his skin contrasting deeply with his black pubic hair and the leathery skins of his captors. Putting down the musket he now held, Burkitt went to adjust Bligh's shirt, hauling it out of the tight lashings. Disregarding Christian's orders to take up his arms again he called down to Sumner for some clothes for the captain, but as John Smith came past he suggested he do this instead. Christian drew out a small pistol that Bligh had once carried and warned Burkitt to take care—he was being watched. Afraid to do otherwise, Burkitt retrieved his musket, and moved away to a less conspicuous place.

Christian ordered the small cutter to be put out and told Hayward and Hallet they were to be among its occupants. Amazement doubled their astonishment at the scenes they had witnessed. Already terrified by Christian's flouting of authority and his use of armed force, they were now asked to leave their ship in mid-Pacific! From this moment until they finally left, the men kept up a continual duet of tearful pleading, asking Christian what they had done to deserve such treatment. He was unmoved. The two midshipmen unwillingly crept below to collect such things as they thought might be useful.

Ellison, once puny but now well filled out, was as frightened and confused as the two sentenced midshipmen. Lashing the wheel and saying he needed to go to the heads, he first found Mills to take over his stint and then went in search of Lebogue, the sailmaker. Lebogue was in no mood to give advice and told Ellison to go to hell. Not daring to ask anyone else, little Ellison made up his own mind and energetically joined Christian's party with a spirited offer to stand guard over Bligh. It must sorely have tried Bligh, for Ellison was a protégé of Campbell.

It quickly became apparant that the small cutter was comically unfit for Christian's purpose. It was so unseaworthy that Norman had to sit in it and constantly bail. Then Christian found others also wished to leave *Bounty*. This was a complication and perhaps a disappointment to Christian. But he listened to the requests and suggestions of both the mutineers and those who wished to leave the ship all morning, further indication that he was as unprepared for mutiny as anyone.

The large cutter was ordered out to replace the small one, and Michael Byrne sat in it to keep it off the ship. Isolated by his poor eyesight and inability to hear what was happening on deck, he cried miserably, terrified he would be forgotten. It had taken time for the cutter to be launched and now a considerable number thought they would join Bligh's party. Of course, they were being loyal to themselves and to the king as well as to Bligh. At this stage there was no question that Bligh would attempt crossing half the South Pacific to Timor and so the choice seemed simple. Should they renounce their duty and stay aboard or loyally sail to Tofua with their captain? England was a long way off, perhaps never to be seen again whichever course they took. The only men likely to have followed Bligh through true personal loyalty were his servants Smith and Samuel, although the latter had to be forced overboard. Hayward and Hallet tearfully did not want to go over the side, but they had no choice. When told the large cutter was not big enough to hold those who wished to leave Fletcher Christian must have been sorely exasperated. What began as a small and simple act of personal revenge was getting out of hand.

The launch was the most valuable part of the ship's furnishings and Fletcher Christian was adamant that it should not be given the sailing party. He most especially did not want Bligh to have it. There was pleading and discussion and after much hesitation Christian eventually gave the launch to those who were following Bligh.

For the third time the troublesome and heavy task of putting a cumbersome wooden boat into the ocean was undertaken. To encourage the men, Christian ordered Bligh's servant to give a dram to each man under arms. This does not mean the mutineers quickly became drunk, incapable of decent or reasonable behaviour. A dram means a tipple, a mouthful. A dictionary defines it as only one-eighth of a fluid ounce but it is hardly likely there was much measuring on *Bounty* that morning. From the evidence of men who were there, only one bottle was fetched, and if John Smith did bring glasses, they would have been small. In any case, to men who were drinking at least half a pint of rum every day a quick refresher of spirits would be only a psychological lift. If Fletcher Christian had ordered a serving of grog it would have been a very different matter, and suggestions of drunkenness would be hard to dismiss. The imprecations hurled at Bligh and others were more likely to have been a result of exhilaration and the unfamiliar privilege of freedom of speech.

It took far too long, but eventually the launch was out and it slowly filled with men and their possessions; only Bligh took most of his. Bligh's selfish gathering of unnecessary bits and pieces was a major contributory factor to the boat's overloading, discomfort and subsequent danger to its passengers.

Earlier Fryer had wanted to stay and had attempted to reason with Christian. For some time he had pleaded to be let out of his cabin so he could speak to Fletcher but had been refused. When Christian relented, and he was escorted to the quarterdeck, Fryer said: 'Mr Christian, consider what you are about.'

'Hold your tongue,' was the sharp reply. 'I have been in hell for weeks passed, you know Mr Fryer. Captain Bligh has brought this upon himself.'

Fryer persisted, telling him his disagreement with Bligh need not result in the ship being taken. He suggested Bligh could be put in his cabin, adding he had no doubt they would soon all be friends again. Once more he was ordered to hold his tongue. Threatened if he said a thing more, Fryer risked injury by making one of the first pleas that Bligh be given something better than the leaky small cutter and made a motion to speak to Bligh. Christian aimed his bayonet at Fryer's heart and told him if he advanced one inch further he would be run through. The moment passed. Fryer was returned to his cabin and a third sentinel, John Millward, was added to those already guarding the aft ladderway and the master.

When the time came for Fryer to be escorted to the ship's side, Bligh ordered him to stay aboard for the safety of the ship and in the hope that he might retake it. The master, anxious to obey, implied to Christian that without his skills Christian could never be master of the ship. Insulted, Christian once more brandished his bayonet at Fryer. 'Go into the boat or I will run you through.' Fryer now thought of his young brother-in-law Tinkler and begged he also be allowed to leave. Churchill, who as master-at-arms should have been the first to defend Bligh, protested. But Christian once more relented. When Fryer eventually reached the side and peered over into the full boat he was amazed that so few armed men had been able to take the ship and turn so many out of her. He was one of the few who realized this.

There was also argument as to whether Purcell should be allowed to go or stay. It is apparent that if Christian were perplexed or conciliatory during the morning, Churchill was not. Careful reading of the evidence shows he clearly understood the consequences of the mutiny and advised Christian of the practicalities required for their uncertain future. If the carpenter were allowed to leave with his tools he could easily oversee the building of a vessel by the castaways. Compromising, Christian agreed to let Purcell go but kept most of his tools and both his assistants. He also kept Coleman, the armourer, on board, and he was a most useful man in the days to come. It was Churchill, too, who ensured young Peter Heywood and George Stewart stayed on board, below deck; they were essential to the safe sailing of the ship, insurance against any future incapacity or loss of Fletcher Christian.

Throughout the long and unexpectedly complicated arrangements to get rid of Bligh, Christian had to withstand a constant tirade. Bligh was later proud he shouted himself hoarse trying to rally action and support on the ship, but there was precious little to generate such pride. There was no response. He alternated these fruitless efforts with attempts to humour and dissuade Christian, which was only to be expected. Losing the breadfruit and *Bounty* was serious, and anything Bligh could do to avert it was fair; but fairness had never been one of his virtues, and his protestations were ignored.

The day before, Bligh had pointedly refused to answer Christian when asked the reasons for his ill-treatment. Today, Christian clearly and repeatedly answered Bligh's same enquiry in a manner that left no doubt about his reason for the seizure. The only cause of the mutiny was Bligh and his behaviour towards Fletcher Christian. It was said so often in the evidence and reaffirmed so clearly by Rolf du Rietz in 1965 (in *Studia Bountyana*), that I never fail to be amazed at the number of books that still pretend to search for the mutiny's cause. The answer was given during the first few minutes of its execution and has always been plain to see. It lies in one word, one man—Bligh.

The biggest reactions raised by Bligh's shouts for assistance were abuse and bad language. It was quickly obvious to the men on both sides there was to be no reversal of the situation. The defiance that men had suppressed so long now poured forth. Christian was advised to 'shoot the bugger', at least. Bligh was taunted with his handling of the food rations and there was satisfaction that he would have to try to survive on reduced rations and only three-quarters of a pound of yams a day; even Midshipman Edward Young taunted his captain about rations with his rotten mouth. The show of solidarity must have secretly pleased Christian, but he was not going to be pushed into more dramatic or bloody events, and it is apparent that only his personal command and self-control prevented this. He was being unduly modest when he told men that something other than fear prevented someone from acting against him: his determination and threats were awe inspiring enough.

Just as Christian ignored suggestions of what he might do to Bligh, Bligh ignored the invective. He had more important matters to attend to: he wanted his freedom and his command back. When Bligh wrote about the dramatic morning he omitted to mention that all three boats had been put out, for only the immediate putting out of the launch would support his belief in the story he wanted the world to accept— that he was the victim of a plot, a well-laid scheme to which more than half the ship was party. Edward Christian thought many readers of Bligh's *Narrative* had the perspicacity to realize that it was not possible for twenty-five people to have conspired in such a plot without a single man resisting the temptation to tell the captain. But Bligh was convinced otherwise. Bligh also published a memorable paragraph: 'Notwithstanding the roughness with which I was treated, the remembrance of past kindness produced some signs of remorse in Christian . . . I asked him if this treatment was a proper return for the many instances he had received of my friendship. He appeared disturbed at my questions and answered with much emotion, "That Captain Bligh—that is the thing: I am in hell—I am in hell." '

As is always the case with Bligh's published recollection of events that might have dishonoured him, there are other, fuller accounts. Most of those which follow were collected from men who were not party to the ship's seizure.

Purcell said of the confrontations between the two men, one so pale, one so swarthy: 'Captain Bligh attempted to speak to Christian, who said, "Hold your tongue and I'll not hurt you. It is too late to consider now. I have been in hell for weeks past with you." '

From others on deck at the time Edward Christian also collected memories of a similar conversation and the details confirm Purcell's version. Bligh is said to have addressed himself to Christian, saying: 'Consider Mr Christian, I have a wife and four children in England and you have danced my children on your knee.'

'You should have thought of them sooner than yourself, Captain Bligh. It is too late to consider now, I have been in hell for weeks past with you.'

Thomas Burkitt, who was to be hanged for his part in the insurrection, gave an even more poignant account. While the second of the three boats was being hoisted out he said he heard Bligh say the following (and like the rest of these reports it is more likely to be in the words of the storyteller than of Christian and Bligh):

'Consider what you are about, Mr Christian. For God's sake drop it and there shall be no more come of it,' said Bligh. It was a seductive plea but Christian was immune.

''Tis too late, Captain Bligh!'

'No, Mr Christian it is not too late yet. I'll forfeit my honour if I ever speak of it. I'll give you my bond that there shall never be any more come of it.' For Bligh to speak of honour was dangerous. In defence of his duty to the king he could do whatever he thought fit. No sooner was he free than he could have pursued Christian with every means at his disposal, and would not have had the slightest qualms about forfeiting his honour. Christian was right not to trust his word. Men who did so later in Bligh's career regretted it deeply. It was too late. Mutiny had had its day. Nothing would wipe it away. And Bligh's *lack* of honour had been one of its causes.

Perhaps the most telling illustration of how almost the entire ship's company knew, and understood, Fletcher Christian's personal situation—even if they did not agree with his solution—came when Cole and Purcell, party to Christian's initial plan, begged him to stop. Christian reminded them that they well knew how he had been used. When Cole answered he settled once and for all the cause of the mutiny.

'I know it very well, Mr Christian,' he said. 'We *all* know it, but drop it for God's sake.'

If pride had driven Christian to mutiny, pride was going to see him carry it through. To Bligh, Christian seemed to be 'meditating' destruction on himself and everyone else. Bligh played for time by asking for arms, a request greeted by derisory laughter. It was domineering Churchill who forced the climax, when he told Fletcher Christian that the heavily laden boat waited only for Bligh.

'Come, Captain Bligh,' said Christian. 'Your officers and men are now in the boat and you must go with them. If you attempt to make the least resistance you will instantly be put to death.'

Without further ceremony, a group of armed mutineers untied his hands and forced him over the side. Once Bligh was in the boat the jeering and ridicule increased. There was some bargaining for possessions, Christian giving Bligh his own compass. Further food and clothing were thrown down and they were grudgingly given four cutlasses.

There was a plan to tow them closer to Tofua but Bligh was terrified that the noisy men on board would shoot into the boat; now the captain had gone there probably was some heavy drinking. After pitiless hours the boat was cast adrift on the open ocean. Ellison climbed up to unfurl the main top gallant sail and Bligh says he saw George Stewart come on deck and dance in the Otaheitian manner. In Bligh's words *Bounty* was now in the hands of twenty-five men 'the most able men of the ship's company'. He fancied he heard cries of 'Huzzah! for Otaheite', and may well have. For whatever side a man was on, once Bligh had left, Tahiti was sure to be the goal. In the strange, strained exhilaration of those first independent hours, the indolence and flesh of Tahiti would have been specially attractive. It was the only concrete thing there was after the mutiny.

Bligh's immediate and consoling thought was that Tahiti's allures were the cause of the mutiny and that there had been a conspiracy by the majority to throw out a loyal minority. It is not true that Bligh falsified his published accounts, for they were largely written or edited by James Burney in his absence. It is perhaps more accurate to say that rather than publishing the truth Bligh allowed the dissemination only of his perceptions of the events, which were then polished or clouded by others' opinions; something largely beyond his control, and against which he did not complain. It was biased rather than dishonest. It never occurred to him that he might have been the cause of Fletcher Christian's mutiny. The motive had to be less personalized, far more dramatic. It had to include everyone left on board or it was too shameful for words. Only a conspiracy of the majority served as the perfect salve to his private pride and public reputation.

Professor J. C. Beaglehole, who was Emeritus Professor of British Commonwealth History at the Victoria University of Wellington, gave an enlightening lecture on 3 August 1967, 'Captain Cook and Captain Bligh', in which he contrasted one with the other. Cook was certainly far more cruel physically and had a smouldering irascibility that made both him and others jump up and down when he was in a rage; but he was a 'character'. His men, whom he flogged until their ribs were exposed, loved him, calling him 'the old boy'. Cook had charisma. He was well over six feet tall, naturally commanding and dignified, and it was this that made him especially admired on Tahiti where height was akin to godliness; it was presence and the natural ability to command respect which recommended him to the men before the mast, where manliness was highly regarded.

Bligh was short. With the unusual combination of blue eyes, delicate white skin and black hair he looked like a doll. He never understood the finer points of human behaviour and naively believed aping of Cook would bring similar adulation. Presence cannot be learned like navigation charts. When Bligh went into a Cook-like rage he merely looked silly. And his tongue made it worse.

Bligh must have developed his legendary linguistic ability consciously, as a weapon against the attacks on his vanity he so feared. A spirited coward attacks before he is threatened and Bligh so developed his arsenal of insult that the most hardened users of foul language were stunned by his inventiveness. Bligh did not just use esoteric and arcane obscenity. He constructed such intricate combinations of physical defects, such complexities of unnatural relationships, it took your breath, and ability to reply, away. It was startling to hear filth pouring from such decorative lips. The contrast made him more, rather than less, ridiculous.

Much of Bligh's conspiracy theory relied on his absolute belief that his constant aspersions on the abilities and reputations of his officers and men were justified. Professor Beaglehole points out:

'Bligh habitually talked to his officers, and wrote about them afterwards, as if it had been the special purpose of the Divine Power,
for some unrevealed reason, to inflict upon him for every voyage
a unique collection of fools and knaves as his subordinates. It is
unlikely that this is the case.' And it is interesting to note that the
men about whom Bligh was most vitriolic went on to pursue blameless and distinguished naval careers. He, however, continued to be
accused of the same faults wherever he went and whatever position
he held. In 1805, when he was a full post captain he was court-
martialled for insulting behaviour and language to an inferior officer,
and found guilty.

Bligh's overriding and fatal characteristic was vanity. It was perpetual, self-righteous, and consuming. This is why he could not
delegate authority—he simply could not bear to see others excel.
This is why he had to wound constantly—to prevent others' competitive feelings of personal superiority. He never mellowed.
Beaglehole says that after Bligh's second breadfruit voyage, 1791–
93, '. . . (he) made no more discoveries—except, one is tempted
to say, of his own limitations, and of those he was always
incredulous'.

The William Bligh who found himself sitting cramped and half-
clad among his hastily packed possessions and with men for whom
he had daily expressed contempt, had a great deal of work to do
to patch up his pride. Almost immediately he cross-questioned the
boatload to reinforce his suspicions. He was convinced of a conspiracy and that both George Stewart and Peter Heywood were
hard core plotters. Relying on evidence of their companionship with
Fletcher Christian, many men and women still believe this, but it
is not so.

Captain Edward Edwards of *Pandora* who was sent to the Pacific
to find *Bounty* and arrested some of the men, made abstracts from
Heywood's and Stewart's journals and also talked to Heywood at
some length. Heywood's story does not waver and the men who

accused Heywood of complicity at their trials were later to express regret for presenting suspicion as fact. There is another, most important, document from Captain Edwards' hands that supports Heywood's innocence. It is a draft of a letter he wrote to 'C. Christian.' It has never been established exactly who this was.

Apparently the addressee and a woman called Mrs Christian wrote to Edwards as soon as he returned to England, inquiring about Peter Heywood, whom they knew to be a friend of Fletcher Christian. The only C. Christian I can identify at the time who had a living wife or mother was Charles Christian, Fletcher's brother; and the woman would be his mother, living on the Isle of Man. Or perhaps she had fled to her son in Hull at the news of the mutiny and they had stayed together for some time. This is unimportant compared to what Edwards says; it is also one of the few letters of which he made a copy, on 17 July 1792.

He begins by letting them know that 'the unfortunate young man Peter Heywood whom you mention' was aboard a guardship in Portsmouth. He goes on:

> I apprehend he did not take an active part against Captain Bligh. How far he may be thought reprehensible for not taking an active or decided part in his favour in the early part of the business will depend on the construction the court may put on the evidence and the allowance that may be made in consideration of his youth, should that also be made to appear. I have had some conversation on the subject with Cmmnd Pasley with whose family the Young Man has some connection ... he has been informed the Young Man was only seventeen years old at the time of the mutiny—I have only to observe that he appeared to be much older and I understand he passed for and was considered to be so on board the *Bounty*. Whatever ... his conduct ... he certainly came on board *Pandora* of his own accord almost immediately ... it is greatly to be lamented that

youth through their own indiscretion or bad example should be involved in such difficulties and bring ignominy on themselves and distress to their friends.

Coming from such a man whose reputation for cruelty and insensitivity surpasses that of Bligh, this is praise indeed. It is scraping the barrel to say Heywood's crime was not to assist his captain. This is true of two dozen others; Bligh had little true support among his officers and crew. No wonder he had to invent false plots and non-existent villains.

20

A Uniform Goal

Fletcher Christian had never thought of mutiny as a practical solution to his anguish, but he had certainly mused many times about what he would do if he were in charge of the ship. To do so is typical of the second-in-command on any ship, then or now. Many of his early actions as the new commander of *Bounty* clearly show a measure of detailed forethought about the situation, but not necessarily about how it could arise.

Once *Bounty* was his, Fletcher Christian's speculations became reality. Quickly he made gestures large and small that demonstrated his ability to assume command, to comfort and to deserve the approbation of the men aboard; he also needed to calm them so that he could order his own mind as full comprehension of the enormity of his act dawned.

It is said Christian sat below, his head on his arms, and gave orders in monosyllables. Yet there was no slackening of discipline. Avoiding comparison with Bligh's autocracy, he encouraged meetings of the men to decide broad issues. New watches were appointed, new responsibilities agreed upon. Acting master's mate George Stewart was chosen as second-in-command. He was not a mutineer and he was unpopular with some of the men because of his severity, but he was acknowledged as perhaps the finest sailing man aboard. Captain Christian risked personal unpopularity by insisting upon Stewart, convincing the others it was for the good of themselves and the ship. Most would have preferred Peter Heywood (another non-mutineer) to be second-in-command, but as the crew now had to stand only two watches, Christian wisely thought him far too young to assume such responsibility.

The twenty-five men aboard were certainly *Bounty*'s 'most able', to quote Bligh. They were a little community of craftsmen and tradesmen, but like no other on earth. Most were tattooed, most were scarred. If their faces were not deeply pitted by smallpox, like Adams, Burkitt, McIntosh and Norman, they had wounds of old fights, of abscesses and accidents. Brown had a remarkable scar that contracted his eyelid and ran right down to his throat, the result of scrofula.

Henry Hillbrant was Hanoverian and spoke little English and that with a heavy accent. Heywood had a broad Manx accent, Martin was American, John Williams was from Guernsey and spoke French as easily as accented English. Edward Young had played an active but quiet part in the mutiny, standing on the quarterdeck armed with a sword behind Christian and his prisoner. Always said to be one of the first to follow Christian, he was perhaps the most evil looking man on the ship. Dark complexioned, probably because he had some West Indian blood, he had lost most of his front teeth and those that remained were rotten. His speech was flavoured with the argot of the West Indies.

The other officers were not all that prepossessing either. Apart from Heywood, who was described by Bligh as fair-skinned and well proportioned although still growing, perspiring Fletcher Christian was bow-legged, and Stewart was bottle-shouldered.

Their tattoos were as varied as their personalities. Men who had quickly been seduced by Tahiti were the more heavily decorated. Adams was tattooed on his body, legs, arms—even his feet. Morrison, the boatswain's mate, who was never despised for having to perform the floggings Bligh ordered, showed his superiority by more than the remarkable journal he later wrote; he was tattooed with the insignia of the Order of the Garter. He had a star on his breast, a garter on his leg and the complete motto (*Honi soi qui mal y pense*) had been spelt out to the Tahitian practitioner so it could be punctured into his leg.

They were a rum lot, but perhaps no worse than most sailors of the day. It was their tattoos and the way they used Tahitian words and phrases, rather than their scars and native accents that made them unique. That, and the fact that the ship was theirs only by an act of piracy.

The desire of academics for order divides these men into opposing parties, mutineers and loyalists, after the event. But once Bligh had gone they were united in a need for survival. Two warring parties would have meant suicide. This is not to say there was no mumbling and dissension. But neither was there any sharp division. If there had been, how would the 'innocent' men have ensured their own ultimate return? They all needed each other, and co-operated.

Sources for the post-mutiny episodes have generally been accounts written by Adams on Pitcairn and by Peter Heywood and Morrison on their return to England. Recently more contemporary records have been discovered, including Captain Edwards' abstracts from journals kept on a daily basis by both Peter Heywood and George Stewart; the originals were lost with *Pandora*.

The quotations from Heywood's journal are detailed and give new slants on many things that followed; Stewart's are mainly a recital of dates. They both generally support the content of Morrison's journal. It is not surprising that Morrison gets his dates wrong from time to time; Heywood and Stewart do the same. This does not affect the content of each story, or have any bearing on the veracity of any account. If readers find my version varies from what they know, it is because I have used the abstracts from Heywood's journal as my touchstone.

Only two days after the mutiny, on the 30th, Fletcher Christian ordered the royals cut up so they could be made into uniforms for all hands, and gave his own blue officer's outfit so it could be used as edging. At that time only naval officers wore uniforms; seamen wore simple working clothes. Morrison tells us Christian observed 'that nothing had more effect on the mind of the Indians than a uniformity of Dress, which by the by had its effect among Europeans as it always betokens discipline especially on board British men-of-war'.

The second part of the statement is Morrison's private observation, but it is acute and relevant. Christian's uniforms would bind his crew of mutineers and loyalists together quite as much as it would impress Polynesians. In his journal, George Stewart adds that on 2 May they cut the mizzen and main staysails to make more jackets. This tattooed assortment of brigands and young gentlemen, tradesmen and seamen, sitting crosslegged in semi-circles to sew jackets under the probable supervision of William Muspratt, a tailor, as *Bounty* sailed east in the pleasant days of the early dry season provides one of the few amusing pictures of the entire saga.

The sewing bees were interrupted. On 1 May, all but a few of the breadfruit plants were thrown overboard. On the 6th and 7th, the men divided 'the pleasing apparel of the People and Officers' who had preceded the breadfruit. The curios, woven mats and tapa cloth were also divided, but not evenly: Morrison says that those of Christian's party always got the biggest and best. The loot— there is no other name—was stored in the newly empty Great Cabin. Then Fletcher Christian moved into Bligh's small book-lined cabin, the most tangible demonstration of his new position and responsibility. He was more than just a new commander faced with the safe and healthy transportation of men and goods from one part of the globe to another. He also had to master and use to his advantage high emotion and unfettered speech, shipmates no eighteenth-century captain would freely choose.

If there had been undercurrents and factions aboard *Bounty* before the mutiny, there were more after, and they were dangerous. The ease with which the ship had been taken would surely strengthen mutinous resolve on the part of other men, newly or permanently disaffected, whomever they earlier had supported. Fletcher Christian had the crew in his care but he was also in their power. Rash decisions pandering to agitators might lead to *Bounty*'s discovery. The mutineers, having wrenched their freedom from Bligh, had fettered themselves with the heavier shackles of avoiding the consequences, and it was Fletcher Christian's responsibility to make sure they did not throw these off early or easily.

As master of the ship, Christian had to make sure no other man outmanoeuvred him. The decisions facing him would have been cruelly complex for an experienced sea captain. He was still only twenty-four, and there was absolutely no precedent for what he had done or for the situation in which he now found himself. The only consolation is that the twenty-five men on board were a more cohesive group than might have been expected.

Bounty was the first European ship to be totally free upon the Pacific. No other band of men had ever had the choice of where they went and when. They were masters of all they could survey and most of that had never been seen by an Englishman. It was at once intoxicating and beyond simple comprehension. Yet, if the men had supported the mutiny so they could return to Tahiti, their piratical seizure of the ship meant it was forever forbidden them. It was no enviable task to tell men who had broken the law that they had done so in vain.

There were navigational guidemaps and accounts of earlier voyages to the South Pacific in Bligh's cabin. His books, which had once helped Christian learn the finer points of seamanship, now became the tools of his escape. Alone in the ill-lit, unventilated cabin with the reminders of Bligh's earlier role as benefactor and teacher, Fletcher Christian must have fought with his conscience as he made his first major, unilateral decision about the ship's destination. Emerging from the cabin he told them the ship was to sail to Tubuai, 350 miles south of Tahiti.

The announcement that their new commander had a particular island in mind quickly polarized some of the more spirited men; having proof that they were to disappear in the Pacific they planned to overthrow Christian and his followers. But the so-called 'plot' was a feeble affair. The men involved vaguely talked of getting rid 'of those we did not like by putting them on shore and that in all probability our design might be favoured by an extra allowance of grog'. If it were so easy, it is astonishing no attempt was ever made to do it.

The tale comes from Morrison. He defended himself at his trial by saying he stayed aboard *Bounty* so he could retake her in the name of Justice. But Justice needs braver fellows to serve her. One author wrote that Christian 'was incapable of keeping control of his men, just as he could not control his passions', and cited the above plot as evidence; to call it a plot is to dignify it more than it deserves.

Much to the plotters' 'unspeakable surprise', the whispers were discovered by Christian, who began carrying Bligh's pistol in his pocket at all times and also ordered his followers to arm themselves. Churchill slept on the arms chest and, whenever two or more of the plotters were gathered together they were joined by one of Christian's men. In some way the situation was probably a relief, for Christian now knew what he was up against, knew which shoulder to look over. But the threat was not, in fact, all that serious.

21

Bloody Bay

O n 24 May, *Bounty* made Tubuai, and the next day prepared to move into the lagoon and anchor.

Few authors other than Professor Maude have written in full about the Tubuaian events, and most of those who have twist the account by Morrison into a sustained and malicious attack on Christian. Of course there was dissension on *Bounty* after the mutiny. At times, Christian's ideas about power sharing were dangerous to his position. Yet he did establish a settlement on Tubuai, the first English colony in Polynesia. When it was abandoned he was still alive and had mastery and ownership of *Bounty*, clear proof of the durability of his command.

If Cook had landed when he discovered the island twelve years earlier, Christian would probably not have. But knowing nothing of the customs and conditions on shore, he hove to outside the reef and ordered the small cutter to be launched so that George Stewart might locate an opening. There is only one of consequence, and once inside a sailing ship is still far from safe, for the lagoon is treacherously uneven, with a sunken patchwork of ragged shallows and sudden shoals amid depths of over 40 fathoms. If clouds scatter the water with shadows, or if the sun is not high and bright, disaster is always a possibility.

The inhabitants of Tubuai had seen sailing ships. But they were not pleased to see another and paddled across the lagoon to attack the cutter. To Stewart it must at first have looked as though this was the end. The Tubuaians' canoes were like nothing he had seen before: each was 30 to 40 feet long with a high prow carved into an animal's head and a tall scroll at the stern. Painted red and decorated with pitch, fish scales and shells, each carried up to twenty warriors with long spears of dark polished wood.

After mobbing the 16 foot cutter, the Tubuaians boarded it, thus giving the Europeans a strange safety: at close range the islander' 18 foot spears were useless. The *Bounty* men were even less well armed, for they had foolishly left the ship with only a brace of pistols, one of which did not work; the other misfired. In the mêlée one of the boat's crew was wounded and the misfiring pistol wounded a Tubuaian. The boarding party tumbled back into their canoes, capturing only a jacket.

The attack was not enough to deter Christian and next day the ship carefully worked its way further into the lagoon, to anchor in sixteen fathoms a quarter of a mile off what Morrison calls a sandy bay but which is more properly described as a slightly deeper curve in the unbroken ribbon of white sand that circumscribes the island. Tubuaians assembled from every district, crowding the beach and flocking about the ship in their canoes, wailing and hooting with great conch shells. Six months in Tahiti had made Fletcher Christian and several of the ship's complement passably fluent in its language and Tubuaian was close enough for the two parties to understand one another. No inveiglement persuaded any of the Polynesians to come on board. By their dress they were warriors. It was apparent that war was on the Tubuaian mind.

Battle was important to the islanders. They constantly bickered and skirmished, although the Englishmen later discovered that property was never damaged. The Tubuaians simply let blood, then retired until there was some new contretemps in which involvement was obligatory. During the lulls, the men attended to their forbidding fighting costumes.

Like the canoes, the 'armour' was largely red and white, and it took some time to don. First, pieces of red dyed bark cloth or coconut fibre were wound around the body and held in place at the waist with a plaited sash, tassled with coconut fibre. The shoulders were bare and unencumbered, and the folds in the cloth were used to carry stone projectiles. Across the chest was suspended a pectoral, sometimes of pearl shell, always highly decorated. On his head each man wore a helmet of woven and matted coconut fibre shaped like a beehive. Some were covered with white cloth and crowned with black man-of-war bird feathers. They could ward off a cutlass swipe; those decorated with a pearl shell and a semi-circle of wild duck wings were later found to be more vulnerable.

This was not the haven Fletcher had hoped for. The *Bounty* men must have stood night watches and as the sun rose next morning would have seen the number of canoes increased considerably. At last an old man, probably a chief, came aboard. 'He appear'd to view everything with astonishment and appear'd frightened at the Hogs, Goats, Dogs etc, starting back as any of them turned to him.' Tubuai had no native mammals other than rats, not even the pig; to the visitor the goats and hogs aboard were just as likely to be gods as the men who sailed the large ship, except they did not speak his language.

Fletcher Christian made gifts to the man, who was not so overwhelmed that he did not carefully, but too obviously, count those aboard. He promised to return and in the meantime the ship's arms were 'Got to Hand', for such an occasion was not likely to be one of welcome; that could be inferred from the islanders' weapons. As well as the long spears, they also displayed a far more dangerous weapon. About ten feet long, it was finely worked into a club at one end and flattened and pointed at the other. A warrior clasped the weapon with his arms spread and swung it. Alternately clubbing and stabbing, he maimed and killed with ease.

At noon on 27 May, the canoes were launched. Among them was an unusual double canoe, carrying mainly women decorated with flowers and pearl shells. They were young and handsome, with black hair that hung to their waists in waving ringlets. As they approached *Bounty*, the girls stood and beat time while one of their number, a chief's daughter, sang her siren's song.

Christian had ordered all hands to change their clothes, presumably into the new uniforms, and mounted a guard. The eighteen women and five of the men who had paddled them came on board so readily that the ship's suspicions were aroused. Sure enough, about fifty canoes—containing perhaps 1,000 men—had glided up to the other side of the ship and began blowing conch horns. The precautions Christian had taken were noticed and the war party chose not to board, even though the odds were massively in their favour.

The women were treated civilly and given presents. Stilted conversations of compliment and deceit were exchanged; the pretence had to be played out. The men who accompanied the women were pests, stealing anything they could: the glass of the compass was broken, one of them stole the compass card but was noticed by Fletcher Christian and in the struggle for its return it was torn. The Tubuaian was a 'stout fellow' and disliked being thwarted. A scuffle followed, but Christian's well-documented strength got the best of the thief who was sent smartly off to his canoe with several stripes from a rope end; the women and the remaining canoeists quickly followed. Once they were in their canoes the men in others brought out and brandished the weapons they had been hiding.

The afternoon of a tropical island in May is heavy and hot. Tensions and fears are multiplied by the sheer difficulty of exertion. In the moments of relief that followed the departure of the boarding party, Fletcher Christian noticed one of the buoys that marked an anchor being cut away. He fired a musket at the offender and ordered the firing of a four-pounder which had been primed and loaded with grape shot. Terrified, and sustaining many injuries, the canoeists hastened ashore, but Christian pressed his advantage further. *Bounty*'s two boats were quickly manned with armed men and pulled to shore in pursuit. The boats were pelted with stones until muskets were fired into the crowd. In a few moments the beach was deserted.

Although they had seen only two men fall, eleven men and women had been killed by *Bounty*'s men; remarkably few considering grape shot had been fired into open canoes at very close quarters. Was Fletcher Christian being bad tempered or undisciplined in firing at the Tubuaians? With so few men aboard, *Bounty* was extremely vulnerable and survival was more important than relationships with unfriendly people. There were no guidelines on making initial contacts with Pacific islanders. Some were friendly and trustworthy. Others were bellicose, deceitful and trusted only power. Tubuaians were of the latter. When they threatened the ship and damaged its equipment, the time had come for *Bounty* to assert itself. Even Captain Samuel Wallis, discoverer of Tahiti, had had to defend himself with firearms.

Determined to find some basis for discussion, Christian ordered the nine canoes left on the beach to be collected and made fast behind *Bounty*, hoping that in negotiating their return the islanders might be persuaded to talk in broader terms. That night the wind swung to the north-west, filling the canoes with water and they were released. Driven on to the shore, they were ignored. Cords had been found in each of them, which the *Bounty* men presumed were intended to bind them. If Fletcher Christian had not used first care, and then force, the whole group might have died. From this time on the place was called Bloody Bay, a name chosen by consensus, rather than by Fletcher Christian.

For two more days Christian attempted to make contact. The two cutters sailed around the eastern end of the island showing a Union Jack and a white flag. Christian landed in several places and pushed through the thick fringe of undergrowth and trees to find houses and to leave gifts of hatchets, but he saw no one. Unbeknown to him, many of the 3,000 islanders had come to the uncultivated swamp behind Bloody Bay. They stayed there for several days and 'for want of their usual bedding they caught Colds, Agues, and Sore Eyes, Running at the Noses' which was interpreted as some sort of punishment from the men on the ship. There was going to be no immediate contact with such powerful visitors. Fletcher Christian's firm action was having a salutary effect, a classic story of first contact in the Pacific that was to be repeated hundreds of times.

What Christian saw on Tubuai, apart from the natives, he liked, and his determination was so fixed, he 'dream't of nothing but Settling on Toobouai'. There were no quadrupeds for food, but that was easily fixed. He thought, incorrectly, the island was sparsely populated, persuading himself that it could be induced to friendship, either by persuasion or force. As to its position, he considered the difficulty of anchorage would deter ships which could go easily on to Tahiti. He was certain he could rest peaceably and permanently here. Heywood says that there were discussions about the lack of women as well as suspicions of plans to take the ship, but by whom was not transcribed by Edwards.

Having landed a sickly young goat and two hogs, *Bounty* weighed anchor and headed for the green peaks and warmer welcome of Tahiti. Her pigs and her women would ease most tensions.

The diplomatic persuasiveness that Fletcher Christian had lately forsworn was successfully put to use on Tahiti. Teina, Tu's father, welcomed Titreano and *Bounty* with such pleasure that it dulled his ordinary sense of curiosity and critical ability. Christian lied that they had unexpectedly met Captain Cook, who the Tahitians believed—having been persuaded by Bligh—was still alive and discovering islands. He was said to be furnishing a new settlement in a place called Aitutaki, and had taken Bligh and his breadfruit to help. *Bounty*, with Christian in command, had ostensibly been sent back to top up supplies, and then return.

Teina believed all he heard and was exceedingly active in attending to *Bounty*'s requirements. He quickly packed *Bounty* with 312 pigs, 38 goats, 8 dozen fowls, and the bull and cow left by Cook which had either never mated or had done so to no effect. Dogs and cats were taken, and many of the empty pots in the great cabin were planted with flowers and tubers. If he could not have the real thing, Christian was certainly taking much of Tahiti with him.

There were differences of opinion about the number of animals gathered. The numbers above are from Peter Heywood's journal, and seem quite enough for a vessel of this size.

After an initial scare, when *Bounty* seemed likely to ground on Dolphin Bank off Point Venus, necessitating the cutting of a cable and the loss of an anchor, the ship headed south for Tubuai. The dates for all these events are given by Stewart a day later than in Heywood's account; he says they arrived on 7 June and left on the 20th.

Two weeks in Matavai Bay had not been the orgy of eating and sex that might be imagined. To protect his plans, Christian kept an armed guard at all times and his people were forbidden to tell the truth on pain of death. Presumably, his own faction was occasionally allowed on shore, but even if not, women were enjoyed. They came on board, but not to stay. They had had second thoughts about these Europeans, and the idea of sailing away to live permanently with them was far less appealing than spending the occasional night afloat. There was no point having a white lover and collecting large quantities of iron nails in return if their families and friends could not see them doing it. So *Bounty* sailed with only nine women. Adams had Jenny, McIntosh a woman he called Mary, and Fletcher Christian now had Mauatua, soon to be called Isabella. There were eight men and ten boys as well.

Heywood says he thinks most of the Tahitians on board came

voluntarily so possibly Fletcher and Isabella were renewing a friendship. She and Jenny were easily the two most influential Tahitian women who went to Pitcairn and I find it interesting that they should so early have been the consorts of the two men who successively took the leadership on the island.

The voyage back to Tubuai held several surprises and much discomfort. First stowaways were discovered, including Hitihiti, a young chief from Bora Bora who had once been especially friendly with Bligh. It was too late to return, so Christian, warning everyone they would never see Tahiti again, at the behest of some of his shipmates included them in his party. Morrison says he was amazed that neither Hitihiti nor his retinue ever showed the slightest regret at leaving their friends.

The sea was more troublesome than their unexpected companions. Pigs and goats were so tossed about they trampled upon each other, but only five were lost. The bull, which could not keep its footing and obstinately refused to lie down, fell several times and died. They heaved the carcass overboard; it was easier to dispose of it than to attempt to salvage the better parts of its overfed flesh.

On the first day out Stewart says the remainder of the slops were equally divided after first clothing the Tahitians.

By the 26th, *Bounty* was once more anchored at Tubuai and this time she was welcomed. Even if there had been subterfuge in the islanders' manner it was soon dispelled by landing the cow and 200 of the pigs; they were far more terrified of these than they had been of the firearms, the more so because the animals were let to run loose. Most of the other animals were taken to the small keys in the lagoon to the east of Bloody Bay, where they were easier to husband. This took two days and the Tahitians soon learned to adapt their Polynesian to that of the Tubuaians.

From Edwards' abstracts of the journals of both Heywood and Stewart, we learn that considerable discontent broke out very soon after *Bounty*'s second arrival. The mutineers probably thought their freedom, long overdue, was now upon them. There must have been great tension between those who wished to escape the world and those who had no wish to do so.

On 5 July, some began to be mutinous and, on the 6th, two were put into irons by a majority vote; Christian was still a believer in collective action.

The problems were drunkenness, fighting and threatening of each other's lives, so that Heywood said those abaft were obliged to arm themselves with pistols. Normally those 'abaft' would be the officers, but on *Bounty* they could have been the hard core mutineers. On the other hand, it is just as likely that a chosen few of those uninvolved in the mutiny, but responsible for duties aboard, might have been armed; Stewart, for instance. They had had plenty of chance to escape in Tahiti, by swimming ashore at night, so it is unlikely that any of them had the courage to try to take the ship by concert or force. Christian was sensible enough to know that it was also important for men who were not entirely on his side to have some protection from the worst of those who were. On 7 July, matters were so bad that a sort of truce was declared. Christian, together with Churchill who supported Christian in the manner he should have supported Bligh, drew up articles which specified a mutual forgiveness of all past grievances which every man was obliged to sign. Only Matthew Thompson refused.

Christian must have been working from dawn to dusk, believing that a permanent settlement on shore would alleviate the tensions on board. It would indeed have been wonderful if a man so young, so beset by the threats of co-mutineers and perhaps the pangs of conscience, had planned the establishment of a settlement that satisfied everyone on board. Yet, at first glance, the island of Tubuai did seem to offer precisely this possibility.

22

'He always took a part'

At a distance, Tubuai looks as if it might be two islands, one flat with a great central outcrop of rock, the other high and rocky. But this is an illusion caused by a combination of volcanic and coral origin, and the single island is enclosed by a reef from one to three miles from its shore. At its furthest points it is five miles by three miles wide. The dazzling, narrow white beach that surrounds almost all the island was then the best access from one place to the other, for a strip of timbered lowland up to one and a half miles deep also encircled the island and the thick undergrowth made passage difficult. The western end is the flatter and more fertile, but in most lowland places the soil is a rich black mould changing towards the foothills into a red earth that supports ferns, bamboos and reeds. The interior of the west leaps up in three naked rocks of hard stone. The east is generally more mountainous, emerging from the verdant lowlands to look like the pastel peaks of Cumberland.

The island produced perfumed flowers and nuts, breadfruit, coconut, yams, taro, plantains and everything else common to Tahiti. Within the reef there were fish, and shellfish and large turtles which were held sacred and forbidden to women. Throughout the island were innumerable rivulets which, having been banked up for the cultivation of the swamp taro, gave shelter to wild ducks and a profusion of eels, prawns, shrimps and freshwater fish. Morrison's estimate of 3,000 inhabitants seems to have been quite accurate.

The Tubuaians were more robust and savage looking than the Tahitians, an impression heightened by their use of turmeric and oil to dye their clothes which gave them 'a Yellow disagreeable look'. The women were considered more handsome than any the *Bounty* men had seen and were somewhat more decorous. There was no lewdness in their dancing even though the women were considered 'equally good at the diversion'.

If the men were more warlike than the Tahitians, their society was, by our standards, more humane. There was no infanticide, the family was not so extended, parents looking after their own children 'tenderly'. There was no acknowledged form of marriage; while a man and woman agreed, they lived together. If they parted, the men took the boys and the women took the girls and neither was a hindrance to further alliance. The islanders were less sophisticated, and both dirtier and smellier, than their neighbours to the north. Tubuai had no tattooing, no supercision of the foreskin and no societies of *Aroi'i*. They did pluck their body hair, but they bathed infrequently, rivers being too shallow for that purpose. Wherever they went they carried a length of purple bark cloth, glazed to make it waterproof. So efficient was it that the Tubuaians scorned gifts of European cloth. They also preferred their own tools of stone.

Their oval houses looked like haystacks thatched right to the ground on one of the forty to eighty feet long sides, at both ends, and to within six feet of the ground along the front, which was provided with several shuttered openings, carved and painted red. A tier of stones divided the men from the women of the house. At the men's end was another area fenced with standing stones four or five feet high. Here the male heads of the house were buried, and here their images were kept, carved and decorated with hair, teeth and nails.

The natural and physical glories of the island by day were scarcely matched by its nocturnal features. None has ever described the misery better than Morrison: 'and when they go to sleep they beat the musquettoes out and make a fire at each Door to keep them out—as they are very troublesome and together with Fleas and lice keep them employed till sleep gets the better of them and the Rats run over them all night in droves, but as we left several cats it is possible they may reduce their numbers.'

Although so different in comfort, hygiene and custom from Tahiti, Tubuai was similar in the way it was ruled. There were three clandoms. That which included Bloody Bay, which is almost on the dividing line between east and west, was the biggest, comprising most of the western end. The chief was Tamatoa and he made great demonstrations of friendship. Fletcher Christian was taken to Tamatoa's marae and seated on a large parcel of cloth. After being presented with a young plantain tree as a symbol of peace, he was given a root of yava (from which a narcotic drink is made) and exchanged names with the chief. The chief's relations gave Christian plantain, yava and lengths of cloth; fifty of the landed ra'atira followed, each with servants carrying more cloth and each with two baskets of provisions, including baked and raw fish, breadfruit and all the produce of the prolific island. There was more. The wives of the chiefs came to make similar presentations and then the huge pile of gifts, and the chief, were taken to Bounty.

The chief Tamatoa remained on board all night, most of which he spent in prayer at Fletcher Christian's bedside. In the morning Christian made gifts in return: hatchets, red feathers, Tahitian cloth and matting; the feathers were the most popular, a point quickly noted. The pleasantries and prayers over, Fletcher and Tamatoa returned to shore to fix on the site for a settlement. Finding none suitable in Tamatoa's western district, Fletcher Christian then made the move which doomed the project. He went to the next clandom, smaller and poorer, and ruled by Taaroa.

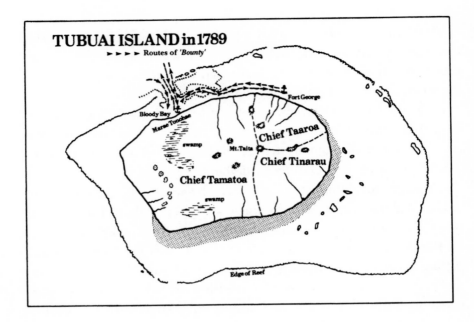

Taaroa was not allied with Tamatoa and quickly seized the opportunity to score over his adversary by first welcoming Fletcher Christian and telling him to choose the land he liked. Then he performed a name-changing ceremony. Tamatoa was furious. Unable to get Fletcher Christian to change his mind, he and the chief of the third district, Tinarau, joined forces and prohibited the people in their districts, the majority of the population, from going to the ship or having anything to do with the visitors.

Fletcher Christian was so intent on planning the settlement he did not at first notice the effect this ban was having on supplies. When he did, he tried approaching Tinarau but he and his family always fled. Anxious to establish himself ashore, Christian decided the best plan was to be firmly settled before solving the problem. He ordered a careful and frugal rationing of the ship's provisions and greater care of the stock, something which scarcely endeared his plan to men who were by no means attached to it or its execution.

The site Fletcher Christian had chosen for his settlement was some miles east of the reef opening and Bloody Bay, and to further his plans, the ship was moved closer to the site. This proved laborious and dangerous, far more difficult than moving Bounty from Matavai to Pare. There are so many coral shoals on the course that it is impossible to move in a direct line, making progress under sail out of the question. From 10 or 11 am until 4 pm the ship could not move because of the strong sea breeze. The only way to move a ship in the circumstances is to haul it along, first throwing out anchors and then winching in the line, leaving the anchor attached to the lagoon bottom. That they moved the ship safely indicates that Christian was the accepted leader and had plenty of co-operation.

The sea is so shallow on the way it became necessary to lighten the ship, first by pumping out the water used as ballast, and then by jettisoning the fresh water. The spare booms and spars were put overboard and moored to a buoy, but they went adrift, to the horror of some but unconcern of Christian, who thought it no great loss as he never intended to go to sea again.

By 10 July, according to Morrison's reckoning, Bounty was anchored only 100 yards from the shore. Met by Taaroa, Christian chose the exact site for his fort, abreast of the ship, and was given permission to do with the land as he thought proper; it is probable he purchased the site with red feathers.

It was no time for sighs of relief. When Christian returned aboard, Morrison says he found Sumner and Quintal had gone ashore without permission and it was not until next morning they returned. When they were called aft to explain their absence, they said, 'the ship is moored and we are now our own Masters'. Christian clapped the pistol he carried to the head of one, saying 'I'll let you know who is Master', and they were both put into leg irons. When they were brought up next morning the resoluteness of Christian's behaviour had convinced them he was 'not to be played with'. They begged pardon and promised to behave better in the future.

It is possible that this disagreement is confused with one on May 6, when two men were put in irons by 'a majority of votes'. Heywood says it was May 9, when the ship was kedged up to the fort site, close enough for there to be confusion. One incident or two? I think two, as I do not feel Morrison would confuse a joint decision with one made solely by Christian.

The reporting of this Quintal/Sumner incident is one which illustrates how other authors colour events to favour or denigrate a character. In *Bligh* by Gavin Kennedy, which makes it clear that Morrison is the source of the anecdote, the original telling of the story and the author's version are quite at variance. Morrison says, 'He [Christian] called them aft and enquired how they come to go on shore without his leave.' In Kennedy's book this appears as 'Christian demanded to know on what authority they had gone ashore.' He goes on, 'Christian went into a rage'; there is no suggestion of demand or rage in Morrison's journal. Fletcher Christian may well have been in a rage, but no one has told us so; it is just as likely that he enquired quietly in the way of a stronger, and to use Morrison's own word, a more 'resolute' man.

Christian acted to help prevent such frustration happening again by giving leave for two hands to sleep on shore each night, as had been Bligh's custom at Tahiti, and as many as pleased to go ashore on Sunday on condition that one of them inspected the livestock at the keys.

The next man Christian had to deal with was Tom Ellison, who now seems to have been his servant for he is described as 'Thos. Ellison, who waited on him and was frequently there'. Knowing the popularity of red feathers on Tubuai, Christian distributed some to all hands which gave them status and bargaining power when on shore, another thoughtful and placatory gesture. Then some of Christian's feathers were suddenly missed from his cabin. Ellison was accused of being the thief. He was stripped and tied, ready for flogging, but as he was so persistent in declaring his innocence, and as no other man could say he had seen the boy with what might have been stolen feathers, he was released.

Work now began. The forge was set up and Coleman, the armourer, first made iron rammers for the muskets and then altered axes for felling trees. William Brown, assisted by a Tahitian, was to clear a piece of ground to plant yams. Coleman and McKoy were to work at the forge making spades, hoes and mattocks. Hillbrant was the cook, Byrne and Ellison with some of the Tahitian boys cared for the boats, and the rest were sent ashore to work. Arms were to be carried and left under the care of a sentinel while ground was being cleared. To protect the boats and the ship while the men worked, one of the cutters was to be anchored near the beach, the other was to return to the ship.

On the first day of work the party was met by the chief and some friends who presented Christian with two plantain trees as peace offerings. The ground for the fortress was measured, a clod was turned as symbolic of possession, a Union Jack was hoisted on a makeshift flagpole and the place named Fort George; Christian had mutinied against Bligh but he remained a patriot, loyal to his king. An extra allowance of grog was given and drunk. Because the place was overrun with rats, several cats were brought on shore and let loose.

The ceremony and celebrations were interrupted by hideous shrieks and yells, which the celebrants took to be war cries. Quickly they grabbed their muskets and sent some Tahitians to find out what was happening. It was simply a local funeral, a time when relatives and friends of the deceased rent the air with horrid cries, 'cutting their heads and breasts with shells and smearing their bodies with blood; after which the grave is filled up and they departed . . . having this information we returned to our work'.

Once the ground had been cleared, the fortress was laid out. The front was only about 50 yards from the beach and Morrison says it was to have been 100 yards square, measured outside the ditch which was to surround it. This ditch would turn out to be more of a moat, for the ground was very wet. Indeed when I visited Fort George in 1980, I discovered it had an independent spring in the middle of it; Fletcher Christian chose this site for the great advantage of reliable fresh water. In times of strife the water supply could not be interrupted or contaminated. Critics claim he chose this site through ineptitude, misunderstanding the political balance and internecine tension on the island. By going there myself, I found a more practical reason for choosing this site, and one which showed that by now he was again thinking clearly and decisively.

The ditch which became a moat was to be 18 feet wide, enough to ensure it was not easily crossed, wet or dry. The walls were to be monumental—20 feet high, measured from the bottom of the ditch, 18 feet wide at the base and 12 feet at the top. The exact height the walls reached has never been established but in 1902 the wall was 6 feet 7 inches high and the ditch about the same again,

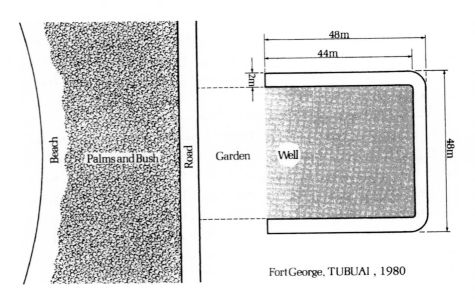

Fort George, TUBUAI, 1980

about two-thirds of the original target. The ditch seems never to have been more than 6 to 8 feet wide.

The notes from Heywood's journal cast fresh light on these specifications, for he says the fort was only to be 50 yards square. This is more practical than Morrison's 100 yards square and is also close to the reality of the remains, which are 48 yards square inside the ditch.

Defence consisted of a drawbridge on the north side facing the beach and mounting of the ship's ordnance on the walls: a four-pounder on each corner and two swivel guns on each side, with two of the latter always in reserve for reinforcement. Each direction was thus protected by at least two four-pounders and four swivel guns.

There was a professed dearth of knowledge about fortification, but work proceeded. Stakes and battens were cut, sods were dug and carried; barrows were made and timber was cut for the gates and drawbridge and, presumably, for the one long and two short huts that the Tahitian woman called Jenny said were built. This was not a Wild West fort of split timber; the only place wood might have been used is as a palisade atop the earth walls, but such a plan has never been recorded.

Fletcher Christian was no idle spectator. 'He always took a part in the most laborious part of the Work.' To encourage his men amid the heat and insects he allowed them an extra half-pint of porter, a strong, dark bitter beer, twice a day.

From this time on, about the beginning of August, the reports vary a great deal in their dates but more or less coincide concerning actual events. I think it likely that Captain Edwards was as slack in copying correct dates as he was in applying the third person singular only to Heywood.

The timing of what follows, which includes new incidents reported only by Edwards/Heywood, is entirely mine.

At the end of July, some of Christian's party had been waylaid on their way to feed the cow and shot an islander in the back. (This incidentally is a murder that Kennedy attributes to Christian, but there is no such suggestion in Edwards' abstracts.) Early in August a party went ashore to take women by force, and meeting with expected opposition, shot another Tubuaian and wounded one with a bayonet. Christian's strict rationing of time ashore must have been relaxed for Morrison says, 'We remained quiet some days, but as the people were fond of sleeping ashore, some of them were decoyed by the Weomen into Tinnarow's district, where they were strippd.'

This was vexatious and when Adams was actually imprisoned in Tinarau's own house, Christian was obliged to assert his authority on behalf of the men. He assembled a party and marched into Tinarau's district. The chief fled at his approach but the woman who had enticed Adams brought him to Christian wearing only his shirt. The rest of Adams' clothes had been taken by Tinarau's men. Christian sent messengers asking for their return and suggesting that both sides should make friends. It was a game of patience and Christian waited hours, sending repeated placatory messages. All were refused.

Christian ordered Tinarau's house to be burned, a serious action made more insulting to the chief by the removal of his revered ancestor images. Just as he had hoped the canoes he took on the first visit might stimulate conciliatory conversation, Christian thought these immensely valuable objects would perform the same task. The party returned to *Bounty* accompanied by the woman who had lured Adams. She was afraid of being punished for leading him back to his companions. Once aboard she found friends she knew, and was perfectly pleased to stay—it is apparent that some of the men had managed to lure local women into their hammocks.

By the early days of September, work on the fort had slowed but the gate posts were fixed and three-quarters of the walls completed. On the 2nd, Tinarau and his attendants came with baskets of food as a peace offering to Fletcher Christian. He wanted his household gods. Christian agreed to return them provided women were allowed to go freely with the *Bounty* men; he also wanted his men's stolen clothing returned and a promise there would be no more inveiglement or ill-treatment in Tinarau's district. Tinarau agreed and proposed they should drink yava together to seal the bargain.

When Christian refused the beverage, Tinarau was furious and swept away in a passion; not because his offer was spurned but because he knew the trick behind his visit had been discovered. One of the Tahitian boys had seen the food carriers secrete weapons close to the fort; when the Europeans were under the narcotic effect of the yava they were to be exterminated. Once informed of this, Christian went through the greeting ceremonies but ordered his men to take positions atop the works. Seeing this made Tinarau so angry he left without formality.

The boy who had brought the information had then been sent out to the ship with orders for Coleman. As soon as the Tubuaians appeared on the beach he was to fire a shotted four-pounder at them. He did, and their exit was considerably hastened. No damage to flesh was inflicted but some of the shot passed through a house and cut away a rafter to which a man was hanging a gourd of water. He was terrified, of course. He could not see the ship and did not see where the shot went; as far as he was concerned it was something supernatural and he never returned to his house again.

23

The Dream Abandoned

The 'royal' family of the district in which the fort was situated was always loyal and friendly to Christian. They made a special visit a few days after Tinarau's failed ploy. Taaroa brought his old father, his own daughters, and the usual retinue of attendants bearing provisions. Taaroa's daughters sang and danced for Christian, then the compliment was repaid by the Tahitian women. Not feeling he had entertained enough, Christian invited his noble guests to return the next day for a Tahitian *heiva*, a far grander and more formal entertainment. Special attention was paid to the costume of the entertainers; two women were 'neatly dressed' and two of the men donned the astonishing mourning dress of the Tahitians, the *pari*. *Bounty* had loaded some as gifts for King George. But even a *heiva* on Tubuai could not now be all fun; while the Tahitians sang and danced the entertainments of their homeland, the Europeans were under arms.

Then mutiny bubbled to the surface again. So advanced was the fortress, and so singleminded its architect, there was finally talk of removing the masts from *Bounty*. The ship was to be dismantled so that its timbers might be used for proper houses. Morrison records that he entertained the idea of sailing back to Tahiti in the ship's large cutter. He spoke to Stewart who said Heywood and he had formulated the same plan. To prevent their being pursued Morrison suggested he would sabotage the ship's lifting blocks after the masts had been removed, thus preventing their replacement. It was first decided to make the cutter shipshape, but Christian ordered that the boats were not to be repaired until all were settled safely ashore. The trio of plotters, feeling others had the same plan, thought they might be better off simply risking the voyage with the boat as it was.

Morrison wrote: 'tho the passage was short and it might perhaps be made with safety in 5 or 6 days, yet had we the Chance to Meet with bad weather our Crazey boat would certainly have made us a coffin . . .' But the situation on Tubuai was soon to change and they were unable to make the attempt.

From the recollections of both Adams and Jenny there seems to have been at least one more battle, perhaps two, not mentioned by Morrison, Heywood or Stewart. Adams says the Tubuaians believed a rumour which suggested the ditch around the fortress was to be a mass grave and that the European visitors planned to exterminate the entire population. Jenny says there was a conspiracy between the Tubuaians and one of the Tahitians to do the reverse, that is to murder all the Europeans and divide their goods. Isabella is said to have told Christian of the conspiracy, neglecting to mention it was one of her countrymen who was the traitor. It is possible that both Adams and Jenny are speaking of the same battle for there are reasons enough in their tales for both sides to wish to attack the other in the interest of their own survival.

The lack of women had never been solved. They would not join the *Bounty* men, although they were happy to sleep with them at their own houses, which was not quite good enough. There was even a plan to make slaves of the Tahitian women, men and boys and to cast lots for them, or to land with a party led by Christian to try again to capture women by force. Fletcher would have none of this even though he was told they would do no more work until each man had a wife.

Heywood and Morrison agree that Christian's desire was to persuade rather than to force the Tubuaians, which is hardly the decision of a man 'who could not control his passions or men'. His reason for not turning the Tahitians into slaves was obvious—he could lose Isabella. Work did stop and three days were spent debating; exercising their tongues was as thirst-making as labouring with their bodies and the men demanded more grog. Christian refused what he considered yet another absurd demand, so they broke the lock of the spirit room (presumably on the ship) and took it by force.

To humour the men, perhaps playing for time while they cooled their tempers, Christian ordered a double allowance of grog to be served every day, but to no purpose. Foiled again, he called yet another meeting of all hands on the quarterdeck, asking their opinions. At first the men wanted to move to Tahiti where they might get women without force, but this was overruled. Next day the proposal was revived and on a show of hands the idea was accepted—sixteen voted for Tahiti, nine to stay with *Bounty*. The details were quickly settled. Those electing Tahiti were to be given supplies and arms and a share of everything on the ship. Fletcher Christian was to have the ship in seagoing condition and eight men agreed to sail with him.

Among those who wanted to settle on Tahiti were Churchill and Thompson. From their later behaviour Christian was well rid of them; they were probably more destructive to the Tubuaian settlement than those who had opposed Christian's mutiny.

There was now action and unity. Water was collected, the sails were bent. A party under the command of, or including, Hitihiti was sent to collect stock and to find the cow, which had not been seen for some time. They were set upon by islanders who beat and plundered them, insulted Hitihiti and had the additional audacity to send a message with the bruised men that they would treat Christian the same way. Meanwhile the Tubuaian woman who had come aboard because of her friendship for Adams had abruptly departed.

Bounty's commander was not to be intimidated. He sent the men back to complete their errand. Twenty were armed and, taking the nine Tahitian men and four of the boys, one of whom always carried the Union Jack, they marched off to retrieve some of their roaming stock and to chastise the offenders. The insults to Hitihiti, a chief, were especially to be avenged.

Just a mile from their landing place they were ambushed by about 700 men. The war party fought with stones, clubs and spears but with more fury than judgment, retiring with great loss; and some stock was collected with no further trouble. Further ambush being expected, each European was issued with twenty-four rounds of ammunition, and Hitihiti, being an excellent shot, was armed with a musket. Arriving safely at the fort, they found Taaroa with his aged father and young brother, Taaroamiva. They had come to explain that *Bounty*'s stock was the bone, and the flesh, of contention. Tinarau was determined that the animals which roamed into his territory were his property and he was arming more men.

Christian was not going to leave without resolving the question of mastery. He needed to show leadership to his own party as well as to punish Tinarau. If Christian had upset anyone on the island it was Tamatoa, but this chief had kept his distance. It was the lesser Tinarau who had always been the primary taunter and teaser. Christian asked his Tubuaian friends to remain in the fortress to avoid accidental injury. Then he drew up his party into ranks with one Tahitian between two of his men, and armed the former with clubs. In silence they marched through the thick woods towards Tinarau's district.

When they reached a path with dense bush on each side, caution suggested an extra careful lookout. Burkitt, thinking he heard something stir in a bush, stepped to look and received a spear wound in his left side. In seconds there was bedlam. The Tahitian beside

Burkitt levelled his attacker and took his spear. Tubuaian warriors rushed in with 'great fury and horrid yells'. Christian's party halted and, like the famous military square, faced different directions and fired several times. The Tubuaians were so angry and determined they continued attacking from all quarters.

The *Bounty* men retreated safely to rising ground a short distance to their rear, by which time the Tahitians were armed with Tubuaian spears, which they employed 'manfully'. The islanders attacked the hillock with redoubled energy, not the least perturbed by the growing number of their own dead. The retreat had to be continued, for thick bush above the place the *Bounty* men had chosen proved an excellent cover for the attacking Tubuaians. Several of the Tahitians were now wounded and Christian had injured his hand on his own bayonet.

They fell back through the bush to a taro ground 200 yards away, keeping up a constant rear-guard fire. Once there they protected themselves behind the banks built to irrigate the taro ground; it was trench warfare, and, it worked. The Tubuaians followed in hot pursuit until they reached the edge of the bush, and then halted to throw stones. Although the fighting had been furious and apparently without order, the Tubuaians were actually organized into parties of twenty to twenty-eight men, each of which had a leader whose orders were followed.

One of the leaders, a chief, bravely began to rally his men by venturing from the cover of the bush. Even though some distance away, he was shot dead. Seeing that each man who came into the clear was killed or wounded, the Tubuaians began an overdue retreat. It was just in time, for Burkitt was growing faint. Skinner, who had a disabled musket, was able to assist him to the ship while the rest waited to see if they were to be attacked again. It was soon apparent that the small band led by Christian had beaten the men who outnumbered them by more than ten to one and there were three rousing cheers.

The Tahitian men and boys immediately began to collect spoils of war. They did not get all they wanted. One asked permission to cut out the jawbones of the dead so they could be hung around the ship as a deterrent to other troublemakers. It must have been tempting to Christian, thinking of the troublemakers among his own party, but the request was denied, so incensing the man that he had to be threatened with his own death; yet he still begged to excise just one for himself. The other Tahitians were happy with spears and clubs. They met no opposition when they finally gathered the animals they wanted, including the nomadic cow.

Burkitt had had the narrowest of escapes. The spear had struck, but not broken, a rib and he healed in a short time. Morrison says the affair gave them a very mean opinion of their bayonets for although several men had fallen by them, the blades always broke off and remained in the body. The length of the Tubuaians' spears was such that bayonets were generally no use against them. If they had not had firearms, everyone in the *Bounty* party would certainly have died.

On the 14th, the day after the bloody battle, they killed the cow, which proved excellent meat; butchering it ashore was preferred to manhandling it back on board. For safety they were all living on the ship and while they were enjoying their beef, young Taaroamiva came aboard to tell them the outcome of the fighting. Sixty Tubuaian men had been killed (fifty according to Heywood), as well as six women who had been supplying them with spears and stones; many had been wounded. Among the important men who had fallen was Tinarau's brother. Taaroamiva had been so loyal to Christian that he feared for his life and asked if he and two friends could join *Bounty*. When told the ship was bound for Tahiti they were doubly pleased.

Bounty weighed anchor and made her way relatively easily to the opening, being lighter than before. When clear of the reef, they lay by and 'filld Saltwater to keep her on her legs and at noon made sail, leaving Toobuai well Stockd with Hogs, Goats, Fowles, Dogs and Cats, the Former of which were increased to Four times the number we landed . . .'

The battle with the Tubuaians surely convinced Fletcher Christian that his settlement had failed, even if the unhappiness of the men in his own party had not done so. But vital lessons had been learned. The blame for the failure of the brave experiment cannot all be laid upon the young shoulders of Fletcher Christian. The friendliness of the Tahitians would seem to indicate that settling on some other close Polynesian island was a simple proposition. Naturally there were those aboard *Bounty* who might have sabotaged the Tubuai settlement, but in the main they only nagged and complained about the lack of women. Fletcher unknowingly had a far greater and more powerful enemy than either his companions or a universal ignorance of the complexity of Polynesia. The priests of Tubuai were determined he would never live on their island.

The priests had virtually all the authority on Tubuai and seemed to be nearly on a footing with the chiefs. Once they had seen the Europeans were, as Morrison observes, 'Common Men and liable to accident like themselves' they could not bear to see 'such Superiority as the Europeans in general usurp over those who differ from themselves'. Because the Europeans ignored and ridiculed their authority, the priests used every means to prevent the chiefs making friends, believing that if the visitors remained, their own power would be lessened; Morrison adds 'which in all probability would have been the case'.

If there had been fewer in the party, they might have been absorbed into the community and things might have been different. A foreign community, initially dependent for supplies upon the inhabitants, was less likely to succeed. It could have done so on an island as fertile as Tubuai but for two mistakes—the loosing of the animals and the antagonism of Tamatoa, the most powerful chief, by settling outside his domain. The first action affected every Tubuaian, for having no large mammals on the island they had no fences. The 200 rooting pigs and browsing goats must have damaged property and gardens badly. Snubbing Tamatoa was just the push the priests needed to help slam the chiefs' open door of welcome. If they lived the next thirty years they may well have wondered who had the final victory. *Bounty* left them with venereal disease and dysentery. The effects of both afflictions were compounded when a vanguard of the London Missionary Society chose Tubuai for their first establishment. By 1823, the population had been reduced from 3,000 to 300.

If Fletcher Christian had not ruled firmly on Tubuai, the people aboard *Bounty* would also have been decimated, a proposition firmly supported by the Tubuaians' action of the last few days. Those who moaned about Christian's restrictions may well have lived only because of them. His plan had been precocious. That he succeeded in persuading such a disparate group to labour in tropical conditions, while pestered by insects and Tubuaians, was at least a personal success. Many a lesser and older man would have crumpled. Fletcher Christian, frustrated but not beaten, still had the ship.

But they were now returning to Tahiti, where they would separate. By the 20th, they were in the lee of Mehetia, where the remaining trade goods, arms and ammunition, alcohol, clothes and practical goods were divided. On the 22nd, they were back in the sweep of Matavai Bay and the belongings of those headed for shore were unloaded before nightfall.

Peter Heywood, quoted by his step-daughter Lady Belcher in her book about the mutiny, remembered how difficult this was. There was a high surf on the day and only one of *Bounty*'s boats was considered safe to 'swim'. Fearful of travelling in the canoes, even though they admitted the Tahitians handled them better in those conditions than they did their own boat, the Europeans waited endlessly as it made trip after trip. Only when everything else was on shore was the ammunition landed.

Among the things they took were carpenter's tools, as well as some belonging to the armourer, a pig of iron for an anvil, a grind-stone, some bar iron (probably ballast bars), a suit of clothes, some iron pots, a copper kettle and about three gallons of wine per man. Each man except blind Byrne had a musket, pistol, cutlass, bayonet, cartridge box, seventeen charges of powder, a quantity of lead to make bullets and some spare belts; there were three extra firearms, which went to Heywood, Norman and Burkitt. The eighteen men also asked for saws, of which there were a 'whip' and a 'cross' aboard, but Christian wanted these and gave them instead extra trade items, two spyglasses and an old compass. He offered them some of the swivel guns but these were declined; instead they took and divided a portion of the canvas and sails. The two household images belonging to Tinarau were given by Christian to Peter Heywood as a present for the young king, Tu. Hitihiti made the presentation on behalf of the *Bounty* men and the objects are said to have caused a sensation.

Naturally there was visiting in both directions; Hitihiti and most of the Tahitians who had been to Tubuai went ashore, delighted to be back. As Tubuaian women other than Adams' friend had been on the ship, they may also have sailed to Tahiti for safety. Altogether *Bounty* probably had over sixty people aboard on her return, as well as a good stock of animals and plants.

The Free Grammar School in Cockermouth, now demolished: Fletcher's time there in the early 1770s coincided with the much younger William Wordsworth.

Mr. Jackson, my teacher at Owairaka School, Auckland, in 1951 was first to awaken my interest in ancestors: I am third from the right in the front row.

Ewanrigg, close to Workington in Cumbria, the Christians' enormous mainland mansion where Fletcher's father Charles was born and brought up. Originally it was Unerigg, but the family's favourite name of Ewan made a change inevitable. Today only part of the façade remains.

Charles Christian died in 1768 when son Fletcher was four. His showy table grave in Brigham Churchyard sports a bold Christian coat of arms and the inscription carefully points out that he was an Unerigg Christian.

Milntown, outside Ramsey on the Isle of Man, passed directly from father to son in an unbroken line of 24 recorded generations of Christians from 1368 to 1904.

Moorland Close, birthplace of Fletcher Christian, sits on a hill outside Cockermouth in England's Lake District and is still a working farm. When the house seen was built outside them in 1709, the brick walls still enclosed the ruins of medieval buildings entered only through the small door of the square tower.

Bounty's objective was to collect breadfruit trees from Tahiti and deliver them to the West Indies, providing cheap and nutritious food for Britain's sugar plantation slaves and making them independent of supplies from the revolutionary American colonies. When freshly baked, breadfruit has a curiously yeasty smell and taste and is a Polynesian staple, but the West Indian slaves refused to eat it.

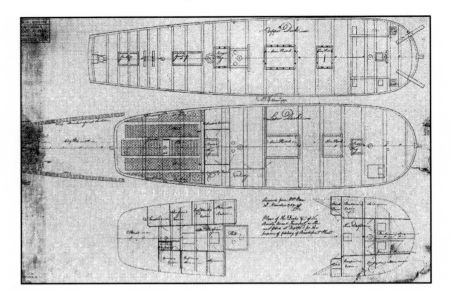

The plans of the converted *Bounty* show how two extra platform decks were built fore and aft, below the already dark, airless lower deck, to compensate for the space taken by the extension of the great cabin to make a green house for the storage of the bread fruit trees.

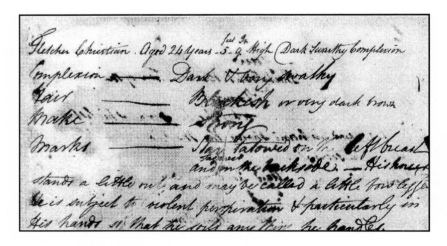

Bligh wrote many descriptions of Christian to help officials track him down. But only Bligh ever mentioned Christian's problems with heavy perspiration, a clue to his personality and behaviour which has only now been fully explored, giving new insight into Fletcher Christian and why he mutinied against a man who had once been his friend and mentor.

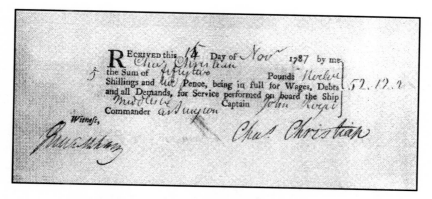

Fletcher Christian's brother Charles was two years older and a surgeon. Fletcher's last night in England was spent talking to Charles, who had recently mutinied against a difficult captain aboard the East Indiaman *Middlesex*.

John Adams signed on *Bounty* as Alexander Smith and was the only mutineer still alive when Pitcairn was rediscovered in 1808. This original drawing by Capt. Richard Beechey RN (c.1825) shows stronger features and a more aquiline nose than engravings copied from it. Adams died four years later aged 65.

Adventure Bay, Tasmania: in August 1788 it was the last major wooding and watering place for *Bounty* before the long eastwards haul to Tahiti. Boatswain's mate James Morrison says it was here that the 'seeds of eternal discord' were sown when Bligh insulted both officers and men by confusing their roles. Painted by artist George Tobin in 1792.

Robert Dodd's original 1790 oil painting of Bligh being cast adrift, which remains in private hands. Fletcher Christian stands with a cutlass on his shoulder where Bligh had a private long-drop lavatory, perhaps an 18th century visual pun. By 2 October 1790 Dodd was selling engravings of the picture, cashing in on the huge interest in Bligh's narrative of the mutiny, quickly published by the British Admiralty.

Tahitian women were not the cause of the
mutiny. But when we discovered Teura in
Papeete's flower market I understood how
they might have been. The Tahitian women
who went with Christian guaranteed the
success of the mutineer's revolutionary colony
and were the true social pioneers.

Fort George, Tubuai, where Christian
first attempted to settle after the mutiny.
Now a sweet potato patch surrounded
by the shallow remains of the moat
which once protected high earth walls.
The rough patch in front of the
breadfruit tree is the spring, probably
Christian's major reason for choosing
the site.

Expedition members carefully mapped the remains of Fort George but couldn't establish how deep the moat had been: locals had only recently filled it in, some said to stop drunks accidentally drowning.

Adamstown, the only area ever settled on Pitcairn, as seen from Christian's Cave, where the mutineer is supposed to have brooded on his fate. The mutineers and their Tahitian companions first hid behind the thick coastal bush, lighting no daytime fires for fear smoke would reveal their hideout. The lower peak on the right is Ship Landing Point.

Viewed from Ship Landing Point, Adamstown stretches for almost half a mile towards Christian's Cave, high on the peak of Lookout Point in the distance. Actually a scoop in the rock rather than a cave it is a perfect spot for musing one's fate, but not the hideout it's often said to be.

Mainmast's Pool, Pitcairn Island. Tom Christian first helped work out that Mumma's Pool was a corruption of Mainmast's Pool, and then excavated the man-made shape, hacked out of rock and filled by a spring. Made by Christian for Mauatua, who was also called Mainmast, perhaps because of her upright bearing. Or simply a favourite spot? No-one knows.

This engraving of the original school building in Adamstown helped us find where Mauatua and her second son Charles 'Hoppa' are buried. The building has gone, the banyan tree moved down the hill and the gravestones are under what is now a meeting hall, but the site was still called 'The School' by older Pitcairners.

CHURCH AND SCHOOL-HOUSE, PITCAIRN.

Sarah Christian Nobbs, daughter of Charles 'Hoppa' and Sully, was a granddaughter of Fletcher and Mauatua, and sister of my great-great-grandfather Isaac. Within the family it is said she looked a lot like Mauatua.

Elizabeth 'Betsy' Mills (centre foreground), first girl born on Pitcairn, only daughter of mutineer John Mills and Vahineatua and one of my great-great-great-grandmothers. Photographed on Norfolk Island in 1862 with other Pitcairners and officers of HMS *Pelorus* when she was about 70.

Sons and grandsons of mutiny. This 1862 photograph shows first and second generation Pitcairners: from right, Arthur, son of mutineer Matthew Quintal and Tevarua, George, son of John Adams and Teio (another of my great-great-great-great-grandmothers), Arthur's son John Quintal and George's son John Adams.

The original 1814 watercolour of Thursday October Christian, Fletcher and Mauatua's first born. The awkward shoulders and arms show that the artist, British naval visitor Lt. John Shillibeer, was no draughtsman, but the strong features echo descriptions of both his parents.

On the right, my great-grandparents, Godfrey Christian with his wife Frances; the wedding couple is my grandparents, William and Evelyn. When Godfrey and Frances married they united two of the South Pacific's earliest pioneering families.

Duddie, one of Fletcher Christian's grandsons, in 1911. He clearly remembered his grandmother Mauatua, who died when he was 20 and spoke of her to Pitcairners who were alive when we visited in 1980.

Windermere Lake.

The end of another theory. If Fletcher Christian escaped from Pitcairn Island he couldn't have hidden in the trees around Lake Windemere hoping to see his lost love, Isabella Curwen. This 1795 engraving of Isabella's fanciful round house Belle Isle shows there were virtually none at the time: in fact, her husband John Christian Curwen was planting most that we see today.

Is there where Fletcher Christian was murdered and then buried with the beheaded bones of his followers? After identifying this dried-up pool on the site of Christian's original land holding, only time prevented the expedition digging to prove my belief he never escaped Pitcairn, and that this great lonely rock became the greatest mausoleum one revolutionary young man ever had.

24

A Private Message

D id Fletcher Christian go on shore in Matavai Bay that day? Christian is quoted as saying he could not face the chiefs to whom he had lied on his last visit. On the other hand, Heywood says he came to say a final goodbye to himself and to George Stewart; it is possible Christian did this under cover of darkness.

When their leave taking was almost finished, Heywood said Christian took him to one side on the black sands of Matavai, absolved him of any complicity in the mutiny and told him to give himself up to the ship that was bound to arrive in search of *Bounty*. Heywood said he was also entrusted with a message to pass on to Christian's family, relating circumstances that might extenuate, though they could not justify, the crime he had committed against the laws of his country.

Heywood kept the meeting secret until well after his subsequent trial in 1792. It was only sensible to distance himself from Christian, who had been such a close friend that Bligh could—and did—regard them as allies. There was no point in giving Bligh further ammunition against himself. Heywood apparently lied about his age and he was no angel; his name is one of those that appear on the venereal list. But he was a gentleman of honour and kept his word, given on the Tahitian sands, to his lost friend. When Heywood finally revealed the conversation—but not the details—the conjecture began.

In the 1930s, it was said that Christian's wild-eyed look and mutinous behaviour might have been caused by syphilis. The shame of this was thought to have been too much for Christian to bear, so, rather than facing society and his mother, he mutinied and took the ship to sail into a hidden shame. It is unlikely in the extreme that Fletcher Christian was suffering from tertiary or neuro-syphilis, the stage of the disease that can turn the mind, and when death, if not imminent, is inevitable. The most licentious of men would not be in this state in his mid-twenties for, although this final stage can appear within five years of initial infection, it usually takes ten to forty years, and the longer time is the more usual by far.

Fletcher Christian, sensitive to criticism as he was, would not have mutinied because he had syphilis or any other venereal infection. If he had the disease he would have known so for many years, and there were less dramatic ways of evading social condemnation; like his brother Charles he could simply have remained abstinent and kept his secret.

In 1965 Madge Darby first expressed the theory that Heywood's message concerned a homosexual relationship between Bligh and Christian. This theory is not easy to dismiss. If Bligh and Christian were homosexual lovers, much of the so-called mystery of the mutiny can be explained. The friendship between these two men demonstrably exceeded the norms. Bligh had promoted Christian above others who might be thought to be more deserving because they were more senior. He dined him regularly on *Britannia* as well as on *Bounty*, where he had been allowed unlimited access to his liquor chest. Christian had been a visitor to Bligh's house in England, as shown in Bligh's remark, 'You have danced my children on your knee'. Christian was the ideal protégé, loyal, charming and a quick learner. In the long days and exhausting nights of sea passage under sail, special relationships can flower into a sexuality two men would never consider when ashore, whatever the opportunity.

Bligh and Christian were both young, healthy and passionate, and had every opportunity to explore homosexuality. Let us assume it to be true. If Bligh were the instigator and made his young friend pay for privilege with his body, or even if Christian seduced him, Bligh behaved in Tahiti in a decidedly strange way. By placing Fletcher Christian, and most of the other young boys, on shore while he remained on the ship, Bligh denied himself the pleasures he is supposed to have demanded at sea and also ensured he would have none of it again. For, on Tahiti, and this is not supposition, Fletcher Christian developed into full, independent manhood, and lived the life of a squire such as he might aspire to in England.

To continue the assumption, once *Bounty* sailed for England, Bligh would demand a resumption of their sexual relationship, only to find Christian now refused. Passions which had bound and comforted these men across the world's great oceans now soured to the point where Bligh nagged painfully at Christian and Christian couldn't stand the sight of Bligh. So, in a fit of pique, Christian petulantly stole his ex-lover's ship. Or so the theory goes, and it does make sense in a simple modern way. But, apart from their special friendship, the theory of a physical involvement is totally unsupported by any contemporary evidence.

But I do think the intensity of their friendship contributed strongly to its breakdown. Bligh was certainly a man's man and felt happier in men's company, hence his suitability for a naval career. Betsy had given him only daughters. A frustrated and tortured feeling for his young wards, part paternal, part sexual, might explain why he was so vitriolic about Heywood on his return. He could also simply be smarting under a wounded vanity.

Fletcher Christian, ten years younger than Bligh, grew up largely without the interest of an older male member of the family, at least not of the father-figure type whom it is permitted to clasp emotionally and physically. This psychological void, combined with the practical need for a patron, would certainly recommend Bligh's interest as worthy of encouragement. Bligh fits well into the role of a surrogate father to Fletcher Christian. The reciprocated and loyal interest of a bright young man from a good family, who was also a good sailor, would serve only to flatter Bligh. He needed, or enjoyed, the feeling of having a surrogate brother or son, too. Such situations are more fragile and more explosive than the real thing.

But young men must one day grow away from their parent figures; the wrench is more difficult for the latter, for whom it is a retrograde step to loneliness. The independence which Bligh gave to Christian on Tahiti also became an unwished for independence of himself. After six months ashore, Christian was thinking his own thoughts, which, turning the pyschological tables on Bligh, saw him considering himself better able to command than his erstwhile father figure and discarded friend.

Back aboard *Bounty*, it would have been mutually agonizing. Something had to give. Fletcher Christian had one way to salvage his sanity. He followed the usual pattern of such relationships, by doing the equivalent of leaving home.

There were many associated with *Bounty*, in particular Peter Heywood, Fryer and Purcell, who could vengefully have used the homosexual accusation against Bligh. If they had he would have been ruined. But never in his long career was there a breath of such a thing.

The message Heywood is thought to have taken home contained nothing about syphilis or homosexuality. As soon as Heywood was free he went to Edward Christian and simply gave him first-hand background information revealing that Bligh's published narrative was far from the full story, thus stimulating Edward's search for the truth.

Fletcher Christian had made it quite clear to Heywood that the blame was all his. He knew he should have been strong enough to weather the daily storms that Bligh sent his way. But he was provoked beyond his ability to cope and Heywood made certain Edward Christian knew of this. Fletcher was aware that under normal circumstances his behaviour was not just illegal, but eccentric and unjustifiable. He trusted his friend Heywood to let his family know the circumstances were anything but normal, even by the brutish standards of daily naval life. By quietly explaining himself only to Heywood, he showed he was not pursuing a personal vendetta; while, in sharp contrast, Bligh needed to defend his actions publicly.

25

Oblivion

The eighteen immigrants who left *Bounty* were not the first white men to be turned off a European ship to live on Tahiti. Somewhere else on the island was a trouble maker called Brown, who had been left behind by a ship called *Mercury*, a few months earlier. Fletcher Christian did not meet him. If he had he would have realized that he was better off away from Tubuai. For while he was building Fort George he had missed discovery by the slenderest of margins.

On 9 August 1789, in the afternoon, *Mercury*, commanded by John Henry Cox, sighted Tubuai some eleven leagues distant. By the time the ship was within a couple of miles it was eight at night and dark. Seeing lights on shore the ship fired two guns but appeared to get no reply. Having sailed too close to the reef, she had to bear off to avoid an accident and then continued on to Tahiti. In daylight she might have sailed around the island, seen *Bounty* and stopped to pay a social call. A little less attention and she might have been wrecked on the reef. Fortunately, neither happened and at Tahiti the men on *Mercury* were confused at stories of *Bounty* returning there under command of 'Titreano', Bligh's second-in-command.

The risk of discovery grew the longer Christian stayed at Tahiti. The men he was leaving behind were bound to tell the truth this time, and Tu or others might feel obliged to revenge their friend Bligh. At the very least they could take advantage of Christian's small crew to seize the vessel and its treasures, a highly likely event. As well, Christian could not rely on the men who had said they would stay with him. For all his brave speeches about being left to run before the wind which Edward Christian says he made, Fletcher needed help in sailing the ship. But it was not even as simple as that. He knew that these men needed women, and talk on the island could well dissuade possible mates for the men. The men and women who had been on Tubuai would quickly have told of the drunkenness and fighting, the battles. Yet, if Christian wanted men he had to have women. To get women he would have to kidnap them.

Early on the morning of 23 September 1789, Fletcher Christian cut yet another cable, leaving a second anchor at Tahiti, and *Bounty* slipped through the reef. (Bligh was later told that he sailed so hurriedly because Isabella discovered a plot among the Tahitians to take the ship.) On board were his eight companions, plus six Polynesian men, nineteen women and a little girl, thirty-five people in all.

The remaining members of *Bounty*'s crew were Edward Young, John Adams, William McKoy, Matthew Quintal, John Williams, Isaac Martin, John Mills and William Brown.

Taaroamiva was almost certainly on board by choice with his two companions, and presumably Jenny and Isabella were content to be with their European lovers.

During the latter part of the twentieth century some writers began to suggest that Christian and Mauatua were married by now. The first was Robert Nicholson in his 1965 book, *The Pitcairners*, although he offers no evidence to support this assertion. In spite of this, Nicholson's claim was used in an application to the College of

Arms in London which hoped to prove Fletcher's descendants had the right to bear the Christian family's arms of a unicorn crest over a shield of three bishop's cups. Bluemantle Pursuivant, the College Herald who examined the claim, told me that the question of their marriage was irrelevant. An unmarried couple, even if accepted by their peers as being man and wife, is disqualified from passing on noble titles, but is able to pass on the right to bear arms; their bastard children simply add a bar sinister to their coat of arms' shield. In my view there was no marriage by any of *Bounty's* men by this time: if Christian had made a Tahitian-style marriage, it is exactly the sort of occasion James Morrison would have remembered and recorded, but he did not.

So, other than Jenny and Mauatua, the rest of *Bounty's* passengers had been tricked but it's unlikely this was deliberate. They had been invited on board the night before for a farewell celebration and taken to bed believing the ship would be moving only down to Pare the next day; but in the morning they were actually a mile outside the reef, heading past Moorea. One woman immediately jumped overboard and swam for the reef. Others would have followed if they had had more courage. The captain sailed relentlessly on, making the atoll of Tetiaroa late in the morning, but still the kidnapped women could not bring themselves to jump overboard.

Something happened to change Fletcher Christian's mind. Perhaps a combination of noise made by the unhappy women who were 'much afflicted' and some natural selection. Each of the white men chose a companion and three more women were selected for the six Polynesians. Then *Bounty* turned back to Moorea where a canoe put out and the six 'rather ancient' women were released. When *Bounty* turned and sailed away from the turreted twins of Tahiti and Moorea, she was never to see them again. No man was to know her destination or the fate of the men and women aboard for twenty years.

The *Bounty* that sailed Fletcher Christian into oblivion on that late

September day would hardly be recognized as one of His Majesty's naval ships. She bore no resemblance to the smart expedition vessel Bligh had boasted about in his letters to Banks almost two years before. Certainly there were plants and animals aboard. But there was only one truly seaworthy small boat, many of the sails had been cut up or given away, booms and spars had been lost at Tubuai. Long months in the tropics without proper maintenance meant the ship needed recaulking. The deck timbers would have shrunk and, in a heavy sea, water would drip through the deck onto the accommodation below.

And who was there to sail her? Who to keep watch? There were few charts of these seas, little to indicate shoals and reefs. Considering the voyage *Bounty* made, her crew of men and women must have worked day and night; for in his search for a home, Fletcher Christian was to guide the ship over nearly 8,000 miles of Pacific water. It is a story pieced together only in 1958, and even now is so little known that recent books still show *Bounty* somehow taking four months to sail south-east to Pitcairn from Tahiti, a distance of 1,200 miles.

Professor H. E. Maude of the Australian National University in Canberra spent some years on Pitcairn Island during the Second World War, and helped to set up its popular philatelic service. Using his knowledge of Pacific history to locate and interpret new sources of material, much of it records of oral tradition, he finally pieced together the extraordinary journey of *Bounty*, corroborating previously misunderstood—or more generally ignored—references to islands and incidents made by the Tahitian Jenny, when she later spoke of their search for a hiding place.

When he left Tahiti for the last time, Christian knew he had to find an island that was uninhabited, difficult of anchorage and well off the beaten track. It seems a simple aim when you have the whole Pacific at your disposal. It is not.

First he thought of sailing up to the glorious Marquesas, hoping on the way he might find a suitable island that was closer to Tahiti. But this invited early discovery and instead they looked for islands said to have been discovered by Spanish explorers. These were not where they were supposed to be, and the ship simply sailed westwards with the wind from the Society group to the Tongan archipelago.

There have never been any reports of tension at this stage of the voyage but it must have been bizarre on board as both groups continued to learn each other's customs and language. The Polynesian men and women had slowly to adopt a new attitude to taboos concerning food and to each other. The English men were probably being taught Polynesian navigation, watching waves and currents, birds and clouds, stars and planets, instead of relying on a compass needle. Undoubtedly, Christian used Polynesian traditional talents and rote-learned information to chart his course to island after island; otherwise, it was easy to sail and see no land in these vast expanses.

From accounts that Professor Maude collected, he deduced that *Bounty* must have passed through the Cook Islands. Several accounts of floating islands with rivers and taro swamps had been collected in 1814 and 1823, and led Maude to the conclusion that Fletcher Christian was the discoverer of Rarotonga. Not only that, *Bounty* also introduced the orange to the island; and now the export of that fruit's juice is the mainstay of its economy. There was bartering on Rarotonga and *Bounty* sailed on to an island Jenny calls Purutea, and she gives some detail of an unfortunate incident there.

She said that a canoe came from the island bringing a pig and some coconuts. One of the canoeists came aboard and was delighted by the pearl shell buttons on Fletcher Christian's jacket—the uniforms were still being used in port, it seems. Christian gave the jacket to the man, who then stood on the gunwale to show it to his friends, when one of the mutineers shot him and he fell into the sea. With loud lamentations the body was put into the canoe and the islanders who came bearing gifts paddled back to shore with only a dead companion for thanks. Christian was indignant but, 'He could do nothing more, having lost all authority, than reprimand the murderer severely'. The context in which this statement was made and by whom, must be very carefully considered. Jenny gave her interviews around 1818, and whatever her understanding of Europeans was later in her life, it cannot have been very great in 1789. To a Tahitian, authority meant autocracy, and as Fletcher Christian did not flog men, or put them in irons the way he had in Tubuai, he would undoubtedly appear to have lost authority in her eyes. She would expect a wrongdoer to be punished and the fact that Christian simply shouted at him would not be enough.

From a European view it might be considered differently. What should he have done? Killed the murderer? Locked him up? There were not enough people on board for him to have done either, and I think to have done so would have been dangerous. Considering they were less than half way through their voyage it is obvious that Christian cannot have lost all authority. If he had they would never have achieved what they did. No one else was capable of sailing the ship. Even if they were, there is general agreement that Christian was the one who chose and steered them to their final destination. Jenny's statement must be considered as either misreporting or a subjective Polynesian interpretation.

They moved on to Tongatabu, where Jenny said they stayed two days, then continued further westwards; by now they were more westerly than when the mutiny had occurred off Tofua. On sighting a small low island, Christian proposed to stop there but a brief visit showed it was well populated and would not do, but they got eggs, birds and coconuts. Evidence points to this lagoon island being either Vatoa or Ono-i-Lau, in the Lau Group in the south of the Fijian islands. It is just as well they did not stop, for the inhabitants were almost certainly cannibalistic.

This marked the end of their westward cruise. It was two months since they had left Tahiti and they had been at sea almost all the time. The ship, although protected from worm by its expensive copper sheathing, would nevertheless be deteriorating. The animals and plants on board needed constant water and feed, and, without the meticulous hygiene and care of Bligh, the ship was probably as noisome and unhealthy as most others on the sea. After so long at sea without the inhibitions of dress required by their ex-captain, the Europeans would have been tanned deeply over most of their bodies. Except for the times they wore uniforms while calling at islands, they had probably already adopted the free and comfortable Tahitian loin cloth, or like so many modern sailors on the Pacific, wore nothing at all.

Did Christian turn *Bounty* to the east because he knew there was little hope of finding an island that was safe in the western reaches of this ocean? Or had he already made up his mind to find Pitcairn?

Choosing Pitcairn and then convincing his companions to accompany him there required enormous courage on Fletcher Christian's part, courage and tremendous faith in Christian by the others. It meant well over a month more at sea without the possibility of a single respite. To get to Pitcairn, 2,000 miles to the east, they would have to loop far south into cooler climates to find hospitable winds; there would be no islands. It was even worse than feared.

For two exhausting and dispiriting months they tacked into the chill teeth of the south-east trades. Discouraged, the party 'therefore thought of returning to Tahiti'. Even Fletcher Christian must have been tempted, but sailing there would not have been any more pleasant. They were cold and bored. Not even the wines of Tenerife could temper the fatigue and the monotony. There was no escape from the whine of the wind in the rigging, none from the wretched complaints of the spent timbers. There could be no respite from duty, no refreshing uninterrupted sleep. And Christian could never relax his vigilance. The sails of a faster ship—and most were faster—would signal the end of *Bounty*'s voyage.

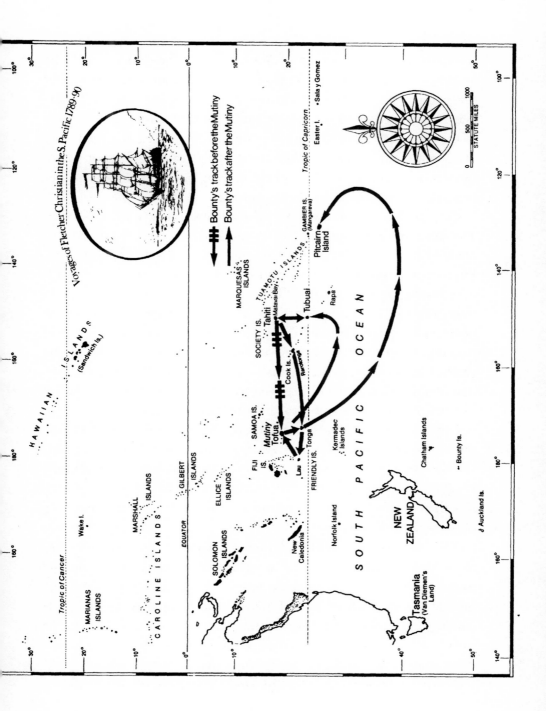

Voyages of Fletcher Christian in the S. Pacific 1789-90

Bounty's track before the Mutiny
Bounty's track after the Mutiny

There were many weeks of unhappiness before *Bounty* could be headed out of the Pacific's grey southern waters. As December dragged on, the days became increasingly hotter and another Christmas Day passed amid pagans and sunshine. Days after the dawning of the new year of 1790 there was sudden hope born of unexpected disappointment. *Bounty* and her crew finally reached the spot where Pitcairn was said to be. They found nothing but more water, further horizons of anguish and unkept promise.

Yet, to Christian this was the most encouraging event for months. The description he had read of Pitcairn by Carteret, who had discovered it in 1767, but who could not land, made it sound perfect. Pitcairn was isolated by unimaginable stretches of water, its smallness making it even more difficult to find or stumble across than most islands. It was pounded by violent unhindered surf, which made landing treacherous if not impossible. It looked fertile, had running water, and it seemed uninhabited. If it were also to be charted incorrectly, it was virtually undiscovered. If Fletcher Christian could find it he would have sailed his ship and himself right off the face of the earth and into the oblivion he wished.

Deducing it was almost certainly the island's longitude that Carteret had mistaken, Christian zigzagged along the line of latitude. On the evening of 15 January, he saw Pitcairn at last. It was pitifully small to be the object of such excitement. It is but a lonely rock less than two square miles, misplaced, like the discarded plaything of a forgetful Leviathan.

The gods were determined to extract every ounce of patience from Fletcher Christian. After a voyage of almost 8,000 miles and four months, there was to be no simple finale. For forty-eight hours he and his ship where hurled about in a violent swell that made landing impossible; yet because they saw no signs of life on the thickly-clad peaks that loomed over the lofty sea cliffs, each hour's delay made the island only more attractive.

A truly safe and calm day for landing at Pitcairn occurs only a few times in the life of a man. At last Fletcher Christian took advice from his Tahitian companions that conditions had subsided to the point where an attempt was worthwhile. The wind must have been blowing from the cold south or the east for they rowed through the surf to Tedside on the west of the island. Here was the only possible alternative landing site to what became known as Bounty Bay on the eastern side.

Christian, Brown, Williams and McKoy, together with three Tahitians, guided their boat through the sea to land on sharp but slippery boulders, grotesquely gnawed and perpetually drenched by surf. Then they pushed their way through the resistant undergrowth and began climbing the unwelcoming slopes, a glissade of rotting leaf and viscous red mud, the island's final protection against the wounds of men. For two days they fought their way around the towers and secret passages of this fortress. They must have seen most of the island in their uncomfortable, tense exploration. Ancient paths, made by someone or some animal long gone, were overgrown, narrow and easily lost. The mid-summer air was humid and enervating, for sea breezes do not penetrate the canopy. And there was the constant fear of angry animals or attacking men. But by the time they stumbled back onto *Bounty*, they knew Pitcairn was everything that they could wish for. There were mulberry trees for making cloth, candle-nut trees for light, pandanus palms for thatching. There was water. Fruit and vegetables grew wild and there were no animals, no mosquitoes. There were coconut trees in abundance and breadfruit, too. With the mangoes and plantains, oranges and sweet potatoes, hogs, goats and chickens aboard *Bounty*, they would live like tropical kings.

It was simple to follow the example of the unknown earlier inhabitants and choose to settle on the few relatively easier slopes that stretch about half a mile along the north-east coast, beginning just above the other, comparatively safe anchorage. There the remains of old gardens were most noticeable. The rich red earth was deep and well drained and water was close. Bounding one side of the site was a high peak, from which a lookout could be kept.

Everything Fletcher Christian had identified as crucial to his survival was here. The island was solitary, almost impregnable and uninhabited. It was also fertile, temperate rather than tropical, and it was unknown. Pitcairn signalled a new beginning for them all, far beyond practical expectations. For Fletcher Christian it promised the return of all he cherished, all he had abandoned. Here on Pitcairn, with a wife, with land, friends and freedom, he might once more live with dignity. It must truly have felt like Paradise found; but it was a fragile Paradise and it would shatter.

III

Serpents in Paradise

26

Roots

The early days on Pitcairn were hard. January is by far the hottest month of the southern summer, and although the temperature on Pitcairn rarely exceeds 90°F in the shade, this is burden enough when you are quickly relieving a 215-ton vessel of everything movable—animals, plants, provisions, fittings and tackle. As well, a tense, two-way watch was being kept. On land, signs of habitation were apparent everywhere, not recent certainly, but the island was so densely forested, so rugged, there was no sure way of knowing who or what might be hiding. While they were unloading the tattered ship, they were at their most vulnerable should they be spotted by another, for the masts and spars of a square-rigger are etched all too obviously against even the roughest lines of nature; but to remove them too soon would make escape impossible.

Day after wearying day, all hands were employed fetching and carrying, filling and emptying the boat that threaded its way over Bounty Bay's surf and through the treacherous rocks it concealed to the tiny arc of beach amidst the eastern hills. Tradition records that Teio's baby daughter, Sully, was taken ashore in a barrel, but I cannot see that this was safer than a boat. It soon became apparent to the group that a change in the weather could prove as disastrous as the crashing sea, at best delaying them for a few days, at worst exposing them to the fury of a hurricane, for this was the season. The longer the ship rode the waves, the greater the risks.

Bounty was run on to the rocks of Bounty Bay some way to the left of the beach, directly below a 700 foot peaked cliff, now named Ship Landing Point. A narrow flat shelf of fertile land gave way to the terrible half-hidden track that crawled perilously along the cliff-side. Even after this had been cleared of centuries of overgrowth, most men and women needed help to get up or down until new muscles and techniques developed. But at the top there were rewards aplenty.

Shelters had quickly been made of palm fronds and *Bounty*'s sails, hidden in the trees well back from the cliff edge. It is easy to imagine the moments of leisure they snatched amid the anxiety and pressure. After three and a half months of all-round deprivation since they left Tahiti on 23 September, they would again enjoy true privacy, eat fresh fruits and vegetables, bathe, drink fresh coconut milk or water—Brown, the gardener, had quickly discovered an excellent source close to the camp.

The seas were full of fish, the rocks encrusted with shellfish and alive with succulent crayfish. There were sea birds and their eggs. Now that the animals could be fed, fattened and bred properly, they could probably afford to slaughter a pig or goat for a gigantic pit-oven feast. How much the traditions of Polynesia dominated at this stage is unknown, but judging by Pitcairn today, there was some segregation of sexes at eating even though the taboo that prevented men and women touching the same cooking vessels and implements must have vanished aboard *Bounty*.

But the attractions of solid ground and of nature's liberality may not have been satisfaction enough for someone. On 23 January, less than two weeks after they had arrived, the ship was ablaze, her sun-bleached and warped timbers spurred to greater conflagration by the tar used on the decks and caulking. Was it an accident? This seems unlikely, and the ship must have been cleared, for no artifacts that would suggest otherwise have ever been recovered from the floor of Bounty Bay. Quintal is discredited with responsibility for the fire, over-anxious about discovery and retribution, possibly because there was some discussion about preserving the vessel. Abetted by constant sea breezes, the fire consumed *Bounty* down to the copper sheathing of her hull, and easily burned through the heavy hawsers of rope that had steadied her to trees. Apparently she drifted back and forth but the seas forced her to the shore; whether the hulk sank of her own accord or was holed by her erstwhile masters, the remains lie remarkably close to land in water less than ten feet deep. The twisting of the nails and sheets of copper recovered from the sea-bed bear testament to the brutality of the flames.

The finality of their situation can hardly have been lost on the twenty-eight stranded souls as they watched their only means of escape angrily devoured. They were thousands of miles from any-where, committed to doing what had only been spoken of; they had to settle on the island.

At an early stage, Pitcairn Island was divided equally between Fletcher Christian and his eight white companions: the six men from Tahiti, Tubuai, and Raiatea, some of them chiefs, were given no land. By one decision they became servants and labourers forever. It would be unfair to lay the blame for this unfortunate decision only on Fletcher Christian. Now the party was on land his authority was diminished and the group, mainly common seamen, expected a say in things. An entirely new social order was emerging, and dealing with it was probably difficult for an officer and a gentleman who had always known where he was with these men; but they saw new horizons. As simple seamen they had never had much to lose. As the landed gentry of a new Pacific kingdom, they had everything to gain by questioning the authority and position of others, including friends.

It is clear that McKoy and Quintal had brought Polynesians along as servants from the start and they at least were determined to follow a life of personal status and ease. Just as Fletcher was consciously or unconsciously creating for himself the estate denied him at home, his followers were establishing themselves as gentlemen of property, something barely possible and unlikely to have been tolerated in England.

The idea of democracy and the equality of men taking root in the newly independent states of America, and in France, had no place here. The taste of equality has always been sweetened by denying it to others. It is most likely that in dividing up the island among whites, Fletcher Christian was only partly acquiescing in the wishes of others. There was no precedent anywhere in the world for black men to be equal with white; things were revolutionary enough as it was.

Fletcher's Isabella became pregnant as soon as they made landfall, and by the time the baby was born on a Thursday in October 1790, the settlement had a routine of sorts, with couples taking turns to keep watch from Lookout Point, almost the highest on the island and just to the north-west of the village. Fires were lit only at night and the dogs had been killed, in case the smoke of one, or the noise of the other, advertised domestication where none should have been.

No pregnancies occurred during the four month trek about the South Pacific, and Fletcher and Isabella had been together on Tubuai for three months, too. But almost exactly nine months after they arrived on Pitcairn, the leader's wife gave birth, as though confirming a hierarchy. There must have been other pregnancies; it can only be assumed that all earlier ones were terminated by the Tahitians' deep-massage methods and by infanticide. It would have been impractical to be pregnant if the ship were ever endangered, or if stranded on another island, perhaps inhabited, with a half-caste child at the breast; white was by no means always associated with might on islands other than Tahiti.

The arrival of babies may be thought to have given a sense of permanence to the settlement; it is, rather, the other way about. Once they realized the settlement was permanent, it is probable that some Tahitian women were happy to do what was expected of them. Perhaps they too wanted the pleasures of bearing and keeping their children, instead of having them immolated before or immediately upon birth. The Tahitian women were not mute and obedient handmaidens. They too saw new freedoms for themselves, and pursued them passionately.

The first-born Pitcairner is almost as well known as his father Fletcher, mainly for the eccentricity of his name—Thursday October Christian. Because this name can only have been chosen by his father, it is a sad commentary on Fletcher's inability to accept his new life. Naming babies for the day they are born was a common form of protest among West Indian slaves. The idea of Thursday October's name as a quirky compromise between naming the boy in Tahitian or English cannot be supported, for no Pitcairn child was ever given a Polynesian name. It must also be remembered that though three Tahitian women were servicing six men of their own race, there was never a full-blooded Polynesian child born there, and this can only have been by design. What began as a preference for the attentions of white men eventually became an abhorrence of black men by the whole community, even though every native-born Pitcairner had the blood of Polynesian women.

It is not surprising that Fletcher Christian was suffering remorse for his actions which only now he had time to ponder. The birth of a son and heir must have reminded him of the family forbidden him forever, even by correspondence. Was he by now publicly branded a murderer? And if so, of how many men? To his own knowledge, well over sixty Polynesians had been killed as he searched for a home. It might be possible to excuse the battle deaths of the Pacific Islanders, but what about Bligh and the others? Were they alive or dead? Perhaps some of them had survived to tell the world—and his family—of the young man whose emotional turmoil had changed all their lives. Such mental agonies, for which there was no resolution, must have been deeply distressing and ample reasons for black depression. Yet there was precious little time for wallowing in self-pity; there were problems enough under Fletcher Christian's very nose.

It would have been strange indeed if there had been no clashes of temper, no equivalents of the ritual sprayings of territory by tomcats. There had never been a community like this before and each day meant either adjusting to the problems or hiding from them, both courses that required effort.

But for the moment, life was not too bad. Whereas ambition evaporated with indolence on Tahiti, fishing, farming and fencing prevented most quarrels on Pitcairn. Quintal and McKoy fathered sons, and Mills a daughter. In 1792, Isabella bore another son, Charles, and in late 1793, was due to give birth to her third child, the sixth on the island. It is apparent that in the early years on Pitcairn, most women were reluctant to bear children.

Once they had built more permanent homes, the mutineers are said to have given the canvas sails to their women, to make clothes. They were thrilled, for otherwise they had laboriously to manufacture their draperies of tapa, the bark cloth, which took weeks.

As the settlers explored and marked out gardens and animal pens, they found constant reminders of their predecessors who had left some time before 1350. They discovered countless stone chisels and hatchets, and a marae platform on which stood four stone images, each about six feet high. The idols were crude representations of the human form, as were those also found on the much bigger marae site on the steep western side of the island. But any religious significance was discounted by both Europeans and Polynesians, who used the stones as foundations for buildings. There were other piles of rocks about the island, whose sea-pounded smoothness indicated they had been dragged up the slopes with great labour. Beneath these cairns there was always a skeleton; indeed skeletons turned up in all manner of places and some of them had a pearl shell under their skulls. There are no pearl oysters around Pitcairn so this probably indicates that these men were from the island of Mangareva.

While Christian wondered about Bligh's fate, England was guessing the arrival date of *Bounty*, and Bligh was pondering how far the king would support him in pursuit of the criminals who had subjected him to trouserless indignity and an open boat voyage of Odyssean suffering. On 17 February 1790, the *Cumberland Pacquet* reported that *Bounty*, although 'retarded beyond the proposed period' was bound for the West Indies via Cape Horn, news that can only have come from Tahiti or from a journalistic surmise, based on knowledge of the earlier delays in 1788, but on ignorance of the return route *Bounty* was supposed to have taken. Nobody panicked when a sailing ship was overdue in those days, so there was no anxiety when 1789 dawned and progressed without word from the little ship; the world was totally unprepared for the story it was soon to hear.

27

'Bailing with horror and anxiety'

We left an astonished Bligh and eighteen companions making slowly for volcanic Tofua, where they were made anything but welcome. Norton was killed in a rock-throwing battle and they had to jettison extra clothes and equipment as temptations to their pursuers, thus deflecting them. News of Bligh's treatment of the Nomukan chiefs is thought to have preceded him and they were lucky to lose only one man. Thus warned of the dangers of these islands, Bligh announced to his frightened charges that he saw no hope of succour closer than Timor, some 1,200 leagues away.

This was 'Foul Weather Bligh' at his most magnificent. According to his assiduously kept notes he had on board 150 pounds of ship's biscuits, 28 gallons of water, 20 pounds of pork (presumably salted), 5 quarts of rum, 3 bottles of wine, some coconuts and some breadfruit. Conditions were so cramped that no one could lie down to rest, not even one at a time. Yet, he writes that:

> . . . all agreed to live on one ounce of bread and a quarter pint of water a day. Therefore, after examining our stock of provisions, and recommending this as a sacred promise for ever to their

memory, we bore away across the sea, where the navigation is but little known and in a small boat twenty-three feet long from stem to stern, deep loaded with eighteen men; without a chart, and nothing but my own recollection and general knowledge of the situation of places, assisted by a book of longitudes and latitudes to guide us. I was happy, however, to see everyone better satisfied with our situation in this particular than myself.

The confidence of these men in their ridiculed commander was well placed, for he did have knowledge of the area and was an ace navigator.

The misery of this boat voyage can scarcely be imagined. Bedevilled by rain for twenty-one out of forty-three days, they laboured towards the eastern Australian coast, weakened by hunger, tortured with bowel pains, and constipation, all carefully noted by Bligh in his impersonal manner. He meticulously divided each day's rations in makeshift scales of coconut shells with a bullet as a weight. Although they constantly trailed a line over the stern, they caught none of the fish they knew abounded beneath them.

With few words, Bligh summons up pictures of the dreadful conditions:

> ... so covered with rain and sea that we can scarce see or make use of our eyes ... Sleep, though we long for it, is horrible ... we suffer extreme cold and everyone dreads the approach of night ... the least error in the helm would in a moment be our destruction. The misery ... has exceeded the preceeding ... The sea flew over us with great force and kept us bailing with horror and anxiety ... another such night would produce the end of several.

By 25 May, after almost a month on the open sea, Bligh had to cut rations even further, which he described as feeling like taking life itself from his haggard companions. Four miserable days later, after negotiating the treacherous Great Barrier Reef, they landed on the Australian coast. As with any interlude in a difficult sea voyage, a change of mood overcame the men when they were on land. There were disagreements about the proportions of an oyster stew; someone stole several of the remaining few pounds of pork. There were even factions aboard the little boat; the majority supported Bligh; the rest looked to Fryer, the master, for leadership. There were constant complaints about who was collecting the most food, who was eating too much—the excusable petty niggles important only to men who, famished and dispirited, faced anonymous death for reasons not of their own making.

Further up the coast, on 31 May, Purcell's temper erupted into mutiny when he said to Bligh he was as good a man as he and that, anyway, they would not be here if it had not been for Bligh. Bligh wrote: 'I saw there was no carrying command with any certainty or Order but by power, for some had totally forgotten every degree of obedience'. Bligh had sympathy, yet it is natural that the men might doubt that his every command was right. No man likes to feel his life wholly dependent on just one other, even less so when the situation is so dramatic. If Bligh had such severe disciplinary problems with weak, undernourished men lacking firearms, it is not surprising that Fletcher Christian, on the other side of the Pacific, had to rule his stronger group by pistol. It is the way of seafaring men when on land, and 'the only wonder is those who wonder at it'. Henceforth, Bligh always carried a cutlass.

Bligh's manly courage at a time when he could have been murdered did little to encourage tighter order or respect. Yet, as well as having to contain passions that would turn even the most phlegmatic into an apoplectic, he had the self-discipline to write down regular reports, observations and sketches, noting details of current and coastline, fixing his daily position as well as he could.

Once the boat sailed away from the north-eastern tip of Australia and he and his companions were on the open sea again, Bligh noted it seemed as if they 'had only embarked with me to proceed to Timor, and were in a Vessel equally calculated for their safety and convenience'. Days later the condition of his men had weakened alarmingly, legs were swollen and there was much of the terrible sleepiness that often precedes the body's predisposition to surrender. Bligh, too, was becoming seriously ill.

On 12 June, Timor was at last sighted. Bligh wrote that it was scarcely believable that this should have taken only forty-one days. By his reckoning they had made about ninety miles a day. But if land was in sight, co-operation and comradeship were not. Fryer and Purcell demanded that they should land immediately, a patently absurd thing to do on an island both unknown and inhabited by tribesmen; still they were filthy, starving and exhausted and to be denied respite when so close to land must have been agonizing. In a nice turn of phrase and using further reserves of courage, Bligh severely reprimanded the master, telling him 'he would be dangerously troublesome if it were not for his ignorance and lack of resolution'. A few hours later Peckover and Cole were sent in to a small settlement where they learned that Kupang was just along the coast, and a local agreed to tow the boat there once he had sight of Bligh's parcel of Rix dollars, some of the money the Admiralty had given him to buy additional plants for the West Indies and Kew Gardens from this part of the world.

The pitiful cargo was towed into Kupang as day broke on 14 June.

Bligh's attention to detail and duty now assumed the trappings of a fully mature mania. For even though he and his men were desperately ill, he raised a pennant of distress and prepared to wait at sea for formal permission to land. The signal was quickly spotted, fortunately, and there was little delay in landing, upon which Bligh was astonished to be greeted in English by a sailor from his own country. The sailor's commander, a Captain Spikerman, organized an English breakfast—with pots of tea—and asked Bligh to invite his men up, too. Extraordinarily, Bligh ordered Fryer to remain on board to watch the little boat and its meagre contents. As Bligh had belongings in the boat, Fryer demanded that Bligh's servant, John Smith, should also remain.

The two deserted and starving men were noticed and brought a kettle of tea and some small cakes by a soldier. Fryer, moved to tears by the man's thoughtfulness, began to thank him in Dutch but was surprised when the man answered in English. His father was English and he liked people from England, he said.

It was some hours before Dutch soldiers told Captain Spikerman that there were two men still in the boat. He was amazed, thinking the breakfast party in his house represented the intrepid little boat's full complement. Tea and bread were immediately sent out, but only the tea was ingested as the two men sensibly felt that to eat too much would endanger their health further. There now being little else to do but wait, Fryer shaved himself. Learning that Smith did not think himself capable of doing the same to his own very large black growth, Fryer set to and within a half hour had given the man a smooth and clear face. He adds, 'all this time I might have gone to the devil for my good friend Captain Bligh'.

In describing the events that found him in a part of the world he never expected to be, Bligh noted his disappointment in Ellison, saying he felt he had been run down by his own dogs. He makes enigmatic reference to a problem with Hallet and Hayward, but never expanded. It is clear that nothing deflected him from his impression that the mutiny had been planned, and by a large group.

The Governor, Adrian van Este, was sick, but put a big house at Bligh's disposal. Bligh had to invite his haggard crew to share it, for there was no other comfortable space available. Bligh continued his manic industry, quickly laying down the foundations of his defence as he began making statements to his hosts, writing a full report of the mutiny, descriptions of the mutineers and letters of excuse. He had plenty of time. Inquiries showed they would have to sail to Batavia to ensure passage to England, and Batavia was 1,800 miles away. Such a sea voyage was inconceivable with his men in the condition they were. For two months the men convalesced and Bligh self-righteously crammed his logbook with the minutiae of life in the settlement; history, growing rice, Chinese burial customs, the slave trade and market prices. On 18 July, David Nelson, the botanist, who had been collecting breadfruit shoots, died after an attack of fever, and Bligh seems to have been touched by his death.

It was not until the day before they sailed for Batavia that Bligh wrote to Betsy, his wife. His expectation of sympathy in this letter is obvious, but understandable; his other priorities of money and position are neatly woven into a missive that is a masterful manipulation of events and the reader's emotions. When observing Bligh at this time and over the next year or two, it is only fair to remember that he was doing more than fighting for his reputation, he was fighting for his future. When I first heard Bligh had sailed from Kupang with a collection of plants, including more breadfruit, I thought it a sad attempt to prove his worth to his masters. This was unfair. Bligh's was a typical eighteenth-century mind whose overriding curiosity gave the world so much of value.

After a month at sea in *Resource* which he had bought at Kupang, towing *Bounty*'s launch, they reached Surabaya and Purcell and Fryer were misbehaving again; this time Bligh marched them below at bayonet point. It seems Bligh's men were expecting to be treated better than usual, considering the hardships they had endured. Bligh might have been compliant; but when he sent for Dutch officials to come to his aid in dealing with the two men, he learned that calumny had been spread in the township, suggesting Bligh would be hanged or blown from a cannon's mouth when he returned to England.

Next day a court of inquiry made up of the Dutch army

commander, a captain and the master attendant of the port put questions, wrote down answers and had the proceedings certified. Fryer accused Bligh of overcharging the Admiralty for items purchased in Kupang and produced a paper that seemed to implicate Governor van Este in the slander. Bligh countered by producing his receipts and vouchers which had been signed by Fryer himself, as well as by the boatswain and two respectable residents of Kupang. Fryer begged forgiveness, ending a note to Bligh, 'if matters can be made up, I beg you will forward it'. But Fryer had done him wrong in Kupang, too, where he had suggested that no bill would be honoured by the Admiralty if it had only Bligh's signature. The two men were then reduced to the silliness of communicating solely by letter. Now Fryer wanted assurance that Bligh would forgive. Bligh would not, and wrote back saying he was too busy to see him. Purcell and Fryer were put onto separate Dutch ships, which would also be sailing on to Batavia. Bligh did visit Fryer eventually, only to hear more disavowals of the infamous reports he had spread, then ordered the convoy to sail. At Samarang on 22 September, Fryer apologized properly and was released but Purcell remained in irons until they reached Batavia on 1 October.

Here, Bligh soon became feverish. His condition deteriorated, so he obtained a medical certificate to prove it and to explain his haste in departing and leaving the rest of the men in Fryer's charge; he had a piece of paper to account for his every action. All he could raise for the *Resource* and the launch was $295.

It was 16 October before he sailed with Samuel and Smith, his two servants, on the *Vlydte*. By now Thomas Hall, the ship's cook, had died and before the rest of the group departed, Elphinstone and Linkletter also perished. Robert Lamb died during his passage home and Ledward was never seen again—he might have jumped ship or been drowned. Of the nineteen men who were turned off *Bounty*, twelve returned to England.

On 14 March 1790, Bligh landed on the Isle of Wight, and days later arrived in London. The interest in his story was enormous, but publicity was not necessarily what Bligh wanted. It was more important that Sir Joseph was still prepared to support him. After receiving letters from Bligh, Banks was persuaded to put the best face on it, for he, too, was no happy man so long as the breadfruit plants were in the South Pacific.

The press had a heyday and soon most people knew about the mutiny and the boat voyage. Bligh had only adulation and sympathy, not an unreasonable initial reaction.

Quite what Fletcher Christian's immediate family made of Bligh's story is largely unrecorded, but one of the supposed results that has been widely advertised is quite untrue; his first cousin John Christian XVII did not change his name to John Christian Curwen because of the mutiny. The announcement of both events was simultaneous, which may have led to the confusion. A simple attention to relevant records explains the matter. The *Cumberland Pacquet* for 3 March 1790 records: 'Mr Christian of Workington will shortly take the name of Curwen. His Majesty's Royal Licence and permission respecting same will probably be announced in the next Gazette [the official court newspaper]'. On March 17th it was announced that the change had been celebrated 'by a large party of principal inhabitants at the Indian King on Monday last'. John had been preparing for the change for some time and had formalized the Christians' coat of arms in 1788. It is fatuous to suggest that John Christian had tried to hide behind a new name for shame. He was already far too well known as a politician to hide behind any name and anyway always retained Christian as part of his surname. He was simply getting things straight between his two families.

The next issue of the *Cumberland Pacquet* on 24 March contains the news of the mutiny. Although John Christian Curwen is mentioned in the same issue there is no linking of the two and of all the *Cumberland Pacquets* I read which mentioned *Bounty* or Fletcher Christian, there were few that did not also mention his first cousin.

As a rich and famous MP, John had news value, but no one connected him publicly with his mutinous first cousin.

The only first-hand account we have of a family member's reaction comes from Charles Christian, Fletcher's mutinous surgeon brother. By 1790 he was in Hull, where he says he was well known for 'the successful Extirpation of two Women's Breasts, one just broken into an open cancerous state, the other an immense excruciating painful schirrous Enlargement . . .' He continued though to have trouble with the jealousies of others and writes of the latest intrigue which involved 'the circulation of . . . malicious poetic productions' to the effect that Charles had gotten a widow pregnant, then arranged her marriage to another man so he would not have to care for the child. He writes:

> When my mind was in a state of extreme soreness from the invidious and malignant attack by a villain whom I had never spoken to, came the heart-rending account of the *Bounty*'s mutiny.
>
> I was struck with horror and weighed down with a Sorrow to so extreme a pitch that I became stupified. It was hard to bear, but I thank God, strength was given to me equal to the burden.
>
> I knew that this unfortunate occurrence, following so close on the heels of my late eventful and disastrous voyage [in *Middlesex*], would occasion the lies which had been spread abroad in consequence to assume the aspect of Truth. I have in bed perspired with agony of mind till I thought my nostrils were impressed with a smell of Death—such was the peculiar sensation I experienced.

There was similarly melodramatic, but more serious, reaction by another brother. According to genealogical notes written in the nineteenth-century transcript of the diary of the boys' first cousin Jane Christian Blamire, Humphrey, 'then at a station on the coast of Africa, being in very bad health, died shortly after reading the account of the mutiny'. Edward, by now a Fellow of St John's and confirmed as a Professor of the Laws of England at Downing, appears to have made no immediate comment.

When Charles recovered he wrote to Dr Betham, William Bligh's father-in-law and

> ... firmly prophecied that it would be found that there had been some Cause not then known that had driven Fletcher to this desperate step. I was enabled to form the just presage from what I had so recently observed possible to occur on Board of Ship where Strife and Discord prevailed. I told Betham that my feelings were so harrowed up with this unlooked for and unhappy intelligence that I would have him consider that instead of Ink, it was my Heart's Blood I wrote with.

This sanguine exertion in pursuit of an early identification of the truth was in vain. For Betham had died of 'dropsy of the breast and terminated his existence by suffocation' almost a year earlier, on 3 June 1789. This was one champion Bligh would sorely miss.

With the undue haste that scandal excites in the thespian world, the Royalty Theatre in London dramatized the events with *The Pirates! or The Calamities of Captain Bligh*; you could see *Bounty* sailing down the Thames, an Otaheitian Dance, the seizure of Bligh, the distress of the boat at sea, their miraculous arrival and friendly reception. In the interests of drama the latter two events are said to have happened at the Cape of Good Hope (which would indeed have been a journey to write about!) so that the final scene was one of the Hottentot dances and ceremonies on their departure. Most intriguing of all was the final line of the bill poster, 'Rehearsed under the immediate Instruction of a Person who was on-board the *Bounty*, Store-ship'. A short time later a Parisian company went further and set the whole spectacle to music.

In June, Bligh's first book, *A Narrative of the Mutiny on board His Majesty's Ship Bounty*, was published by the Admiralty, obviously cashing in on the best story of the century, too.

By 21 July, the news had sped across the Atlantic to the United States. On that date the *Columbian Centinel*, printed and published on State Street, Boston, Massachusetts, devoted more than a column to the story. (On the front page President George Washington was announcing that monies collected during 1789 by Congress were to be used to pay arrears to officers, non-commissioned officers and privates for services in the years 1782 and 1783; another announced the imposition of a duty on goods imported into the United States via the State of Rhode Island and Providence Estates.)

By 2 October, Robert Dodd had painted and then engraved what was to become one of the most famous images of the period, that of Bligh with hair streaming down his back standing in the launch, a protective hand raised as he looks at a man whom we can only presume is Christian, standing high on the stern of *Bounty* with his cutlass laid back on his right shoulder; in contrast, the others on the ship are brandishing their arms wildly. The picture raises an interesting point.

The engraving (far better known than the original which is in private hands) is dedicated to the West India Planters and Merchants who had started the whole venture, and the purchaser is referred for further information to Bligh's *Narrative*; so it has some claim to being an official, or at least approved, image. The face of Bligh is not unlike some of his portraits and considering the interest in the story, Dodd seems likely to have consulted Bligh for his blessing and advice. Allowing for the vagaries of the engraver's instrument, are we also seeing Bligh's recollection of Fletcher Christian? If so, it is the only image we have of him; I look at my hand-coloured original of the engraving, still in its eighteenth-century frame and glass, and wonder if I am looking at my great-great-great-great-grandfather.

Much later I realised this picture could have another significance, hidden to us but well recognised by savvy Georgian society who were used to gross cartoons from caricaturist Thomas Rowlandson and others. This is not an accurate image of *Bounty*. In a complicated visual pun, Christian stands precisely where the real *Bounty* had a private long-drop lavatory for Bligh's use—you can see it clearly on the conversion plans and in sketches of the completed ship. It might just be artistic licence, but it could also be wicked visual comedy by Dodd, even if only Bligh and his shipmates understood the barb.

Bligh had to face a formal court martial for the loss of *Bounty*, which was held at Spithead on 22 October 1790, well after artists of canvas and stage had trumpeted heroically on his behalf.

He was then obliged to state whether or not he wished to charge any of the officers or men among the eleven survivors now in England. Details of his low opinion of Fryer and Purcell had been published in his *Narrative*. Thus, it might be thought he would have charged Fryer, but he did not, seriously diminishing his published criticisms of the man, which were common knowledge. Purcell, less highly ranked, was charged on six counts but the prosecution was so mild he earned only a reprimand. Was Bligh being conciliatory? Had he mellowed after his harrowing experiences? It was more likely he was protecting his career by avoiding long trials in which the accused might make counter accusations. The advice of others must have swayed him; and one of these must have been Banks.

Not unnaturally, relatives of the men who had not returned with Bligh wrote asking for news of their sons, husbands and fathers. In the few of Bligh's replies that survive wounded vanity is venomously compressed into a few words. Peter Heywood's mother, recently widowed, received the following:

> London, April 2nd, 1790
> Madam, I received your letter this day and feel for you very much, being perfectly sensible of the extreme distress you must suffer from the conduct of your son Peter. His baseness

is beyond all description, but I hope you will endeavour to prevent the loss of him, heavy as the misfortune is, from afflicting you too severely. I imagine he is with the rest of the mutineers, returned to Otaheite . . .

To Colonel Holwell, an uncle of Peter Heywood, he wrote:

. . . your nephew Peter Heywood is amongst the mutineers. His ingratitude to me is of the blackest dye, for I was a father to him in every respect, and he never once had an angry word from me through the whole course of the voyage, as his conduct always gave me much pleasure and satisfaction. I very much regret that so much baseness formed the character of a young man I had real regard for, and it will give me much pleasure to hear his friends can bear the loss of him without much concern.

This really puts an end to the idea that Bligh was a humanitarian. He moans for sympathy rather than giving information, ever the wounded, never the wounder. And worse, he was vilifying a young man unable to defend himself. When that was a possibility—as with Fryer and Purcell—Bligh stood back and said nothing.

On 24 October, Bligh wrote to reassure Banks he had been honourably acquitted at the court martial. He said he had held back some of the evidence against Purcell, 'for it threatened his life'—surprising in view of Bligh's vindictiveness in print.

Bligh went from Spithead to Lord Chatham, who assured him he would be promoted to post captain as soon as Chatham had seen the king; Bligh proudly added in his 24 October letter to Banks that he was to be presented to His Majesty on Wednesday. An enigmatic section in the letter seems to show that Banks and Bligh were not on the best terms. Bligh writes, 'I am concerned at losing your kind assistance just at this time . . .' but nevertheless makes suggestions about how Banks might help his promotion. Why and how Bligh had lost his assistance is not explained.

Bligh was presented to King George III, who was enjoying a spell of popularity and clarity between losing the American colonies permanently and misplacing his reason temporarily. He was quickly promoted to commander and then to post captain, the usual conditions of service being waived.

Bligh and Betsy and the girls lived for five more months on the £600 given him by the Jamaican Government in commiseration, plus half pay. On 16 April 1791, Banks had him appointed commander of a new breadfruit expedition. His ensuing absence prevented both offenders and offended from receiving a fair and balanced trial in courts, ward rooms or drawing-rooms. Mutiny was common at the time, and it was just as common for mutineers to countercharge their captain and for him to be punished as harshly as he had expected the mutineers to be. The Navy was the Senior Service and, although not always the case, an appearance of fairness and justice was vital for the security of the nation. If Bligh had been present at the trials, history and his future are likely to have been markedly different, and that would have reflected very badly on Sir Joseph Banks, for his judgment, too, would be called into question.

I think Banks was aware of the danger of too much countercharging which would be just as troublesome for him as for Bligh. After all *Bounty* should have had marines, the ship should have been bigger, it should have had fewer 'gentlemen' aboard. If blame eventually had to be attached to the organizers rather than to Bligh, the opprobrium would certainly be attached to Banks; he had written so before *Bounty* sailed. It was better for all if Bligh were out of the way, and it is not unlikely that he was persuaded to go in return for promises of continued patronage by Banks and further promotion.

It did not work out quite like that. The second breadfruit expedition was successful—apart from the exasperating refusal of the

West Indian slaves to eat the stuff—but when Bligh returned from his third South Pacific voyage he found public opinion had swung heavily against him. It never swung back and it was largely his own fault; he thought he had told the truth about the mutiny—but it was not the whole truth, nor was it nothing but the truth, and he had been discovered.

28

Pursuit and Capture

George III was easily persuaded to order Fletcher Christian to be pursued; the newspapers reported his decision as early as 24 March 1790, ten days after Bligh's return. For this task the Admiralty appointed Captain Edward Edwards, a martinet if ever there was one, but a commander who in no way equalled the talent of Bligh as navigator. Bligh arrogantly doubted Edwards' ability even to find his way to and from Tahiti, and said so publicly.

Edwards' expedition sailed in *Pandora*, a frigate of 24 guns and 160 men; it resulted in the apprehension of a few of the fugitives, but it cost almost as many men as had originally sailed on *Bounty*, and was a far more horrid illustration of the barbarity of the Royal Navy than conditions on *Bounty* had been.

Edwards is not a reliable source for details of the voyage. Both Morrison and Heywood furnish us with accounts of their treatment—or lack of it—at the hands of this man, treatment which John Barrow, Second Secretary to the Admiralty, described as having 'a rigour which could not be justified on any ground of necessity or prudence'. Edwards based his justification on something other than necessity or prudence: fear of another mutiny. Edwards had been the object of one himself in 1782 aboard HMS *Narcissus*. Six of the mutineers were hanged, one sentenced to 500 lashes and another to 200.

Pandora anchored in Matavai Bay on 23 March 1791, after rounding the Horn and sailing close enough to Pitcairn to have warranted investigation; but Edwards ignored it. Edwards' success must have seemed assured in the first hours of his visit to Tahiti. Straight away, Coleman put out in a canoe and although he was almost drowned when the canoe capsized, he climbed aboard. To his astonishment he was arrested. Next George Stewart and Peter Heywood arrived in a double canoe. They asked for Thomas Hayward, *Bounty*'s sleepy midshipman, now a third lieutenant whom they had been told was sailing with Edwards, and expected him to protest their innocence. But they were disappointed. Heywood wrote later, 'he (like all worldlings when raised a little in life) received us very coolly and pretended ignorance of our affairs!' Stewart and Heywood were clapped in irons. Then the unsuspecting Skinner arrived and joined them in bondage.

Ten more *Bounty* men remained on Tahiti. They were all in Papara, acting as mercenaries and helping prepare for a major massacre. Just as Christian's force had been embroiled in Tubuaian politics, the men he had left behind on Tahiti became involved in the inter-clan squabbles there. With arms and ammunition they were a prize beyond price for any man with ambition, and were used to help permanently change the social structure of Tahiti.

Edwards knew enough about Tahiti to note there was no important man among those welcoming him. Teina, father of Tu, was nowhere to be seen. He was in hiding, in fear of his life. His brother, Ariipaea, was in charge of his district and acting as regent for Tu, still only seven years old.

When Christian sailed away in September 1789, Ariipaea quickly realized the value of the abandoned men, and tried to entice as many as possible to Pare, the district of his clan and site of the second breadfruit camp. At first, only five were tempted by his offers of land—Muspratt, Hillbrant, Byrne, McIntosh and Norman. The others stayed closer to Point Venus. Morrison, who somehow became the acknowledged leader, actually lived with Poeno, chief of Matavai district; and so did Millward, who had formed a liaison with one of the chief's wives.

Stewart and Peter Heywood—perhaps because of their officer status—stuck together, remaining slightly aloof from much of what was to follow. They stayed close to Matavai, with another chief; and Stewart was married in Polynesian fashion to that chief's daughter. Heywood was conspicuously industrious about establishing himself as a Tahitian squire. He set up his own household at the foot of a small hill, the top of which afforded him a fine and useful lookout post. The garden and avenue to the house were well tended and planted with decorative and useful trees and plants, the first amalgam of Polynesian vegetation and the English cottage garden.

Conscious of their status as visitors, and perhaps heeding the advice of the diplomatically astute Hitihiti, all the men went to pay their respects to the boy Tu, whose full name, says Morrison, was something like Toonoeaiteatooa. They wore, and then shed in his presence, cloth shoulder mantles, gave gifts of iron, and handed over the household gods from Tubuai. Churchill was sent off to find and pay his respects to Tu's father, Teina.

Morrison quickly decided a boat should be built in which they could sail home. He was joined by everyone but Heywood and Stewart, who were prepared to wait for the man-of-war they knew would eventually be sent from England. On 12 November 1789, the keel was laid for a thirty foot vessel, which the men had to convince their Tahitian hosts was purely for pleasure and for sailing around the coast. If the Tahitians suspected the men wished to sail away, they would have done everything to hinder the construction for they wanted their fire-power for battle. For three months the Englishmen laboured incessantly, exciting the astonishment of the local men and women, not only by their craftsmanship but also by their application to toil for so long a period.

Then Thompson shot a Tahitian, and the child he was holding, after the man had ignored Thompson's command to leave the boat builders alone. Thompson considered it expedient to move into the interior, accompanied by Churchill, who shortly afterwards became a chief when his blood-brother or *taio* died. His new-found status was of little advantage. After Thompson discovered Churchill had arranged the theft of his muskets (for self protection) he shot the white chief through the back. Although Churchill was unpopular, and his theft of the muskets had been exposed by a Tahitian he had ill-treated, his murder had to be avenged by his subjects. Thompson was pinned to the ground with a branch of wood across his neck and his brains beaten out with stones.

With the two violent men gone, the boat builders worked in peace. By 30 April, the boat was fully planked and the gum of the breadfruit was laboriously collected for caulking. On 5 August, the vessel, complete with bowsprit, masts, booms and a rudder, was blessed by priests who threw boughs of plantain over her. It took half an hour of vigorous pushing to move her the three-quarters of a mile to the sea. Then she was christened with cider they had made and named *Resolution*, a sensible reminder to their hosts that they were associated with the great Cook.

Trouble with finding suitable sails—not even the local matting worked—meant Morrison had to abandon his attempt to sail first to Batavia and then to England. But *Resolution* soon had other voyages to make, other tasks to perform.

In September, an entirely new battle was to be fought on Tahiti. The forces of Teina and Tu, encouraged by the way their European allies had carried the day in previous skirmishes, now planned more decisive military action. While engaging their enemy on land in the traditional way, they also attacked from the sea with a fleet of forty canoes, assisted by *Resolution*. The Parean forces triumphed. Teina felt he could now move even further towards dominating the island.

One of the spoils of his victory was a *maro ura*, a simple plaited belt of pandanus leaves decorated with red feathers, as significant as the English sovereign's sceptre and orb, for it was a symbol of power and position. Change of ownership whether by inheritance or force was accompanied by a ceremony in which lesser chiefs acknowledged their new allegiance. There were a number of such belts on Tahiti, and only a few people swore fealty to each holder. But the *maro ura* that the Teina clan had just won had belonged to a highly important family. This, combined with the courage given him by English musketry, convinced Teina to do something never before attempted. He sent his son Tu around the entire island so that every chieftain could pay homage to him, thereby acknowledging him as first paramount chief or king.

Undoubtedly flattered by the political and military importance with which they found themselves endowed, all the Englishmen attended the first of these ceremonies and to the *maro ura* was now added a new regal symbol—a feather-decorated Union Jack. The boy, the belt and his flag progressed around the island with little trouble and less true submission. To underline what had happened, Teina proclaimed that all the island's chiefs should also come to his marae to acknowledge formally the supremacy of Prince Tu. There was never any question that this would work. But Teina simply wanted to identify those chiefs who were not his allies and friends.

On 13 February, on a newly consecrated piece of ground, the great ceremony took place. Tu was invested with the belt. Three human victims were among the offerings from the loyal island of Moorea. Their eyes were removed as the boy sat with his mouth open, a symbol, it is thought, of ancient cannibalistic rites. The rest of the loyal chiefs followed, bringing their own sacrifices of one or two bodies according to the size of their territories. The total was thirty corpses, some of which had been killed a month before.

The absence of the chieftains who would have nothing to do with Teina's *folie de grandeur* was happily taken to be mortally insulting to Tu, and the *Bounty* men began to help with plans to defeat them. Heywood, Stewart, Cole and Skinner refused to have anything to do with these machinations.

The plan was for all Teina's followers to gather for a celebration in the Papara district close to that of their enemies. The festivities would hide the positioning of a large attacking force backed by *Resolution*. However, they had hardly finished a tremendous banquet on 24 March when a messenger arrived with the news that an English sailing ship had anchored in Matavai Bay.

Resolution's crew of Europeans first panicked and sailed out of the lagoon. Only Byrne refused to go, and fuddled his way back to Matavai Bay. The home-made ship was unprepared for a lengthy voyage and soon sailed ignominiously back to Papara. The Tahitians were now torn between saving the extraordinarily useful vessel, and saving their friends. They also kept an eye on *Pandora* in case it could offer bigger and better rewards. Some of *Bounty*'s men hid in the mountains. Morrison, Norman and young Tom Ellison remained on *Resolution* but were quickly arrested by Tahitians, who did not want their new warship damaged in any attempt to capture their erstwhile friends.

Morrison's trio was helped to escape, found one of *Pandora*'s boats, and were as surprised as the rest to be put into irons. Norman, like Coleman, expected Bligh to have spoken up for them. In fact he had, but not strongly enough, and Edwards was ordered to treat all the men he found as mutineers. The opportunist Teina came to offer his help in rounding up the rest of the Europeans, but he was not needed.

Teina quickly saw that his hegemonistic aspirations were dashed and begged Edwards to take him away. The captain refused, and once more Teina had to head for the hills. Tahiti returned to its previous state of petty clandoms. But young Tu and his advisers had learned from the experience. By careful cultivation of the English captains and missionaries who subsequently came to the island, and the building of a loyal body of mercenaries, Tu eventually did conquer the entire island and founded the Pomare dynasty, which later sold out to the French 'for protection against the English'.

The men from *Bounty* were treated insufferably. They were chained and forbidden to speak in English or Tahitian under pain or instant death. Edwards was terrified that his own crew would be persuaded to mutiny. The hammocks they were given were verminous; they were unable to change their clothes because they were bound so tightly. The foul air and enervating temperature of their floating prison must have been torture enough to men who had so recently been free in the perfumed air of Tahiti; but enforced silence and lice made it intolerable.

Edwards was not certain the prisoners were fully secure and ordered the construction of the infamous 'Pandora's box'. On the after part of the ship's quarterdeck, 18 feet by 11 feet and only just taller than a man, the box was entered by a scuttle less than 2 foot square and had only two scuttles 9 inches square for ventilation. Iron grates effectively halved the amount of air that could pass. The box held fourteen men who were constantly protected by a musical comedy trio; two guards stood on top and a midshipman marched around the four sides. When the weather was calm the heat was so intense that sweat ran from the suffering men in streams to the scuppers. When it rained they were soaked. Nothing stayed wholesome, so they preferred to sit and sleep naked on the bare deck. For their personal functions there were two basins. The prisoners were allowed all the food their friends brought them, but the foul conditions must have killed much of their appetites.

This unwarranted torture continued for two months while *Pandora* was refitted. George Stewart was so shaken by the tormented cries of his wife he begged she should never to allowed to come aboard again. Even good behaviour did not stimulate any remorse or sympathy in Edwards. When McIntosh's leg slipped out of irons, as he slept, everyone's irons were tightened further. When their wrists began to swell they were told the handcuffs were 'not meant to fit like gloves'.

Pandora sailed out of Matavai with her pitiful cargo on 8 May 1791. Edwards had to try to find Christian but had only faint suspicions and rumours to go on. At the beginning of August he gave up and ran for home. When near the Great Barrier Reef, he foolishly made inadequate safety precautions one night and *Pandora* ran aground, tumbling her terrified, manacled prisoners upon one another. Somehow they managed to shatter their irons, but they were bound again. Though the water rose higher and higher, more guards were placed over the prisoners. Unbelievably, Edwards ordered them to be shot or hanged if their irons were broken again. By six-thirty in the morning it was apparent that *Pandora* was lost. Edwards finally gave the order to abandon ship and jumped over the side with his officers, giving the order for the prisoners to be released.

An armourer's mate scrambled into the box. Muspratt, Skinner and Byrne struggled out first, but then a ghastly turn of fate occurred. The master-at-arms, who seems to have been even more heartless than Edwards and unaware of his order, closed the hatchway. The moment he did this the ship lurched and threw him overboard. The prisoners were locked in again—with the man who was to release them. The ship was sinking but the armourer's mate worked in a frenzy to unshackle the men. At the very last minute William Moulter, a sailor, shouted to the prisoners that he would release them or go down with them and wrenched the bolt off the hatchway. Amazingly, everyone escaped but Hillbrant, who was still fully shackled.

When Edwards finally arranged a roll-call on a sandbank three miles from the wreck he found thirty-five of his men had been lost including four prisoners—George Stewart, Hillbrant, Skinner and Sumner.

Edwards' vile treatment of the prisoners continued. They were naked, but were refused permission to shelter from the fiery sun under a sail. Rather than expose themselves to severe sunburn and sunstroke they were forced to bury themselves in sand. As scape-goats for the entire disaster, the *Bounty*'s men were cruelly and ruthlessly treated as Edwards led a hungry and thirsty flotilla of four open boats containing ninety-nine men across the sea to Kupang. For the odious Hayward it was his second such arrival there.

It was not until the prisoners were aboard HMS *Gorgon* in March 1792 in Cape Town that they were treated with any humanity at all. They arrived at Spithead on 19 June, and shortly afterwards transferred to HMS *Hector* in Portsmouth Harbour.

29

Fire and Water

Of the twenty-five men left on *Bounty* when Bligh was turned off, only ten were to be tried. Some should not have been but Bligh had forgotten to speak up, or did not do so loudly enough. For three months they were confined aboard HMS *Hector* in Portsmouth harbour. Things were not too bad, for they were allowed writing paper and ink and some visitors. Some were astonishingly industrious. Morrison composed his *Memorandums*, wrote his own defence and helped others construct theirs. He was also working on his *Journal*, an astonishing record of all his experiences since December 1787. He had plenty of time and help from the others; Heywood was working on his dictionary of the Tahitian language.

It was difficult for the prisoners or their counsel to plan suitable defences since Bligh could not be cross-examined. After reading Bligh's *Narrative*, which was admissible as evidence because it was 'official', they knew they would have a great uphill battle. Public opinion was decidedly against them, and Peter Heywood, the only officer to be tried, particularly expected to be made an example.

Two days after Edwards' court martial for the loss of *Pandora*, which clearly showed there was no sympathy for the men of the *Bounty*, not even the ones Bligh conceded were innocent, the ten survivors were brought to trial aboard HMS *Duke*. On 12 September 1792, each was charged with 'mutinously running away with the said armed vessel (*Bounty*) and deserting from His Majesty's Service'. If they were found guilty, death was the sentence, but recommendations for mercy could and would be heeded.

The minutes of the trial are a treasure trove of fact. What was said was taken very seriously at the time, as it should be now. Much detail from the trial has been incorporated into my narrative of the mutiny and I hope it will now suffice if I briefly describe what happened to each prisoner.

Peter Heywood was doubly damned, by Bligh's acts of commission and omission, especially when the captain did not publish in his public versions of the mutiny some lines from his original manuscript. The most relevant was: 'As for the officers . . . they endeavoured to come to my assistance, but were not allowed to put their heads above the hatchway.' If Bligh had published that sentence, his story that everyone left on board was associated with the mutiny would not have been sustained. Allowing the suppression of the sentence was as foul a piece of unfounded spite as the letter he had written to Heywood's frantic, widowed mother.

Heywood was further damned by the evidence of Hayward, who, overlooking his own tearful begging to stay aboard, said he supposed Peter Heywood *must* have been a mutineer, simply because he stayed. Hallet said he saw Heywood laughing when Bligh spoke to him on the brief occasion that Heywood had come on deck to see what was happening. Both these men later expressed remorse for their statements. Nor was Heywood helped by the defence statement read on his behalf and written by his counsel. It was mawkish, relying largely on appeals of youthful indiscretion rather than hard evidence which clearly showed he was forced to remain below. There was just enough suspicion of collusion, based mainly on the extraordinary idea that this boy should have led a counter-revolt, for him to be found guilty, but recommended for mercy.

The king heeded this request and Peter Heywood was granted a free pardon on 24 October; later there were some legal wrangles which resulted in the declaration that the King's Warrant was not so much a pardon for a crime committed as a quashing of the conviction. Heywood went on to a distinguished career in the Navy; but first he quickly told Fletcher Christian's family the truth about *Bounty*. Having himself been a victim of Bligh's post-mutiny malice, he did everything he could to prevent his friend Fletcher Christian being damned more than necessary; he was honourably keeping a promise he had made the last time he saw Fletcher Christian.

Morrison was found guilty, but also given a free pardon, for various reasons. Norman, Coleman and McIntosh were acquitted, as was the fiddler Byrne, but given no compensation for their appalling time aboard *Pandora*.

There was too much evidence against young Ellison so the court did not feel they could take his age into consideration. The verdict of guilty was not accompanied by a recommendation for mercy. The most convincing statement against him was made by Hayward, who said he saw Ellison arm himself and run towards Bligh saying, 'Damn him I'll be sentry over him.'

Burkitt, who had equivocated and covered Bligh's exposed genitals, found that this was not enough to outweigh his having been with Christian when Bligh was seized. He was convicted, and so was Millward, who had stood guard over Fryer while the master was detained in his cabin. Muspratt was also convicted but he had been defended by Stephen Barney, who was responsible for transcribing minutes of the court martial's prosecution proceedings. Barney managed to get Muspratt discharged because there was a technical irregularity in his trial.

The pardoning of Heywood, in particular, has been put down to family influence. This may be true to some extent, but it is in no way unusual for a young man to wish to live, or for his family to support him in this. Although the death sentence was mandatory for many crimes in both the civil and martial courts of the eighteenth century, there were thousands of precedents for it not being carried out. It has been estimated that fewer than fifty per cent of those sentenced to death in the civil courts were actually executed. All that was needed for a reprieve were connections, but not necessarily in high places. A mother, a brother, or anyone else of honest and industrious standing in the community, could vouch that they had some need or care for the condemned person. This was all the 'connection' the courts looked for. The only people who could be assured of execution were those for whom no one spoke up. Of course, money and titles helped, but thousands of men and women who had no access to either escaped the death penalty simply because they had friends.

No friend was prepared to speak up for Ellison, Burkitt or Millward.

On 29 October 1792, the three men were hanged publicly aboard HMS *Brunswick*. Seamen from every other naval ship in the port were present. Millward is said to have made the following stirring and penitential speech to the assembled tars. It sounds unlikely, but several people vouch for its veracity; perhaps it was penned by Morrison.

Brother seamen, you see before you three lusty young fellows about to suffer a shameful death for the dreadful crime of mutiny and desertion. Take warning by our example never to desert your officers, and should they behave ill to you, remember it is not their cause, it is the cause of your country you are bound to support.

The 'shameful death' the onlookers were about to see was an example indeed. Naval hangings were not a sudden drop into oblivion. Instead, a cohort hoisted you agonisingly aloft from deck level, so that the slow choking and the facial discolouration, the bowel and bladder voiding, and the futile struggling against suffocation were all public and prolonged.

Within days of being released, Peter Heywood wrote a moving letter to Edward Christian, which, when published in the *Cumberland Pacquet* was the first intimation the public received that all was not well. Equally telling, Fryer went immediately to see a relative of Fletcher Christian. But first, Heywood's letter.

Peter Heywood wrote to Edward Christian on 5 November 1792, from Great Russell Street in London:

> SIR, I am sorry to say I have been informed you were inclined to judge too harshly of your truly unfortunate brother; and to think of him in such a manner as I am conscious, from the knowledge I had of his most worthy disposition and character (both public and private), he merits not in the slightest degree; therefore I think it my duty to undeceive you, and to rekindle the flame of brotherly love (or pity) now towards him, which, I fear, the false reports of slander and vile suspicion may nearly have extinguished.
>
> Excuse my freedom, Sir:— If it would not be disagreeable to you, I will do myself the pleasure of waiting upon you; and endeavour to prove that your brother was not that vile wretch, void of all gratitude, which the world had the unkindness to think him; but, on the contrary, a most worthy character, ruined only by the misfortune (if it can be so called) of being a young man of strict honour, and adorned with every virtue; and beloved by all (except one, whose ill report is his greatest praise) who had the pleasure of his acquaintance.
>
> I am Sir, with esteem
>
> > Your most obedient humble servant
> >
> > P. Heywood

Edward Christian must have been astonished. Although his brother Charles thought there were extenuating circumstances, Edward, like everyone else, believed the worst about his brother.

But now he learned that 'the dreadful mutiny on the *Bounty* originated from motives, and was attended with circumstances different from those which had been presented to the world'. He was at Gray's Inn, but went to see Mr Romilly of Lincoln's Inn and then took advice from a more senior legal man who had been present at the trial; this seems to have been Sir Archibald McDonald, Attorney-General. At almost the same time, Edward learned that Fryer had been to see Joseph Christian of No. 10 The Strand. Joseph Christian told him Fryer also painted a new and different story. There may have been an element of revenge in the actions of Heywood and Fryer. But they were also interested in putting the story straight. Bligh's reputation was a casualty, but not the target. They acted with speed. Edward Christian acted with caution. The 'scoop' he had was extremely dangerous if mishandled. He apprised the public at large of his intention by releasing Heywood's letter to the *Cumberland Pacquet*. The *Pacquet* published it and other papers later reprinted it.

Imagine the feelings of Sir Joseph Banks when he read the following, late in November, with Bligh far away at sea. He cut the reprinted piece out of a newspaper, the name and date of which he omitted to note, and kept it to show Bligh. The article said among other things:

> Though there may be certain actions which even the torture and extremity of provocation cannot justify yet a sudden act of phrenzy, so circumstanced, is far removed in reason and mercy from the foul deliberate contempt of every religious and virtuous sentiment and obligation excited by selfish and base gratifications.—For the honour of this county, we are happy to assure our readers that one of its natives FLETCHER CHRISTIAN is not that detestable and horrid monster of wickedness and depravity, which with extreme and perhaps unexampled injustice and barbarity to him and his relations he

has long been represented but a character for whom every feeling heart must now sincerely grieve and lament . . .

Heywood's letter then followed, but, apart from saying he was an officer on *Bounty*, his identity was not revealed. The article goes on to say that since receiving the letter, Edward Christian had spoken to three officers and two seamen from *Bounty*, the only men who were in the London area. McIntosh alone is quoted, having said about Fletcher: 'Oh! he was a gentleman, and a brave man, and every officer and sailor on board the ship would have gone through fire and water to have served him.' The newspaper article concluded by saying the mystery was soon to be solved and that shame and infamy would be distributed in the just proportions it had been earned.

It was to be almost eighteen months before these revelations were published. Edward Christian had no need to hurry, for others were equally interested in telling versions other than Bligh's. But it is naive to call everything written by other men an attack on Bligh. Why should not Fryer and Morrison and Heywood wish to defend themselves more publicly than the trial allowed? If Bligh was entitled to publish his opinions, why should not others be heard?

It is likely that Morrison's *Memorandums*, a good basis for counter charges against Bligh, was circulated during the trial and was one of the 'various reasons' contributing to his pardon. There was plenty of precedent for counter charges at mutiny trials and it was precisely this kind of nastiness that Banks would want to avoid. Read in conjunction with the trials' evidence, Morrison's outline of what *could* be said in reply (even if not substantiated), showed it would be troublesome to convict men about whom there was any possible doubt. They, then having nothing to lose, would counter claim. In some cases the captains against whom counter charges had been made were found guilty and dismissed from the service. Banks could not afford to let this happen to Bligh. But gradually, the news of what Bligh had not said was repeated in well-informed and gossipy naval circles.

✦

Unaware, Bligh was once more cursing and swearing his way to and from the South Pacific. This time all the precautions that should have been part of *Bounty's* preparations had been taken. Bligh was a full post captain, and so sailed with a number of lieutenants. The first lieutenant was a man called Francis (Frank) Godolphin Bond, a step-nephew of Bligh and thus a protégé. The others were Lieutenant Tobin, an excellent water colourist, Lieutenant Guthrie, whose health was broken on the expedition and who died in Innsbruck soon after returning, and Lieutenant Portlock; also aboard as a midshipman was Matthew Flinders, off for his first look at a part of the world he would make very much his own. There were also marines, and even a second ship as a tender. This little brig was appropriately called *Assistant.*

The second breadfruit expedition sailed on 2 August 1791, well before anyone knew what had happened to *Pandora.* The departure was hardly the relief to Bligh that it was to Banks. He was suffering terribly from intense and recurring headaches and fever, and should have stayed at home in bed. But it was a healthy respect for patronage and promotion rather than for doctors that made him go.

The expedition returned to England via the grateful West Indies towards the end of 1793, and was a resounding botanical success. When *Providence* and *Assistant* were paid off at Woolwich, the *Kentish Register* of 6 September 1793, reported that Bligh was cheered, which made a good impression on everyone. But sailors know it pays to be nice to superior officers in public; and, as far as the complements of *Providence* and *Assistant* were concerned, Bligh was still a hero in England. They were quickly to be disabused. So was Bligh.

The court martial had radically changed opinion about Bligh throughout the Navy, where it counted. He found he was neither welcomed nor given audiences at the Admiralty. His lieutenants discovered his recommendations for promotion were almost useless. And whatever the men of his ships did in public, they said different things in private.

Charles Christian wrote that he spoke to a captain of marines from the second expedition; that man had said 'from Bligh's odious behaviour during the voyage, he would as soon shoot him as a dog, if it were not for the law'. Lieutenant Bond wrote much more in that vein. Although he undoubtedly aired his opinion in private, he did not do so in public, so it had no immediate effect.

While Bligh was away, Sir Joseph Banks received a welter of correspondence and documents concerning the *Bounty* affair from Edward Christian, and he asked Bligh to answer the allegations and questions they brought up. For eighteen months Bligh had little else to occupy his time. He was on half pay, with no offer of a command. It is not clear why this should have been so. He had promised Betsy that if he was returned safe from the *Providence* voyage, he would forswear the sea, but that was ages ago and past promises were the blight of his life. His long furlough may also have been an unofficial punishment or expression of displeasure at least, after the publication of alternative versions of Bligh's *Narrative*. All are likely; none is certain.

We have Bligh's draft replies to Banks concerning three separate sets of documents. First, he sketched answers to three letters addressed in December 1791 to Banks by Edward Christian. Christian seems to have revealed all the information he had collected from ex-*Bounty* men in London to which the newspaper article alluded, and which he wished to publish. From these we learn there was correspondence with John Christian Curwen, head of the Christian family and MP for Carlisle, but none of this has survived. I cannot think why these notes have not been given more importance.

Wishing to keep the interest of Banks, Bligh self-righteously goes further towards allowing for the possible veracity of other men's stories than anywhere else. In some places he positively contradicts his public statements. Bligh had already dissembled; to retain his position he had to resort to the truth.

It was in one of these notes that Bligh asserted he was Fletcher Christian's sole patron and had employed him in the Merchant Service for three years—a convenient lapse of memory as the correct length of time was nine months.

Bligh scratchily makes the major confession that the mutiny might possibly have been caused solely by Fletcher Christian's desperation, but rather snidely dismisses it simply because *he* was not aware of it: 'What Mr Christian calls his Brother's being drove to desperation must have been a very sudden impulse, for it is certain that Capt. Bligh's usual invitation to dinner and supper with him was sent to him the day before the mutiny happened.' A dinner invitation is proof enough to him that Fletcher Christian was not being driven to despair! Elsewhere in the notes Bligh admits he had words with his officers and men about coconuts, but does not elaborate, even in his own defence.

The most vital note immediately follows the one quoted: '. . . and Mr (Edward) Christian knows from his Brother's Note of Hand (which he received) that he was supplied by him with what money he wanted.' This finally gives real credibility to stories that Bligh and Christian had argued about money at Cape Town. Bligh's exaggerated comment that he 'for three years kept [Christian] employed', and Christian's need to borrow money from him, both explain why Bligh considered Christian so obliged to him.

Bligh also reveals that he argued with Christian after they left Tahiti, another important admission, and further proof his *Narrative* was by no means exhaustive, or balanced. Bligh shifts his ground on other points but keeps his paranoia firmly in place. He constantly says in his defence to Banks that many of the men now criticizing him should have done so at the court martial for the loss of *Bounty* in 1790. The fact they did not proved to Bligh they had no just complaints and had subsequently been suborned. On the other hand, Bligh had not taken that opportunity to prosecute Fryer or others, but he conveniently overlooks this.

He also moves the theory of concerted action against him first from Tahiti to *Bounty* and then to England. Once the prisoners from *Pandora* arrived, he said they and their friends formed connections to prevent the mutineers from being hanged. And why not? It would have been very silly for Fryer and Purcell, for instance, to have attacked Bligh at the first court martial without the supporting evidence of others who were involved. It would be strange if there were not a degree of collusion among the defendants and possibly the prosecutors, too; some men felt more revengeful than others. But there are two important points to remember. First, Bligh did not accept that those men had any right to defend themselves; his *Narrative* was 'sacred truths'. Yet he had defended and dissembled, and he should have expected others to do so too.

A second more important point also escaped Bligh's attention. If the prisoners were simply plotting to save their lives, they could have done so in a far less dangerous way by blaming everything on Fletcher Christian. They could have made him out to be a temperamental, inconsistent and disloyal second-in-command, and Bligh would have had to support them. Or they might have played the homosexual card. The penalty for homosexual behaviour on a naval ship was death and even the suspicion of such acts would have been fatal to Bligh's career. If there had been a homosexual relationship between Christian and Bligh it's just as likely one or the other would have tried to net others into his sexual lair, yet there is no evidence of this.

There is another theory that Christian was perhaps withdrawing from addiction to opium or laudanum, a liquid draught containing the drug. The suggestion is as much an insult to Bligh's command

and extraordinary attention to detail, as it is to Christian. The only source of these drugs was the medical supplies in the ship's stores, which were the eventual responsibility of the captain. If any crew member had been able to use these supplies to feed such an addiction, it would suggest that Bligh had either allowed this to happen or had been negligent, and would represent a serious abrogation of Bligh's duty to ensure the safety of both ship and crew. The unlikelihood of this is compounded when you consider that control of the ship's supplies is what would make Bligh's eventual profit from the voyage. In any case, in the cramped confines of a small ship, alongside an increasingly tense and hostile crew, how could Christian possibly have been addicted and escaped notice or subsequent mention?

Even though their very lives were at stake, none of the accused used the damning counter-charges of homosexuality or drug addiction in self-defence. This in itself should have prevented such theories ever being aired.

Bligh said Peter Heywood's evidence from the court martial incriminated Fletcher Christian in the fullest manner. That Heywood went on to write the letter to Edward Christian simply confirmed Bligh's belief that the evidence had been tampered with. Bligh was sure that Edward (and Peter Heywood) believed Fletcher was innocent. This is totally untrue. Edward Christian knew his brother was a mutineer and did not defend him; he simply wished the world to know some of the reasons why the crime had been committed. If he damaged Bligh's reputation in the process, that was unavoidable; had not Bligh already done this to almost everyone aboard *Bounty*? I must again refer to the comments of Professor Beaglehole on page 186. The low opinions Bligh had of everyone who sailed with him were subsequently shared by very few others; the low opinion of Bligh was extensive in and out of the Navy throughout the rest of his life.

In Bligh's remarks to Banks about the court martial, he refers once more to the conspiracy he thought was planned on Tahiti, and goes on to comment about Fletcher Christian and women, certain that Christian did have a particular female on Tahiti. He wrote that Coleman remembered her and that Lebogue, who had gone out in *Providence* with Bligh, had actually seen her at Otaheite on his last voyage. 'She went with Christian always untill his last Departure, which was sudden and unknown.' More contradiction. Mauatua/ Isabella went with Christian to Tubuai and then to Pitcairn; but Lebogue and Bligh agree here that his favourite was left behind when he sailed for Pitcairn. It is noteworthy that Bligh never reported asking this favourite for information about Christian.

For quite unfathomed reasons Bligh includes in his notes to Banks two new snippets of information about Fletcher. First he writes, 'Christian stood godfather to Peter Roger's child my boatswain who was a very low man and was connected in plundering sugar belonging to Mr Hibbert £17—as Mr Lamb reported.' Presumably Bligh is attempting to show that Christian was also 'low' because he stood godfather to the son of a dishonest man. If Rogers was low it would have been an extremely important compliment to him to have Fletcher Christian as godfather to his child; it was another form of patronage and Christian was obliged to do it whatever he thought of the man. Bligh was probably jealous. This all happened aboard *Britannia* and the Mr Lamb referred to was chief officer. Bligh additionally wrote, 'Christian also had a hoard of provisions aboard *Britannia*', perhaps supporting his belief that Fletcher was likely to steal coconuts.

Having seen Edward Christian's evidence and answered Banks' questions, it is surprising that Bligh did not foresee what was about to happen. Perhaps he thought his influential friends would calm things on his behalf. It was not so. In the middle of 1794, Edward Christian published Stephen Barney's *Minutes of the Proceedings of the Court-Martial* and to this he attached 'The Appendix'. The rumours, gossip and contradictions of private and naval circulation were made public. Society was transfixed.

30

Edward Christian's Defence

At first Edward Christian had asked permission to reprint the Admiralty's official minutes of the court martial, but he was refused on the reasonable grounds that public records could not be released for private publication. So Edward presented himself to Stephen Barney, the counsel for Muspratt. He had taken copious notes throughout the proceedings and although they were incomplete, with discrepancies and mistakes, they were better than nothing for Edward Christian's project; he wanted to use other men's words uttered under oath.

To this publication Edward Christian attached a pamphlet known generally as 'The Appendix'. In an introductory page dated 15 May 1794, Edward thanks Barney, acknowledging that the notes had been taken with no thought of future publication. Edward also makes it perfectly clear that he alone is responsible for the accuracy of what he says, and that the information was obtained exactly how and by whom he says.

'The Appendix' is quite unequivocal about how abhorrent was the crime of mutiny. But, Edward pointed out, the trial's only concern was to establish who did what on the morning of the mutiny. There was no interest in preceding events. Most of what

Edward Christian published has already been incorporated into the body of this book. It is useful here to show who Edward Christian used to help him collect information and to whom he spoke.

Edward Christian, aware of the delicacy of his operation, collected a group of men of impeccable reputation. Almost every time he spoke to someone from *Bounty* about his brother, one or more of these men were present. The fact that these men were prepared to be named and to bear testimony that what they heard was faithfully represented in 'The Appendix' must not be underrated. It also indicates how well respected Edward Christian was. The list is impressive. Furthermore, they could easily be contacted for verification, as their addresses or official capacity were clearly stated.

John Farhill, Esq., 38 Mortimer Street
Samuel Romilly, Esq., Lincoln's Inn
Mr Gilpin, No. 432 Strand
The Rev. Dr Fisher, Canon of Windsor
The Rev. Mr Cookson, Canon of Windsor
Captain Wordsworth, *Abergavenny* [an East Indiaman]
Rev. Mr Antrobus, Chaplain to the Bishop of London
John France, Esq., Temple
James Losh, Esq., Temple
Rev. Dr Frewen, Colchester
John Atkinson, Esq., Somerset Herald [a position at the
    College of Arms rather than a provincial newspaper]

Most of the men had connections with St John's, Cambridge, and with William Willberforce, the great opponent of slavery. There is considerable circumstantial evidence, as outlined in C. S. Wilkinson's *The Wake of the Bounty*, to support the claim that Edward Christian was able to gather these men because they were so opposed to the business interests of Bligh's earlier patron and relative by marriage, Duncan Campbell. It may have been one of the things they had in common, but I cannot believe that an anti-slavery campaign was their motive. They would have said so. Many of the men had connections with the Wordsworths, but Edward had, after all, won their famous case against the Earl of Lonsdale in 1791, and William Wordsworth was also a St John's man.

Both the Canons of Windsor were very close to the king, far too sensitive a position in which to join in perjury. Dr Fisher was known, according to one source, as the 'King's Fisher'. Antrobus was from Cockermouth; and Romilly, later Sir Samuel, became a famous law reformer.

They must have been formidable to meet, and perhaps some of *Bounty*'s men did alter their stories slightly 'to please the gentle-men'. But it was not just able seamen who were interviewed; Edward Christian also made a point of publishing the addresses or whereabouts of each man to whom he spoke. The only thing he hid was who said what; but there were very good reasons for that, as will later be shown. The *Bounty* men interviewed were:

John Fryer, the master
Thomas Hayward, midshipman
William Peckover, gunner [who lived with some nicety
  in Gun Alley, Wapping]
William Purcell, carpenter
John Smith, cook
Lawrence Lebogue, sailmaker

All had returned with Bligh. Edward also spoke to:

Joseph Coleman, armourer, tried and acquitted
Thomas McIntosh, carpenter's mate, tried and acquitted
Michael Byrne, musician, tried and acquitted
Peter Heywood, midshipman, pardoned

William Muspratt, able seaman, might have been convicted but
   for a legal error
James Morrison who wrote to Edward Christian.

Of these only one—Muspratt—might conceivably have been a
mutineer.

After giving the names and addresses of the men who accompanied him and the men who had helped him, Edward Christian then
went on to re-tell the whole story.

A particular paragraph in which Edward Christian discusses his
brother's relationship with women has always created problems.
The sentence that has continuously been misinterpreted is one in
answer to Bligh's report that Christian had a favourite female and
that his desire to return to her occasioned the mutiny.

> As this paragraph contains an assertion that Christian had a
> favourite female at Otaheite, it is proper it should be known
> that although Christian was upon shore, and had the command
> of the tent all the time that Captain Bligh was at Otaheite with
> the *Bounty*, yet the officers who were with Christian on the
> same duty declare he never had a female favourite at Otaheite,
> nor any attachment or particular connection among the
> women. It is true that some had what they called their girls
> or women with whom they constantly lived all the time they
> were upon the island, but this was not the case with Christian.

Even if it was, Bligh tells us that this was not the woman who went
away with him.

The usual interpretation of this passage is that Christian had
nothing to do with women on Tahiti, but this is not Edward Christian's meaning. He is simply saying Fletcher Christian seemed to
have no regular or favourite female companion and thus could not
have mutinied for the sake of a woman.

Edward's last few paragraphs are worth reading:

The writer of this Appendix would think himself an accomplice in the crime which has been committed, if he designedly should give the slightest shade to any word or fact different from its true and just representation; and lest he should be supposed to be actuated by a vindictive spirit, he has studiously forborn to make more comments than were absolutely necessary upon any statement which he has been obliged to bring forward. He felt it a duty to himself, to the connections of all the unfortunate men and to society to collect and lay before the Public these extraordinary circumstances.

The sufferings of Captain Bligh and his companions in the boat, however severe they may have been, are perhaps but a small portion of the torments occasioned by this dreadful event: and whilst these prove the melancholy and extensive consequences of the crime of Mutiny, the crime itself in this instance may afford an awful lesson to the Navy, and to Mankind, that there is a pressure, beyond which the best formed and principled mind must either break or recoil. And though public justice and the public safety can allow no vindication of any species of mutiny, yet reason and humanity will distinguish the sudden unpremeditated act of desperation and phrenzy from the foul deliberate contempt of every religious duty and honourable sentiment; and will deplore the uncertainty of human prospects, when they reflect that a young man is condemned to perpetual infamy, who, if he had served on board any other ship, or had perhaps been absent from the *Bounty* a single day, or one ill-fated hour, might still have been an honour to his country and a glory and comfort to his friends!

It was Bligh's opportunity for a full-blooded public defence. He had, after all, written his refutations in strong, positive terms to Banks. They could have been suitably edited and published with speed and efficacy. Instead, he published a series of miscellaneous correspondence and orders that have no cohesion and upon which he does not comment. Some of them even tell against him, such as Heywood's letter to Edward Christian, which Bligh does not counteract by comparing it with Heywood's evidence in court. His answer made little impression. Once again he may have been advised not to go too far. He would have been better off not answering at all. The few comments he did make were meant to debunk Edward Christian's method of collecting statements. Bligh suggested he withheld facts about who said what to obfuscate the truth and to prevent perjurers being brought to justice. This was a dangerous thing to say about any man of the law and reckless to say about two Canons of Windsor. Bligh was more or less publicly calling them liars. To him it was all another plot.

Edward Christian quickly published a *Short Reply to Capt. William Bligh's Answer*. Even Christian's foes admit it is brilliantly argued, but they do not say that it also removes once and for all any suspicion that Edward Christian kept his quotations anonymous for any but the most noble reasons; without a guarantee of anonymity the men would not have spoken at all. And one at least, McIntosh, had actually been threatened for what he had said to Christian. One of Edward's informants, Bligh's servant John Smith, had come to see Edward Christian of his own accord.

The *Short Reply* is one of the rarest and most expensive pamphlets in the world. Only 150 were printed and today only three are known to exist. Its rarity is possibly why it was not included when 'The Appendix' and Bligh's 'Answer' were published in *A Book of the Bounty* and perhaps why authors have overlooked its important substantiation of everything in 'The Appendix'.

Kennedy and others have suggested that *A Short Reply* was meant to sting Bligh into taking legal action. Bligh could then have been properly cross-examined as he tried to disprove the allegations in 'The Appendix'. But he said nothing and was quickly given a command. At the end of April 1795, he joined as captain a ship newly named HMS *Calcutta*. Off he sailed, far less trouble to the authorities when he was at sea than when ashore.

31

'The fury of an ungovernable temper'

W hen I began this book I expected to have to blacken Fletcher Christian's reputation and to defend Bligh to some degree, an unusual position for a member of the Christian family. It was amazing how short a time I was able to maintain that expectation. The available evidence seemed to prove overwhelmingly the traditional harsh view of Bligh, except that he was never as physically cruel as films made him out to be. I was rather worried about this. Because I had found so much new material about Fletcher Christian, I wanted to say something new about Bligh. Recent works gave no clues to new sources; all the research seemed to have been done. Yet, when I was at the Australian National Library in Canberra, an assiduous librarian pointed out some extraordinary material. Some of the original documents are in the Greenwich Maritime Museum and copies are available on microfilm around the world. But, although discovered and published in 1953 and 1960, they had been largely ignored by Bligh's apologists in 1978. The first and only scholar who had so far realized and strongly argued their tremendous evidential significance was the Swedish historian Rolf E. du Rietz (in 1963 and 1965), who has also clearly defended Edward Christian against his attackers.

The material in question is the draft of a letter plus journal notes written by Lieutenant Francis (Frank) Godolphin Bond, first lieutenant on *Providence*, the ship commanded by Bligh on the second breadfruit voyage. His official position aboard *Providence* was the same as that of Christian aboard *Bounty*. But he had not sailed with Bligh before, and there was no passionate friendship. Most important of all, there was no humiliating reliance for funds upon Bligh. These differences are important.

The first document is a draft of a letter Bond wrote to his brother in 1792, during the late days of the expedition, when *Providence* was sailing through the Atlantic towards the West Indies. In its original form it is extremely dense, so I have divided it into paragraphs.

To say a southern voyage is quite delectable is also to say you have every domestic comfort; but on this score I must be silent, for at present I mean to say but little of our Major Domo (i.e. Mr. Bligh) . . . Yes Tom, our relation has the credit of being a tyrant in his last expedition, where his misfortunes and good fortune have elevated him to a situation he is incapable of supporting with decent modesty.

The very high opinion he has of himself makes him hold everyone of our profession with contempt, perhaps envy: nay the Navy is but [a] sphere for fops and lubbers to swarm in, without one gem to vie in brilliancy with himself. I don't mean to depreciate his extensive knowledge as a seaman and nautical astronomer, but condemn that want of modesty in self estimation. To be less prolix I will inform you he has treated me (nay all on board) with the insolence and arrogance of a *Jacobs*: and notwithstanding his passion is partly to be attributed to a nervous fever, with which he has been attacked most of the voyage, the chief part of his conduct must have arisen from the fury of an ungovernable temper.

Soon after leaving England I wished to receive instruction

from this imperious master, until I found he publickly exposed any deficiency on my part in the Nautical Art etc. A series of this conduct determined me to trust to myself, which I hope will in some measure repay me for the trouble of a disagreeable voyage—in itself pleasant, but made otherwise by being worried at every opportunity.

His maxims are of the nature that at once pronounce him an enemy to the lovers of Natural Philosophy; for to make use of his own words, 'No person can do the duty of a 1st lieut who does no more than write the day's work of his publick journal'. This is so inimical to the sentiments I always hope to retain, that I find the utmost difficulty in keeping on tolerable terms with him. The general orders which have been given me are to that purport—I am constantly to keep on my legs from 8 o'th'morning to 12, or noon, altho' I keep the usual watch. The Officer of the morning watch attends to the cleaning of the Decks; yet I am also to be present, not only to get it done, but be even menially active on those and all other occasions.

He expects me to be acquainted with every transaction on board, notwithstanding he himself will give the necessary orders to the Warrant Officers, before I can put it into execution. Every dogma of power and consequence has been taken from the Lieutenants, to establish, as he thinks, his own reputation—what imbecility for a post Capn! The inferior Warrants have had orders from the beginning of the expedition, not to issue the least article to a Lieut. without his orders so that a cleat, fathom of log line, or indeed a hand swab, must have the commander's sanction. One of the last and most *beneficent* commands was that the Carpenter's Crew should not drive a nail for me without I should first ask his permission— but my heart is filled with the proper materials always to disdain this humiliation.

Among many circumstances of envy and jealousy he used to

deride my keeping a private journal and would often ironically say he supposed I meant to publish. My messmates have remarked he never spoke of my possessing one virtue—tho' by the bye has never dared to say I have none. Every officer who has nautical information, a knowledge of natural history, a taste for drawing, or anything to constitute him proper for circumnavigating, becomes odious; for great as he is in his own good opinion, he must have entertained fears some of the ship's company meant to submit a spurious Narrative to the judgement and perusal of the publick.

Among the many misunderstandings that have taken place, that of my *Observing* has given most offence, for since I have not made the least application to him for information on that head, he has at all times found illiberal means of abusing my pursuit; saying at the same time, what I absolutely knew was from him. Tir'd heartily with my present situation, and even the subject I am treating of, I will conclude it by inserting the most recent and illegal order. Every Officer is expected to deliver in their private Logs ere we anchor at St Helena. As our expedition has not been on discoveries, should suppose this an artibrary command, altho the words, King's Request, Good of the Country; Orders of the Admiralty &c &c &c are frequently in his mouth—but unparrelled [sic] pride is the principal ingredients in his composition.

The future will determine whether promotion will be the reward of this voyage: I still flatter myself it will, notwithstanding what I have said. Consistent with self respect I still remain tolerably passive; and if nothing takes place very contrary to my feelings, all may end well: but this will totally depend on circumstances; one of which is the secrecy requested of you concerning the tenor of this letter.—My time is so effectually taken up by Duty that to keep peace I neglect all kind of study; yet the company of a set of well informed messmates makes my moments pass very agreeably, so that I am by no means in purgatory ... The 2nd August [1791] we left England and had pleasant w[eather] to Teneriffa, where Captain B. was taken very ill, and from particular *traits* in his conduct believe he was insane at times.

That is strong stuff, but there is more, which elaborates further. The above letter was written towards the end of his voyage with Bligh. But Lieutenant Bond's son, the Rev. F. H. Bond, had in his possession his father's daily notes. In 1960, George Mackaness, who wrote the only important book about Bligh, published a paper written by F. H. Bond, in which Bond summarized what he had been told by his father about Bligh and supported this with quotations from the notes, which have not, incidentally, been made public *in extenso*, nor is their whereabouts presently known. Most of what follows are the words of F. H. Bond, those that are underlined are direct quotations from Lieutenant Bond.

Though a prime seaman, however his [i.e. Bligh's] passionate temper and violent language were so uncontrolled that he was hardly ever employed without exasperating his officers and ship's company. The story of the Mutiny on the *Bounty*, the immediate causes of which were an outburst of temper on his part and grossly insulting words to one of his officers, and the marvellous voyage of the *Bounty*'s launch for 4,000 miles are so well known that they need only be referred to here. This extraordinary feat of seamanship was now on everybody's lips and Bligh was universally commiserated. He had of course told his story in his own way and was, like many violent tempered men, perhaps really unconscious of the amount of provocation he had given. He had represented the mutiny as the result of his crew's experience of the delicious climate and the life of the island of Otaheite ...

The most perfect harmony was luckily maintained among the Lieuts throughout [the *Providence* voyage], a matter of immense importance for a reason which must unfortunately be presently noted . . .

During the voyage to the Cape of Good Hope, Bligh transferred Bond to *Assistant*, which was something of an insult. Once at the Cape, Bond was returned to *Providence*. His comments in notes made at the time were full and hasty and his son declines to quote them as Lieutenant Bond had written under the influence of strong feeling. He merely wrote of the notes:

It will be enough to show that there was great cause for discomfort.

Hardly had the voyage commenced when Cp. Bligh's arbitrary disposition and exasperating language began again to render his ship a most unfortunate one for his officers and especially for his First Lieutenant [Bond] who from his position was brought into closer contact with him. Orders of an unusual nature were given with haste and in a manner so uncalled for and so devoid of feeling and tact as to occasion very great irritation.

The short exchange with the *Assistant* was felt at the time quite a relief and his resumption of duties as First of the *Providence* was attended with discomfort which he speaks of as frightful. A dictatorial insistence on trifles, ever-lasting fault finding, slights shown in matters of common courtesy, strong and passionate condemnation of little errors of judgement— all these stung the hearts of his subordinates and worked them up into a state of wrath which would probably have much surprised Bligh himself had he known it.

Instances are given of his want of courtesy. At a ceremonial visit to the Governor of the Cape, Bligh takes the opportunity of snubbing Lieuts Portlock and Bond by presenting them after a junior Lieut, and the Commander of the *Assistant* last, quite against the rule of etiquette. At Teneriffe he refused to present two of his officers to the Governor, who thereupon corrected the intentional blunder and presented themselves. The Governor, it is added, received them well.

Refusals of leave to land, apparently without cause, which annoyed at the Cape, were felt still more strongly at Otaheite, when frequent leave was naturally expected during their 3 month stay. One other point was very trying to Bligh's nephew, the great inconsistency of his conduct. He says that in prosperity Cap. Bligh was all arrogance and insult, despotic insistence without explanation, advice or show of kindness; often an hauteur and distance which utterly ignored the nephew as well as the rank of his First Lieut.

In time of real danger what a change to cordiality and kindness! The Devil's Hole for example! 'Oh Frank! What a situation; into what a danger have I brought you! God grant that we may get safe out of it.'

I replied, 'No sir, we shall do very well; I don't see that there's any real danger to the ship.'

The event which called for this conversation is not given; but there is the hint that the danger was caused by the helm being put the wrong way through mistake.

. . . The serenity of the weather gave us the most flattering hopes of a safe passage; but several affairs have lately occurred to prevent the cordiality which should have existed between my commander and myself, and his remarks tended to deprive me of self-confidence. I was e.g. reproached and threatened because my men on the Fore Tops yard were beaten by Tobin's and Guthrie's, the carpenter was abused for acting on my orders and ordered to take the skippers out; the boatswain was similarly treated. The usual etiquette in our respective positions was quite set aside.

There is little I need add to the words of the Bonds.

Lieutenant Bond tells us the truth about Bligh. Bond did not mutiny simply because he was *not* in purgatory; he had more peers aboard, and he also had no close ties of friendship with Bligh.

On later ships there were continuing complaints about Bligh's manner of command, his inconsistency and insensitivity, but the problems they caused were never again so public, except when he was court martialled for abusing an inferior officer. It does not follow that Bligh grew less irascible, but only that on larger ships the commander was more remote.

Indeed, remoteness might be the key to why there was not as much turmoil on *Providence* as there was on *Bounty*. The logs show Bligh was not in direct contact with his officers on a daily basis because he was so seriously ill and confined to bed for most of the time. Other men would probably have refused the command, perhaps even disembarked before it was too late. But not William Bligh. When he had orders he fulfilled them whatever the personal cost. It was hell on his inferiors, but exactly what Joseph Banks wanted for two reasons: Bligh could be relied on to do the job and it kept him well away from any trial of the *Bounty* mutineers.

The appointment of the ailing Bligh to this second breadfruit expedition might be seen with hindsight as selfish of Banks, but is also an odd compliment to Bligh. Understanding this dichotomy finally gives an answer to a question that has perplexed many writers. Just why was Bligh later appointed Governor of New South Wales?

In 1804 Bligh faced a court martial over his verbal abuse of a lieutenant and was convicted and 'reprimanded and admonished to be in future more correct in his language'. Yet, by 1806 he was ensconced in Sydney as Governor, living in considerable style and wielding tremendous power. Some say the British Establishment just wanted him as far away as possible, some that the appointment was an overdue reward for what happened on *Bounty*, others believe it to be a punishment for *Bounty* and all the other incidents.

Curiously, it is more likely Bligh was appointed because of *Bounty* and other incidents, not in spite of them, and for this important insight I am grateful to Paul Brunton, Curator of Manuscripts at the State Library of New South Wales and a noted Bligh scholar. Brunton explains that the Governorship of the colony, which was in deep strife at the time, was in the personal gift of Sir Joseph Banks. Whoever he recommended for the post, the Crown would accept. Banks, of all people, knew Bligh could be relied upon to tackle the challenge fearlessly, for precisely the qualities and reasons that made him unpopular—he had an absolute belief in the written law, and was insensitive to the opinions of others. Whatever the rights or wrongs of his motives, Bligh was nothing if not magnificently courageous and would wade in where others would fear even to tread. As far as Banks was concerned, the man the rest of the naval establishment still called 'that *Bounty* bastard' could be as horrible as he liked as long as he did the job.

Banks tempted Bligh with a greatly increased salary and the guarantee that his place in the Navy List would not be compromised. Like every other naval officer Bligh's eventual promotion to Vice-Admiral would come through simple seniority, by outliving contemporaries, not as any reward for duty done, so this protection of his precedence was understandably important to him.

Just as it had been cruel to send the sick Bligh on the second breadfruit expedition it was deeper, calculating self-interest for Banks to send him to New South Wales because if this colony failed, Banks himself would fail. It is likely that Banks believed Bligh alone had the ruthless focus to confront and ultimately tame the factions that were tearing the colony apart. Anti-British sentiment combined with the greed of privileged settlers and the venality of the powerful New South Wales Corps had created a hell for ordinary freemen and for transported prisoners alike.

Bligh constantly had to ignore jeers as he walked in the streets of Sydney, sometimes because he had ordered full ceremony, of pipes and bands and guards of honour, wherever he went. But he did what he was sent to do. He stood up to the troublemakers and began the long process of turning the penal colony into a calm and profitable settlement. Even it were true that he was found under a bed when the NSW Corps eventually mutinied against him, it would not have been through cowardice, as is commonly claimed, but because he was determined to protect the written records of his administration, which he clasped to his breast. They represented vital proof that he had done his duty, quite as important as the journals he so doggedly kept during his open boat voyage after the *Bounty* mutiny.

Throughout his life, Bligh trusted the opinions of no other man. Every action he took was based entirely on the written word, and thus the unwavering support Banks and his official orders gave him provided the armoury he needed to begin the taming of New South Wales.

On 26 January 1808 Bligh was arrested for tyranny by the NSW Corps and its supporters, marking the beginning of the Rum Rebellion. This was the second mutiny against Bligh, yet he made no attempt to avoid conflict or change his behaviour in any way. In fact he was so difficult about the conditions under which he would agree to leave the colony that he remained a prisoner in Sydney until February 1809 when he finally signed an agreement with the NSW Corps to quit the colony.

In *Distracted Settlement*, published in 1998, Dr Anne-Maree Whitaker introduces the previously unpublished journal of Lt James Finucane, who was in the colony at the time. He said Bligh 'eventually entered into a most solemn engagement to leave the Colony on the 20th of this month [February 1809] . . . and proceed to England with all possible expedition, not to touch at nor return to any part of this territory without receiving His Majesty's orders . . . and not to interfere in any manner or under any pretext . . . with the Government of the Colony'.

Bligh sailed for England on *HMS Porpoise* on 17 March 1808, but the moment his ship was out of Sydney Harbour he went back on every aspect of the agreement, arguing on board that it was extracted by force and was thus not binding. He sent letters proclaiming the officers of the NSW Corps and several others as traitors and rebels, and continued 'cruizing in sight of land' for almost a year, most of it in and around Tasmania, believing he should be reinstated as Governor. On 12 May 1810 he was finally convinced to sail for Britain and trial, accompanied by the 102nd Regiment. It is sad that the important changes Bligh began before the colony's mutiny have become so tainted by his actions after it, but the world has always preferred bad news to good. The man who so vehemently condemned others for failings of duty and honour had diminished his triumphs by breaking his word. It is no wonder there is so much ambivalence about him.

Thus, what Lieutenant Bond says about Bligh's behaviour in his draft letter, and what his son subsequently wrote, dramatically confirm every point made by Morrison, Fryer, Edward Christian, Peter Heywood and other men who were aboard *Bounty*. And the autobiography of Charles Christian gives us further and unexpected illumination of the dramatic situation on *Bounty*. With hindsight, and to listeners who were not officials, Bligh eventually gave a different reason for the mutiny from the ones given in his published works. Charles reports a conversation between Major Taubman of the Isle of Man and Captain Bligh. Taubman had been instrumental, you will remember, in putting Fletcher Christian aboard *Britannia* when he made his first voyage with Bligh. When Major Taubman asked Bligh what could possibly be the cause of his defection, he replied: 'It was Insanity.'

'He spoke right,' says Charles. 'But who was it that had drove him into that unhappy state?'

Bligh knew the answer, for he had been told by Christian and the evidence heard at the court martial clearly showed Christian had been forced into an abnormal state of mind—by Bligh. Charles

Christian adds that when Fletcher was a boy, he was 'slow to be moved'. On board *Bounty*, 'Jealousy and Tyranny had produced Ill Usage to so great an Excess . . . and Revenge ensued as an Effervescence from the Opposition of good to bad Qualities.'

32

Driven to 'that unhappy state'

The question of whether Christian might actually have been insane was never fully explored in the first edition of *Fragile Paradise*. I regret that I had not collected enough research on either the medical or the mental condition of Christian to do so. Well, now I have.

First, Fletcher Christian's physical state. In the notes he made in the open boat after the mutiny, Bligh tells us that Christian was 'subject to violent perspiration and particularly to his hands so that he soils any thing he handles'. In another description written in Timor, Bligh describes 'violent perspirations'. The simple explanation is that Christian suffered from hyperhidrosis, but there is no evidence to tell us how long this condition had existed, for no other person ever mentioned it.

Hyperhidrosis is the medical term for excessive sweating. It can be caused by diseased vital organs in some conditions and at the time was also associated with opium taking. But this is unlikely in Christian's case without also believing that Bligh condoned and accepted Christian was using the opium in *Bounty*'s stores for recreational purposes. Excessive sweating is also associated with diabetes, but this would probably have led to coma and eventual death in those days.

Hyperhidrosis can affect the palms, the armpits, the feet or the face. Some sufferers are struck in just one of these areas, some in all. Essentially there is no escape. It is chronic and goes on all day and all night. The affected areas are colder than other parts which, together with the constant dampness, makes them seem clammy. Like all sweating, hyperhidrosis gets worse in times of emotional pressure or conflict and thus can be a terrible social handicap, commonly leading to withdrawal and the complications this can cause both professionally and domestically. It is common for sufferers to develop a fear even of accidentally touching the one they love most.

If Christian's basic condition was so extreme that he was noted as dirtying everything he touched, at a time when hygiene and nicety was minimal, he was either in a bad way or Bligh was being impossibly prissy. We know Bligh used personal debt to wound Christian. What if Bligh added insult to injury by mocking his sweating—few men and women can bear being mocked for something they can do nothing about. It's telling that Bligh was the only person to mention it. On the other hand, the fact that the condition was impossible to conceal, even if only minor, made it excellent evidence for use in identifying Christian if ever he were captured, and perhaps this is all that should be read into Bligh's comments.

Although the pathology of the condition is now understood and some cases can be helped with surgery to sympathetic nerves, the genesis of most hyperhidrosis remains a mystery, except to say it commonly appears in puberty and it may improve or even disappear in the late 20s and 30s.

It is extremely important to understand that hyperhidrosis is not a symptom of some psychological or nervous disorder. I once thought this and it was also suggested in Montgomerie's *William Bligh of the Bounty in Fact and Fable* (1937). But this conclusion represents the classic mistake, accepting a generality as a relevant explanation of a specific. It was only when I consulted an acknowledged expert in the field, Professor John Ludbrook, Professor

Emeritus at Adelaide University and Professorial Fellow at Royal Melbourne Hospital, that the distinction was clarified.

But if hyperhidrosis is not a symptom of nervous disorder, the social consequences of being a sufferer can certainly lead to some degree of psychological or nervous disorder, and the order of the appearance of the two has often been confused. Excessive sweating in mentally insecure patients is much more likely to be a side effect of their medication or of some medical condition. Or they might suffer hyperhidrosis as well as their other affliction.

The clear documentation that Fletcher Christian was admired physically and socially on all his other voyages and by all but a few of those aboard *Bounty* suggests he did not always suffer from the condition or that, if he did, it was minor or he and others were able to ignore it. The conflict which developed between him and Bligh after they left Tahiti—and perhaps previously—was ideal for making the condition increasingly severe. In times of stress sufferers of hyperhidrosis of the face can look and feel as though they have been rained on, and the acidity of the sweat pouring into their eyes can make these flaming red with irritation. And isn't this how Christian is described as looking on the day of the mutiny? Apart from a sleepless night, his eyes 'aflame with revenge' might just have been emotion. They were much more likely to be red because of the violent perspiration that the situation aboard *Bounty* had generated. His long hair would have been sodden too and his shirt drenched alarmingly from his armpits. We would all sweat more in the situation: Christian poured with it. Even if he were utterly sane, he would have looked mad.

Combined with the dread seriousness of what Christian was doing, and what everyone on board had been recently enduring, this further explains why so many of *Bounty*'s crew preferred to watch him take the ship from Bligh rather than dare challenge him.

But was Fletcher Christian actually insane? Perhaps he was, at least for a while.

Dr Sven Wahlroos' *Mutiny and Romance in the South Seas: A Companion to the Bounty Adventure* (1989), combines a chronological account of the mutiny events with an exhaustive encyclopedia of every person and every place associated with it. A practising psychologist, Wahlroos was the first to use these professional skills to analyse the mutiny. He concludes that everything points to Christian having a borderline personality disorder. The clinical description he cites of this condition, as defined by the American Psychiatric Association, is telling:

> Interpersonal relationships are often intense and unstable with marked shifts of attitude over time. Frequently there is impulsive and unpredictable behaviour that is potentially physically self-damaging—the borderline person will often go from idealising a person to devaluing him.*

The mutiny can then be seen as a predictable outcome if Christian were pushed too far. In Wahlroos' professional opinion, Christian suffered a 'brief reactive psychosis'. He quotes the American Psychiatric Association again to support this:

> The essential feature is the sudden onset of a psychotic disorder of at least a few hours but no more than two week's duration . . . suicidal or aggressive behaviour may be present . . . Individuals with Borderline Personality Disorders are thought to be particularly vulnerable . . . situations involving major stress predispose to development of this disorder.*

Clinical psychologist Paul J. Rodriguez agrees with Dr Wahlroos' basic diagnosis. But he adds that many people diagnosed with

---

* Reproduced with permission from the *Diagnostic and Statistical Manual of Mental Disorders*, Third Edition. Revised. Copyright 1987 American Psychiatric Association.

Borderline Personality Disorder have commonly experienced child-hood neglect, abuse and conflict. Often they have lost one or both parents when young. Fletcher Christian's father died when he was four and he later lost his family home through a combination of mismanagement by his mother and profligacy by his older brothers, both of which can be construed as abandonment through neglect of his welfare. Thus, explains Rodriguez, if Fletcher felt he was in further danger of being abandoned aboard *Bounty* or believed he was being neglected or demeaned, particularly by someone he once idol-ised, his inherent instability would have predisposed him to behave in extreme ways, especially during times of stress. On *Bounty* in late April 1789, there seemed to be stress everywhere Fletcher Christian turned. As Rodriguez states:

> Fletcher Christian would have responded to events on *Bounty* with feelings of deep emptiness and may have had considerable diffi-culty controlling his anger. He would have dramatically altered his attitude towards the person whom he believed to be aban-doning him, from intense admiration to intense devaluation.
>
> When faced with considerable stress—the sort of events which almost anyone would find difficult to endure—a Border-line person may suddenly lose touch with reality. This is usually short-lived and can involve deep feelings of detachment from events and people, or grossly inappropriate behaviour.

Brief Reactive Psychosis, the diagnosis by Dr Wahlroos of Fletcher Christian's condition during the mutiny, is now known as Brief Psychotic Disorder with Marked Stressors, a mental state which commonly includes paranoid or grandiose delusions and irrational behaviour. The duration of this sudden-onset condition can range from at least a day to less than a month, after which the person returns to his or her previous pattern of behaviour. This all fits pretty well with what we know of Christian's behaviour.

However, if Fletcher Christian did suffer from this condition, there would have been a long-standing and inflexible pattern of instability in his relationships, emotions, self-image and control of his behaviour. He would have exhibited characteristics markedly different from our own expectations of behaviour. Instead, every contemporary pre-*Bounty* account describes him as someone particularly affable, charming and socially sensitive, who went out of his way to understand others, especially those of lesser position. The explanation of this dichotomy, says Rodriguez, is fascinating: 'Individuals with Borderline Personality Disorder may appear charismatic, which masks or makes acceptable behaviour which would otherwise have been judged unsuitable'.

And that is the final piece of the jigsaw puzzle. The very characteristic which could have led to a greater and earlier understanding of Fletcher Christian is precisely that which has led writers and historians astray for over two centuries. Most wouldn't have it any other way. I believe many were simply more interested in telling a gripping tale than history or truth. For that, their hero—particularly a hero of protest—has to be as normal as the rest of us.

So, just as Bligh said to Major Taubman, the man who first introduced the pair, Christian probably was insane on the day of the mutiny. Taubman's reaction is not known, but Fletcher's brother Charles, who had also been driven to mutiny against the captain of *Middlesex*, used this personal experience to ask the most important question of the entire saga: 'But who was it that has drove him into that unhappy state?'

The clear answer is that it was Bligh's treatment of Christian. Regardless of what Christian or Bligh said or did or achieved at any other time of their lives, this time it was their relationship which led to the tragedy, and nothing else. Christian said again and again he had been in hell for weeks and no one did much to resist Christian when he took the ship from Bligh. Everyone knew that Christian had good reason to be in his state, even if they did not agree with it or fully understand it on the day.

The exact details of what went wrong cannot be known, except that the men who were there thought that the animosity between the two men was long-standing. To this we must add that for most of his naval life Bligh had a reputation for bullying and mentally torturing other men, even those he considered friends, and that Christian was by every account a special target for this behaviour: imagine your own response if you were personally victimised on board *Bounty* as well as daily enduring the bullying inconsistencies Bligh displayed on *Providence*.

We simply cannot accept Bligh's protestations that because he had no inkling of the mutiny he could not be held to blame. I believe that it was Bligh's duty to have had that inkling, but he lost his ship because of this essential personality defect, an inability to listen to others. By offering sympathetic treatment to his former disciple when he needed it most, Bligh might have headed Christian off, but Bligh was not interested in helping Christian or acknowledging that his deteriorating mental state, obvious to everyone else on board, had anything to do with him. Indeed, Bligh seems to have worked Christian even harder and insulted him even more grievously.

Bligh's failure to recognise approaching danger from Christian is not the only time he suffered because of his inability to see another man's point of view. He simply expected others to think the same way he did and could not understand it when they did not. These days it might be described as being in denial. He applied the same selective thinking to objects as well as to people.

In his account of the mutiny, *A Voyage to the South Seas*, published in 1792, Bligh wrote that until the day of the mutiny he considered 'the voyage had advanced in a course of uninterrupted prosperity.' Broadly speaking, this is poetic licence. His belief in himself as a faultless administrator and captain was misguided and sorely exposed before and after the mutiny. In Tahiti sails were found to have rotted and, although he blamed others, the responsibility as commanding officer was ultimately his. Much worse was the discovery during the mutiny that one of the ship's cutters was not seaworthy.

Now let's see what psychologist Dr Sven Wahlroos has to say about Bligh in *Mutiny and Romance in the South Seas*:

> Bligh probably did not have any clear-cut mental or emotional illness but he did show prominent compulsive, narcissistic, histrionic and somewhat paranoid tendencies. A major part of his interpersonal problems lay in his almost total lack of understanding of the impact he had on others. His focus was always on himself ... he felt he had nothing to do with the misfortunes which befell him during his life.

Of all the many supporting sources for this view, Wahlroos quotes just one. In his 1976 book *Captain Bligh*, Richard Humble wrote 'a man who is pathologically unable to accept imperfection is a permanent martyr to himself: he has an enormous cross to bear ... [Bligh] was not only unable to face up to this [making mistakes], he recoiled from the very idea. From this mental block sprang his tendency to arrogance and diversion of the blame on to others; whatever went wrong it could never be his fault. Inconsistent though he was, he was never inconsistent in this.'

On 28 April 1789, Bligh's conceit and self-deceit took a terrible toll. Other men would also pay the price. Not least was Fletcher Christian, who had come aboard *Bounty* regarding Bligh as a mentor but who was then driven insane because of the way he had been treated by him.

33

The Wretch at Cadiz?

The burning of *Bounty* at Pitcairn Island, in January 1790, isolated her complement even more than their dearest or worst hopes. For almost twenty years the community remained unknown as it writhed bloodily until succumbing finally to an all-pervasive form of Christianity that was either inspiring or sickening. It was called both.

Only two ships accidentally found Pitcairn during its anonymous infancy. Both thought it uninhabited, even though one actually sent men ashore to collect coconuts. They did not detect any sign of habitation. Neither did the other ship, which was prevented from landing by violent swells. The next day was apparently the calmest since *Bounty* had arrived, but fortunately the intruder had sailed off.

Then, on 6 February 1808, an American whaling ship, *Topaz*, Captain Mayhew Folger, chanced upon the incorrectly charted rock. For reasons never explained, but probably connected with the younger inhabitants' dangerous mixture of naivety and piety, the Pitcairn community made itself known to the astonished sailors. Folger quickly knew he had solved the fate of *Bounty*, and he sent his news back to England via the Consul in Valparaiso. But few were interested. France and Bonaparte were causing trouble again.

It was not until 17 September 1814 that men again sighted the peaks of Pitcairn where none should have been. This time it was an altogether more serious encounter. There were two ships and they were both English naval frigates, *Briton*, Captain Sir Thomas Staines, and *Tagus*, Captain Pipon. The ships had been hunting for an American man-of-war, *Essex*, which had been worrying English whalers.

Sultan, Captain Reynolds, which like *Topaz*, hailed from Boston, raised Pitcairn in 1817. This was the last contact made by a ship that did not know of the island. By now the publication of the visit of *Briton* and *Tagus* was causing a sensation around the world, and callers became increasingly common. They thirsted for gossip and mystery, for a look at what was vaunted as the world's most perfect community, and for good meat, fruit and vegetables. In return, they were expected to behave, to keep their libido, blasphemy and innuendo to themselves, and to give such practical things as nails, tools, clothes and religious tracts.

Not unnaturally, these early visitors besieged the islanders with questions. The fate of *Bounty* had been a favourite topic in the inns of ports and the wardrooms of naval ships for two decades. The enquirers learned much, but little of the truth.

That something awesome and Biblical had happened between 1790 and 1808 was certain. Pitcairn was not the expected group of middle-aged men and women and their children. Instead, the island was populated like an embryonic Eden, largely by children and teenagers; the oldest was nineteen. The only adult women were four Tahitians, and there was but one adult male, a corpulent European, who epitomized preconceptions of what the patriarch of an Elysian nursery might be. The other fourteen men who had sailed from Tahiti were not to be seen. As for Fletcher Christian, everyone told a different story about how and when he died. It made men wonder if he *were* dead.

Indeed, the world had been fed with possibilities of his escape from self-inflicted exile since as early as 1796. Some time about

September of that year the British public was tempted with a slim volume with a long title: *Letters from Mr. Fletcher Christian, containing a narrative of the transactions on board His Majesty's Ship Bounty, Before and After the mutiny, with his subsequent voyages and travels in South America.*

On Tuesday, 13 September 1796, *The True Briton* (*Nolumus Leges Angliae Mutari* was its motto), devoted half a column to a report based on the pamphlet, saying that Fletcher Christian, this 'extraordinary Naval Character' had at length transmitted to England an account of himself. It said that after obtaining command of *Bounty* he had visited Juan Fernandez and other islands off the west coast of South America before being shipwrecked while rescuing Don Henriques, Major-General of the Kingdom of Chili [sic]. Suitably grateful, the Spanish Government lucratively employed Fletcher Christian, who was shortly to sail from Cadiz to South America on their behalf.

The True Briton says that Fletcher's *Letters* were published in Cadiz and that, 'we are candidly told by this enterprising mutineer that the revolt . . . was not ascribable to any dislike of their Commander but to the unconquerable passion he [Christian] and the major part of the ship's crew entertained for the enjoyments of Otaheite. . . "It is but justice that I should acquit Captain Bligh in the most unequivocal manner . . ." '

Extracts from the *Letters* were published everywhere. The gentle-manly defence of Bligh makes one think that perhaps the commander himself, or someone close to him, had encouraged the publication, perhaps as an overdue response to Edward Christian's damaging texts.

A copy was sent to Bligh by his publisher, a Mr Nicol. On 16 September, still defending himself, Bligh wrote to Sir Joseph Banks.

Mr Nicol has been so good as to send me down a pamphlet called Christian's Letters—is it possible that wretch can be at Cadiz and that he has had intercourse with his Brother, that sixpenny Professor, who has more Law about him than honour—My Dear Sir, I can only say that I heartily despise the praise of any of the family of Christian, and I hope and trust yet that the Mutineer will meet with his deserts.

Clearly the pamphlets of Edward Christian had wounded Bligh more than he had publicly admitted. Bligh was quite prepared to accept the *Letters* as authentic and the passion of his correspondence with Banks is thought by Gavin Kennedy to prove the work did not come from Bligh's camp. That is doubtful; but it does prove that memories of the mutiny still stung.

Among the journals that published extracts from the *Letters* was *The Weekly Entertainer*. This was seen by William Wordsworth, who was at Racedown, Dorsetshire. The November 1796 issue of this 'agreeable and Instructive repository' published a letter from him that has excited much conjecture, now if not then.

Sir, There having appeared in your Entertainer (vide the 255th page of the present volume) an extract from a work purporting to be the production of Fletcher Christian, who headed the mutiny on board the Bounty, I think it proper to inform you, that I have the best authority for saying that this publication is spurious. Your regard for the truth will induce you to apprize your readers of this circumstance. I am Sir, Your Humble servant, William Wordsworth.

This was not the only rebuttal of the *Letters'* authenticity. On 23 September, *The True Briton* now wrote:

Letters pretended to have been written by Mr Fletcher Christian having been advertised and an extract from them having been inserted in some of the Public Prints, it is necessary to assure the Public, as we do, from the best authority, that since

Christian landed at Otaheite in September, 1789, that part of
the ship's company who were afterwards brought to England
by Captain Edwards, neither he nor the *Bounty* has ever been
heard of. In a matter of so great seriousness, the Public ought
not to be trifled with nor imposed upon by idle fabrications
and scandalous falsehoods.

The authority quoted by Wordsworth was undoubtedly Edward
Christian, the family mouthpiece. The Christian family had not
heard from Fletcher Christian. It was unthinkable they should not
have done so if he were alive and well in Spain: his argument was
not with them.

On 15 April 1815, *The Aberdeen Chronicle*, reporting the visit of
Briton and *Tagus*, said:

The mutineers were unheard of for several years. At length,
some accounts, which we do not distinctly recollect, represented Christian, the ring-leader of them, to be subsisting by
piracy; but this was contradicted, upon the authority of his
family, who knew him to be dead at that time, 1804 . . .

That was a worrying thing for me to find. How did they know he
was dead in 1804? They did not even know where he was, let alone
possess details of his mortal state, unless he really had managed to
be get back to Europe, returned to his family, and there died. But
perhaps the anonymous Aberdonian journalist, lacking access to
family information, was simply filling an empty column, an un-
romantic but far more plausible theory.

Of course, not everyone who read or heard about the *Letters*
would know that they were thought a forgery; and another such
narrative, with an even longer title, was successfully published only
two years later in 1798. So convincing are the accounts that it is
easy to believe they are true and I am sure they are what led to

the belief that in 1808 and 1809 Fletcher Christian was back in Cumbria. There is no contemporary evidence to support this and it was first reported as late as 1831; but the rumour was never substantiated, then or subsequently. The two bogus pamphlets are notable for one thing, though. They are remembered not for their exoneration of Bligh but for suggesting Christian had escaped retribution and was off adventuring. Adventure, defiance and romance were what the public really wanted.

Just over a decade after the *Letters* were published, in February 1810, the *Quarterly Review* reported Folger's discovery of Pitcairn Island. Fletcher Christian's children were from then on the object of great interest and represented as 'very handsome, their features strongly partaking of the English: the beauty of one of them, a girl named Mary Ann Christian, for which she is termed "the maid of the South Seas" is said to invite the same admiration which is offered to the most favoured of our own fair country women'. The news was barely noticed except by Mary Russell Mitford, who wrote 'Christina, The Maid of the South Seas: A Poem', which was published in 1811 (Samuel Taylor Coleridge helped her with it). The first stone of a real avalanche of romantic Pitcairn trivia had been dislodged.

Late in 1815, a man called Porter published his narrative of a cruise, which covered the call of *Briton* and *Tagus* at Pitcairn. The *Aberdeen Chronicle* introducing three long extracts said: 'we are now enabled to complete (the mutineers') history and to describe their present condition'. In fact, the truth was farther away than ever. The history of the Pitcairn community will never be known in full, for from the start there was a deliberate campaign to smudge the past, and that provided even more fuel for the romantics.

From the *Topaz* visit we are told the following different stores:

• Six years after they arrived their servants (the male Polynesians) attacked and killed all the English except Adams who was injured.

- Four years after they arrived, the same revolt of all the Polynesians occurred, with only Adams being spared, although injured.
- Christian became insane shortly after their arrival and threw himself off the rocks into the sea.
- They all lived in tolerable harmony for several years under Christian's government; and then he became sick and died a natural death. This was followed by two massacres when the Tahitian men killed the Europeans, and were in turn killed by the Tahitian women.

Folger stayed at Pitcairn only four or five hours so we must suspect both the reliability of those who told the tales and those who reported them. Captains Pipon and Staines fared a little better. The main discrepancies between the stories they collected concerned the times that certain people were killed. Christian was said to have been shot in the back by a Tahitian man 'three or four years' after arriving on Pitcairn, 'eleven months' and 'about two years' after arrival. These two visits resulted in seven different times of death; five were murders, one a suicide, one a natural death.

A further enigma arose from confusion over what had happened to Fletcher Christian's wife. Several stories said the reason for Christian's death was that he tried forcibly to seize the wife of a Polynesian after Isabella died, giving birth to their first son. This was given credence by a report from Lieutenant Shillibeer, who was with Staines on *Briton* but did not land, interviewing Pitcairners on board instead. He was told that Fletcher Christian's eldest son did not know his mother, for she was dead, and no one contradicted him.

Still, even these confused and contradictory stories may have been some comfort to Fletcher Christian's family in Great Britain. Although we do not know exactly when or how his family learned of Pitcairn and the sad possibility of his having been murdered, the details were published well before the deaths of his brothers Charles and Edward. Extraordinarily his mother was still alive, too.

Ann Christian is perhaps the saddest of all the characters in this long complicated tale. At last she had news of her son Fletcher, and now, in extreme old age she also learned he had given her grandchildren, her only ones. Half way around the world were the three half-caste children and a Tahitian daughter-in-law she would never see. And no one could tell her whether Fletcher was really dead, or how he had died. Ann, a widow for fifty years, died aged ninety in the house in Fort Street, Douglas, that she shared with Charles, on 30 March 1820. Although she had two other famous sons, the local newspaper noted her only as Charles's mother. He died on 14 November 1822 and the same newspaper noted only that he was the brother of Professor Christian, Chief Justice of the Isle of Ely. There was no wish for the relationship with Fletcher to be publicized.

On 13 December, the *Douglas Advertiser* announced a sale of the contents of Charles's house. It can only be imagined what material from or about Fletcher Christian was sold or destroyed.

Professor Edward Christian died the following year in 1823, the last of the clan and thus the natural repository of family papers and possessions. From his Will, I hoped to glean some further clue to Fletcher Christian, and what his family had done about his effects when they resigned themselves to his permanent banishment from the country.

Instead of revelation I found something far more disconcerting that, far from helping pinpoint the fate of Fletcher Christian on Pitcairn, strongly suggested he might, after all, have returned to England. Neither Ann, Charles nor Edward left a Will—a mystery since the Christians from the earliest times were a law-oriented clan. Edward was a Professor of Laws as well as a judge, and had a wife and possessions. I had found the Will of his father, Charles. After him neither his wife nor children had made Wills, yet each of them had possessions and close family when they died.

Since 1796, there had been rumours that Fletcher Christian was not in the South Seas. Could it be, I found myself wondering, that he had really managed to get back to England, and instead of dying before 1804, had lived on, the secret recipient of his dead family's possessions? Peter Heywood is one man who would have agreed wholeheartedly with the possibility, but his opinion was not published until 1831, after he and all the Christians were dead.

Sometime in 1808 or 1809, Peter Heywood had had a startling experience. He was walking down Fore Street in Plymouth Dock when his attention was caught by the appearance of a man whose shape so reminded him of Fletcher Christian that he involuntarily quickened his pace. Both men were walking very fast, and the rapid steps behind him roused the stranger's attention. He turned, looked at Heywood, and immediately ran off. His face was as much like Christian's as his back, and Heywood, exceedingly excited, followed. Both ran as fast as they were able but the stranger had the advantage, and after making several short turns, disappeared.

That Christian should be in England Heywood considered highly improbable, though not out of the realm of possibility; for at this time no account had been received of him. The resemblance, the agitation, and the efforts of the stranger to elude him were too strong not to make a deep impression on him. At the moment his first thought was to set about making some enquiries but on reflecting upon the pain and trouble such a discovery must occasion him, he considered it more prudent to let the matter drop; but he never forgot the incident.

There is nothing sinister about Heywood not following up this intriguing encounter, or in its not being made public for twenty years. The reports from *Topaz* made it quite clear that the Pitcairners at least considered Fletcher Christian dead. If he was not, then the 'pain and trouble' Heywood feared would fall mainly on his old shipmate. Anyway, Fletcher Christian could not have long been in England before finding out that it was Heywood who set into motion the endeavours of Edward Christian to expose Bligh and to publish alternative stories about the mutiny. My opinion is that if the stranger really had been Fletcher Christian, he would have embraced Peter Heywood, rather than fled, and I am sure Heywood thought so, too.

Heywood maintained a keen interest in the Pitcairn community, which was continued by his widow and by his step-daughter, Lady Belcher, who made a point of seeing any captain who had called there. In the Mitchell Library in Sydney, there are several letters which Mrs Heywood wrote in 1852 to George Hunn Nobbs, the lay-pastor on Pitcairn who had come to England to be ordained, inviting him to come and see her. Determined he should have no doubt about who she was, she described her husband as one of the 'Bounty mutineers'. An intriguing remark, considering that in her book, *The Mutineers of the Bounty*, Lady Belcher stated most definitely that Heywood was not a mutineer. Presumably the old lady was determined to get attention at any cost; and it would seem that by then fascination for Pitcairn's model community had lent a certain respectability to those who had been associated with events leading to its foundation.

Or could Heywood have been a mutineer, and had he actually seen Fletcher in Devonport?

34

Massacre

The best accounts of the events on Pitcairn Island between 1790 and 1808 would obviously be those given by people involved. This effectively rules out all but the adults who arrived on board *Bounty*. The age of most inhabitants of the island made it clear they were born after the main turbulence; even those who were alive at the time can have been only three or four, so their tales were second-hand.

The surviving European male, John Adams, said he had been born at Stanford Hill in the Parish of St John, Hackney, of poor but honest parents. His father was drowned in the Thames leaving John and three other children orphans. He was brought up in the poorhouse, where he received rudiments of education and religion. He was in his early forties when Captain Folger met him. A theory has emerged this century that Adams was Irish, and a runaway from trouble in his native village. I have seen much circumstantial evidence that a 'Jack' Adams did go to sea, but there is nothing to link him with the *Bounty* one; but a recent article in the *Mariners' Mirror* shows that it is likely that John Adams' father was the runaway Irishman 'Jack'. John Adams had signed on to *Bounty* as Alexander Smith, and was known to Folger under this name. He may have used an alias because he deserted another ship. When Staines and Pipon called, he used his real name.

Adams was in a real dilemma. Twenty years had passed since he had sailed from England. Here he was with new scars, tattoos, and confronted by a ship full of men who hung on his every word. How much did the visitors know about events aboard *Bounty*, and his part in them? What had happened to the open boat—was he party to mass murder as well as mutiny? And were events on Pitcairn likely to be judged under English law? In short, was he liable to arrest and punishment?

He personally believed he had atoned for his few crimes; he protested he was innocent of complicity in the mutiny, saying he was in his hammock at the time, even though some visitors knew better. Being the only Pitcairner who knew about the world, he monopolized and was monopolized by the visitors. That way he knew what was said and to whom, and cunningly gave the answers that men expected.

Of course, he could not be everywhere and some visitors spoke to the Tahitian women. They managed some general corroboration, but the women were forbidden to speak Tahitian and could barely speak English, using instead a confusing mix of eighteenth century English and Tahitian. Their children merely repeated what little they had been told, and added to the confusion.

It took Adams and his flock seventeen years fully to believe he would not be taken off the island. When it had earlier been suggested, and he agreed, there had been such a wail from his islanders that the suggestion was dropped. By the time Captain Beechey arrived aboard *Blossom* in 1825, Adams was certain that the cross-examining was academic rather than incriminatory and began to give fuller and more accurate accounts. But he still preferred to draw a veil over most of his own involvement in the horrors which emerged.

The other eye-witness accounts are by Jenny, who had first been with Adams during the Tubuaian experiment and then gone with *Bounty* to Pitcairn. She was always fiercely independent, a leader of the women: but she had never been a mother and left Pitcairn in 1817 aboard *Sultan*. Subsequently, she talked to a Captain Peter Dillon who translated her account from the jumble of Tahitian and English in which it had been given. The details she remembers are about people rather than dates and places, and thus are all the more believable. They helped me discard much generally accepted history as fable.

Apart from the educated Christian and Young, the rest of the white settlers of Pitcairn Island were from the lower classes. Their island hideout provided expectations far beyond those to which they had been born. The pursuit of a more self-indulgent way of life is why they had followed Christian in the first place. The slightest diminution of their new status was likely to spark violent protest.

There is conflicting opinion about the behaviour of Fletcher Christian on Pitcairn. He is either morose and brooding or a happy, active, natural leader. Both pictures were given by Adams: the former was probably what the upright and sermonizing nineteenth-century interviewers wished to hear. But Fletcher Christian was a believer in deeds, not words. A busy organizer, digging his garden, building his house, delighting in physical activity of any kind is the more likely picture. Yet he was human and he had done something quite spectacular; he would have been a less than sympathetic man if he had not sometimes yearned for his home and the freedom he had before he became an outlaw. At such brooding moments, he was said to retire to a cave in the sheer side of Lookout Point, close to his house. There he had erected a small watch house and kept a store of provisions. Beechey thought it so difficult to access that a single occupant could hold off a party whatever their size as long as there was a supply of ammunition.

One other source of reliable Pitcairn stories, although second-hand, is John Buffet, who settled on Pitcairn in 1825. He became much respected and trusted, and as many of his stories were collected after Adams' death, when Adams' editing of the truth was no longer possible, they must be given much credence. One of Buffet's most important discoveries exposes another reason for Adams' later exaggerated loyalty to Fletcher Christian—he always referred to him as Mr Christian, even after the mutiny. At one point Adams is said to have refused to mend part of his fence through which the free-ranging hogs might have damaged Fletcher Christian's garden. Christian warned him that if any pigs did get through the fence, they would be shot. 'Then I will shoot you,' Adams replied. Immediately the others—not Christian, you will note—bound Adams and sentenced him to be set adrift on the ocean, which would have meant certain death. Fletcher Christian intervened.

The real problems of Pitcairn were not petty squabbles about hogs and fences. There were three more men than women and some of the men were white. It meant that six Polynesian men had to share three Polynesian women. Although this was something Tahitians might ordinarily have done by choice, here it was a further underlining of the lowly status of these men. Slowly their position as friends and accomplices was eroded. They became slaves. It seems even the women regarded them as second best.

The pattern of inter-racial strife, based on the determined pursuit of guaranteed sexual intercourse, could be discerned soon after they arrived at Pitcairn and Jack Williams' wife died. Williams arrogantly demanded one of the women shared by the Polynesians. Christian refused, and it was suggested that Williams wait for Sully, the infant who had come ashore in a barrel. She was possibly as old as three, but even that meant a wait of ten years, and Williams was not prepared to accept a decade of celibacy. The white men capitulated and the three 'spare' women were taken and lots cast. The lot fell to Nancy, unfortunately, not a shared wife, but the consort of the only Polynesian man who had a wife to himself. Though she liked the idea of increasing her status, her ex-husband was deeply wounded. Weeping with anger and humiliation he took to the hills. Three days later he returned and by force or sweet words took Nancy back. But, like Fletcher Christian once before, he had been pushed too far. His smouldering anger kindled a plot to kill the white men.

Ingeniously the women let their white husbands know by incorporating clues into the songs they extemporised as they went about their daily tasks: 'Why does black man sharpen axe? To kill white men.' There was little subtlety and less time to waste. Christian seized a musket and went to find the conspirators. Most of the Polynesian men lived communally in a large house above Bounty Bay. To intimidate the first of them he met, Christian discharged his gun straight at him. It had been loaded with powder only, as a deterrent; Fletcher was not willing to jeopardize his position by killing in anger. His target misunderstood; and mocking Christian's bad aim, he turned and ran to join Nancy and her husband in their hideout.

When the remaining Polynesian plotters realized their plan was discovered they quickly extracted a promise of forgiveness in return for an act of treachery against their own countrymen. They agreed to kill both Nancy's husband and his companion. First, there was an ineffectual attempt at poisoning. Anxious to break the tension so all could sleep easily, Christian ordered the men to be shot. The Polynesian he chose to do this was told that, if he failed, *he* would be shot. Strong language and action, but it was respected by the Polynesians. The renegades were shot and the island was safe once more.

Nancy went to live with Williams. One of the plotters was put into irons for a while and a couple of years of relative tranquillity ensued. At the end of the wet season in 1793, there were five children. The Christians had two boys, McKoy and Quintal each had a son and Mills a daughter. Fletcher Christian's wife was due to have another baby at the end of September and Mills's wife was also pregnant again.

Quintal and McKoy are universally blamed for finally pushing the Polynesians to murder. They were both cruel and thoughtless towards their 'slaves'. If Quintal's man did not prepare his food sufficiently quickly or well, he was severely flogged. When the man was bleeding and whimpering, unable to defend himself, Quintal would rub brine into the lacerations. McKoy was just as free with the clout and lash.

At the end of September 1793, the black men had had enough. Posing as a thoughtful servant, one of them borrowed a gun to shoot a pig for the white men's dinner. Once armed they bided their time. The women did not suspect their intentions, or did not care. When they left the village to collect eggs, their European husbands were working in the plantations. Fletcher Christian worked close to his home, at the request of his wife, who did not go with the other women as she expected the birth of their next child at any time, an exact three years after the arrival of the first.

Williams was the first victim. When he heard the shot, Martin exclaimed they could all expect a glorious feast that night, believing it was meat and not man that had fallen. The three murderers then asked if their companion, who was helping Mills in his garden, could help them carry the animal they had supposedly shot. The quartet moved to the yam plantation where Fletcher Christian was working. As he struggled to remove roots from some newly-cleared ground he was shot from behind and fell down. To finish the job, he was disfigured about the head with an axe, and left for dead. As he was shot or as he lay bleeding in the freshly-turned red earth, Fletcher Christian groaned loudly. McKoy recognized it as the cry of a dying man, but Mills contradicted him, saying it was only Isabella calling her children to dinner. Reassured, McKoy went back to work with Mills.

The Polynesians were still outnumbered and feared meeting the

Europeans who remained in a group. First McKoy and Mills were separated by a ruse. When they then shot at McKoy, they missed. He fled to raise the alarm but seeing the apparently dead Christian, he found Quintal, and the two hid some way from the village.

Mills had been warned by McKoy but trusted his friendship with the Tahitian men. Shortly afterwards he died at their hands. Martin was shot next but managed to get to Brown's house. When he fell after a second shot, he was beaten over the head with a hammer until he was still. Then Brown was beaten with stones. An ally told him to feign death; but he moved too soon and another shot him. Five white men were now dead and the numbers were even. Only two more deaths were required for the Polynesians to be masters.

Adams had been warned of the troubles by Quintal's wife, and took precautions to secrete himself in the bush with a supply of provisions. But he too exposed himself precipitately and was shot in the shoulder. As he fell he was attacked with the butt of the gun and broke two fingers warding off the murderous thrusts. The gun was put to his side—but misfired twice. Shocked, but stimulated by fear, Adams leapt to his feet and found enough strength to outstrip his would-be assassins.

Finding themselves unlikely to prevail, his pursuers offered Adams protection. Exhausted, Adams accepted and was helped to Christian's house, where most women had sheltered. Some accounts say he was spared only when the women flung their bodies across his. He was not the only one the women championed. Young, said always to have been a special favourite of the Tahitian women, had been protected from the start; he may even have planned the entire coup, for one of the men pursuing Adams was supposed to have apologized, saying he had forgotten Young had said Adams was not to be harmed. It is very difficult to understand why Young, who had rotten teeth and an 'evil' look, should have been so favoured. Perhaps his West Indian blood helped forge a closer tie? Or he may simply have been a better lover.

When a truce was agreed upon, there were plenty of women for the remaining eight men. Yet plenitude brings its own complications. The Polynesians quarrelled as to who would have which widow. They doubtless had competition from Young and Adams, too. The most troublesome of the victors was a young man called Menalee. He soon shot one of his countrymen while he accompanied the wife of Young on the flute. When another consoled Young's wife—for she had been fond of the murdered musician—Menalee attacked again. This time the women protested at his brutality and the man survived. Fearful of retribution from black and white alike, Menalee escaped into the mountains to form an unlikely alliance with McKoy and Quintal, who were both too frightened to reappear in the village.

No one had really won, and from now on lives were bargained and spent recklessly. First either Adams or the women got a message to McKoy and Quintal that they would be welcome to return if they disposed of Menalee. They shot him forthwith: but, still suspecting the remaining two black men, they remained in the bush.

The Tahitian women soon realized how great was the loss of the Europeans they had called husbands, and they helped to bring matters to a conclusion. One of the remaining Polynesian men was axed by one woman as he lay sleeping with another. The other was straightaway shot point-blank by Young. The hands and heads of the two had to be taken to McKoy and Quintal before they returned, on 3 October. Nine men had been slaughtered.

On the day of the first massacre, a girl had been born to Isabella, and called Mary Ann. Not long after her birth, John Mills II was born. Now there were seven children on Pitcairn and the oldest, Thursday October Christian, turned three a few days after the murders ceased. The situation was now reversed. The Polynesian women could choose their men. Adams and Young were each joined by three, McKoy and Quintal each two. Slowly life settled down.

In December of the same year, Young began a journal, which only Captain Beechey reported seeing. Most of the details are domestic and banal. Houses were rebuilt for the newly expanded families, new divisions of land were fenced off and gardens were protected from the pigs by digging pits to trap them. It must have been hard work with only four men, especially as in the next five years thirteen children were born. Several of the women were almost constantly pregnant, a definite change from the first years.

If there was any discontent, it appears to have been among the women, who lived promiscuously with the men and changed their abodes regularly. But judging by Young's journal, the change of abode may have been accounted for by unhappinesss and ill-treatment rather than sexual boredom. In fact, Pitcairn Island was now a distinctly unpleasant place to be. Astonishingly the bodies of those who had been murdered remained where they were killed. Some had had their heads removed by the women.

On 12 March 1794, Young wrote that he had seen Jenny with a skull in her hand, and discovered it was that of Jack Williams. When he insisted it should be buried, the women with Jenny refused, and asked him why he wanted such a thing when the other white men did not. Young conferred with the other three and said he thought that 'if the girls did not agree to give up the heads of the five white men in a peaceable manner, they ought to be taken by force and buried'. It should be noted that Young nowhere says he *saw* five heads or skulls. Even if he did, there was no way he could be certain one was not that of a Polynesian. What happened to the five skulls, whoever they had once belonged to, is not known. The incident exasperated the women, who resolved to leave the island.

On 14 April, they were so urgent in their demands that the men began building them a boat. The childless Jenny tore off the planks of her house for the craft and endeavoured to persuade her countrywomen to do the same. It was astonishing that the men should co-operate with such a scheme but in mid-April, the vessel was launched. 'According to expectation' it upset and although saved from a certain death during their attempt to return to Tahiti, the women became even more despondent and dissatisfied. They were after all treated rather badly, and frequently beaten by the temperamental Quintal and McKoy.

The day after the abortive escape the bones of the murdered people were gathered and buried. The impression given in most accounts is that Fletcher Christian, at least, was buried in his own garden, close to where he fell. Although there is a definite Polynesian tendency to forget someone once he is dead, it is, nevertheless, an appalling thought that the late husbands of these Tahitian women, the fathers of their young children, lay rotting in the sultry summer of 1793–94.

Quintal was showing signs of mental distress and had seriously proposed that the men should not 'laugh, joke, or give anything to any of the girls'. But on 3 October, he gave a party to celebrate the death of the black men a year before. Only a month later the women were discovered to have a plan to kill all the white men as they slept. The women were not punished but the men agreed that the first woman to misbehave in the future would be instantly put to death. So would each subsequent offender until the 'real intentions of the women' could be discovered. Talk meant nothing to the unhappy women, who made a physical attack on the men on 30 November. More threats were made but now the women seemed to have the upper hand. Whenever they were displeased they collected their children and some firearms and hid in a remote or fortified part of the island until it pleased them to return. By such mercurial behaviour the women were able to keep their men in a constant state of suspense. Nevertheless, Quintal fathered five children and Young, having had four by Nancy, then had three by Fletcher Christian's widow. McKoy only managed one further child and Adams, after a slow start, fathered four.

By 1796 there was a more sociable atmosphere, with the men

entertaining one another in their houses and making life a little more comfortable for their women. Then McKoy distilled alcohol from the sweet syrup of the ti root (*cordyline terminalis*). Drunkenness was added to promiscuity. The raw spirits inflamed McKoy and Quintal. McKoy lost control totally and threw himself off the cliffs just below Christian's house. Quintal threatened to kill Fletcher Christian's children unless he could have his widow. For the protection of all, he was executed by Young. Only now did real peace seem possible.

35

The Enigma of the Ancient Mariner

Young took the opportunity of teaching Adams to read and write better. Within a couple of years, Young died of asthma, the first man to die naturally. Now alone, Adams became an alcoholic. During the most dramatic of his hallucinations, he saw the Archangel Gabriel, sobered immediately and scurried to find the prayer book and Bible that were among the books that had come from *Bounty*.

With his limited ability to read and only cobwebbed memories of religious instruction in the poorhouse and at sea, Adams cobbled together what he thought was a suitably penitential form of Anglicanism and quickly converted the island to a new way of life. The rules included two fast days a week, which resulted in frequent fainting among his too malleable flock as they laboured in their fields to grow what they were forbidden to eat.

Life on Pitcairn did indeed become Paradise. But even Paradise has loins and by now Thursday October wanted to exercise his. In 1806, when he was probably about sixteen, if that, he fathered a child on the Tahitian woman known as Susannah, who had first been the wife of Young and then of Quintal and who was almost certainly the woman who had axed to death one of the last

Polynesian men. She was the youngest of the girls (except for Sully) who had come to Pitcairn but was over thirty when she married the youthful Thursday October. They had six children.

By the time Beechey arrived in 1825, Fletcher Christian's second son, Charles, had also married a Tahitian woman, Sully. Fletcher Christian's many grandchildren were three-quarter Tahitian, and by the time they were old enough to marry, Isabella saw a wedding between her son Edward Young and her grandchild Polly Christian, one of Thursday October's daughters.

In 1825, Adams took the opportunity to ask Beechey to marry him officially to his blind and ailing wife Mary, who had borne him his only son, George.

Beechey was the first fully to explore Pitcairn Island's community, past and present, and he described an idyllic existence. The Pitcairners were innocent and beautiful to behold, golden children of Christian love, who did not lie or gossip. If he asked about another islander, they would answer: 'It will do you no good, it will do you no harm', and refuse to continue. The men wore a loin cloth and the women a long skirt. Both dropped a tunic rather like a short poncho over their shoulders to protect themselves from the sun, but otherwise went naked from the waist up. They wove hats with dexterity and bedecked them with flowers. They anointed themselves with the oils of tropical flowers and entertained with a natural warmth and unaffected Christianity that had many visitors feeling ashamed of their own nodding, bobbing and mumbling on Sundays.

So breathless and admiring are most, if not all, the visitors' journals that the dearth of hard fact is barely noticed.

We know the community lived in bowers in a small group some half mile from Bounty Bay. In front of Adams' house was a large lawn, often mistaken for a village square. At the bottom of the clearing was Fletcher Christian's house and beyond that, the house of Thursday October, who shortly changed his name to Friday

October, when he learned his father had not compensated for crossing the date line.

Beechey described remains of maraes and the strange carvings in the rocks of the virtually inaccessible cove called Down Rope. But he does not mention a grave for Fletcher Christian. Isabella, who was still known as Mrs Christian, was not questioned about it. If Adams' flock was really so Christian, should they not have made some attempt to mark the graves of their forefathers? Paganism and idolatry were all behind them. Pitcairn was now a Christian community, and Christians honoured the dead. This fact, in particular, convinces me that Adams was not a benevolent old patriarch but a hypocritical manipulator of Polynesian women and young children. It can only have been him who led Thursday October to believe his mother was dead, yet called Isabella Mrs Christian. The obfuscation about the early days can be laid at his feet alone; and it was all planned to save his neck. There was nothing to be proud of in what he did, which not only guaranteed his survival, but also served to underline his position in his community as a handy *deus ex machina*.

Adams died in 1829, without ever being exposed as a pious fraud. It is impossible to feel anything but affection and sympathy for those he left behind, who had no way of knowing whether his teachings were right or wrong. At least they knew the rudiments of reading and writing and the language of their white fathers. They were startled to see dogs and cattle and did not know how to open doors. They shamed naval officers by saying grace before and after meals with genuine sincerity. When Thursday October was once served food by a black servant aboard ship, he left his place at the ship's table saying he did not like black men. Adams had managed to put most of the blame for Pitcairn's problems on the Tahitian men, and the prejudice had lasted, even though Thursday October and his brother had both a Tahitian mother and wife.

Once Adams had gone, and lay in a marked grave behind his house, different versions of his stories began to emerge.

In 1831, John Barrow published the first really comprehensive book about the mutiny on *Bounty* and Pitcairn Island. In a footnote he revealed Heywood's reported sighting of Fletcher Christian in 1808 or 1809. Then, in 1834, Dr Bennet, the surgeon aboard the whaling ship *Tuscan*, Captain Stavars, was shown a grave said to be that of Fletcher Christian. But his report was buried in a long *Narrative of a Whaling Voyage*, published in London in 1840, and has been ignored by or unknown to most authors or visitors to Pitcairn, possibly because it was not consistent with other records.

There was one person who could have set the record right— Isabella, the widow of Fletcher Christian. She had not grown fat like most of her countrywomen but remained slim and relatively upright. She had a shock of white hair and was renowned for her stories. But these were told only to her family. The awful truth— at least it is awful to a descendant—is that Europeans could probably not bear to speak to her; she seems to have been a perfect fright in her old age.

In March 1830, a young man aboard the vessel *Seringapatam* wrote in his journal:

An old woman has a world of prejudice to surmount before she can become anything but an object of pity, and often of disgust ... we recall the stories of witchcraft malice and cruelty imputed to the old and infirm of the female sex. She looked so old and corpse-like that I gladly escaped from her awkward expressions of pleasure at the appearance of my clothes, gun, etc.

Naturally, I always rather hoped I would never find proof that the young man was referring to my great-great-great-great-grandmother. But he was.

In 1841, a 24-gun English naval ship, *Curaçao*, called at Pitcairn and stayed a couple of weeks to help with an epidemic of fever and flu. There are many important records of this visit, including the acerbic journal of the ship's doctor, Gunn. He could not help but note the sadness of a Polynesian community that insisted on dressing their children when they swam. I deciphered a previously ignored note in his book, which said that the Christian children were thought to be simple in the head, 'perhaps the influence of their Tahitian mother'.

There has never been any trace of mental deficiency within the family, at least not recognized, and it was only when I was shown a privately owned and previously unknown journal of another of the *Curaçao*'s complement that the reason for Gunn's remark became clear. The author of the beautifully illustrated record of this visit to Pitcairn was George Gardner, apparently one of the officers.

He noted that the females never ate with the males and called it a relic of the barbarianism, a custom of the uncivilized inhabitants of the South Seas handed down from

these peoples '. . . Tahitian parents. There are two of the Tahitian women still living. [One is] Isabella Christian . . . the wife of Fletcher Christian who headed the mutiny. Isabella Christian is the most perfect picture of an old hag I ever saw. She is still surprisingly active. Her age is supposed to be between 80 and 90. She remembers Captain Cook at Tahiti and from what she herself says must then have been a mother. In this tho' there is nothing very extraordinary since they marry even nowadays at the age of 13 or 14.

So—she looked like an old hag. No wonder visitors did not talk to her and thought her children might be mentally deficient. She was certainly over eighty then, and this is the first indication that she might have left children behind on Tahiti. Within a month she was dead, another victim of the epidemic. On 19 September 1841, she was buried. Isabella's son Charles followed her to the grave early the following year; his wife Sully had died in 1826.

Unbelievably, there were more versions of Fletcher Christian's end to come. One of the least known and most fascinating appeared in a book published in 1898 called *The Mutineers: a Romance of Pitcairn Island*. Although turgid with high passion and purple patches in the best manner of the Victorian novel, it purported to be the first true story of what had happened, written by two men, Becke and Jeffery. Becke was an extraordinary Australian adventurer about whom it was said he was 'one of the rare men who have led a wild life and have the culture and talent to give some account of it'. In the Mitchell Library and the National Library in Canberra, I found a great deal of his correspondence, both with his collaborator, who lived in England, and with various critics and associates including his agent in London.

The Mutineer said that Christian survived the gunshot wounds and recovered in his cave. When he was well enough, he attempted to put to sea in *Bounty*'s boat to join a sailing ship sighted off Pitcairn. Adams tried to prevent him to protect the secrecy of the community and in the struggle, shot and killed Christian. Before he died, Christian asked to be buried in an unmarked grave—he did not wish people to point out the grave of 'the mutineer'. No wonder Adams would not commit himself. *He* had killed Christian, albeit accidentally. No wonder everyone else had conflicting stories. They were protecting their patriarch. And it was Christian's own wish that his grave be not known.

It was such a perfect solution, even if found in a 'factional' book, that I had to dig deeper. How had Becke come up with this version? The answer is astonishing—he got it from Pitcairners. Among his correspondence I found a letter to Egan Mew, QC, of 3 Gray's Inn Place, London. He was a writer for *The Critic* which had just given *The Mutineer* a wishy-washy review. Becke wrote in his defence:

I know the descendants of the *Bounty* Mutineers and the *native*
story of Christian and his life better than any man living. This
sounds very egotistical of me but it is true.

And instead of Christian being . . . the 'full-blooded villain'
he was the very reverse. I have been told over and over again
by old natives that Christian was the very reverse of a sensual
man; that he was intimate with only one Tahitian woman
whom he afterward took away with him to Pitcairn; that this
woman was seduced by Young; that the other Tahitian men
and women would have killed Young, but that Christian,
horror-stricken at the bloodshed that had already taken place,
carefully protected the man who seduced his wife; and the
story of his life in the cave as narrated by Jeffery and myself
is *true*—not embroidered fiction.

Furthermore the story of Christian's death by gunshot accidentally received from John Adams/Alexander Smith whilst
endeavouring to prevent Christian from putting to sea in the
Bounty's boat, is I believe, strictly true.

Anyway, I prefer to believe the native account of the *Bounty*
story to the vague surmises of the many authors who have
written on the subject but who only obtained their data from
the Court Martial of some of the mutineers or from John
Adams' carefully considered statements to Naval Officers.
Perhaps you can make an interesting par[agraph?] of this?

Becke's assertions that he heard these stories first hand are proven
by journals which show he did stay on the island, but the exact date
of his sojourn has never been established. Letters that passed
between him and his collaborator clearly show that neither was
above twisting the story for the sake of drama; but Becke passionately believed he had solved the question of Christian's fate.

Is it true, though? Somehow it is *too* true, and, of course, the
'old natives' were anything but witnesses to the events, for Becke's

stay was probably in the 1850s or 1860s, as far as I can make out. All my research into his background and the writing of the book only showed me that I could not lightly ignore this version. Neither could I ignore the other, better known story—that Fletcher Christian did escape and was the inspiration and model for Coleridge's, 'The Rime of the Ancient Mariner'.

This idea was first suggested by a Mr Porter, who did a lot of work to show that Coleridge's so-called fantasy poetry was really based on events and places and people he knew of or had read about—he boasted he had 'read everything'.

The sufferings of the Mariner can certainly be related to those of Fletcher Christian. It is possible to make a strong case for the poem being a description of Fletcher's secret journey back to England. And as well as helping Ms Mitford with her poem about Fletcher Christian's daughter, Coleridge once penned a note to himself about Christian's adventures, making the possibility of a link even stronger. Add to this the friendship of William Wordsworth for both the Christian family and Coleridge, and there is enough substance in the enigma for a book, as C. S. Wilkinson proved with his persuasive *The Wake of the Bounty* published in 1953.

Once I had read it my confusion was complete. Yet I was certain there must be some way of discovering the true fate of Fletcher Christian. It was not until 1975 that I realized there had never been a biography of him. I knew then I had somehow to unearth the truth about my ancestor and to write it.

IV

Oblivion Denied

36

Ignominious Beginnings

I decided finally to begin full time work on discovering Fletcher Christian while I was being starved in the isolation ward of a geriatric hospital somewhere in Ruislip, early in 1978. I had been in Thailand for three weeks, travelling north into the Golden Triangle to visit the nomadic Chinese tribes who were then responsible for growing much of the world's opium. It wakened my taste for adventure again, something I had repressed for three years while operating a delicatessen I had opened just off London's Portobello Road market.

On the 747 flight back from Bangkok, I was struck painfully and feverishly by what turned out to be both dysentery and salmonella poisoning; yet during my long recovery I knew I had to travel again. My next goal would be Pitcairn Island.

As soon as I was allowed to mix with the public again, I called on the only two explorers I knew. First was Robin Hanbury-Tenison, one of the most important—and glamorous—of modern explorers. At the time, Robin was leading the Royal Geographical Society's biggest ever expedition to Mulu in Sarawak, for which he later was awarded the RGS Gold Medal. As luck would have it, he was back in London for a short time and I went to see him at the Society's house, in Kensington.

'What do you think about a descendant of Fletcher Christian . . .'

'Following his ancestor's footsteps? Marvellous! Do it! How about becoming a Fellow of the RGS, too?'

A good start.

Next I went to see Tim Severin, who had just sailed across the Atlantic in an open leather boat, proving that St Brendan, a sixth-century Irish monk, probably discovered America. I had provisioned *Brendan* on the second leg of its voyage from Iceland to the USA, and the grains, smoked meats, sausages and cheeses I had chosen, some specially made, were a greater success than modern foods and a considerable help to both health and morale in the cramped and cold boat.

Tim was as enthusiastic as Robin and after his Atlantic trip was envious that mine would be in warm waters. He offered an introduction to Julian Bach, his agent in New York. Julian met me in London's Connaught Hotel the next week. His interest and excitement spurred me on to write a synopsis of the biography of Fletcher Christian I planned. Various New York publishers were approached, some were less enthusiastic than others, but finally it seemed likely that either New York Times' Books or the Atlantic Monthly Press would commission me to do the book. Confident of a quick and adequate sale, I left for Sydney, Australia, to start my detailed research in the Mitchell Library, which has a magnificent collection of *Bounty* related material.

But negotiations did not move as fast as I had hoped, and by March 1979 I still had no contract and no money, but I had discovered enough new information to convince me I was on the right track; I had already found the Bond papers. So when I was telephoned by New York Times' Books at 3.30 in the morning to tell me that an author who had recently written on the subject advised them not to bother with me, I was stunned. I cabled Julian to cancel further negotiations, borrowed money to return to London and spent the weekend spending my remaining $10. A telegram was waiting for me on Monday when I returned. Certain it contained more bad news, I opened it with forboding. Amazingly, Julian had had an exceptionally good offer for the book from Atlantic Monthly of Boston. I left for London three days later. I had a book to write.

Within six months I knew more about my universally recognized but totally unknown ancestor than anyone who has written about him. Extraordinarily it was easy; sadly, it revealed how many so-called definitive works are merely patched together of old material.

There is a book called *The Yesterdays Behind the Doors*. It was published by Liverpool University Press in 1956 and contains 1,000 years of Christian family history. The book has one astonishing feature—none of the sources is given, not even those of the pictures. It occurred to me that someone must have spent many many years putting the background of this book together—every book is but the tip of an iceberg of labour and paperwork. Perhaps I could find that research? I did, simply by looking at three Wills in Somerset House, and tracing the estate of the woman who had written the work, Susan Hicks Beach, born Susan Christian.

Underneath a grand piano in a bewitching red-brick Inigo Jones mansion outside Newbury, England, I found a veritable mountain of family papers. Included were 500 leather-bound pages of Christian family genealogical fact, dating back to 1380, annotated and verified and brimful with every record of tradition, hearsay or gossip. In neat handwriting, with no mistakes and three colours of ink, impeccable research recorded twenty-one generations of Christians. The last Mrs Christian of the Milntown line and her daughter Rita had spent over thirty years collecting memories, Wills, letters, diaries, paintings, prints, and photographs in the hope that the record would stimulate a member of the family to buy back the estate that they had been forced to sell.

Ewan Christian, who owns this remarkable cache, is considered now to be the head of the family. With enormous kindness he let me take exactly what I wanted and promised that no one else should look at a thing until I had published my book. In any case, one other author had come to look at the papers and dismissed them as worthless.

Using this family history as my base, I traced echoes of stories to their sources, added colour to monochromatic asides produced by shame or a descendant's respect for the dead. Among the trove of letters and notes, the most breathtaking find was the auto-biography of Charles, Fletcher's previously unknown brother, and digging in the treasures hidden between the lines of this led, as you will have read, to the discovery of Charles's mutiny. The original copy of this work was once in the Manx Museum in Douglas but has long since disappeared; again I thank Mrs and Miss Christian who day after day for decades copied each document they found by longhand, tracing signatures and double-checking references.

So now I could tell the world who Fletcher Christian was and could properly assess for the first time what he did, and his rela-tionship with William Bligh. With a distinct feeling of dread, admit-tedly interspersed with excitement, I knew that an expedition to Pitcairn was a responsibility I could not avoid. Without such an attempt to solve the mystery of Fletcher Christian's death the book would not be fully credible; but I could see it would take so much time and money to organize that the writing of the book might well be jeopardized.

The deeper I became committed, the fewer people there were to help; there was no precedent for what I wanted to do. The Expeditions Office of the Royal Geographical Society—Nigel Winser and Shane Wesley-Smith—were superb in their moral support, but as I was not climbing a Himalayan peak or exploring a rain-forest they could be of little specific help.

Suspicious of the attitudes of other authors about visiting *Bounty-*related sites—some were dismissive, some snide and contemptuous of what they found—I was certain I dare not go alone. I was bound to be thought biased, and so I wanted to take a group along to temper, oppose or complement my impressions. That meant organizing my own transport there and back. It also meant raising many thousands of pounds of finance.

Visitors to Pitcairn generally arrive in small sailing vessels on their way to or from South America, but they never stay more than a few days. Even if you can manage to organize a passage on a ship from New Zealand or Panama *and* permission to land—the combination of which might easily take two years to arrange—you can find yourself sailing past Pitcairn because conditions make landing impossible; or, having landed, find yourself trapped for months until the next vessel arrives. It was a great problem. But luck seemed to be on my side.

Through my delicatessen shop, I had met some cousins called Curwen, descendants of Fletcher's first cousin, John Christian Curwen. David Curwen had recently been in Greenwich and was overwhelmed by the sight of a sailing ship called *Christian Bach*. Inveigling his way on board, he learned it was soon to sail for Australia and intended to call at Pitcairn. It was a 120 foot brigantine, beautiful, broad and air-conditioned; each cabin had Mozart and a telephone and refrigerator. It sounded just right for me, who had never sailed on anything less than 25,000 tons and who cannot swim.

I raced down to Ramsgate where she had sailed, marvelling at the coincidence of her name being a combination of my surname and my New York agent's. Too good to be true, I thought. Indeed it was.

After weeks of exciting planning it was agreed we would meet *Christian Bach* in Guayaquil, Ecuador, sail to Pitcairn via the Galapagos and Easter Island, include a stop at Tubuai, and finish the journey at Tahiti. I made a short film for BBC TV, there were pictures published all round the world, and *Christian Bach* sailed back to Greenwich. But my nautical friends were beginning to wag their heads. They felt something was wrong with the ship and could not believe the captain was planning to sail, very shorthanded, back down the Thames at sunset with no knowledge of the tides that particular day. It did not seem so important to me, and having found a ship that was going to Pitcairn, I kept my mouth shut, voicing doubts only to God.

Soon *Christian Bach* was sinking in the Channel and had to be rescued by the Royal Navy. Once she was ignominiously returned to port, a writ for non-payment of bills was nailed to her mast. Fortunately I had not paid over any money, but there my luck ended. From then on the story of the expedition's planning is one of disillusionment, loneliness, fear, sweat and more tears than I knew I had inside me. But once again in my life there was no going back. By now the expedition was officially approved by the Royal Geographical Society—without schedule, without a real budget, without even a vessel; I could not possibly lose face with the Society, having named the project in honour of one of their Founders.

One of the men who formed in 1830 what became the Royal Geographical Society was John Barrow, Second Secretary of the Admiralty, who was at the same time working on his book *The Mutiny of the Bounty*, the first serious work on the subject and still one of the most important. It had seemed to be an excellent idea to make the Fellows and the public a little more aware of this man and his interests in the year of the 150th anniversary of the founding of the Society. It caused no little stir when the prospectus for the Sir John Barrow Commemorative Expedition, 1980, arrived at the Society. Founders are treated with scarcely less reverence than the Creator. But my argument for the expedition's name was accepted and at last I was waiting outside the Committee Room for my official interview, to establish whether they would give me their stamp of approval.

No trial of endurance in the field can have been much worse. I was seated at the middle of one side of an immensely long and thin bank of tables. There was a smell of leather and pipes in the air. In the distance on my left was the serious white head of Lord Hunt, leader of the successful 1953 Everest expedition, amazed at my confidence in raising a budget of at least £15,000. Equally far away, to my right, was Nigel Winser of the Expeditions Office, asking good questions about my commitment to long-term interest in Pitcairn, which I could answer with passion. In between were men of eminence and exploit, who gently probed and questioned with implacable faces. As I answered each question, I tried to look at each man by turning my head so as to answer them equally. It was not unlike being at Wimbledon, except the ball was in my court.

With Robin Hanbury-Tenison's advice and my own wish to contribute something to Pitcairn's future, as well as digging in its past, I had presented a comprehensive programme of tasks we hoped to perform. Making a definitive map of Pitcairn was something I had hoped the committee would find irresistible. It would be the only one and was to be presented to their Map Room, one of the most famous in the world.

Their deliberations and doubts were never revealed, of course, but they did give me their approval. With that I expected my troubles to be, if not over, considerably eased. My expedition was official, and surely that would make other arrangements easier.

37

Tahiti Regained

To complete the voyage and write the book by the end of 1980, I had to be sailing out of Tahiti early in July of the same year. By the time the *Christian Bach* had finally foundered and the RGS had given me their blessing, it was the end of March. I had just over three months to find a vessel and raise the money to charter it. Both are notoriously difficult to do and the trap was tightening—without money I could not charter a vessel; without a vessel and a budget, I could not raise money.

No charter company in London could help—the South Pacific was another world. I knew that Sydney and Auckland were not organized enough to have big chartering services and finally thought my best bet was to try to find a ship on the West Coast of America. Enquiries to quite disparate people came back with the same answer—'see Mary Crowley of Ocean Voyages in Sausalito'. There was no time to worry about further expense. Within a week I was in Sausalito and Mary was calming me. She was very sensitive to the problems of putting a group of people together and what effect they might have on the Pitcairners, for she had sailed on expeditions, led expeditions, done everything I had not. Soon she had chosen eight of her vessels that were suitable and willing to do the trip, and we were attempting to make a decision. But comparing one vessel with another is like comparing a buttercup to a Cadillac. You can't. One was big and strong but the crew was probably not right. Another had a wonderful crew but was ultimately too small or too expensive. Of course to me they were *all* too expensive and I think Mary knew that. But she didn't let on, and we blithely talked about basic costs of £50 per person per day for ten weeks— and agreed that ten people would be about right for the group. I was committing myself to spend (and raise) £35,000, plus air fares, and the inevitable extras.

One of the ships keen to go to Pitcairn and benefit from the eventual publicity was called *Taiyo* (Japanese for Ocean, but also, of course, the Tahitian word for special male friendships), and she was the only one I was able to see. She was anchored at the Sausalito Marina, just a few minutes from Mary's house. *Taiyo* had been built in Mexico only seven years before, to combine the lines of an eighteenth-century brigantine with the advantages of twentieth-century technology and comfort. Reassuringly, she was steel and the sails on her square-rigged main mast could be managed from the deck rather than requiring crew to scuttle up and down ratlines. She had never been fitted out internally, for the shipbuilders in Mexico had gone bankrupt as she was nearing completion and the government impounded her. Her subsequent history was not very much more encouraging. Her last owner was the pilot of the small aircraft that collided with a jet at San Diego late in 1978. Now she was owned by a consortium headed by Mike Dunn, a Pan Am pilot, being fitted out in mahogany and teak and looking for a job.

It was duty rather than interest that saw me following Mary to the docks to see her. I had mainly registered the unhappy aspects of the story, and words like brigantine, square rig and steel had not meant much. I turned a corner to see *Taiyo* dead ahead. I stopped, immediately persuaded. I saw the yard-arms with their furled sails at right angles to the main mast and that was it. Was it some of

Fletcher's blood that made my heart leap so? Who knows? I only know that nothing has so moved me for years as that sight. If the price could be arranged I wanted this ship. It was another immediate and emotional decision. But if the ship's lines did that to me, I hoped they would do it to others, making it easier to build interest and raise money.

Details were completed when I was back in England. It was a tremendous deal for me. *Taiyo* would have a crew of four, and accommodation for an additional twelve. For $30,000 I could have the ship and six others in my party; Mary took it upon herself to find four fare-paying passengers who, because they would have to be subordinate to the aims of the expedition, would pay only $2,500 each.

Once I started fund raising in earnest, the combination of Royal Geographical Society approval and a beautiful ship worked against me; most people thought that RGS approval meant they were paying and I was asking others merely to top up the barrel; some were so taken with the romance of the voyage and the ship that they made promises they should not have. Promises of introductions or contributions came to nothing.

An international airline and an oil company were the most interested potential sponsors, and both asked me not to approach other companies, an encouraging sign. As time passed, I emptied my bank account then borrowed another £5,000, but two weeks before we were due in Tahiti, I still had not paid the final amount to Mary. It took repeated telephone calls to establish that neither the oil company nor the airline was going to help. In one case the decision had been made two weeks before; both the men concerned had over-committed themselves and had been too embarrassed to tell me.

This last fortnight was as bitter and solitary as it is possible to imagine. I barely slept as I tried to raise money. I was hardly capable of making a logical decision, yet was faced with deciding whether to cancel the trip and lose the money I had already sent. I had neither time nor energy to reconsider my motives or the outcome; the path I was on would have to do, whatever other people thought.

Just one week from the deadline, I was able to pay for the expedition myself. Against all odds I had an expedition of eleven, including a three-member film team from Marin County found by Mary.

Exhausted financially and emotionally I packed for this most important trip of my life in less than an hour. There was no time properly to consider the reference books I should take. I hadn't learned to swim or to dive, knew little about sailing and less about most of the people for whom I would be responsible for the next ten weeks. I flew out with Michael Brook, who as a loyal friend and ingenious researcher had been an invaluable support during the past year. When we arrived in San Francisco, there was no one to meet us. We found a cheap hotel, then caught a freezing cable car to Fisherman's Wharf to get drunk and fed economically: I didn't dare use my credit card, the hotel had taken almost all the money we had in our pockets and no one would change travellers' checks.

Next morning Mary found and mollified us in her incomparable way. Hours were spent agreeing to the details of the film contract and by mid-afternoon we had crossed the Golden Gate Bridge twice and were back at the airport meeting the film crew before flying to Los Angeles to meet more expedition members, and flying on to Tahiti. Others came on different flights. In the early hours of the morning of 5 July, we went aboard *Taiyo* in Papeete harbour. I was pleased there was little moonlight, for I could sit in the warm tropical night and cry silently with fatigue and relief, and no one could see. A fine way for an intrepid explorer to behave.

38

The Soul of Polynesia

Our first South Pacific sun came up explosively, lighting in turn the fabled peaks of Moorea across the lagoon, the knife-edged crags behind Papeete, then the masts of *Taiyo* and the faces of the expedition members. We had stayed up the rest of the night, drinking tepid white California wine, talking, and wondering at the great geometric stretch of the Southern Cross.

From London there were Michael Brook, Vivien Gay and Jasmina Hilton. Vivien was thirty and a fairly high-powered travel executive, who had promised to be very seasick; Jasmina, half-Iranian and 'a few years older' was an actress. The film crew was headed by Ted Cochran, a Vietnam veteran who had flown helicopters on Apollo mission retrievals, and was a full-time enthusiast for the trip, the ship and the sea. As cameraman, Ted had brought Kim Hoeg, a young Norwegian who had lived most of his life in America. The sound recordist was Marilyn Waterman, a native-born Californian and star graduate of the Film Faculty at Stanford. These three were virtually unknown to each other, but their professional and Californian jargons gave them an apparent cohesion.

Richard Hudson was a New Zealander with great knowledge of horticultural and agricultural methods that rely on natural techniques. Elliott Smith was another of Mary's finds, a forty-year-old professional photographer from San Francisco who had worked in the Solomon Islands. From Jackson, Mississippi came Mark Balsiger, a thirty-year-old free-lance journalist; from Bedford, Massachusetts, came Andrew Brady, a son of my American editor —he was fifteen, but admitted to sixteen.

Taiyo's captain, Terry Purkiss, was English, the Australian mate was, intriguingly, called Tony Fletcher, the engineer was 'Hop' and Virginian, and the cook, the fourth woman aboard, was German and known as Bina, short for Sabine. Terry and Bina seemed very much in love. Three of the crew admitted to past marriages but were now divorced, the remainder were single.

The perhaps surprising range of age, sophistication, background and culture was the lifeblood of the expedition, the base on which I would, paradoxically, build firm opinions. By drawing on the varied experiences of all my fourteen companions, I was certain to present as objective and balanced a view of Pitcairn as possible.

But first I had to peel the layers of normal life from myself and the expedition members. I wanted them to discard their European and American ways of life and understand the simplicity of Polynesia, to develop a feel for its music and a taste for its luscious food, to understand personally the deprivations and discomforts of life at sea and on a remote island. Only then might we begin to understand more of Fletcher Christian and presume to comment on his Pitcairn descendants.

Papeete and Tahiti for all their past importance to the *Bounty* story were hardly the places to begin our re-education. Airconditioned shopping centres, television, discothèques, transvestite bars, Chinese restaurants, and superlative croissants meant we might have been in any number of provincial French resorts. We would have to deal with the Tahitian aspects of the story later in the voyage. Now I wanted to show the expedition some of the threads of old Polynesia, ones shared by the *Bounty* men. While waiting for jet-lag and shyness to dissipate and stores to arrive, we planned. On Sunday 5 July we had our first serious meeting under *Taiyo*'s striped awning. Terry first needed to establish our several degrees of seamanship; they turned out to be low, with Ted, Richard and Mark being the only sailors. The latter two had both also been to Pitcairn and supported Terry when he warned us of the dangers of the waters through which we would be sailing. One ship in seven that sailed into the Tuamotu Archipelago was wrecked, almost always because of sloppy navigation or inefficient watch keeping.

Terry and I had been working at 'best' and 'worst' schedules. First we plumped for a short shakedown cruise from Tahiti and back, sailing north-west to Bora Bora and other islands of the Society Group. Wednesday morning was fixed for departure and the intervening days were spent visiting Matavai Bay, the kaleidoscope of Papeete's early morning food market, filming, and struggling with the problems of stowage aboard *Taiyo*. It was all a little aimless for, although we clicked as a group immediately, there was still no sense of reality in the adventure.

At precisely 5 am on 9 July *Taiyo* edged out of Papeete's still lagoon past the ugly concrete docks built by the French which scar the town's view of Moorea. It was a sickly sunrise and the dreaded *mal de mer* took a wide and sudden toll, which just as quickly disappeared. By noon we were skirting Tetiaroa, the coral atoll Marlon Brando was allowed to buy after he had played Fletcher Christian in the MGM film made on Tahiti in the early 1960s. Here, just thirty miles from Papeete, was the timeless South Pacific of legend. Most of us were seeing for the first time the startling contrast as the rolling sea of intense blue turned to a still, milky turquoise after thundering over an encircling reef. Behind the sand, here dazzling and white in the high tropical sun, not black like that of volcanic Tahiti. Then, a jumble of greens, as violently stroked and tangled as a Van Gogh, vivid and thick and punctured with the heads of coconut palms.

As we cruised around the reef looking for the sole, narrow entrance we tried to contact the atoll's main island, which has a small airstrip and a few thatched huts that may be rented. I was nursing the hope that I could meet Marlon Brando and had written to tell him of the expedition. There had been no answer and no one knew if he was there or not. Even if he was not, his wife, Tarita, who played my great-great-great-great-grandmother in the film, might be at home. When we made radio contact we were rudely ordered to get off the air—which we did—and that was the last time our radio ever worked, a re-creation of eigthteenth-century marine isolation I could have done without.

Just as Bligh had done aboard *Bounty*, our captain divided us into three watches, so that each group was on duty for four hours and off for eight, in rotation. He had also arranged two 'dog watches' which purposely interfered with the routine by dividing the 4 pm to 8 pm watch into two, so each watch worked a different time on successive days and nights. When Terry had suggested that the cook and I be excused such duties, I accepted without thinking. Later I spent a lot of time reconsidering. Should I not imitate Fletcher Christian and learn to handle a sailing ship, remember the names of lines and sails, learn how to keep safe and awake on the dreaded graveyard watch, from midnight to 4 am? But when I saw how the broken sleep patterns affected the others, I was confirmed in my quick decision. I felt it my responsibility to everyone on board to be as physically and mentally strong as possible; for the expedition's sake I also needed to be well briefed. There were months of thinking and reading to catch up, all the work that should have been done before I left.

Difficult winds, rough waters, seasickness and tiredness persuaded us to make an early landfall at Raiatea. We slipped through its reef late in the afternoon of the 10th and were unable to express our impressions as we sailed through calmer waters past thin black valleys, and luxuriantly draped mountains, flossed with cloud towers of pastel colours. As night fell we tied up at the spartan dock of Utaroa and Marilyn stumbled off to fall on her hands and knees and kiss the solid ground, to the natural consternation of some local children. This is French Polynesia's second biggest town, yet boasts only a dozen or so shops, an endearingly irregular market, and a sprinkling of those untidy, secretive, fascinating jumbles called general stores that germinate throughout the Pacific wherever there are isolated communities and Chinese entrepreneurs; one of these also cooked excellent steaks from locally bred cattle and served them with wonderful chips, thick, dry and crisp.

Next morning enquiries around the town produced a Mr Chang, who owned the most capriciously decorated nightclub and was also the acknowledged expert on the island's most important site, the ruined marae of Taputapuatea. Before Christian missionaries brought newer and more amazing myths, this was the holiest place in Polynesia, a true Mecca for followers of the cult of Oro. For centuries brave, pious pagans sailed their carved and festooned canoes from as far as Hawaii and New Zealand to the sacred ceremonies here. One of the Polynesians who went to Pitcairn with Fletcher Christian was from Raiatea and was accorded special status because of this. Mr Chang, in Chinese-accented French, told us he couldn't come with us but repeated tales of cannibalism that were not true and stories of human sacrifice that were.

We decided to see the marae for ourselves, and amid constant peals of that enchanting easy laughter of all Polynesians, we squashed onto the wooden seats on the back of open-sided trucks which served as buses.

The marae was hot, stifling both in temperature and atmosphere. It was so alien to us that most gave up trying to identify or understand the remains and wandered off to enjoy instead the lagoon-side setting. Close to where sacrificial victims had their heads clubbed in, we were shown how to split open young coconuts and enjoy the cool milk. A girl showed us a special gardenia, with petals on just one side, that grows only in secret glades high on the mountains. We didn't stay long, having easily bribed a driver to run a special service to lurch us back the twenty twisting kilometers to the boat. As we sped through settlements scattering the ubiquitous children, pigs and dogs, I tried to answer questions about the plants and plantations, teaching others to recognize taro and mango, papaya and tobacco, pineapple, banana, plantain, hibiscus and other flowers. In the market of Utaroa we watched the cook bargain for fresh fish and sweet potato and hands of bananas. We learned the pleasure of being greeted by each person we passed, and soon were wishing the Raiateans 'bonjour' in return. By evening it was apparent that the experience had been absorbed. We shared the exquisite calm there is in tropical places of just sitting and watching and endless ravelling and unravelling of cottonwool surf on a reef, or the fast, flashing sunsets.

By now, most of us had discarded our wrist-watches and when Ted Cochran and I bought everyone lengths of printed cloth (the *pareu*) inhibitions went the same way and the 'uniform' was quickly complementing newly-brown bodies. Suddenly we were a group, not a bunch of individuals.

If Raiatea cast the first spell, Bora Bora, our next call, completely enchanted the entire ship. The island was well on the way to the high point of its Bastille Day celebrations and its normally unnoticeable village had been transformed into a fun-fair.

At night golden-limbed men and women entertained with the *tamure*, the famed dance that brings Polynesian music and bodies to their most fevered climax. Soaking myself in the spectacle I crept through a fence and, pretending rather more professionalism with a camera than is the case, popped flashes as I sat in the dust just inches from the incredible vibrations of hips that varied from lithe to gargantuan. Tiny women, some barely teenagers, displayed agility that defied propriety, and huge men conjured thoughts of war and blood as they shook their thighs, rolling their eyes. My Tahitian ancestors had danced like this. Fletcher Christian and his mutinous companions would also have sat on the ground, lit by great flares and been entertained after pit-cooked banquets. I knew what they had made of it all—but what about my companions?

In spite of rain that made the bars ever more tempting, they had watched transfixed for hours, as overwhelmed as I was at the thought of the battering ram effect it must have had on the less worldly minds of eighteenth-century sailors; mutiny would be the least emotion stimulated. I could tell they had seen into the soul of Polynesia and Michael Brook was unusually inarticulate. 'I'm just a boy from a small village in Devon, you have to remember.'

Taiyo returned to Papeete on 15 July, and I took the wheel to guide her back into the harbour. We found the continuing Bastille Day celebrations there more commercial with such twentieth-century phenomena as sky-diving and dodgems. But our recent experience gave us a new perspective.

When Elliot Smith asked me if I would help persuade a young Tahitian girl to pose for his camera, I soon found myself cajoling her on my behalf as much as his—for this was an Isabella if ever there was one. Teura was fifteen, tall, black of hair, and gifted, with a face that would have launched far more than a thousand canoes. She displayed that seductive mixture of child and woman that only the truly innocent dare adopt, sitting sure and erect but giggling behind fingers with bitten nails.

Teura was bought a new *pareu*, put a crown of flowers on her waist-length hair and posed in the flower market against the blooms, buds and leaves that had come from Tahiti's forests and gardens that morning. She confounded us with artless, sparkling smiles and Sphinx-dark stares that no European or American girl of the same age could emulate. She may have been younger than most of the women who went to Pitcairn, but feeling I had the blood of a race who could produce such regal and magnificent women made me immensely proud. As I looked at her through the time-arresting frame of a camera lens, I saw in the eyes of this one girl the certainty of the fulfilment of most men's dreams.

There were few regrets as we sailed from Papeete. It was time to go on. Michael climbed up to *Taiyo*'s yard-arm and threw a lei of frangipani into the water, ensuring we would return. I was happy that by seeing Polynesia *en fête* we had shared a rare insight into the astonishments that stunned Fletcher Christian and his shipmates almost two centuries ago. We had had our first experience of ocean sailing and, like Fletcher Christian, we had stocked up with private stores of treats without which we would have found life at sea impossible—from chocolates and mint tea to camembert, a tape of bagpipe music, chewing gum, Coca-Cola and piles of trashy novels. All knew that 1,200 miles of Pacific lay between Tahiti and Pitcairn. Although I never admitted it, I already suspected the radio was never going to work, despite the attention given it over several days; as well as being dangerous, this meant I could not make broadcasts back to my radio station in London, cutting off a source of income.

And there were definite rumblings about the food—in Papeete the three girls had walked away from one lunch on board, preferring to spend money ashore. It didn't take much to see that I would have to deal with isolation and stresses that the *Bounty* men would have recognized. The first excitements were now over, the span of a normal holiday away from home was complete and I expected the disorientation caused by our continuing flight from familiarity to become threatening. But sickness in the form of a feverish flu, tiredness caused by the watch system, and heavy seas all produced such strain that there was little time, energy or audience for tantrums, and perhaps that was true on *Bounty*, too.

Because I suffered neither the plague nor seasickness, my status as leader of the expedition was unexpectedly enhanced. And knowing it would be counter-productive to assume any kind of command at sea, I decided to capitalise further on the situation by being both strong and silent. I stayed out of sight reading the *Bounty* material, preparing for Pitcairn. Then, realising I had far more time on my hands than I expected, I stopped researching and plundered the ship for the cheap novels I had denied myself for years, and enjoyed a refreshing orgy of trash.

39

Echoes on Tubuai

I n the last minutes before we cast off for Tubuai, Andrew leapt overboard to kiss and give flowers to a young girl who had flirted with him from the dockside for hours. He returned, and Terry and I called a meeting. From that moment we formally became The Sir John Barrow Commemorative Expedition and the project's aims were now to take precedence over those of any individual, indeed individuality itself was to be forsaken. Terry forcefully reminded us of the danger of the sea, the importance of safety procedures and of fast compliance with orders. Then, believing a detailed list of instructions would be counter-productive, I explained the rule on which the expedition would be based. I must always know where everyone was when ashore, so that valuable time was not wasted in waiting or searching for each other. Independent action was to be eschewed if the expedition was to be a success, and awareness of this was vital for the safety and enjoyment of all.

It was the first time I had been so direct and it made a noticeable impact. In the next few days even the sick could be seen reading material about Tubuai and there seemed a definite excitement at the prospect of following Fletcher's footsteps.

It took five days of rough water and starchy, fatty food to reach Tubuai. As it changed from a grey mist into recognizable trees, mountains and plains, I felt the first sense of real achievement. The discussion on deck quickly demonstrated that Fletcher Christian's decision to settle there seemed perfectly reasonable, even sensible to us all. The most startling feature of Tubuai is how un-tropical it looks—if the fringe of palm trees is ignored. Almost immediately behind them rise stark hills of mauve and green and brown.

'My God, we've taken a wrong turning . . . it's Scotland,' said Ted Cochran. Indeed it could have been. Or Cumbria. Or the Isle of Man. Already it was obvious to us how Fletcher Christian might turn his back on England and expect to find happiness in the South Pacific—a great deal of it looked just like the homes of his child-hood. By the time we paid out our anchor in the lagoon, we had identified Bloody Bay and then agreed, on purely topographical grounds, that we too would have built Fort George where Fletcher had chosen. It was the most attractive part of the island, provided great opportunity for secrecy, and was close to the small lagoon islands (keys) where animals could be safely kept.

The little settlement of Mataura, off which we anchored in extraordinarily clear water, has a square with a flagpole and was lined with more of the palm-panelled huts we had seen on Bora Bora. Was Bastille Day celebrated somewhat later down here? No, but they were continuing their celebrations for a while longer to ensure a good send-off for the teams of athletes going to Papeete for the Pacific Games. It suited us well, for we needed a good send-off too, when we left this last touchstone of civilization.

Ted and I donned anoraks and clambered into a small boat to go off in search of an American photographer, Don Travers, who was supposed to live here and who could be helpful; others went on an informal exploration charged with a later report about such facilities as bars, restaurants, banks and the like. What little village there is spreads languidly along the coast and up the one road which heads inland. Hibiscus, bougainvillaea and frangipani crammed the gardens and children smiled before they stared. The Post Office was a walk west; the bank was a mile east but no one knew when it was open. We didn't find Don, but it was established there were no restaurants other than those temporarily operating on the square. We found the one bar almost by accident; we had to walk through the counter of one of the two Chinese general stores to a shed of corrugated iron and wood, some distance from the village centre. Those less devoted to the refreshment offered by Hinano beer would not have found the establishment. Here, convivially crammed onto wooden benches, we learned there was to be more than one discothèque each night and a Miss Tubuai competition—once more we were amid Polynesian party time and could expect to be royally entertained. Already we were being plied with beer by fishermen, who undoubtedly could afford such magnanimity less than we could, but who gave with such pleasure it was impossible to refuse while still capable of speech.

That same day I had to cope with the threats to fly home of Marilyn, who had been perpetually seasick, and with tears from another expedition member. Making the most of the alcoholic cloud under which we all returned to the ship, I continued my diplomatic ploys and arranged to cook for the first time. We sat by candlelight behind the reef of Tubuai and ate sweet-and-sour pork and Terry agreed that I should cook every second day, ostensibly to give the cook a break, actually to avoid a real mutiny. To be fair, cooking for fifteen people three times a day *was* the hardest job on board, exhausting when done seven days a week. Of all Bligh's acute observations on the basic requirements of a viable ship, none is more important than nourishing food, and in the twentieth century it needed to be attractive and varied too. Tomorrow was to be our first working day, so over the conciliatory dinner I repeated my simple request of responsibility to one another.

By 9.30 next morning I was enraged and the day's plans were

in pieces. One member of a small advance party had left after breakfast to follow up leads of people with specialized local knowledge, and on not finding that contact, had picked up a German itinerant and sped off on the back of his motorcycle. Where or for how long, nobody knew. As I had warned, half the rest were angry, the others followed the flagrant example of irresponsibility and wandered off to follow their own interests. Matters were only solved by the final appearance of Don Travers, the photographer. He is a burly, blond ex-sailor who had stopped at Tubuai on his way to New Zealand, where he had planned to go to university using his GI grant. Instead, he fell in love with Jeanette, one of the most attractive Tubuaian women, married her and settled. He used his knowledge of the people and a mixture of English, French and Tubuaian to help collect the group, to arrange transport for our mountain of film and surveying equipment and to deliver us to the site of Fort George, two miles or so from the square.

There was little left to see of that once bold place. Without knowing about the wooden plaque chained to a tree by the National Geographic Society, it is easy to drive past the hedge that hides it. Houses are built close to each side and it was only in recent years that the walls were bulldozed and most of the moat filled—it is said that too many people were drowned there in the rainy seasons. The neat, enclosed square that had been home and refuge to the mutineers and their hostages is now a sweet potato patch.

There is still a well where the original spring had been, and it took some time for its significance to dawn. Christian must have thought all his dreams had come true when he found this site— safe anchorage, handy islets within the reef for the stock, a clear view to the reef entrance and a water source they could control and protect. Fresh water is a far greater guarantee of prosperity than simply being friends with the right chief, even if to ignore that was naive. We all talked about it, and all agreed we would have done what Christian did.

There was enough detail of the moat left for us to make our measurements and map, and Louis, a smiling neighbour, gave us permission to survey and photograph as long as we did not damage the young plants. I was amused to recognize two breadfruit trees growing among the sweet potatoes and wondered at their ancestry. What happened next was not amusing, but illustrated the stunning ability history has to repeat itself.

Leaving Michael, Mark and Richard to map the fort's site, I pushed through the fringe of Toa wood and coconut palm to the narrow, gold-white beach. Less than half a mile to my right were the small keys that had once been the pens of *Bounty*'s animals; the beach to my left was being marked into a grid prior to being searched with metal detectors. It had seemed safer to put the errant, unrepentant, but returned wanderer to work here, away from the rest of the party, to avoid further interruption of their work. Mark suddenly appeared and through his Southern accent informed us that Michael had been arrested and driven off 'by some dude who needed a shave but said he was a gendarme'.

It was difficult to remain cool during the thirty minutes that slowly ticked by before a Land Rover returned carrying Michael, a Frenchman who identified himself as one of the island's two gendarmes, and a surly Tubuaian. I was informed we were trespassing, for Louis, who had given us permission, although of the right family, was from a branch out of favour with that which more properly owned the fort site. The large sulky young man was from the aggrieved branch and kept stealing distasteful glances at Michael's bare feet; at some time during the voyage he had allowed Jasmina to paint some of his toenails iridescent pink.

I was expected to see the mayor. I climbed into the Land Rover feeling far angrier at the toenails than at not having been told what had happened immediately.

First the gendarme had to go home, shave, put on a uniform and apply several handfuls of after-shave lotion in a painful attempt to staunch the flow of blood from his throat, wounded by haste. Then we had to wake the mayor from his post-prandial nap by standing in his lush garden and shuffling. In separate vehicles we rattled back along the pot-holed road to see an old man who sat on his haunches and spat and looked at Michael's toes and refused to give us permission to return to the site . . . he should have been consulted, he was not consulted, and that was that. Further, he was only caretaker of the property on behalf of some 'old ones' who lived in the hills; perhaps if the mayor sent them a telegram . . .

Our gendarme was as amused as we became, explaining he spent most of his time refereeing such family feuds and the continuing flavour of farce helped me forget the time that was being wasted. Then he made a detour to show us an extraordinary, overgrown marae on which the stone paving, the erect back rests and the petroglyphs were still in place. It was a chilling experience, but Michael and I were very grateful for his efforts in showing us and agreed that Tubuai was lucky to have such a sensitive and interested man.

Don and Jeanette had joined the others for lunch in a coconut grove close to the disputed garden. As Michael and I tried to make a meal of the few remaining bananas and some sun-melted salami, Jeanette told us of her great interest in Tubuai and its history, and how she and Don collected stories. Eagerly I explained how much I wanted to identify the site of the battle fought here by Fletcher Christian in which so many islanders had been killed. Surely such an important place would be vividly recalled in oral tradition?

Through the sticky heat of the afternoon, Jeanette drove me to see the island's sages and storytellers. None knew where the battle had been, some didn't even know about it. In fast fading light, we rattled up an overhung track to a collection of huts in a muddy clearing protected from most light and all weather by a high canopy of breadfruit and mango trees. As if on cue, descendants of the mosquitoes that tormented the *Bounty* men emerged; even the smoke from the fire of the open cookhouse was no protection. Stamping, scratching and slapping, sidling from the attention of mange-disfigured dogs, we spoke to the oldest man on the island, while his wife wove a basket; 'If it was in the time of my father or his father I would know about it; before that there was a great sickness and I know nothing'. So much for oral tradition, I thought, by now more interested in whether the mosquitoes in the South Pacific were malarial.

Later, in the circle of light from a paraffin lamp, in the house Don had rebuilt from a shell of coral walls, he, Jeanette and I read the books on the island he had collected and learned why the battles with Fletcher Christian and his men had become so unimportant. When *Bounty* arrived there was an estimated population of 3,000. Less than fifty years later it was only 300; intestinal sickness and fevers introduced by *Bounty*, and then by the missionaries and traders who quickly followed, had massacred both the men of Tubuai and their memories. The island has still not recovered from the interest of the Europeans. Its population today is a bare 1,400, but is at last increasing. I left them a copy of relevant extracts from *The Journal of James Morrison* and they promised to continue the search for the battle site.

Naturally I am very interested in men who leave a European culture to marry a Polynesian woman. Without in any way abjuring their backgrounds—Don loves books and showers, Jeanette nurses her baby while sitting on the floor—they complement one another perfectly. When I asked Jeanette how and why she had learned English, she punched Don in the chest and said: 'Because I wanted him!' Then she laughed that long inimitable fluid laugh of the perpetually happy Polynesian woman. Had Isabella made Fletcher Christian as happy? I wondered.

Next morning the gendarme (we could neither remember nor pronounce his name) told us the mayor had a message saying the 'old ones' had also refused permission. Passions were running high, but thanks to Don we had found out why. A team of journalists had recently use metal detectors on the site while foolishly circulating stories of a large hidden treasure. Greed suddenly flared and came between family factions that had ignored the site for years, and hatred and hopes had been more carefully cultivated than ever the garden had been. Once again a party led by a Christian was the victim of an internecine war it had unwittingly reignited.

I decided to let it rest rather than declare war in the manner of Fletcher. Michael and Mark resolutely walked back to the site with their boards and tape measures and completed the survey in stealth. Later we tracked through the taro swamps, again trying to locate a likely site for the battle and agreed that it could well have been close to the marae our gendarme showed us—the distance from the fort and the terrain fit Morrison's description well.

We spent our remaining short time on Tubuai wishing Fletcher Christian had made things work here. Because of its temperate climate, the vegetation and conditions are less relentlessly tropical than those of Tahiti. There are pastures with indolent cows, as well as pigs wallowing in taro swamps. There are butterflies, lemon trees, roses, flowers, grasses and bushes we recognized. Elliott, Marilyn, Vivien and I walked around to Bloody Bay and identified the Marae of Tonohae, imagining the ceremonies which welcomed Fletcher. They call the bay Murivai, and sitting on its sands we imagined the fright caused by a sailing ship and the horror of the bloody carnage when it hurled death from its cannon into wooden canoes. By this time, identifying with those on land rather than with those at sea, we felt more sympathy for the fear of the islanders than for that of *Bounty*'s crew.

Tubuai's happy blend of familiar and unfamiliar was unexpectedly soothing, and the constant smiles and calmness of life here affected us all. We felt it was a taste of what Pitcairn might have in store for us. But before we left to discover that, Tubuai dramatically demonstrated the brute strength of the sea and the dangers to come.

One of *Taiyo*'s two small boats was damaged as it tried to lace its way through the treacherous coral heads that barred most of the way from our anchorage to the jetty. In case the second boat were also to be damaged, Terry moved *Taiyo* along to the almost completed commercial wharf, less than a mile further east; she was anchored with only her stern to the jetty. That night the winds rose to a full tropical storm and with the reef being no protection against the waves, we were more uncomfortable than we had ever been at sea. It was another extraordinary echo, this time of *Bounty*'s experience in Matavai Bay. An anchor watch was mounted in the slashing rain.

At 5 am I was wakened by a scream of metal and what seemed to be an explosion. Confused both by sleep and adrenalin, I had to decide whether I was more use on deck or in my cabin; in an emergency at sea a non-swimmer on deck can be a dangerous complication. The tumult was too great to ignore, so I rushed out to find a scurry of half-naked crew and expedition members endeavouring to secure *Taiyo*. An enormous gust had dragged her anchor and slammed *Taiyo*'s stern into the lip of the wharf. With each surge of wind and water, the ship was being further damaged.

Terry decided to bring her parallel to the wharf, and, by the time the sun had come up, we were safe, but the horrid squeak of metal against fenders of black rubber was extraordinarily trying, every minute reminding us of the forces we were about to battle. Don and Jeanette drove up early, for they had heard *Taiyo* hammering the wharf above the noise of the storm.

Our ship had done more damage than had been inflicted upon her. A little heavy-duty panel beating and a coat of paint would put things right, and we were doubly pleased to be aboard a ship of steel. A wooden vessel such as *Bounty* would have been wrecked and the expedition would have ended right there.

We were a sobered group as vegetables were delivered and stowed and we walked to the store to buy ourselves treats. Arrowroot biscuits, something I had not seen since I left New Zealand in

1965, had become a shipboard rage, and could be kept down by the invalids. We bought cake mixes, more Coca-Cola, shampoo and sun oil to last almost two months. Just after lunch, Tubuai entertained us with a double rainbow but it was an unkind promise of better things that did not come. We sailed into more rain and mountainous seas. The feverish flu had returned, in some cases combined with seasickness, and it was a tense ship. Earlier, in an attempt to cheer everyone up, I had promised to make lasagne, something I knew I could do extremely well and which was well suited to cold miserable weather. But as we left the lee of Tubuai I knew I had crucified myself. Huge pots of boiling pasta, of bechamel sauce and of tomato sauce plus tumbling canyons of waves are not fit companions for someone cooking on the open sea for the first time. For all that *Taiyo* was beautifully fitted, a basic mistake had been made. Whoever designed the galley forgot that the hob and oven should have been gimballed, freely suspended so that they stayed level whatever was happening to the rest of the ship, just as hammocks do for sleeping men. I managed to get at least as much onto the plates as there was on the walls and floor of the galley. And I remember I once stamped my foot in utter rage and shouted: 'For Christ's sake, stop moving!'

40

A Continuous Puzzle

When we tossed away from Tubuai it was Saturday 26 July and the voyage was fairly much on schedule. On Tuesday we sighted Rapa, an island of startlingly primordial appearance that was to be a temporary respite from the tumbling Pacific swells. Like Pitcairn, it is rarely visited, but here women far outnumber men, many of whom have gone to Tahiti to find work. For the first time we saw what solitariness could mean to an island community and I was agitated in case I found the Pitcairners as depressed and uncared for as the people of Rapa. There was a sadness caused by a rising of expectations that could not be answered by the two or three ships a year that called.

But now we were close to our goal. We fairly flew out of Rapa with winds gusting up to twenty-five knots, followed by mischievous squalls expelled from the mouth of Rapa's harbour like a series of smoke rings. Lying on my bunk the ship gave the same feeling of power as that of a jet as it hurtles itself into the air. We were rock steady and speeding along, and at this rate we could expect to be in Pitcairn in five or six days.

By the middle of Saturday morning, any movement we were making was sideways or up and down—none was forward and for a time we were thrown back towards Rapa. Sunday was no better, so Terry decided we should motor, and the inescapable noise and fumes did nothing to improve tempers or health. Each day Pitcairn seemed further away as we successively wallowed and motored, even though perfectly placed to be pushed by the trade winds. Toward the week's end, it seemed we would get to Pitcairn on Saturday, the island's strictly observed Sabbath. I didn't think this wise and told Terry that for all his efforts to get us there quickly, we would have to stay out of sight until Sunday morning. My precautions were unnecessary. On Saturday the wind died altogether, and when we were not motoring we drifted backwards again. It was galling to be under power in such a magnificent sailing ship. But it ultimately meant more time on Pitcairn and already I feared we might only be able to stay less than two weeks—and that certainly would not have been worth the effort.

Sunday's sunrise deserved trumpets and Handel. Against a pink and puce sky, bubbling towers of molten gold clouds poured ever widening rays of light onto a reflective Pacific. Pitcairn was dead ahead, purple, and back-lit.

I braced myself against the rail, alone in the bow. My own excitement was made greater by watching the expressions of joy and achievement on the faces of the expedition members as they came on deck one by one.

As we sailed along Pitcairn's coast, I was amazed at how big it looked, and wondered why no one had ever written of the ochre-red earth that showed in great gashes. The cliffs were daunting, aloof, forbidding. Even on this relatively calm morning, I could see enormous spumes of spray as the rollers, unhindered for thousands of miles, crashed into this lonely rock. I stood by *Taiyo*'s rail, muttering self-congratulatory expletives, a rather pointless sort of reverie, broken by the start of a partial solar eclipse that ended exactly as the first of two whaleboats full of Pitcairners roared slowly past and told us to continue onto the lee of the island, which that day was opposite Down Rope. Half the passengers leapt from both boats and came on board distributing oranges and bananas. Suddenly it was true. The faces we had seen in *National Geographic*, the people who shared my ancestors and my family names were on board. I stood back for a moment, considering my new responsibilities. At sea Terry Purkiss was the ultimate authority, now it was me.

When I began to introduce myself, there was some amazement—I was expected to be 'a big man', like the Christians of Pitcairn. It made no difference, and soon we were all being plied with questions about the voyage and who we all were. And I felt at home. Warren Christian looked like my grandfather William. His brother Ivan was currently the island's Chief Magistrate, but they are as unalike as it is possible for brothers to be, one with Polynesian features, the other Caucasian. In Tom Christian, the internationally known radio ham, I saw my father's brother Keith. Tom is dark and has black hair, Keith is fair skinned and blond; but they have the unmistakable Christian nose and the same tight curls. Laughing Nola Warren was there, so was her husband Reynold, the Postmaster, and Len Brown, the island's Chief Engineer—when we joined the boats in the lee, the rest poured aboard. Glen Clark, Jay Warren, Brian Young, Rex Whiting, the school teacher from New Zealand and his wife Moira, Pastor Stimpson . . . With a trepidation that was well founded we found ourselves in the famous long boats, sailing back past St Paul's rock into Bounty Bay, through the treacherous entrance, and then being helped onto the jetty.

Damp with spray and fuddled with disbelief, we were swept up by this or that family with invitations to stay, and within hours I knew the long journey was justified. It had made us ready receptacles for the unique hospitality and way of life of Pitcairn and its extraordinary people. After the discomforts of five weeks on a ship, bereft of real privacy or fresh produce, or clean clothing or showers—other than in cold salt water—we were grateful for things as simple as buckets filled with hot water. Plain honest food, at a stationary table with new faces, was a banquet.

By next morning everyone had over-eaten enormously. At Tom and Betty Christian's, Andrew and I had sat down to a table crammed with two types of steak, fish in coconut milk, chicken, home-made bread, perhaps half a dozen or more vegetable and salad dishes, *pilhis* (the baked vegetable puddings described by Bligh), and then apple sponge with custard. Others had equally gargantuan stories to tell . . . and all had biting criticism for recent publications about Pitcairn, and writers who had described it as unwelcoming and squalid.

It is the publishing of such inaccuracies that has made the Pitcairners wary of strangers, and we recognized how their shy self-protection might be misunderstood as unwelcoming. Certainly they hoard everything—string, paper, glass and metal. This is simply facing up to the reality of living in isolation and with the unreliability of the rest of the world. It is the pride of the self-sufficient. In a community where there are no servants, the aged proudly look after themselves and even mothers with babies must sew and dig and harvest the year round. There is bound to be some untidiness, but there is nothing that approaches the filth created by the pigs in Rapa—there are none on Pitcairn—and no sight of the ragged children or disease we saw there, either. Perhaps those untrue things are said of Pitcairn by those who judge solely by contemporary standards of large cities, and who have never seen other Pacific islands.

It is extraordinary to me that so few visitors to Pitcairn even begin to grasp the reality of living in such isolation. Such communities, even land-locked ones, have known since the dawn of man that you will not survive if you have or grow or keep just enough. Whether it is fruit which rots uneaten, vegetables which moulder undug or great piles of old wood and metal, the only reliable key to survival is excess.

During our first night on shore, our first night of clean sheets and proper beds, a tropical storm of high winds and heavy rain blew up. In the warmth of a room that did not move, it was a wicked pleasure to feel sympathy but do nothing for the crew, tossed mercilessly at anchor. By morning all was calm, and apart from our stretched stomachs, we had but one physical complaint—mosquitoes. Almost everyone had suffered dreadfully, and, unfairly, those who had been most seasick were most bitten. The bites were so severe, especially round the ankles, that at least two expedition members were made sick by the discomfort and exasperation. It was only as I read deeper into the books and papers we had brought that I learned Pitcairn had been like Tahiti in *Bounty* days—mosquitoes were unknown, being introduced about a century ago. The Pacific without mosquitoes must indeed have been bliss.

Our first afternoon and morning on Pitcairn were spent wandering, getting land legs and meeting the rest of the islanders. My impressions of these days cling as my most vivid memories of Pitcairn. The storm had churned up the red-clay roads and tracks into a viscous mud; the Pitcairners call it the world's friendliest mud because it sticks so tenaciously. In just a few steps you have a couple of pounds weight of the stuff clumped under each foot. Then the knife that each Pitcairn man always carries slices the worst off and you continue. Bare feet were somehow less attractive to it and easier to clean, too, so they were readily adopted.

Barefoot or shod, on a tractor or the back of a Honda, Adams-town to the visitor is a continuous puzzle of gardens, half-seen houses, dappled vales, banks of red earth, and the protests of disturbed cocks and hens; it stretches for about half a mile along the north-eastern cliff top from above Bounty Bay, westwards, and for a few hundred yards up the slopes from the main road, which in the more populous days was called Coconut Grove until it reached the square and church, and was Pitcairn Avenue from then on. Now it is just 'the road'. Although lined with familiar geraniums and gladioli, it is decidedly tropical, too.

Beside a stately grove of banyan trees, which march across roads
and into gardens with the certain arrogance of all magnificent things,
are low plots of spiky pineapples. Hibiscus bushes with flowers of
flaming coral are tangled with a contrast of vivid blue convolvulus,
that spills further onto those epitomes of the tropics, the banana
palm, just filtering enough of the strong sun through feathered
leaves to light tracks with an unearthly warmth. Suddenly, golden
mandarins and oranges glow through dark leaves Rousseau-like,
papayas cluster atop their branchless supports and unripe mangoes
hang from thin threads.

A few monumentally fat dogs attempt to yap at visitors. Each has
a personality or physical quirk, and there are many cats, but the
horrors of tinned food and cat litter are unheard of. As in any
English village, most houses are ruled by one or two of these creatures. There are rats, too, the only native quadruped, but I don't
think any of us ever saw one. We were too busy looking for the
huge, rattling coconut crab and the spiders said to be five inches
long; the first time you saw one of the latter, you would swear it
was twice as big, especially if that initial encounter was in an outside
lavatory, lit only by a torch, late at night. If the rats were really as
big as cats, as we had heard, we just didn't want to know!

Above the coconut palms we saw Pitcairn's lovely flashing white
fairy terns which spend idyllic days in flirtation, tumbling and kissing
with contagious high spirits. But they, like the few other birds, are
largely songless. The muffling effect of the thick foliage quickly
absorbs even the incessant surf's thunder, so a pause in most walks
reveals a silence that is discomfiting in its primeval quality.

Through the treetops and tracks of the village there is one dominating sight, unavoidable and sometimes menacing—Lookout
Point, which contains the scoop of rock called Christian's Cave.
This peak rears at the northern end of the village. Nothing had
prepared us for such size. If Fletcher Christian did make the difficult
climb to the cave and go to brood for days, it would have been a

very tough man or woman, indeed, who could have ignored his domineering presence; those would have been oppressive days on the island.

As one walks up out of the village, the hills become steeper and much of the foliage changes to the troublesome rose-apple, a scrubby fast-growing tree from Norfolk Island that has become a pest of the first order. It does provide firewood and prevents erosion but is terminally unsightly. When we first walked across the island and up to the ridge that ripples the length of Pitcairn, an unexpected feeling of vulnerability developed. Although there are countless hollows, glades and other secretive places, the very erectness and isolation of the island easily gives the sense of it offering no place to hide.

But our lives revolved around the houses, wonderful, welcoming, jumbly houses that, like Topsy, just growed. Most were of weathered boards that had never seen paint—where would it come from?—some had deep verandahs, some were mixes of old and new. I stayed with Tom and Betty in the oldest inhabited house made of massive timbers, pit sawn on the island over a hundred years ago.

On our first afternoon on Pitcairn, 81-year-old Christy Warren waved us into his house, right on the road. One room endlessly led to another. He seated us at a big table and told us of the hardships of his life, his tremulous tone wavering between pride in the past and sorrow at his present. Now his second wife was dead, he baked his own bread. He proudly showed how clean everything was in the house as he piled the table with cakes and biscuits and served orange cordial. We wanted to stay to hear more of unpopular captains who had been thrown off their ships at Cape Horn, of the sailing ships that had come to this island and stories that made Christy spoken of as the strongest man on the island. But our evening meals were at 6 and we had to scatter to be on time.

Elliott had found his first camera subject, but it took the rest of us several days fully to understand the loneliness of Christy. When you walk about Adamstown, it is not immediately obvious that uninhabited houses outnumber the inhabited ones. We walked into some up shattered steps and through broken doors, even so feeling it was wrong to do so. They had been abandoned with clothes half out of drawers, postcards stuck into the mirrors of dressing-tables and bibles beside beds. They had been forsaken when their owners went to visit a sick relative or spent a few years working in New Zealand or Australia. New ideas, or the simple problems of return transport, turned the visits into exiles, not all voluntary, and the houses slowly sink back into the earth, noiseless and unnoticed, for their enemies are creeping plants and the voracious borer and white ants. Christy had a loving family and supportive community around him, but in his life he had seen the population drop from over a hundred to the current sixty; rather than seeing the continuation of life that can be a comfort in old age, he had seen a continuous ebbing. It was a situation the expedition was committed to understanding and, if possible, helping.

41

Food Hangovers

Our objectives on Pitcairn Island fell into two broad categories, those with roots in the past and those concerned with the present. My personal quest was the grave, if such a thing existed, of Fletcher Christian. As The Sir John Barrow Commemorative Expedition, we planned to make a definitive map of the island for presentation to the Map Room of the Royal Geographical Society; projects and information associated with this map would give us a true picture of life on Pitcairn today and enable us to establish ways in which the advantages of the twentieth century might assist the Pitcairners, if that were their wish.

Each morning the expedition met in the small, paved square of Adamstown, edged on three sides by public buildings—the Seventh Day Adventist Church, the Dispensary, the Library, the Post Office and the Court House, also used for Council meetings and films. Earlier visitors had made maps of Pitcairn and credit must be given to the enormously difficult pioneering work they have done, which made our job simpler. Yet, none of these groups had been as interested as we were in preserving the idiosyncratic place names, or they had misunderstood Pitcairn pronunciation and noted names incorrectly. I knew something of the Pitcairnese language and accent from my grandfather and his sisters. Relying on this and the acquaintance of Richard Hudson and myself with the vowels of the Maoris of New Zealand, we hoped correctly to write down the place names. An example of the complications is easily given; one map indicates a place called Jinser Walley. It is easy to interpret the last word for the Pitcairners persist in both the earlier English and the contemporary Tahitian rendering of the letter 'V' and speak of their 'willage'; Vivien Gay became 'Wiwien', even to us. Jinser is not a name, but a Pitcairnese pronunciation of ginger. Thus the proper way to record this place is not Jinser Walley, but Ginger Valley. Another place is commonly mapped as Garnett's Ridge; this is named for the sea birds that cluster there and so is actually Gannet's Ridge. The definite and indefinite article both become 'ah'—'I'm going to ride ah bike', 'give me ah knife', and so on. Thus Ah Cut, a great notch out of the main ridge, is properly The Cut. Places are frequently preceded by Up or Down, indicating where they are in relationship to the speaker. So you might refer to some place as Up Hulianda or Down Tedside without the first word being part of the real name.

By deciphering all the place names we could, a reliable record would be made while people still remembered; I hoped they might also help in my searches, for names change when they are unwritten and the discovery of original meanings should tell us more of the past.

Pitcairn's place names give fascinating glimpses of daily life over almost two centuries. Some are simply possessive, like Jack's Yam and Big George's Coconut, and it is generally not too difficult to establish who the eponymous owner was. Others record accidents or incidents once thought important—Sailors' Hide, John-Catch-a-Cow, Where-Freddie-Fall or Bang-Iron Valley, where *Bounty*'s forge and anvil formerly stood. Those are obvious in derivation. Others are not, and the delving we did was repaid handsomely.

The most amusing story we unearthed is the origin of the name of a fishing pool, Oo-aa-oo, which when heard could easily be dismissed as some Polynesian word, like for instance, the Hawaiian Oahu. Until you meet Andrew Young. For most of his eighty-one years, Andrew has made it his business to know all there is to know about his beloved 'Pit-kern'. He tired us out as he strode around the island telling story after story with a waving of a knobkerrie and a deep, firm voice that belied his age. With appropriate actions he told us about Oo-aa-oo. Last century, when Pitcairn women wore long skirts and petticoats, Agnes Christian and her husband Samuel Warren went spear fishing at night, in a rock pool where fish were often stranded when the tide pulled away. Women here are strong and Agnes waded through the pool with her skirts tucked up and with Sam on her shoulders, lighting their way with a flare of candle-nuts strung together—here called a rummer. In a moment of rare levity for the time, Samuel reached behind him and touched the warm embers of his dying rummer to her rear. Agnes' sur-prise—and perhaps Sam's as he was tumbled into the pool—created the onomatopoeic name. There are dozens of such stories, and by listening to them we were hearing and recording the island's history in a unique way.

A full survey of the island was a task far beyond our ability and time span. Michael Brook had joined a crash course organized by the Department of Surveying and Photogrammetry at University College, London, and learned the simple method of surveying the British had used to map India. This was to be employed to map the roads of Adamstown only, for the island is incorrectly described merely as rugged; like some crumpled piece of tissue paper, it is a three-dimensional maze of steep twists, turns, passes, valleys, ridges and slopes. Andrew Young guided us about—to Ship Landing Point, where high winds and vertigo reduced me to crawling on all fours to peer down at Bounty Bay, then to the dust bowl of Hulianda and the arid eroded slope of Red Dirt, where only pandanus palms grow. The tempestuous pool behind St Paul's Rocks (about 250 yards long) is almost completely surrounded by a high, jagged escarpment of rock shaped by surf. The sea slams in at one end of the pool, hurtling over barnacled ridges and through fissures, then drains and dribbles out the other until it hits the ocean again in huge vortices. Several men have drowned here, and we spent a long time marvelling at the majesty and danger of the place. We walked through Aute Valley, once entirely cultivated but now a low wilderness, with here and there a well-kept vegetable plot, pineapple plantation or banana grove. We sat on high ridges and cliff edges to look at Down Rope and Tautama, where the earliest inhabitants had found material for their tools of stone. From The Cut and Gannet's Ridge we saw gardens, tracks and hills named after Fletcher Christian's three children.

While Andrew Young guided us on his muscle-stretching tours he also told us a lot about the island's food during the times it was expected to be self-sufficient. He showed us the dandelion greens and other plants they ate or brewed into teas. He told of hard days when fish bones from dinner were boiled to make gruel for breakfast that was poured over potato or yam. I then realized that the unique food of Pitcairn, like their language, a mixture of eighteenth-century English and Tahitian, had never been recorded. Jasmina quickly volunteered and spent many hours with most of the women and some of the men collecting recipes that had never been written before.

Being in the food business, I should have liked to have done this myself. But I had a mountain of talking to do. Every native Pitcairner was a blood relative. I have descent from three mutineers, Christian, Young and Mills, and so could be woven in and out of their genealogical tables in many ways. The continuing marriages between close relatives require new techniques of recording information—some people have seven lines back to Fletcher alone—and we wanted to know about each other.

There are only five Pitcairn family names now—Christian,

Young, Warren, Clark and Brown—and only the first two are *Bounty* names. There are no Adams and the last McKoy left recently. Only first names are used, and since there is a Glen (Clark) on the island, the children made an immediate distinction by dubbing me Glynn-Christian, said as one word. Having sorted out the present men and women, I then had to turn to the men and women at the top of our family trees. That meant more serious talking. On Pitcairn, this means serious eating, and for that there was plenty of opportunity. Every day.

The amount and variety of food offered a visitor to Pitcairn Island is astonishing, due as much to the deep freeze as to local industriousness. As Seventh Day Adventists they are expected to be vegetarians, but this is a recommendation rather than a rule, and the Pitcairners have always had a special dispensation to eat their goats, although few do.

Fish features regularly but shellfish and crayfish are fairly rigorously opposed by the church. When Andrew Brady and I went out to dine one night, we were presented with a huge dish of crayfish, or rock lobsters, each more than five pounds and with wicked giggles were told: 'we're heathens here!' Together with fresh ears of winter corn and juice made of boiled wild strawberries, we dined like kings; there were also other meats, vegetables with coconut milk, apple pie and custard, and the obligatory choice of *pilhis*.

Pilhis are thought by some to be the only bad things that came out of the *Bounty* mutiny. They are all made from starchy vegetables or bananas grated into a purée on a unique instrument called a *yollo*, an oblong of volcanic rock into which a coarse, criss-cross pattern has been cut or etched. The purées are mixed with coconut milk made by soaking and squeezing coconut meat, wrapped in banana leaf and baked. Those made with green bananas are perfectly horrid, even to most Pitcairners, but those made with yam or sweet potato have a fascinating honey-like flavour and became an expedition favourite.

Pitcairn's cooking styles are much more varied than might be expected. The Polynesian pit ovens filled with hot stones and covered with earth are no longer employed, but open fires, known here as bolts, are found in many houses, as are stone ovens. The latter are the oldest types of oven known to western man, and those on Pitcairn are re-creations of the bread ovens built into the outside walls of the houses left by the mutineers in England. Bread cannot be baked a better or sweeter way, and the Pitcairners' wonderful pies and pastries nearly all come from this source. A few kitchens have solid fuel ranges and more are installing modern electric cookers from New Zealand; several families have old and new style kitchens beside one another. Here you need as much capacity as you can get. With sixty people on the island there is an average of one birthday a week. Almost every one is celebrated with a party, and a party means all are invited, and all bring contributions.

At home with the family or on any of these binges, the Pitcairners serve food Polynesian-style, which is also the way it used to be done in eighteenth century Georgian Britain—all the dishes, sweet and savoury, are put on the table at the same time. So, if you have your eye on the passion fruit ice cream, some favourite flavour of jelly or the coconut rice, you can tuck into that before you tackle breadfruit chips and chicken curry—or you can pile all on your plate at the same time. I never got used to seeing Tom enjoying a bowl of fruit, ice cream and jelly from a spoon in his right hand while biting into a slice of bread and yeast extract held in the other. He reckoned the combination was great. In another echo of Polynesia, twice I ate at a table with men only, while the women watched. Pitcairners, of the older generation anyway, tell you this is because God created men first and thus they must come first in everything. This is actually Tahitian tradition with a new set of Christian clothes: men and women ate separately for many reasons, some based on food taboos, some on social status. Even those who ate together did so at some distance from another, so their fly whisks did not inflict accidental injury.

For mutual entertainment, we challenged the Pitcairners to one of their famous cricket matches. Visitors to the English cricket grounds of Lord's or the Oval would not have recognized it as such, and we had trouble too. Teams are as big as can be arranged and the rules are simple—the Pitcairners can cheat, their opponents cannot. Ted put beautiful lettering onto a cracked soup tureen that had been retrieved from a wreck at Henderson Island and the *Taiyo* Challenge Cup Match began at Hulianda at 11 am on Wednesday 20 August. It ended at 4.30 and we lost by several hundred runs in spite of the valiant efforts of our baffled Americans, who had practised secretly for days.

This was the first time a visiting ship had challenged the island for more than ten years. Following tradition, the match was celebrated with a public dinner in the square, and even though the women had been playing exuberantly, extra effort was put into the variety and quantity of food that night.

Gluttony and temptation prevailed. Expedition members were convinced they woke with food hangovers; stories circulated of those who trembled if denied cake and mandarins for more than an hour. More than one pair of sleek trousers was quietly put to the bottom of a suitcase. To do what I had to do I had to talk with my mouth full, or I should have learned nothing.

42

Graves, Pools and Caves

To disperse the miasma of deceit and subterfuge that infects the story of Pitcairn's first twenty years, and to get a clearer understanding of what had happened here and why John Adams dissembled so much, I needed to establish some details of the original settlement. In pursuit of Fletcher Christian's grave, I hoped also to find that of his wife Isabella, and of their son Charles and his Tahitian wife, Sully, my great-great-great-grandparents. I had brought photostats of etchings and watercolours discovered in libraries and private collections around the world. These would be used to site long-gone buildings and help make sense of half-remembered stories. We stimulated the community to find old photographs too, and the combination of pictures, memories and interest produced results to confound those who say the Pitcairners are not interested in their past.

In the photographic collection of Len and Thelma Brown I discovered Fletcher and Isabella's grandson, Thursday October II, known as Duddie. He died aged ninety-one in 1911, and so had been a man of twenty when his grandmother had died. There are men and women alive on Pitcairn who clearly remember him wheezing with asthma and reminiscing; they heard twentieth-century memories of the wives of eighteenth-century mutineers. The Browns' house seems to sit on the edge of the common ground of the first settlement, for around it are, or were, the prison built in Joshua Hill's time, the forge, and the building where sugar cane juice was reduced by boiling to what is here called molasses, but which is a 'mother syrup' as none of the sugar has been removed. Close by is the sugar cane crusher itself, like a gigantic, rimless, spoked wheel, said to have come from the West Indies and to be over a hundred years old.

Warren and Maisie Christian let me look through the remaining archives of Roy Clark, who had died earlier in 1980. For seventy years Roy recorded and wrote of Pitcairn with talent and detail; each of his photographs is captioned and most faces are identified, giving sudden life to the names on the branches of the family tree. I was sometimes uneasy to be sitting on a deep verandah sorting these memories, to be enjoying the sight of hens flying into low trees to gorge on bananas, to be listening to Maisie making her famous guava pastries, or to Warren chopping and whittling at the *Bounty* model he was making for Upton Brady, my American editor. It didn't feel like work. Then I would find the face of a long dead relative. Was I looking at the face of Fletcher Christian in an image of one of his descendants; or did those noble faces look like the unknown chief who was the father of Isabella? There is such a similarity between Christian faces over the generations it seems impossible for there not to be echoes of Fletcher somewhere. With a spread of these photographs in front of me, I knew I was as close to Fletcher Christian as it was possible to be. But the gap would never be closed, something which, although incontrovertible, I still find difficult to accept.

There were a number of gruesome pictures of the laid-out dead, including one of Duddie draped in what looks like lace curtains, and the funeral cortège of one of the Coffin brothers was clearly headed for today's graveyard. This simple bare field, hedged close to the oldest house on the island and under the direct gaze of

Christian's Cave, is muddled with concrete-marked graves, mainly anonymous. You can find Rosalind Young, who wrote so well of her island and collected important stories and evidence. There are other half-remembered names, and sad places where uncertain hand lettering has mis-spelt a surname or copied a verse with loving patience, but little relevance. We could find no tombs older than eighty years, and did not even identify that of Duddie. During the voyage, close scrutiny of one of the etchings I had brought gave clues to what seemed to be another graveyard. If it were different from that seen today, then it was also very much older.

The main clues in the picture are a thatched building, obviously non-existent now but said to have been a church and schoolhouse, and a huge banyan tree. Underneath the tree you can just make out an untidy cluster of gravestones. Although this picture had been used on a recent stamp, no Pitcairner had noticed the graves. None of the banyan trees which still exist stands in the same relationship to Christian's Cave and Lookout Point as shown in the picture, but that could simply be artist's licence. Mark Balsiger confirmed suspicions when he reported several people on the island referring to the square where we met as 'Up the School'. It did not take long to find there had been a school on the square just where the Post Office now stands. And the banyan? Yes, it had stood right on one corner, clearly remembered by those who could not recall the old thatched building other than by usage of the name it had given the square.

Disbelief mounted more quickly than excitement. Rightly so. The Courthouse, and the one before that, *had* been built over the first graveyard. We sent Andrew Brady under the Courthouse and he said there was at least one gravestone to be seen in the rubble. An earlier generation had decided to destroy and build over the other stones, rude though they may have been. I was horrified. Land had never been *that* scarce and these were the graves of their founders! I tried to find ways of explaining or rationalizing what had happened. Possibly a sense of guilt made them ashamed of their rough, unmarried ancestors, but respect for the dead and their tombs was part of nineteenth-century religious morbidity. Only slowly did I realize I was judging and questioning these people by standards other than Polynesian. Polynesian grief for the dead is transitory and, interestingly, the Seventh Day Adventists do not savour death either, teaching that the dead ought to be thought of with happiness, as they enjoy their reward in heaven. Here, at least, the two cultures blend perfectly and on Pitcairn, the living have ever taken precedence over the dead. It was important to have been reminded early of the folly of making judgments about Pitcairn based on the mores of other places.

It was specially galling for me not to be able to identify and somehow mark the grave of the woman called Isabella, Mauatua, Mainmast, or Mi'mitti. That same night we went back to the Courthouse, and joined the Pitcairners atop the remains of Isabella and her son Charles, to watch the film *An Unmarried Woman*; it was extraordinarily unnerving. The longer I stayed on Pitcairn, the more I knew she had been the most extraordinary of women. Of the nine that arrived with *Bounty*, she alone is remembered and constantly appears in conversation. I roundly curse those visitors of the early nineteenth century who described her white hair and story-telling ability—but who didn't record her stories.

Tom Christian, my host, is probably the most sophisticated man on the island, well-travelled and professionally qualified as a radio operator. He is as interested in his heritage and in Pitcairn as I am, and between radio schedules and busy hours talking to the world from his ham radio shack, he put me on the back of his Honda and we explored and identified places that seemed linked with the *Bounty* settlers. In a book called *The Pitcairnese Language* there is a list of place names collected by the school children of the 1950s, but published under the names of Ross, Moverley, et al. It mentions a pool named after Mainmast (Isabella) and I was determined to find it, even though no one on the island could place it, or the pool called Maimas, which might or might not have been the same place. All the water levels on Pitcairn have altered radically over the last century, usually after massive landslides, so a once well-known pool could now be dried up or have slid into oblivion.

One morning, waiting for Tom to be free, I went to talk to the island's oldest couple, 85-year-old John Christian MBE and his wife Bernice, eighty-one. This had not been easy to arrange as they are among the most active on the island, forever trundling their heavy wooden wheelbarrow up the winding tracks and roads that join scattered gardens. After writing my genealogy for Bernice, I joined John as he carved in the dim light of a small window. Almost blind in one eye and troubled with the other, he constructs and rigs sailing ship models that are sold around the world; 'I'm not going to sit around doing nothing, not if I can earn some money!' There's one model he wouldn't sell, made entirely from the last scraps of a breadfruit tree said to have been brought to Pitcairn by *Bounty*. He let me hold the stoneware water jar from *Bounty* that had come to them through Bernice's family, and then I started asking them about place names. Did they know a pool named after Mainmast? 'Of course,' said Bernice immediately, 'that's Down Maimas, over Tedside.'

The western side of the island, steep and forbidding, had never been settled although there are the remains of an important marae there. Once called The Other Side, this had become corrupted to Tedside. It seemed as though Mainmast's pool and Maimas might be the same place. I had also heard Tom refer to somewhere called Mummas, and knew that was over Tedside, too.

'Could what you call Mummas actually be Down Mainmas?' I asked Tom.

He thought. 'Of course, it never occurred to me. Mummas, Maimas, Mainmast!' We sped over the ridge and were soon sliding across a greasy, dangerous slope under tall old trees below the road through Tedside. It had been years since Tom had been there but he was certain he remembered the pool.

He found it, and by the time I arrived, breathless and with bleeding hands after the difficult trek, he was hacking grass and moss away from a pool with his machete. We worked for more than three hours in the sun and in the moments we paused, I was aware of the special stillness of Pitcairn, sometimes calming, sometimes frightening, for the slightest rustle of branches is perturbing and might be someone or something unknown. In the hidden pocket of tall grasses and banana, I understood the horror of the days of ambush and bloodshed.

When the pool had been drained of filthy water and cleaned of six inches of grey slime, we stepped back to see that the rock had been shaped by man into a large bathtub. Shaped by mutineers? By Fletcher for Mainmast? Or was it even older, and simply discovered by Mainmast? It was easy to see her and her companions gathered here to bathe on a languid afternoon, and a beguiling sight it made.

We left the pool to fill with the clear water that dribbled in after running between the rock face and the luscious growth that tumbled down from the road. Two days later I hired the island's tractor— at sixty cents an hour—to carry a party back and to photograph Tom's oldest daughter, Jackie. She hadn't known of the pool and was as touched as Tom and I had been. That seemed to be as close to Mainmast as I was to get and the identification of this pool gave the Pitcairners further confidence in the expedition and its serious interest in their island. The spontaneous help we had been shyly offered now became universal and we were shown more artifacts and photographs with a mixture of modesty and pride that gave even greater joy to discovery. Reynold Warren showed us a *tu'i*, a hand-shaped stone pestle used for pounding fish, taro or breadfruit. This was noticeably more elegant and worn than the few others we had seen and Hop, our engineer and expert in such things, felt secure enough to identify it as being Tahitian and old enough to have been brought by *Bounty*.

This news was soon passed around Adamstown and several of the long oval wooden dishes that had been used as a mortar with a *tu'i* were rescued from back cupboards. A new interest in the artifacts and memories of our Tahitian forebears was rekindled and Nola Warren and Tom Christian were specially pleased to have the value of such things pointed out.

I think the expedition was surprised at the interest shown by the younger men and women on Pitcairn, and it was natural they would be intrigued by our metal detectors, the first seen on the island. We first took them up to Christian's Cave. If Fletcher Christian had brooded there for weeks on end, or if he had nursed himself to health after being shot in the back in the 1793 massacre, there might be some evidence of his ammunition stores or of the lean-to Beechey says he built . . . perhaps he had hidden money from *Bounty* and had died before he could use it to escape. Hours of patient work, based on small grids that were checked with several machines with differing abilities, found little but spent shells from forgotten goat hunts. For all this painstaking work we found nothing, neither treasure nor other artifacts of the early days. The payoff came as we struggled back and forth with aching chests and tortured leg muscles; we formed definite opinions about the cave, and what might have happened there.

Christian's Cave is anything but a cave: there are no narrow passages leading to inner chambers, no bats, no glow worms, waterfalls or cathedrals of lime. It is merely a lofty, triangular chip out of the cliff face, some 800 feet above sea level; but I'll call it a cave for the sake of convenience. It is one of the first spots on the island to be touched by the rising sun, but by afternoon is cold, windy and miserable, a dangerous shock to sweated bodies at the end of a climb.

Access from the village, which sprawls in its camouflage of greens away towards Bounty Bay, begins in thick foliage close to the school and continues around Lookout Point on uncertain paths made by man and animal, shaded and sun-lit, until emerging on the glare of sparse, daunting slopes. I paused, breathless and slightly dizzy on my first climb, then zigzagged the next several hundred feet on loose shingle and decomposing rock; it is steep enough to make progress on all fours both safer and simpler. Twenty feet below and to the right of the cave's final access, I had to clamber on great rocks, negotiate a brief but chilling cliff-face ledge, and finally scale the short perpendicular climb to the few sloping yards of scrub that separate the cave's ledge from the precipice. Satisfaction and relief poured over me in direct relationship to the sweat on my brow, undiminished by the laughter of Pitcairn children and men who had bounced ahead as if jogging in Hyde Park.

A hunted man, armed and provisioned, could undoubtedly defend this place for as long as supplies held out; for no more than one attacker at a time could reach the cave and could be shot at will while doing so. At night, it might be a different story, and with no water handy and no back way to sneak out day or night to gather food, it would have been desperately uncomfortable and exposed. It would also have been necessary to stay in one corner of the cave, for snipers could shoot directly into two-thirds of it from rock outcrops less than a hundred feet away from its maw.

I heard stories from several sources suggesting the cave mouth had been partially obscured by trees earlier this century, and older watercolours seem to indicate this may have been so at other times, too. To hide the cave fully from observers a screen of tall mature trees and thick undergrowth would be needed to ensure secrecy, for even the casual eye is caught by slight movement on the rock face. The idea of there being enough trees to make this a hiding place goes directly against the argued attraction it had to Fletcher Christian, a place to sit and stare at the sea and his new estate, to watch the sun rise behind Bounty Bay and slowly illuminate red gardens and thatched huts. Stories of there being *some* trees up here seem to me to have been amplified to fit an unlikely hypothesis.

This is an important point. If Fletcher Christian miraculously survived the October 1793 massacre he needed to have a secure hideout while he regained strength and health and prepared to sail away in secret. Could someone shot in the back, probably with a shattered shoulder and useless right arm, plus possible head wounds climb to the cave? At night, with infinite care, prodigious recuperative powers and strength, it is just possible, but subsequent dangers inherent in leaving for food and water, crossing cliff faces when sick and injured, would make it a dangerous and painful choice. If he had emerged during the day, he would have been certain of detection; if at night, uncertain of safety.

Before I went to Pitcairn I rather fancied the version of Fletcher's death given by Becke and Jeffery in their stirring but stilted *The Mutineer.* Their tale relies on Christian being succoured by his wife and others as he lay in his cave, and calls for a great number of lightly undertaken sorties to and from the hideout, both by Christian and his confidants. The physical impossibility of such casual and repeated journeys in the time allotted, even for healthy men and women, makes nonsense of Becke's vehement defence of his book's authenticity. Rather than presenting a story that might be taken as a slight bending of fact to flatter a narrative, he has gone far enough towards fantasy to ensure his story cannot be accepted at all; although this is not necessarily the fault of Becke, who might have been misled by others, including those on Pitcairn. Any visitor to Christian's Cave can see the faults in this version; so either Becke did not go to Pitcairn Island, or he stayed a very short time, or, like others, he and his collaborator, Jeffrey, recomposed the story to enhance the drama.

There is another complication, a story on Pitcairn of an alternative way to the cave, down from the peak of Lookout Point. This would have been by way of vines and tree roots, for there is neither an indication of natural paths nor signs that adjacent landslides might have affected past tracks. Anyway, such aerial access would have made the cave even less secret and infinitely harder to defend; it is hardly a good idea to have the uninvited drop in from above. And a man with a bullet-shattered shoulder is most unlikely to have made a cave with such access his goal.

So, as a fortress the cave is a possibility; as the desperate hideout of an injured man, it is improbable; as a place where you can retreat into yourself, it is without peer. Most of the expedition used it thus at some time, wishing themselves in other places or other times, and there are only gannets and soaring bo'sun birds to interrupt your thoughts.

43

A Pool of Information

Constant high seas put paid to our plans to survey *Bounty*'s wreck and to use our metal detectors among the boulders of the foreshore. A brief dive on the one possible day confirmed there is nothing left but the random piling of ballast bars. Other relics must lie on the shelf of the bay, more cannon, more swivel guns, more copper sheathing and nails. But most are in Adamstown and in a sad state of decay, despite repeated requests to England and the USA for material and information about preservation. A cannon lies in the grass outside Len and Thelma Brown's. A swivel gun, pristine only two years earlier, flakes in a shed at Ivan Christian's. There are slowly decomposing balls from both types of gun, hunks of twisted copper and stores of copper nails in most houses. And there are stories of sewing kits and other pieces that were not submerged, but which became victims of the settling of estates or were lost in the depths of stored possessions and the envies of those dead or lately departed.

Day after day Tom and I worked to recreate the first village and to establish the validity of any part of any of the versions of our ancestor's death. There was precious little to go on when we got down to it, but we agreed the accounts given by the Tahitian, Jenny, had the greatest veracity.

The site on which Fletcher Christian was supposedly shot is easily shown to those who enquire and has been agreed upon since Pitcairn's first nineteenth-century visitors. Old Duddie said his father had shown him the site. But his father, Thursday October, was barely three years old at the time of the massacre and, according to Jenny, was playing at his home which is on the other side of the island. But why should the site of only Fletcher Christian's murder be remembered? And if, as Young's lost diary seems to say, he was buried close to where he was shot, why is the site not pointed out as his *grave*? I can't really believe, for all their nonchalance about the dead, his family continued cultivating what was literally the soil of their forefather, and we know this plot did continue to be used as a garden until quite recently. It seemed likely to me that the site was a conspicuously successful red herring of Adams, a sop to the curiosity of visitors which, like good stories everywhere, became accepted as fact.

When we stood on the site which Tom had been shown as a boy, we rehearsed the version of Fletcher's death given by the Tahitian woman Jenny. The day for the murders had been chosen because the women had gone up to the mountains to collect birds' eggs. Here was the first anomaly. If anything could be called 'up in the mountains', this site could. It is only a few hundred yards below the island's long ridge, at the top of John Mills Valley. As in the past, it is fairly well protected by thick bush and totally insulated from the village, which is both out of sight and an arduous hilly trek away.

Fletcher Christian is said to have groaned loudly when he was shot, a sound heard in nearby plots and recognized by some as the sound of a dying man. Others thought it was Isabella calling her two children to eat and dismissed the shot as that from a pig hunt planned by the Polynesians. This all becomes transparently impossible when you are standing on the site.

Jenny's story clearly implies that most men were gardening close to the village, and the women as far away as possible up in the mountain. There was no reason in those days for the men to garden in the hills. There was plenty of ground close to home for so few to cultivate, and any 'gardens' they did have in other parts of the island were simply divisions of naturally occurring fruit trees. In any case, the suspect site is amid especially steep and rugged terrain and it would have been tiresome to walk over to another plot simply to discuss an unexpected sound. The type of territory also makes it unlikely they could have shouted to one another, and for Isabella's voice to have been heard as far away as this, she must have been possessed of something rather more stentorian even than modern electronics can manufacture.

If the groan and the dismissal of it did happen, it was closer to the settlement. Jenny shows this is so, by remembering something both intimate to Fletcher and Isabella and important to a Polynesian woman. She tells us specifically that Fletcher was working close to home that day, for his wife was about to give birth to their third child. That does make sense of the whole story; the women were away in the mountains while the men worked in gardens close to their houses. On the flatter, more open land around the village it would have been easy to saunter over for a chat or to shout at one another; indeed many may well have been working in parts of one of the communal gardens. It would also be possible to mistake a sound from the direction of Fletcher's house and garden as coming from Isabella calling from her door.

There was no doubt in my mind that the site traditionally shown as that where Fletcher was shot was a fiction of John Adams. Where, then, was the site?

Ben Christian, Island Secretary for over eighteen years, let me borrow the record of land deeds. Land is divided among a family's children and then subdivided and so on, thus it was possible broadly to piece together Fletcher Christian's original plot of land in the village. Within this swathe at the northern end of the settlement you find Thursday October's house, the oldest on the island, now uninhabited but still showing the sliding shutters used instead of windows. This in turn is directly below Tom Christian's house which stands on the site called Fletcher's; the exact situation is not known, but this is undoubtedly the vicinity of Fletcher Christian's house. Further afield are gardens still owned by Christians, and like some gigantic barrier, Lookout Point bounds the northern extremity. This provides a simple reason for the naming of the cave; it would be Christian's Cave simply because it was on his land, rather than because he adopted it as a den; indeed it would be unlikely he would have done this if it had been on someone else's property.

His gardens in the area are within shouting distance of his house, so Isabella could have called him at the start of childbirth. If he were shot somewhere in this vicinity, his groan might easily have been mistaken for Isabella, for everyone else was south of this site and both sounds would have come from the same direction.

Edward Young's lost diary said that it was not until the following August that the women buried their dead husbands. It is a sobering thought that rivalry and tension were so high on an island only one by one and a half miles that the bodies weathered a full sultry Pitcairn summer; but having been there, and seen how easy ambush and attack is, I knew the seeming uninterest was probably sensible self-preservation, and we know the Polynesians didn't care too much about burial anyway. The women had managed to collect the heads of their men, which was much more important. When the men killed in October 1793, now all headless skeletons, were buried, it was in a communal grave. Other than vague mentions of Fletcher being buried in his garden there is just one solid clue as to where this grave might be, a casual mention in the journal of Dr Bennet, surgeon on a round-the-world whaling voyage aboard *Tuscan*, Captain Stavers. While writing about the Pitcairn he found in 1834, Bennet tells us: 'Fletcher Christian and John Mills were shot on the same day, by the Tahitians: the grave of the former was pointed out to me: it is situated a short distance up a mountain and in the vicinity of a pond.'

Once more I was searching for a pond, this time certain to be a dry one, for none with water answered the description. Throughout the village I asked about ponds, springs and wells, secretly hoping the 'mountain' might be Lookout Point, for it is the only peak that could be so described, though there are higher points. As the time to leave Pitcairn was fast approaching, I was anxious in the extreme, and steeling myself for failure.

I let my mind cast far and wide, following the vaguest clues. For two days I considered clearing a flat area called Graveyard, towards the centre of the island. This is within such distance of the traditional site of Fletcher Christian's death that it was a conceivable place for a mass grave for victims of murder in the area. Perhaps I was wrong to dismiss that first site? Deeper research into the place name showed it was very old; no one alive had ever heard an explanation of its meaning. Then I remembered the *Bounty* settlers had discovered several graves of their Polynesian predecessors. I crossed my fingers and abandoned that site. In the end I trusted my instincts about Adams—I'm sure he would never have allowed such an obvious and dangerous clue to the truth to exist.

Following tangents simply so I could return to my base with a clear head, I went with Tom to his garden below Christian's Cave; it is an important site for artifacts of the industry of those men whose graves had confused me. Tom was going to point out working sites where stone tools had been shaped, and we hoped to find a partly worked or broken tool for me as a memento. We achieved this and, delighted to have the lower half of a broken stone chisel at least six hundred years old that had been polished with use, I suggested to Tom that we take the path that leads to the Cave, for, some distance along, you come to a dark overhang of rock in which McKoy is said to have set up his still. I hadn't looked

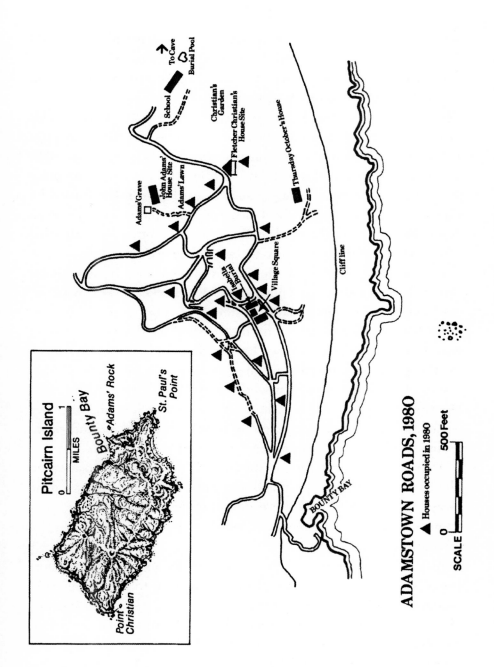

Pitcairn Island

MILES

Bounty Bay

"*Adams' Rock*

St. Paul's Point

Point Christian

School

To Cave

Burial Pool

Christian's Garden

Fletcher Christian's House Site

John Adams' House Site

Adams' Grave

Adams' Lawn

Thursday October's House

Isabella Burial

Village Square

Cliff line

Bounty Bay

ADAMSTOWN ROADS, 1980

▲ Houses occupied in 1980

500 Feet

SCALE

405

at it properly on my peregrinations to Christian's Cave and thought Tom might add some interesting stories to my collections.

Only a few hundred yards after we plunged into the bush, Tom stopped literally open-mouthed. It was the expression I had seen when he realized that Mummas meant Mainmast. I followed his gaze and quickly understood what had caught his attention—as plain a dried-up pool as one could imagine, once one knew. It was right in the middle of Fletcher Christian's original plot, within shouting distance of the original village, close to gardens still being used by Christians, and it was 'a short distance up a mountain', Lookout Point. Not only did the pool fit Bennet's description, it neatly tied a knot with the threads of my theory and Jenny's accounts.

On available evidence both the Pitcairners and the expedition agreed this was all a fair conclusion. We checked every map, re-read every list of place names, listened to more stories—but no other pool seemed to have existed that fitted the description. Now, two days before departure, we had no time for a systematic search for the grave or graves among the banana palms and coffee bushes scattered on the steep hills around the oval pool's crumbling banks. Identifying the pool did not, in itself, prove Fletcher Christian was buried nearby. But discounting one possible murder site and establishing another was a major step forward in my research.

The time had come for me carefully to consider my position on Fletcher's death—was he killed and buried on Pitcairn or did he escape to England? There were more hurdles to clear before I was home on that one, not least of which was the emotional one of leaving Pitcairn.

As early as the second afternoon of our stay, expedition members feared the emotional wrench of saying goodbye to the island. Subsequently, the deepening friendships we made and the insinuating charm of Pitcairn drew more into this band. And when we joined the Pitcairners in the Courthouse Hall to hear them record their famous songs of goodbye, ringing with rich, reedy harmonies unique to Polynesia, there was not one who could say they did not dread the day. It was put off until 28 August, so that Ted and his film crew could record the brief visit of the *Essi Silje*. Now that no British ships are officially thought 'suitable' to call at Pitcairn on their way south to Australasia, the island must rely on the courtesy and personal endeavours of less than a handful of Norwegian sea captains to deliver supplies from the northern hemisphere, an extraordinary situation in which to find a British Colony. We went out to the ship with the long boats and by the time we were delivered to *Taiyo*, salt-splashed and cold, the sun was setting. Some of the Pitcairn women were seasick and so stayed in the long boats, tied up to our ship's side. The rest, most of the island's population, crammed on to our slippery decks for final embraces and tears.

The moment of goodbye, when just we fifteen were left on the deck, was ghastly. We stood mute in harsh floodlight from our mast heads as they sang, 'Goodbye' and 'In the Sweet Bye and Bye', and we were grateful we had some preparation for the raw beauty of unaccompanied singing by almost fifty loved people on the open sea. The long boats' diesel motors roared them out of sight into the darkness, then they turned and swept past for a final wave and last glimpses of favourite faces and faltering smiles. The wrench was much more than just that of leaving friends.

Pitcairn's way of life showed me that the message of basic Christianity can work, that brotherly love and kindness are more sustaining than the rewards offered by industrialized societies. Even though supported by deep freezes and Honda motorcycles, this is a community that largely lives the life of small settlements throughout Europe and America during the mid to late nineteenth century, before the advent of mass media and travel. There is no newspaper, no television and no radio station although since 1980 there are more ham radio operators, most households have video recorders and the single telephone and fax line mean not only better communication but private communication is now possible; email and the Internet will be increasingly possible in the early years of the new century. News comes from intermittent attention to the BBC's World Service, but it does not mean much here, and only great disasters are discussed, not because of morbid interest but because there can be an element of identification with victims of tragedy. The machinations of politics, strikes, and royal processions cannot alter their lives or impinge upon them, but the latter might actually interest these most loyal subjects of the Queen.

The Golden Rule—Do unto others as you would that they should do unto you—is indeed golden here. So is 'Don't Rock the Boat', an unspoken but universally understood aphorism of acute relevance on land and sea; you do not dare make an enemy through criticism or complaint on land when, next day, you may rely on that person immediately understanding your slightest word or gesture in defence of lives at sea. This is not to say there are no undercurrents in the village, but the good of the community is understood to be far more important than the foibles of the individual.

At first we were embarrassed by the generosity and hospitality of the Pitcairners, hardly believing it could be sincere and sustained; but it was. To live in Adamstown is to bathe in a perpetual glow of friendship and trust, with no thought of locked doors or theft, no worries about dark streets or social levels, no fear of loneliness or of wounding gossip. I saw that away from the temptations of self-aggrandisement, men and women are born inherently good and continue that way, a far more triumphant dogma than that of original sin.

44

A Degree of Immortality

In the sixteen days it took to sail back to Tahiti, there was both reverie and discussion on the vessel and little else broke the routine of sleeping, eating and steering except the magnificent attentions of a single albatross. We enjoyed increasing warmth as we bumped north, and pursued suntans with naked determination. Close quarters and the return to duty and discipline brought to festering point the problems of companionship. Yet, none of the potential for explosion brought aboard by fifteen strong-willed individuals erupted to such an extent that the expedition's objectives were seriously threatened. There were few blows other than some irregular and infantile bullying but this was as likely to be verbal as physical. The equivalent situation on board *Bounty* as she sailed away from Tahiti was never far from my mind.

It was a triumph for all on board *Taiyo* that emotions were contained; this is not to say there were not disappointments and short-comings or that there were never ugly moments, but my worst problems all seemed to happen on land.

Tahiti was welcome when we tied up in the first few hours of 13 September, and headed for the food stalls that alluringly scented the air along the strip of concrete between the park and harbour at the eastern end of town. We devoured steak sandwiches, bags of chips and Coca-Cola. Within days we had melted away from one another, Michael and I flying to New Zealand, Australia, Norfolk Island and Honolulu, to complete research for this book.

During those final days on Tahiti, I spent a stimulating and civilized afternoon with Bengt Danielsson and his wife, Marie-Thérèse. Bengt was aboard *Kon-Tiki* in 1947, and since then has become a world respected authority on the anthropology of the South Pacific and the *Bounty* story, as has his wife. We sat in a huge, cool, thatched library and study, one of the scatter of traditional Tahitian buildings on his marvellous estate right on the lagoon. Across the close-cropped grass was an uninterrupted view of Moorea; as we talked of *Bounty* and times past, an outrigger canoe, paddled by a woman with a flower in her waist-length hair, glided across the proscenium of coconut palms. Such diversions and the mirabelle *eau-de-vie* produced by Marie-Thérèse notwithstanding, Bengt went quickly to the heart of my questions. With typical Scandinavian economy he convinced me that the simpler an explanation was, the more likely it was to be true; he gave me examples which encouraged me finally not to fear an unfussy solution to many of the vexed *Bounty* questions. It was deeply reassuring to have the keen interest of Bengt and his wife, and next day he drove me to see the sites he had identified as the breadfruit camps at Matavai and Pare.

In the cocoons of Air New Zealand DC-10s and the welcome of Mary Crowley's house in Sausalito, I carefully reviewed what we had found about the death of Fletcher Christian. Until the time I began my research, the circumstantial evidence was as strong for his demise on Pitcairn as it was for a dangerous undercover return to his birthplace. Since then I had made two important discoveries in England.

The first was the 600-year family history mentioned earlier. At the end of the entry about Fletcher Christian, whom the authoresses dub the undoubted black sheep of the family, they write: 'It is . . .

extremely unlikely that the Pitcairners should have been deceived in the matter of their leader's death. Moreover, had Fletcher got back to England the only motive worth the risk would have been to see his family and of such an event no tradition has been preserved.' I find this completely persuasive, considering its provenance. If there had been the tiniest glimmer of gossip from sources in or close to the family, Vio Christian and her daughter, Rita Christian Browne, would have found it and recorded it.

It *is* extremely unlikely that the Pitcairners could have been deceived as to the death of their leader. And if he had not died on Pitcairn some mention must surely have slipped out in conversation with visitors. Indeed the sense of guilt that Adams' fierce religion instilled into his sheep-like flock suggests they might all have welcomed the chance of excusing themselves of complicity in at least one of the murders. But no hint of an escape has ever come from Pitcairn itself, only Adams' dissembling created a mystery which led others to infer such a possibility.

Heywood's supposed sighting of Fletcher Christian in Devonport is blown out of all proportion by the very thing that was supposed to do the opposite; it was kept secret until after Heywood's death.

It remains strange that Barrow believed in the sighting, or at least in Heywood's telling of it and did not publicise this until 1831. That Barrow wrote *The Mutiny of the Bounty* anonymously is not as suspicious as it seems; most people did in those days when there were terrible laws of slander and libel which could be interpreted too freely for anyone's good.

It is also extraordinary that Sir Jonn Barrow admitted complicity in the 'cover up'. As Secretary to the Admiralty, he might be assumed to be as responsible as anyone in pursuing those who had incurred its displeasure. Perhaps it helped Barrow's career to be uncontroversial, and it was easy to find other explanations for the flight of the man who had surprised Heywood. In Plymouth in the early nineteenth century there would have been many a tar who would run from a naval officer, or any other man, uniformed or otherwise. There were previous shipmates and captains to fear, as well as cut-throats and footpads. There is even the possibility that Heywood saw another member of the Christian family, perhaps Charles, for there was a widespread disability of the knees among males of the clan, which contributed to the peculiar gait imputed to Fletcher and several relatives.

As to Wilkinson's belief in Fletcher Christian as the inspiration for 'The Ancient Mariner', it is as well to consider what the author disarmingly says right at the start: that he has no new information to offer and that he began his research only because he found the signature of an F. Christian in a scrapbook in a Charing Cross bookshop. Not being able to compare this with the autograph of the mutineer, and because it was associated in the scrapbook with the Losh family, who had assisted Edward Christian, he thought it might be the long-lost key to proving the return of Fletcher. He also mentions the existence in a notebook of Coleridge in the Public Records Office of the scribbled note, 'The adventures of Fletcher Christian.'

It is patently absurd to think the latter is anything other than the most basic *aide-memoire*, the sort of thing any writer does constantly. As to the signature, there are a number of other F. Christians of whom I know, and there would have been others besides. I subsequently found two signatures of Fletcher Christian on *Bounty* documents which have survived, but was unable to arrange to compare them with that held by Wilkinson.

And then there is the paper written by William Fletcher MP in 1867: *Fletcher Christian and the Mutineers of the Bounty*. William was a relation of Fletcher's mother and I found a handwritten copy— his, I think—of the work in the archives of Tullie House Library in Carlisle, together with some letters to him from Lady Belcher, who had Morrison's journal at the time; at first she scrawled to say she was not well and could not find the work; but later advised she had sent it by rail.

William Fletcher does not note any sources so presumably the originator of rumours of Fletcher Christian's return to the area current in 1808 and 1809 is Sir John Barrow, who likewise furnished no provenance for his information. I spent many days reading every newspaper I could find that exists from the period and from the area, but there is no hint of Fletcher's return, and I think this is just the type of story that would have been printed if it were actually in circulation. William Fletcher also says Fletcher is thought to have been visiting a favourite aunt. In fact all his aunts were dead. Isabella Christian Curwen was not, but she was only a cousin by marriage.

The continuing thrust of William Fletcher's story is that Fletcher Christian could have avoided discovery by hiding in the thick forest that covered the hills around Lake Windermere and the thirty acres of Belle Isle. It is a melodramatic theory, in the best tradition of the Victorian novel: the repentant mutineer, bullied into abandoning his coloured consort and bastard children, journeys half way around the world in disguise to live out a life of lonely misery within sight of the real Isabella, rich, beautiful but forever unattainable. The descendants of John and Isabella no longer live on Belle Isle, but Windermere still enthrals tourists with the suggestion that Fletcher Christian might have walked where they did, indeed that he might be buried beneath their feet . . . but this is all impossible, as my second important discovery, in a Cockermouth junk shop, helped me prove.

When I was there in late 1979, I visited the antique junk shop in Noreham House on Main Street (which incidentally once belonged to Fletcher Christian's grandparents). In perfect accord with the above type of plot I found, in a remote dark corner, an engraving of Belle Isle dated 1796. There are almost no trees on the island, and most of those to be seen cluster about the round house; nor are there trees to speak of on the hills that surround Windermere. Later research showed it was John Christian Curwen who planted most of the millions of trees that coated Cumberland by 1864, and who had made Belle Isle into a forest of imported specimen trees.

He started planting there in a small way in 1787, and seems continuously to have improved or changed the style of the gardens. The original formal gardens had been demolished in the early eighties and a raised gravel walk a mile and a half long, which William Wordsworth loathed, was constructed to run right around the island at the water's edge. Dorothy Wordsworth gives in her journal for 8 June 1802 the final lie to the possibility of hiding in a dense screen of trees on the island. She writes: 'The shrubs have been cut away in some parts of the island. They have made no natural glades: *it is merely a lawn with a few miserable young trees*, standing as if they were half starved . . . And that great house! Mercy upon us! if it *could* be concealed . . . Even the tallest of our old oak trees would not reach to the top of it.'

This pretty much clinches the impossibility of Belle Isle as a hiding place; if it was not covered with bushes or trees in 1802, it would not be seven years later. Anyway, every traveller with the will could visit the island and it was also the main summer house of the social Christian Curwens who introduced boating regattas and swans to the lake. A fugitive from society on Belle Isle would have to have been as fey as a sprite to avoid detection by the *ton* of Cumbria or the house's servants. By 1809, Fletcher Christian would have been forty-five, which in combination with a crippled right arm would have made him something less than fleet. He could not have rowed himself to the lake shore, or have swum there without great physical difficulty; and when he arrived there would have been little cover.

Nor can it be said that Curwen bought silence from those who might have discovered the presence of Fletcher Christian in Cumberland. As a rich crusader and a distinguished member of the Old Minority of Whig reformers, he had many opponents who would have paid more handsomely for the exposure of his harbouring a criminal.

So there can have been no hiding in Cumbria and little reason so to do. There was no point in skulking elsewhere in England for that would keep Fletcher Christian away from what little family he did have left; if he simply wanted to get away from Pitcairn and be anonymous, he would have been far better off in the West Indies or anywhere in the Americas, where a murky past was not unexpected.

The one person, I think, who might be expected to tell us of Fletcher's return is his brother Charles. The cruel, forced anonymity of a younger brother whom he considered to have been driven to temporary madness by the intemperance of another was too meaty a subject for him to abjure. As a further and proximate example of man's inhumanity to man, his pen would have worried at the idea over many pages. If Fletcher were back, he would have gone to Man to see Charles and his mother; if he did, Charles must have alluded to it. But he did not.

None of Fletcher Christian's supposed hiding places is verified by contemporary printed or written evidence and none of the stories that incorporate such suggestions has an identifiable ultimate source. There is no trace of belief or proof within the family, either in England or in the South Pacific, that he returned. Indeed, my great-aunts from Norfolk Island would redden and refuse to countenance even the suggestion, let alone the possibility. And this was always so within the family.

For all the conflict about the end of Fletcher Christian, his descendants on Pitcairn and Norfolk Island place it firmly on Pitcairn. My corroboration of Jenny's story and the identification of Bennet's pool convince me this is the truth; the enduring myth of his escape originated in England. The seed was planted as early as 1796, with the publication of the fictional *Letters from Mr Fletcher Christian*. Whoever wrote it certainly knew a lot about South America, and many readers must have believed it to be true.

The ultimate wonder is not the contradictions but that there should be such a myth about his escape from Pitcairn. One way to seek the answer to this is to look for precedent; you will find plenty. It seems man has always needed some of his heroes, especially those of protest, to survive. Fletcher Christian was quickly and firmly put into the temporal pantheon because he struck a seminal chord in universal yearnings for adventure and freedom, goals few achieve in reality. The legend of troublesome but admired men and women being reborn—if ever so briefly—is thousands of years older than the story of Jesus. Almost always the victim has been a protester and law breaker, an iconoclast whose adventures give excitement and hope to admirers. They in turn battle on with their hero through adversity and come out the other end, defeating both the system and that more implacable enemy, death.

The hot pioneering courage and imagination of Fletcher Christian when only twenty-four make him worthy of a far more dramatic end than that of perishing with his broken head clubbed into the warm, red earth of Pitcairn, slowly blackening in his own blood and the scorching sun. In the absence of a tombstone to prove such a banal end, the world's romantics have given him the more enduring memorial of making him into a legend, with a distinct extra claim to a degree of immortality, from a literary point of view at least.

There are many things my search for Fletcher Christian did not reveal. I will never know what he looked like. I shall never be able to sit by the grave of his wife or of his son, Charles. I will never know what he thought as he sat in a strip of cloth on the edge of his cave, with the new world he created far below. But I did discover that I have more than the blood of Fletcher Christian. I know his weaknesses and strengths are also mine. And I am certain I would have done as Fletcher Christian did.

Sometimes I feel I must return to Pitcairn and identify his grave, giving him the monument circumstances deny his immediate family. Surely the founder of Pitcairn Island, a man whose exploits have fired the imagination of millions of men and women over almost two centuries, deserves something better than an unmarked pit?

Or, is the great lonely rock of Pitcairn the most extraordinary mausoleum one revolutionary young man ever had?

Epilogue

Pitcairn's Revolutionary Women

Alleged under-age sex crimes against them make Pitcairn Island's women seem victims: but their Tahitian foremothers were leaders, creating a society of unique privilege and status for women

There's a bronzed memorial on a stand at the top of The Hill of Difficulty, the steep red-mud track from Bounty Bay to Adamstown, the only settlement on Pitcairn Island. Proudly, it lists Fletcher Christian and the eight Englishmen who settled the island with him after they took HMAV *Bounty* on April 28ᵗʰ 1789. Also there are the specifications of *Bounty*: the ship is glorified, her white men remembered; but there is no mention of the young Tahitian men or women who also arrived in her.

These young women were far more revolutionary than any French woman of 1789, who at least knew what she wanted from revolution, and some lived to be first in the world to have the vote by law, more than fifty years before NZ women. Without them there would be no Pitcairn Island, no Pitcairners – no me. Ask most *Bounty* descendants and they can tell you which mutineers' blood they have: ask from which Tahitian women they are descended, and only a handful knows.

It was a few days over eight months from the 1789 mutiny until the arrival of *Bounty* at Pitcairn Island early in January 1790. Some of the women had been with one or another of the white men almost as long or longer. Yet, amongst the nine European men, six Tahitian men and 12 Tahitian women who landed here, no woman was pregnant and the one infant was 10 months old.

It's impossible there had been no conceptions aboard *Bounty* in the months between leaving Tahiti and arriving at Pitcairn. The clue to what had been going on was the birth of Thursday October Christian, the first Pitcairner. He was born to 'chief' Fletcher Christian and his consort Mauatua almost exactly nine months after the Pitcairn landing. It was 1791 before the next child was born. It's clear the Tahitian women had a hidden agenda and the means to implement it: there would be no families until the sailing stopped and they were settled.

Tahiti seemed like paradise to the 18th-century European men who were its first white visitors. No one seemed to work, for you could scoop fish from the sea and whatever could grow there grew with almost no attention. Curiously, both men and women dressed in swathed togas of white cloth beaten from the bark of a sort of mulberry tree. They were tall too, and like ancient Greeks preceded nouns with an 'o': ask a Tahitian the name of their island and they would say Otaheite; I would have told you my name was Oglynn. It was as close to classical Greece as could be imagined.

Tahitians had perfect teeth, bathed in fresh water twice daily, and extracted all their bodily hair. They seemed to have great sexual freedom but this was a European misunderstanding. There were three distinct social classes, each taller and paler than the last; if you were caught with someone of the wrong caste you might be stoned. In any case, all children conceived of such couplings had to be aborted by one of several methods, or killed at birth.

Individual Tahitian women are recorded as having killed as many as eight babies at or before birth: as long as the baby had not taken its first breath they believed it had no spirit or independent life. It's quite probable most children conceived on Tahiti did not live.

Scratch the surface and Tahiti was a tearful drudgery for its women, made worse if they had a daughter permitted to live because she was perfectly formed, long and the right colour. Many female births were refused life simply because daughters ate only food gathered and prepared by their mother, so a daughter was a prison for her mother until she eventually left home to have children of her own. Neither was every son a balancing, personal joy, for once he was through puberty he might be beaten to death by priests, as a temple sacrifice.

Before they married Tahitian girls were encouraged to a free sexual life from a very early age, as long as they had many partners and not just one: this, their parents believed, prevented early pregnancies. Once married, Tahitian women first mourned for children who were conceived but aborted, or born but not permitted to breathe, then they mourned their own lost lives whilst mothering daughters, and might also suffer the loss of murdered sons.

Only six Tahitian men went to Pitcairn Island, few of them enjoying choice. They had to share three Tahitian women, nothing unusual for either sex, and so full-blooded Tahitian children must have been conceived. None was ever born or permitted to live. Once they were happy to have children, the Tahitian women clearly wanted only babies with more godly pale skins, and did what they had to do to ensure this. Once the Tahitian men were all murdered, these Tahitian women then became the first to keep all the children they conceived. Mauatua's second son Charles, nicknamed Hoppa, was born with a clubfoot. On Tahiti he would have been killed before he took his first breath, but he lived and became my great great great grandfather and the antecedent of almost everyone called Christian on Norfolk Island, the other *Bounty*-descendant settlement.

Some of the women had actually agreed to sail away on *Bounty* and had possessions with them, but most were spirited away without warning. When sailed back to Tahiti on September 22nd, 1789, Fletcher Christian was told of a plot to seize the ship from him and secretly slipped anchor.

Simply to survive, *Bounty*'s captured women had to overcome major taboos about clothing, food and eating. They had to rethink what they ate and how they cooked it: women were proscribed from touching much food, making it taboo or inedible if they did. They had to rethink their religion, their gods, their spirituality and their domestic, maternal and sexual roles - and to do this during months on a fleeing, under-manned sailing ship where even their basic Tahitian daily ritual of bathing twice in running fresh water was impossible. It's hard to imagine what they endured on stinking, leaking *Bounty* as it searched for a safe haven from the British Navy and its king. They didn't even have a language in common with its sailors.

Bounty's men, men, who would rarely have bathed or even washed their clothes, had terrible teeth, gums and breath, unwashed foreskins (Tahitian boys were supercised) and hairy bodies, but they were pale-skinned and had a big ship. Extraordinarily, Tahitian priests had foretold pale-skinned men with clothes that covered their bodies, who would come in a big canoe with no outriggers.

We must not judge 18th, 19th or even 20th century views with our own sensibilities. Finding themselves sailing away on *Bounty* was quite possibly the most thrilling thing imaginable for Mauatua and her companions, like us discovering the man at the door was Christ returned. Suddenly they were part of a story every bit as fantastic as the legends they had been told around fires: they seemed to have been chosen to be first to share the paradise in which these gods lived. That there should have been human frailties, pain and deceit in the lives of these gods would have been no surprise, not when you knew how Tahitian gods behaved

In Pitcairn's first years massacre and pain were the norm as a struggle for supremacy fermented between the white men and between the white and black men. It was the black women who nurtured Pitcairn Island. The black men were all quickly dead and even if they had passed their knowledge on to those white men who survived the first massacre, the European survivors were commonly drunk or determined to be idle kings of their new castles. It was as well Tahitian girls were brought up the same as boys, taught how to grow and harvest and fish and carve, to swim and to surf on boards. Only the women can have known how best to grow and tend and harvest and fish on a South Pacific island.

The most telling clue to the extraordinary determination and vision of these women - for their children I believe, rather than for themselves - is their belief in voting. This can be directly related back to Christian and the way he ran *Bounty* from the moment she was first his in 1789. In the year of the French Revolution he revolutionised a British naval vessel, allowing its early mix of mutineers and non-mutineers to vote on decisions: he also had them sew uniforms of canvas piped with the blue of his officer's jacket: democratic *Bounty* was also the first British naval ship ever to have a uniformed crew rather than just uniformed officers.

No-one knew what had happened to *Bounty* for almost twenty years. When Pitcairn was rediscovered by *Topaz* in 1809 only one man was alive, mutineer John Adams. He met these first visitors wearing a loincloth of beaten mulberry bark. If it had been up to Adams, Pitcairn's first generation would have claimed to be English and to believe in Christ, the Union Jack and the king, but would have been naked. Seven of the Tahitian women were still alive with a flock of 24 offspring aged from 19 downwards.

For the next thirty years ships came and went, usually just for the day, and a few Europeans stayed longer or shorter timers, often with disastrous social effects on the community, yet an important seed, sewn decades ago, was about to flourish.

In November 1838 HMS *Fly* called at Pitcairn Island, and Captain Elliott was asked to help with writing into law the right of all women to vote and that education for both boys and girls be both free and compulsory. For elderly Mrs Christian and her daughter-in-law Susannah, the only surviving Tahitian women, this was the culmination of a life's work. They had created a new ethnic group with unique ethics, language and culture and, now, unheard of rights. It was not the mutineers, but these Tahitian women who had the last laugh on the British.

Today's focus on Pitcairn Island is less heroic. In September courts may try Pitcairn men for allegedly having sex with under-age girls. The community has had to endure protracted torture to get to this stage, initiated by Whitehall men and women with no idea that for generations neither men nor women had anyone independent to approach for advice or with complaints. The schoolteacher doubled as a representative of the Pitcairn Administration in Auckland, in turn only there to represent Britain's interest: the Administration and the schoolteacher handed out paying jobs, so no Pitcairner dared be any trouble to them. Pitcairners didn't even have a policeman, and this was not for lack of asking. For all the 20th century they had not one person anywhere in the world who officially represented them and their interests, rather than the interests of Britain. When the colonial Hong Kong Government wanted help they chartered a 747 and went to London to get it. When the Prince of Wales married Lady Diana Spencer the intensely royalist Pitcairners asked if it would be alright to send a gift: it was but they were not invited to have a representative at the wedding.

The alleged cases have finally stirred the conscience of Blair's government a little. The purse so freely spilt to protect the future of Iraqis might at last protect and support one of Britain's much older responsibilities. New infra-structure, an airport, wind or solar power, medical care and the dignity of self-determination have long been promised and could now happen, encouraging a new flourishing, even a resettlement of Pitcairn. There is some strong legal argument Pitcairn is not actually British, but this shouldn't matter – promises have been made for decades, and for decades promises have not been kept. It's not like that in Baghdad.

The great surprise to those intrepid enough to visit Pitcairn is there is so little to tell you quite where you are. There is only one first settlement gravestone, for Adams. There is no memorial – not even a mention - of the Tahitian women who first fed and clothed and then brought peace, democracy and compulsory universal education to this dot of volcanic rock, and who did this for the sake of the children whom once they might have killed.

It would be a good, enhancing thing if *Bounty*'s Tahitian women were remembered daily on Pitcairn Island, as Pitcairners speak the language they created from Tahitian and English, eat the food grown in their gardens, look out over the vast seas whence they came. Few people in the world can have such extraordinary examples as foremothers.

The rest of the world might then reconsider its long-held view of Pitcairn Island, famous for the naval revolution of the men who settled her, but more worthy of fame and respect for the social revolutions of its Tahitian women settlers.

This article was first published in CANVAS, the Saturday magazine of the NZ Herald in 2004. Subsequently a new memorial has been added, with the names of the Tahitian men and women who arrived on BOUNTY.

Tahitian Women of Bounty

Mauatua (Isabella, Mauatea, Mainmast, Maimiti)
Consort of Fletcher Christian (two sons, one daughter) then of Edward Young (one son and two daughters). Died 14 September 1841. She is said to have remembered Cook's last visit to Tahiti in late 1777 and also to have left one or two children behind there. She was older than Christian, but by how much is not certain.

Faahotu Fasto)
First consort of John Williams – she left no children. Died 1790/ 1791.

Mareva
Shared consort of Manarii, Teimua and Niau, later lived in Adams' household – she left no children. Died between 1808 and 1814.

Puarei (Obuarei)
First Pitcairn consort of John Adams – she left no children. Died 1790/1791.

Teatuahitea (Sarah)
Consort of William Brown. She left no children. Died between 1808 and 1814.

Teehuteatuaonoa (Jenny)
Consort of John Adams of Tubuai and then of Isaac Martin. She left no children. Date of death uncertain.

Teio (Mary)
First consort of McKoy (a son and a daughter). Later lived with Adams and bore his only son, George: Adams and Teio were married in 1824. Died 14th March, 1829.
Teio arrived on Pitcairn with a baby girl Sully, who subsequently married Fletcher Christian's second son, Charles 'Hoppa' Christian, and had four sons and four daughters by him. Thus her son George Adams and her McKoy

children were all half siblings to Charles' wife even though Sully was a
full-blooded Tahitian.

Teraura (Susannah, Taoupiti, Mataohu)

First consort of Edward Young (no children) and then the second
consort of Matthew Quintal (one son). When she was about 30 she
married Thursday October, Fletcher's elder son who was about 16
at the time (three sons, three daughters) Died 15 July, 1850.

Tevarua (Sarah or Big Sully)

Original consort of Matthew Quintal (two sons, two daughters,
infant son) Died 1799.

Tinafanaea

First the shared consort Titahiti and Oha she was then given to
Adams, which began the events of Massacre Day in 1793. She left
no children. Died between 1808 and 1814.

Toofaiti (Nancy, Hutia, Toohaiti)

First the consort of Tararo, she was then given to Williams after
Faahotu died. After Massacre Day she was one of Young's consorts
(three sons, one daughter). Died in Tahiti 9 June, 1831.

Vahineatua (Prudence, Balhadi, Paraha Iti)

First the consort of John Mills (one daughter, one son) she then
had three daughters by Adams. Died before 1809.

Sully

Came to Pitcairn as a baby, the daughter of Teio and subsequently
married Charles 'Hoppa', second son of Fletcher Christian (four
sons, four daughters). Died 7 March, 1826.
Note that although it is said she was the daughter of McKoy, it is more
likely she was a full-blooded Tahitian.

Postscript

Pitcairn: Safe at Last?

W hen I sailed away from Pitcairn in 1980 I was fired with ambition to change what I had found. Here was a community with the same status in the British Commonwealth as Gibraltar, Hong Kong and the Falkland Islands, yet aged women still carried water on their backs. While Hong Kong's Administrative Council could charter a Boeing 747 for discussions in London, and millions were spent on the Falklands War and its aftermath, Pitcairn Islanders pitifully asked me if they were *allowed* to send a gift to the Prince of Wales' marriage, and they were not represented at the ceremony. Pitcairn Island is undoubtedly one of Britain's most famous possessions, but its romantic association with the mutiny on *Bounty* had somehow prevented the world seeing the harsh reality.

Most people I talked to in England believed Pitcairn was prosperous and well looked after. But in 1980 it was one of the world's most neglected inhabited islands, relying on charity to survive. During the 1960s and 1970s, the cargo and passenger ships which called fortnightly were replaced by jets, and by container ships whose huge operating costs made charitable detours impossibly

426

expensive. Pitcairn Island was reduced to relying on supplies delivered only a few times a year through the office of the Commissioner for Pitcairn Island in Auckland. This was not enough to support the island, and the population declined dramatically. The remaining Pitcairners had to resort to illegal commercial use of ham radio friends around the world to order goods from Europe and the United States. The delivery of these goods relied on the charity of passing ships, usually Scandinavian, which diverted without permission of their owners.

The wood-planked long boats on which the island relied to take them to and from these ships were getting old, and the suggestion they might be replaced by metal ones had caused only consternation. How can you ask the men of such a remote place to agree when they had never seen a metal boat, and had no access, as we would have, to comparisons. It seemed Pitcairners had only to do what they were told, like schoolchildren. Nanny Britain knew best.

On my return to London I set up the Pitcairn Island Fund as a starting point to alert people to the plight of the Pitcairn Islanders and campaign to help them fund new ways to guarantee supplies, and to improve healthcare and housing. The essential problem was that although there was a Commissioner for Pitcairn Island based in Auckland, his job was to represent Britain and the Foreign and Commonwealth Office and there was no structure for hearing the voice of the Pitcairners other than through the Commissioner. Britain was represented, the island was not. *The Times* helped begin the campaign with an article that clarified the colony's position.

I was joined in my campaign to change this situation by others with first-hand experience of Pitcairn Island, and we took our case to the Foreign and Commonwealth Office in London. However, when we warned an official that the Pitcairners' stoic refusal to complain meant that Pitcairn needed proactive government to survive, she laughed. Proactive was the old-fashioned way, she said, not far removed from 'ruling', something Britain no longer did.

Passsive administration was to be the thing, and in retrospect perhaps this was not surprising because in the 1980s colonies and the word 'colonial' had become distinctly unfashionable. Indeed, after several meetings we gained the impression that the British Government would be happier if Pitcairners lived elsewhere. This is precisely what the Pitcairners I had talked to did not want—at any price.

But even though I was only doing what most Pitcairners had privately asked me to do, some reactionary factions in Britain and New Zealand persuaded the Pitcairn Island Council to write to me saying they had no need of an independent voice or independent help. The council is elected on the island by Pitcairners, but it is not autonomous and has little ability to achieve any degree of self-determination because they have no control of the island's finances; they are merely an advisory committee to the Commissioner. Without the explicit support of the council, the Pitcairn Island Fund could do nothing, so the money we had raised was sent to the island and I shut up. Factions and rumours cause untold trouble on a small island and I did not want to make matters worse when I had only wanted to make them better.

Twenty years later much has changed. And this time it is very much for the better. First there has been a huge shift in attitude in London, an admission that Pitcairn is different from Britain's other colonies and must be administered differently, taking into account its unique culture and its remoteness. Add to this a new Commissioner in Auckland and the future of Pitcairn looks great.

Commissioner Leon Salt trained as a teacher specifically so that he could live and work on Pitcairn Island. It's not an idle interest. His family background comes from Norfolk Island, where so many *Bounty* descendants settled in 1856, and he has the blood of mutineers Christian, Adams and Quintal. Thus he understands the special way of thinking of the Pitcairners and knows how best to interpret both what is said and, more importantly, what is not said.

Over the past twenty years, the once dangerous dock has been strengthened and extended, metal boats supplied and a medical centre built. But Commissioner Salt has been looking at more than infrastructure. For example, legal advisors are proposing new laws which will separate the office of Magistrate and Chief Officer: in the rare times of trouble this will ensure the safety of both perpetrator and victim. The position of police officer on the island is increasing in status and regular re-training visits are planned. The first visit by WPC Gail Cox of the Kent Constabulary, Maidstone, Great Britain, was a resounding success and it's hoped she will return.

The island has voted to allow the consumption of alcohol which has also meant introduction of laws against drunkenness. It is also reviewing gun licensing. The realities of the outside world, like massacres in remote communities, can no longer be ignored. Other new laws are being proposed which will bring basic human rights legislation into line with the rest of the world. Pitcairn cannot remain a quaint echo from the past, living the old way, when the new way is constantly knocking on its door, through travelling and travellers.

However, shipping to and from New Zealand, the island's official lifeline, is getting worse. Modern container ships are increasingly bigger and more expensive to operate and thus there are fewer and fewer stops at Pitcairn Island. As well, new route-tracking systems are reducing unscheduled stops of vessels which have given the supplies and trading opportunities that official channels cannot provide. Now well-meaning captains will be penalised for diverting to supply or help Pitcairn. Soon the island could be more isolated than a hundred years ago.

So what is to be done? Clearly the answer lies in some sort of self-sufficiency for Pitcairn Island, a return to the idea of a vessel of their own perhaps, or a small landing strip. Both are being investigated. Now that Commissioner Salt is finally tackling the question of land ownership and use, it might be possible to free up a site for the strip.

The problem of land ownership was something Pitcairners were concerned about during my visit in 1980, and now finally something is being done to address it. Generations of inheritance mean plots are divided into ribbons so newly married couples find it hard to identify any space large enough for a house and garden. It's not a matter of sensible swapping because the many years of colonial neglect has meant absent landowners and many land holdings without apparent owners. After much consultation new laws are being proposed that will guarantee any Pitcairner or their children and grandchildren land for building and growing as long as they live there, and this is perhaps the single most significant advance of all for the island.

There is increased hope at every turn. The Pitcairners have more to sell than stamps and carvings. Their honey is amongst the most pure in the world and their bees amongst the most placid. Honey exporting has terrific potential, as does a trade in queen bees. Dried fruit, especially bananas, is a growing export and there is more to come.

Commissioner Salt also believes that if Pitcairn is to survive, it must stop looking to New Zealand, more than 6000 kilometres away, and instead turn its face east and northwards to French Polynesia. For example, Mangareva, which has an air strip, is only 500 kilometres away and could benefit from Pitcairn's resources. Mangareva has problems with coral poisoning in their fish and grows no vegetables. Just as it was to nineteenth-century whaling and sealing ships, Pitcairn could once again be a providore of fresh vegetables, fruit and fish.

With land available, with agricultural and fishing enterprises and their own vessel, it will be possible for Pitcairners to achieve their dreams and to live there safely and comfortably—and for those off the island to return and to do the same thing.

And then there is tourism. Those who rail that tourism will spoil the island are talking claptrap. It is the lack of visitors caused by reduction in shipping that has so put the island in peril. It is increased trade which will save it. As this is Commissioner Salt's vision, Pitcairn will now prevail, of that I am certain.

Satellite technology is improving so quickly that email services will be a reality within a few years. At last it is possible to telephone and to fax Pitcairn direct. But there is just one line and it costs Pitcairners many dollars per minute so don't expect replies. Just as unfairly, it costs a great deal to fax to and from Pitcairn via the satellite service. Those least able to afford it are charged most.

Far better to direct enquiries, especially about buying stamps, carvings and other exports, to the Commissioner's Office in Auckland. For here beats the very heart of Pitcairn's future. How gratifying that a community forged from conflict and revolutionary social experiment should be once again reinventing itself, and that the orchestrator should have the blood of its founder, Fletcher Christian.

PITCAIRN ISLAND CONTACTS

General enquiries
Commissioner for the Pitcairn Islands
Office of the Governor of Pitcairn, Henderson, Ducie and Oeno Islands
Private Box 105 696
Auckland, New Zealand
Ph (64 9) 366 0186
Fax (64 9) 366 0187
Email: pitcairn@iconz.co.nz

Philatelic, collector coin and phone card correspondence
Pitcairn Islands Philatelic Bureau c/o the above address, or:
Email: pitcairn.stamps@iconz.co.nz

Web site
http://users.iconz.co.nz/pitcairn.
This is developing and includes philatelic details, historic, tourist and general information.

Pitcairn Island via Inmarsat satellites
INMARSAT A: between 1730 and 0500 UTC
Phone: +872 144 5372   Fax: +872 144 5373

INMARSAT M: usually 24 hours a day
Phone: +872 7612 24115   Fax: +872 7612 24116

While INMARSAT M generally has the lowest charges, fax transmission speed at 2400baud can be up to a quarter the speed of INMARSAT A, thereby eliminating any apparent per minute charge advantage.

Sources and Bibliographical Note

The bibliography of the *Bounty*/Pitcairn story is enormous, over 2500 major books and articles. To say I had read them all would be as specious as publishing an extensive list and implying by silence that I had done so; even if I had, this book would not have been better or different. Most works on the subject are variations of someone else's themes or the expansion of slim theories in the hope they will become fat facts.

I almost always used primary material, including transcripts and published works. This is simple with today's international network of microfilm exchange agreements. Thus books were used more to track other men's interpretations rather than as reference. In any case, as no other author really knew much about Fletcher Christian, their views were automatically less interesting than had once been the case. And most seemed disinclined to believe what Edward Christian and Francis Bond had to say about Bligh (if, indeed, they knew about the latter). Once I found my new Fletcher Christian material I had to forge a very new frame upon which to tell the story for the first time.

In general I have mentioned my sources during the book, to avoid the disturbance of footnotes. Those who wish to disagree with me, or who care to check up on me, or who want to start at the beginning themselves, will appreciate the following summary of the books and sources I found most useful. If I do not mention a well-known or respected book, no disrespect is to be inferred: I may have read it and enjoyed it, but found it published what was largely known from other, more primary sources.

The major source for my information about the Christian family and the Isle of Man is the private collection of Ewan Christian, which had been used as reference for *The Yesterdays Behind the Door*, Susan Hicks Beach (University Press, Liverpool, 1956). These remarkable documents have now been generously donated by Ewan Christian to the Manx Museum in Douglas, Isle of Man. The MSS accession number is 9381 and the microfilm references are MIC69 and MIC70.

North Country Life in the 18th Century, Vol. 2 by Edward Hughes (Oxford

University Press, 1965) is packed with important Christian family material, and the sources for this are all in the Christian Curwen and the Senhouse MSS in the Cumbria Records Office in Carlisle Castle. The papers of William Fletcher MP are across the road, in Tullie House, Carlisle.

Details of Naval life were mainly taken from *Sea Life in Nelson's Time* (Methuen & Co., London, 1905) by John Masefield.

Several articles published in *The Mariner's Mirror* over the years give excellent insight into the fitting out of *Bounty*.

The background to classical Tahitian life was drawn from the three volumes of Professor Douglas Oliver's *Ancient Tahitian Society* (University Press of Hawaii, Honolulu, 1974) and cross-checked with several of his sources, which include the manuscripts and published works of Bligh and James Morrison, *Bounty*'s boatswain's mate.

What Happened on the Bounty (George Allen & Unwin, translated, London, 1962) by Bengt Danielsson and Rolf du Rietz, clearly presents the complicated story of what happened on Tahiti after *Bounty* left; incidentally all my spelling of Tahitian personal names are those of Bengt and Marie-Thérèse Danielsson, who know best.

As sources for what happened on the day of the mutiny I used Bligh's works, Owen Rutter's edition of *The Court-Martial of the Bounty mutineers* (William Hodge & Co., Edinburgh, 1931), *The Voyage of the Bounty's Launch—John Fryer's Narrative* edited by Stephen Walter (Genesis Publication, Guilford, Surrey, 1979), *The Appendix* by Edward Christian (London, 1794). The latter must be regarded as primary material, not just for what it reports, but also because of the dramatic revelations and corroboration of Edward's subsequent pamphlet *A Short Reply to Captain Bligh's Answers* (J. Deighton, London, 1975). This second, exceptionally rare and rarely used pamphlet reveals the methodology of the first, explains the danger and disgrace risked by the eminent men who helped collect evidence if they were to be found liars, and even shows that Bligh's servant went independently to the Christian family to give a version of the mutiny different from that of Bligh. *A Short Reply* also reveals that McIntosh was threatened for talking to Edward Christian and demolishes the methods with which Bligh appeared to get some men (e.g. Lebogue) to retract earlier statements.

Edward Christian's two short works in explanation of his brother are transparent, clearly argued documents that cannot be dismissed as vindictive and/

or called dishonest. Although a determined eccentric, Edward Christian published some of the most respected papers and legal opinions of his time. He wrote definitively on the origins and privileges of the House of Commons and the liberty of the subject; and in 1807 he published *A Vindication of the Right of the Universities of Great Britain to a Copy of every new Publication* which encouraged Cambridge University to claim their right to a copy of every published work.

Edward Christian and his associates had no need, and would not dare, to risk opprobrium by falsifying evidence in pursuit of a vendetta. Together they worked to publish facts which otherwise would have been suppressed. Journalists get prizes for that today.

The travels of Fletcher Christian after the mutiny were not fully known until the brilliant detective work of Professor H. E. Maude, which was published as 'In Search of a Home' (*Journal of the Polynesian Society*, Vol. 67, No. 2, June 1958, Wellington). James Morrison gave excellent anthropological detail about Tubuai. The abstracts made by Captain Edward Edwards of the journals of George Stewart and Peter Heywood are in his papers, which were recognised in the Admiralty Library, London, by Bengt Danielsson.

For events on Pitcairn Island there are many manuscript sources, and more turn up all the time. Each of those mentioned in this book has something to offer and F. W. Beechey's *Narrative of a Voyage to the Pacific and Beering's Strait in His Majesty's Ship Blossom . . . in the Years 1825 . . .*, 2 Vols. (Henry Colburn & Richard Bentley, London, 1831) is by far the fullest. I decided to accept as most authoritative the versions given by the Tahitian woman Jenny; and my expedition to Pitcairn Island proved I was right to do so. The easiest place to read what she said is the *United Services Journal*, London, November 1829, Part 2, pp. 589–593.

The most masterly and thorough interpretative and critical works published about *Bounty* and her men are by the Swedish bibliographer Rolf du Rietz, based in Uppsala. As well as a series of small articles and pamphlets he published *Studia Bountyana* (Dahlia Books, Uppsala, Sweden, 1979, Vols 1 & 2) and had begun a new series titled *Banksia*. *Banksia* 1 (Dahlia Books, Uppsala, Sweden, 1979) is 'Thoughts on the Present State of Bligh Scholarship', and this puts into focus the problems of writing about a figure who is so well known. A work on Fryer was due in mid-1982.

William Bligh has had many enthusiastic biographers and apologists. None has been more honest or painstaking than George Mackaness, who wrote *The Life of Vice-Admiral William Bligh* (Angus & Robertson, Sydney, 1931. New and revised edition 1951). He subsequently found and published the startling Bond material published in *Fragile Paradise*—the originals are in the National Maritime Museum, Greenwich. As this material was not known to Gavin Kennedy, he did not discuss it in his rich biography *Bligh* (Gerald Duckworth & Co., London, 1978), so a reassessment of his subject could not be made. Gavin Kennedy's later book, *Captain Bligh: The Man and his Mutinies* (Gerald Duckworth & Co. Ltd, London, 1989) incorporates the material and is an important reference book.

Sir John Barrow's *the Mutiny of the Bounty* (John Murray [pub], London, 1831) remains one of the best works on the subject overall, and covers a much wider spectrum than my book.

The Heritage of the Bounty by H. L. Shapiro (Simon & Shuster, New York, 1936) gives an excellent perspective on Pitcairn's development and David Silverman's *Pitcairn Island* (World Publishing Company, Cleveland, 1967) is a worthwhile collection of often overlooked sources. *The Pitcairnese Language* by A. S. C. Ross and A. W. Moverly (Andre Deutsch, London, 1964) includes some excellent essays by Professor Maude and his son and is worth the trouble to track down. The simple style and genealogical charts of *The Pitcairners* by Robert Nicholson (Angus & Robertson, Sydney, 1965) make it important, but the marriage date he gives for Fletcher Christian is 'entirely his own work' and unsupported. The famous article by Luis Marden 'I Found the Bones of the Bounty' in the *National Geographic Magazine* in December 1957 has dated well.

The only other book I know written by a descendant of the mutineers is *Mutiny of the Bounty and Story of Pitcairn Island* by Rosalind Amelia Young (Pacific Press Publishing Assn, Mountain View, California, 1894), who was born and brought up on Pitcairn and who is buried there. It gives details and facts not otherwise collected and even though published last century remains an excellent and entertaining book. Otherwise I find books about Pitcairn Island fail accurately to represent the island and its people.

Naturally William Bligh has been a major source for this book and most of his important papers are in the Mitchell Library, Sydney. His own letters and correspondence with Banks are most fruitful, and much work could still be done. These are collected on three reels of microfilm:

MLMS C218 (Reel FM4/1756)
MLMS Safe 1/35 (Reel CY 178) Bligh documents and correspondence
MLMS A78 4 (Reel FM4/1748) the Banks Brabourne papers, and contains
much of relevance.

There is other Bligh material in the Dixson Library, Sydney, and in the National Library, Canberra, you will find the Rex Nan-Kivell Collection, which includes a deal of interesting secondary material and some outstanding illustrative material.

The Dawson Transcripts of Banks letters, which are held in the Natural History Museum are little referred to in connection with *Bounty*. But this is where you will discover the letter in which Banks says he expected to be blamed if anything went wrong with the breadfruit expedition. These transcripts also show that the letter of 7 September 1787 in the Banks Brabourne papers, thought to be from Sir Joseph Banks to Sir George Yonge, is the reverse; it is a copy of Yonge's letter to Banks about the former's visit to *Bounty*. Banks had actually sent the original on to Evan Nepean. The complete correspondence (DTC 5:245–9 and DTC 5:259/60) seems to show that Bligh was playing these two men off against one another, pretending, for instance, to Yonge that he had no idea where he was to go or to where he was to return.

The quotation from Dorothy Wordsworth's journal is taken from *Wordsworth's Hawkshead* by T. W. Thompson (edited by Robert Woof, Oxford, 1970) a book which contains much detail of meetings between the Wordsworths and the Christian Curwens.

For the new illumination on Fletcher Christian's medical condition, I consulted Professor John Ludbrook, MD ChM DSc MMedSc FRCS FRACS, Professor Emeritus, University of Adelaide and a Professorial Fellow, University of Melbourne Department of Surgery, Royal Melbourne Hospital. Professor Ludbrook is a vascular surgeon and vascular physiologist with professional experience of hyperhidrosis. (The curious connection between a sweating syndrome and vascular surgery is that hyperhidrosis is often accompanied by blushing.) He not only taught me much but also checked my wider conclusions.

Much of the material on Christian's mental condition came from professional psychologist Dr Sven Wahlroos PhD and his masterly *Mutiny and Romance in the South Seas: A Companion to the Bounty Adventure* (Salem House

Publishers, Div. of HarperCollins, Topsfield, Massachusetts, 1989). He, in turn, quotes from the *Diagnostic and Statistical Manual of Mental Disorders* (third edition, revised, Washington DC, American Psychiatric Association, 1987). There is now a fourth edition. Dr Wahlroos' work is a vital reference book, both the only chronological account and a detailed encyclopedia, and is well overdue for republication. Further insight and help came from clinical psychologist Paul Rodriguez, BA (Hons) MPsychol MAPS.

For greater clarity on the effect Bligh's command might have had on *Bounty* after it sailed from Tahiti, I am grateful to my loyal friend and full-time *Bounty* enthusiast Topher Russo, who gave me access to his unpublished Master's thesis, 'Mr Bligh's bad discipline: laxity and recklessness on the high seas' (University of Hawaii, Honolulu, 1994). Similarly, Tasmanian historian Ian Campbell is responsible for new perspectives on Bligh's health and his behaviour during the second breadfruit voyage on HMS *Providence* in his paper 'Mr Bligh's bad health'. Based on his BA Honours thesis (University of Tasmania, Hobart, November 1994), it is available in full on the Internet at the following website:

www.wavefront.com/~pjlareau/bounty1.html

New first-hand accounts of Bligh as Governor of New South Wales are from *Distracted Settlement*, edited and introduced by Dr Ann-Maree Whittaker (The Miegunyah Press, Melbourne, 1998).

For an extraordinary expansion of the story and its players, with fascinating excursions and diversions into many related subjects including the later films, there is nothing better than *Mr Bligh's Bad Language* by Professor Greg Denning (Cambridge University Press, 1992).

I hope the preceding will show upon which authorities I have based my book; undoubtedly there is still more information to be found, which may change my views. I look forward to seeing that material, which is probably amongst the whaling and sealing archives of the United States. But, much more, I look forward to the day when there is no longer the urge to cast Bligh or Christian as black or white. They are men who are remembered. Few men who are remembered can have been wholly one or the other.

Picture Sources and Acknowledgements

Any picture or image not accredited is owned by Glynn Christian.

In order of appearance:

Full reproduction and close-up of Fletcher Christian in the 1790 Robert Dodd painting of Bligh being cast adrift from *Bounty* by permission of The Clyde Bank Collection, Sydney. Transparency courtesy of Sotheby's Picture Library, London.

Painting of Adventure Bay, Tasmania by George Tobin 1892 (PXA-555f.18) by permission of Mitchell Library, State Library of NSW, Sydney.

Painting of breadfruit by George Tobin (PXA555f.2) and painting of Point Venus, Matavai Bay, Tahiti by George Tobin, 1792 (PXA555f36) by permission of Mitchell Library, State Library of NSW, Sydney.

Plan of converted *Bounty* courtesy of National Maritime Museum, London.

Extract from Bligh's list of mutineers (MS5395) by permission of National Library of Australia.

The paying off slip of Charles Christian reproduced courtesy of The India Office

Original drawing of John Adams by Captain Richard Beechey RN (P2/82) by permission of Mitchell Library, State Library of NSW, Sydney.

Photo of sons and grandsons of the mutiny (Q980/c) by permission of Dixson Library, State Library of NSW, Sydney.

Original watercolour of Thursday October Christian by Lt. John Shillibeer (Pd 70) by permission of Dixson Library, State Library of NSW, Sydney.

Engraving of original school building in Adamstown, *Pitcairn: The Island, the People and the Pastor* by Rev. Thos. Boyles Murray.

Photo of Sarah Christian Nobbs (PXA4358-1) by permission of Dixson Library, State Library of NSW, Sydney.

Photo of Elizabeth Mills (Q980/c) by permission of Dixson Library, State Library of NSW, Sydney.

Index

Weights and Measures

Linear Measure

1 inch	=	1000 mils	=	2.54	centimetres
12 inches	=	1 foot	=	0.3048	metre
3 feet	=	1 yard	=	0.9144	metre
220 yards or 660 feet	=	1 furlong	=	201.168	metres
8 furlongs or 1760 yards	=	1 (statute) mile	=	1.6093	kilometres

Square Measure

144 square inches	=	1 square foot	=	929.03	square centimetres
9 square feet	=	1 square yard	=	0.8361	square metre
4840 square yards	=	1 acre	=	0.4047	hectare
640 acres	=	1 square mile	=	259.0	hectares

Nautical Measure

6 feet = 1 fathom   = 1.829 metres

100 fathoms = 1 cable's length

(In the Royal Navy, 608 feet, or 185.319 metres = 1 cable's length)

10 cables length = 1 international nautical mile = 1.852 kilometres

1 international nautical mile = 1.150 779 statute miles

(the length of a minute of longitude at the equator)

60 nautical miles = *1 degree of a great circle of the earth.*

= 69.047 statute miles

Liquid and Dry Measure

1 gill	=	5 fluid ounces	=	0.1480	litre
4 gills	=	1 pint	=	0.568	litre
2 pints	=	1 quart	=	1.136	litres
4 quarts	=	1 gallon	=	4.546	litres
2 gallons	=	1 peck	=	9.092	litres
4 pecks	=	1 bushel	=	36.37	litres

Weights

		1 ounce	=	28.3495	grams
		1 pound	=	453.59	grams
14 pounds	=	1 stone	=	6.35	kilograms
112 pounds	=	1 hundredweight	=	50.80	kilograms
2240 pounds	=	1 (long) ton	=	1016.05	kilograms
2000 pounds	=	1 (short) ton	=	907.18	kilograms

Temperature

Fahrenheit → Celsius: $°C = \frac{5}{9} \times (°F - 32)$

Lightning Source UK Ltd.
Milton Keynes UK
UKOW051813241111

182634UK00002B/20/A